OXFORD COMPARATIVE CONSTITUTIONALISM

Series Editors
RICHARD ALBERT
*William Stamps Farish Professor of Law,
The University of Texas at Austin School of Law*
ROBERT SCHÜTZE
*Professor of European and Global Law,
Durham University and College of Europe*

Responsive Judicial Review

OXFORD COMPARATIVE CONSTITUTIONALISM

Series Editors

Richard Albert, William Stamps Farish Professor of Law,
The University of Texas at Austin Law School

Robert Schütze, Professor of European and Global Law,
Durham University and College of Europe

Comparative constitutional law has a long and distinguished history in intellectual thought and in the construction of public law. As political actors and the people who create or modify their constitutional orders, they often wish to learn from the experience and learning of others. This cross-fertilization and mutual interaction has only accelerated with the onset of globalization, which has transformed the world into an interconnected web that facilitates dialogue and linkages across international and regional structures. Oxford Comparative Constitutionalism seeks to publish scholarship of the highest quality in constitutional law that deepens our knowledge of local, national, regional, and global phenomena through the lens of comparative public law.

Advisory Board

Denis Baranger, Professor of Public Law, Université Paris II Panthéon-Assas

Wen-Chen Chang, Professor of Law, National Taiwan University

Roberto Gargarella, Professor of Law, Universidad Torcuato di Tella

Vicki C Jackson, Thurgood Marshall Professor of Constitutional Law, Harvard Law School

Christoph Möllers, Professor of Public Law and Jurisprudence,
Humboldt-Universität zu Berlin

Cheryl Saunders A.O., Laureate Professor Emeritus, Melbourne Law School

ALSO PUBLISHED IN THIS SERIES

Deliberative Peace Referendums
Ron Levy, Ian O'Flynn, Hoi L. Kong

Eternity Clauses In Democratic Constitutionalism
Silvia Suteu

Scales of Memory
Constitutional Justice and Historical Evil
Justin Collings

The Global South and Comparative Constitutional Law
Edited by Philipp Dann, Michael Riegner, and Maxim Bönnemann

City, State
Constitutionalism and the Megacity
Ran Hirschl

Constitutional Change In The Contemporary Socialist World
Ngoc Son Bui

Poland's Constitutional Breakdown
Wojciech Sadurski

Abusive Constitutional Borrowing
Rosalind Dixon and David Landau

Responsive Judicial Review

Democracy and Dysfunction in the Modern Age

ROSALIND DIXON
Professor of Law and Director of the Gilbert + Tobin Centre of Public Law, UNSW Sydney

OXFORD
UNIVERSITY PRESS

Great Clarendon Street, Oxford, OX2 6DP,
United Kingdom

Oxford University Press is a department of the University of Oxford.
It furthers the University's objective of excellence in research, scholarship,
and education by publishing worldwide. Oxford is a registered trade mark of
Oxford University Press in the UK and in certain other countries

© Rosalind Dixon 2023

The moral rights of the author have been asserted

First Edition published in 2023

All rights reserved. No part of this publication may be reproduced, stored in
a retrieval system, or transmitted, in any form or by any means, without the
prior permission in writing of Oxford University Press, or as expressly permitted
by law, by licence or under terms agreed with the appropriate reprographics
rights organization. Enquiries concerning reproduction outside the scope of the
above should be sent to the Rights Department, Oxford University Press, at the
address above

You must not circulate this work in any other form
and you must impose this same condition on any acquirer

Public sector information reproduced under Open Government Licence v3.0
(http://www.nationalarchives.gov.uk/doc/open-government-licence/open-government-licence.htm)

Published in the United States of America by Oxford University Press
198 Madison Avenue, New York, NY 10016, United States of America

British Library Cataloguing in Publication Data

Data available

Library of Congress Control Number: 2022934445

ISBN 978-0-19-286577-9

DOI: 10.1093/oso/9780192865779.001.0001

Printed and bound by
CPI Group (UK) Ltd, Croydon, CR0 4YY

Links to third party websites are provided by Oxford in good faith and
for information only. Oxford disclaims any responsibility for the materials
contained in any third party website referenced in this work.

Acknowledgments

This book has been a long time in the making. In many places it draws on work I did during my doctorate/SJD at Harvard under the generous supervision of Frank Michelman, Martha Minow, Richard Fallon, Richard Goldstone, and Jacqui Bhabha. It also reflects time spent thinking and writing as an assistant professor and professor at the University of Chicago and University of New South Wales (UNSW) in Sydney, as well as during several visits as a visiting professor/fellow at Chicago, Harvard, and Columbia Law Schools. The attention in the book to the realities of democratic politics, and various possibilities for democratic experimentalism, is largely due to the intellectual influence of the University of Chicago and Columbia Law School. The enthusiasm for ideas about responsive law and regulation is shaped by many generous colleagues at UNSW, especially Theunis Roux and Martin Krygier.

The comparative method, and sensibility, I owe to many people around the world both near and far—including colleagues at UNSW and Melbourne, many fellow members of the International Society of Public Law. Many of the ideas have also been shaped by valuable conversations over many years with colleagues such as Richard Albert, Micaela Alterio, Gabrielle Appleby, Ori Aronson, Ben Berger, Carlos Bernal Pulido, Nina Boughey, Sean Brennan, Dan Brinks, Jessica Bulman Pozen, Lisa Buton Crawford, Cora Chan, Adam Chilton, Mathilde Cohen, Victor Comella, Joel Colon Rios, Adam Cox, Javier Cuoso, Grainne de Burca, Maartje de Visser, Sujit Choudhry, Melissa Crouch, Erin Delaney, Evelyn Douek, Anna Dziedic, Richard Fallon, James Fowkes, Stephen Gardbaum, Roberto Gargarella, Conor Gearty, Claudia Geiringer, Jake Gersen, Tom Ginsburg, Mark Graber, Jamal Greene, Michaela Hailbronner, Andrew Harding, Ran Hirschl, Aziz Huq, Helen Irving, Samuel Issacharoff, Vicki Jackson, Aileen Kavanagh, Tarunabh Khaitan, Madhav Khosla, Paul Kildea, Jeff King, Heinz Klug, David Landau, David Law, Hanna Lerner, Daryl Levinson, Sandy Levinson, Ron Levy, Peter Leyland, Vanessa MacDonnell, Frank Michelman, Martha Minow, Sarah Murray, Jaclyn Neo, Roberto Niembro, Aoife Nolan, Kate O'Regan, Will Partlett, Rick Pildes, Iddo Porat, Eric Posner, David Pozen, Kent Roach, Yaniv Roznai, Ruth Rubio, Wojciech Sadurksi, Adam Samaha, Cheryl Saunders, Jeff Seton, Amelia Simpson, James Stellios, Scott Stephenson, Kristen Stilt, Adrienne Stone, Lior

Strahilevitz, David Strauss, Julie Suk, Mark Tushnet, Mariana Velasco Rivera, Sergio Verdugo, Mila Versteeg, Joseph Weiler, Lulu Weis, and Po Jen Yap, among many others. I am especially grateful to David Dyzenhaus for encouraging me to return to work on the book after a long delay, and to Mark Tushnet for his encouragement and guidance at many different stages of the project.

The book also reflects the intellectual debt I owe to a number of close colleagues and co-authors. The book inevitably reflects and has parallels with the work of many of those scholars who I most admire in the field, and it draws explicitly at a number of points on ideas developed in joint-authored work with Michaela Hailbronner, Samuel Issacharoff, Richard Holden, Amelia Loughland, Theunis Roux, Adrienne Stone, Mark Tushnet, and especially David Landau, and I am particularly grateful to these co-authors for so many helpful conversations and their permission to draw on those ideas as part of this project.

The book also draws directly at various points on articles previously published in the *Cardozo Law Review*,[1] *International Journal of Constitutional Law*,[2] *Federal Law Review*,[3] *Law & Ethics of Human Rights*,[4] *Osgoode Hall Law Journal*,[5] and *Virginia Journal of International Law*,[6] as well as various edited volumes.[7] Chapters 2 and 3 draw directly on developed in *The Supreme Court of Canada and Constitutional (Equality) Baselines*, 50 Osgoode Hall L.J. 637 (2012) and Rosalind Dixon and Michaela Hailbronner, *Ely in the World: The Global Legacy of "Democracy and Distrust" Forty Years On*, 19 Int'l. J. Const. L. 427 (2021), and Rosalind Dixon and Amelia Loughland, *Comparative Constitutional Adaptation: Democracy and the High Court of Australia*, 19 Int'l. J. Const. L. 455 (2021). Chapter 3 draws on *The Core Case for Weak-Form Judicial Review*, 38 Cardozo L. Rev. 2193 (2016) and Rosalind Dixon and David Landau, *Abusive Constitutional Borrowing: Legal Globalization and the Subversion of Liberal Democracy* (2021). Chapter 4 draws

---

[1] Rosalind Dixon, *The Core Case for Weak-Form Judicial Review*, 38 CARDOZO L. REV. 2193 (2016).
[2] Rosalind Dixon, *The Forms, Functions, and Varieties of Weak(ened) Judicial Review*, 17 INT. J. CONST. L. 904 (2019); Rosalind Dixon, *Creating Dialogue about Socioeconomic Rights: Strong-form versus Weak-form Judicial Review Revisited*, 5 INT'L J. CONST. L. 391 (2007).
[3] Rosalind Dixon, *The Functional Constitution: Re-reading the 2014 High Court Constitutional Term*, 43 FED. L. REV. 455 (2015); Rosalind Dixon, *Calibrated Proportionality*, 48 FED. L. REV. 92 (2020).
[4] Rosalind Dixon, *Proportionality and Comparative Constitutional Law versus Studies*, 12 L. & ETHICS HUM. RTS. 203 (2018).
[5] Rosalind Dixon, *The Supreme Court of Canada and Constitutional (Equality) Baselines*, 50 OSGOODE HALL L.J. 637 (2012).
[6] Rosalind Dixon, *Constitutional Design Two Ways: Constitutional Drafters as Judges*, 57 VA. J. INT'L L. 1 (2017).
[7] ROSALIND DIXON, *Functionalism and Australian Constitutional Values*, in AUSTRALIAN CONSTITUTIONAL VALUES (Rosalind Dixon ed., 2018).

on *Calibrated Proportionality*, 48 Fed. L. Rev. 92 (2020) and *Constitutional Carve-Outs*, 37 Oxford J. Leg. Stud. 276 (2017). Chapters 4 and 5 incorporate and expand arguments made in *Creating Dialogue about Socioeconomic Rights: Strong-form versus Weak-form Judicial Review Revisited*, 5 Int'l J. Const. L. 391 (2007), David Landau and Rosalind Dixon, *Abusive Judicial Review: Courts Against Democracy* 53 U.C. Davis L. Rev. 1313 (2020), and Rosalind Dixon and Rishad Chowdhury, *A Case for Qualified Hope? The Supreme Court of India and the Midday Meal Decision*, in A Qualified Hope: The Indian Supreme Court and Progressive Social Change (Gerald N. Rosenberg et al. eds., 2019). Chapter 6 draws on *The Forms, Functions, and Varieties of Weak(ened) Judicial Review*, 17 Int. J. Const. L. 904 (2019). Chapter 8 reproduces and extends prior arguments made in *Strong Courts: Judicial Statecraft in Aid of Constitutional Change*, 59 Colum. J. Trans. L. 299 (2021). And I am indebted to various referees and editors for these publications for their role in refining and improving the work.

Many colleagues have also given their time and intellectual insights and read (sometimes multiple) versions of the book in draft, and I am especially grateful to them. My special thanks in this context to Lynsey Blayden, Cora Chan, Erin Delaney, Stephen Gardbaum, Claudia Geiringer, Mark Graber, Michaela Hailbronner, Ran Hirschl, Richard Holden, Madhav Khosla, Vicki Jackson, Martin Krygier, David Landau, Brendan Lim, Roger Masterman, Christoph Möllers Theunis Roux, Kent Roach, Reva Siegel, Adrienne Stone, Mark Tushnet, and Po Jen Yap, and participants at the Melbourne Institute of Comparative Constitutional Law, in December 2019 and UNSW Comparative Constitutional Roundtable in December 2020. I was also generously aided in understanding specific comparative issues by Asli Bâli, Vicente Fabian Benitez Rojas, Siddarth Narrain, Oren Tamir, Sergio Verdugo, and Po Jen Yap, and at various points by a range of outstanding UNSW graduates and graduate students, including Ariella Buckley, John Lidbetter, Karie Mayman, Dessislava Otachiliska, Elizabeth Perham, Veronica Sebesfi, and Melissa Vogt. Melissa Vogt in particular contributed outstanding research assistance throughout the project, and in the context of many of the articles that were a precursor to it.

To them all, I offer my sincerest thanks.

Finally, to Isobel and Hartley—thank you for always coming with me to constitutional law conferences that help make my work better, and for enduring my desire to be on my computer during every spare moment during COVID, and to finish home-schooling on an accelerated timetable. Without your understanding and flexibility, the work would never have been possible—and certainly not nearly as enjoyable or worthwhile!

Table of Contents

1. Introduction   1
   - A. Courts and Democratic Dysfunction: Promoting Democratic Responsiveness   2
   - B. Responsiveness to Context and Limits on Judicial Capacity   8
   - C. Responsive Judging: Responding to Litigants (and Disappointed Parties)   11
   - D. A Sometimes View of the Promise of Judicial Review   13
   - E. Structure of the Book   16

PART 1 DEMOCRATIC FOUNDATIONS

2. Constitutions and Constructional Choice   25
   - A. Judicial Review and Constructional Choice   27
     1. Abortion, sexual privacy, and same-sex marriage   27
     2. Implied speech and equality rights   33
     3. Structural social rights   33
     4. An unconstitutional amendment doctrine   36
   - B. Constitutional Theory and Constructional Choice   37
     1. Abortion   40
     2. Sexual privacy and equality   41
     3. Structural social rights   42
   - C. Why Courts? Constitutional Choice and Democracy   43
   - D. Ely's Response   47
   - E. Criticism of Ely's Approach   52
   - F. Representation-Reinforcement Beyond Ely   54

3. Defining Democracy and Democratic Dysfunction   59
   - A. Defining Democracy   60
   - B. Democratic Dysfunction: Antidemocratic Monopoly Power   65
     1. Electoral monopoly   72
     2. Institutional monopoly   74
     3. Monopoly: Intent versus effect   78
   - C. Legislative Blind Spots and Burdens of Inertia   80
     1. Legislative blind spots   82
     2. Legislative burdens of inertia   84
   - D. "Deliberate" versus Interconnected Democratic Blockages   88

PART 2 COURTS AND DEMOCRATIC RESPONSIVENESS

4. The Scope and Intensity of Responsive Judicial Review — 95
   A. The Legal and Political Legitimacy of Judicial Review — 96
   B. The Political Legitimacy of Constitutional Implications — 99
   C. Responsive Review in Practice — 102
      1. Abortion rights — 102
      2. LGBTQI+ rights — 108
      3. Implied rights to freedom of expression and equality — 115
      4. Structural social rights — 117
      5. Unconstitutional amendment doctrine — 122
   D. The Intensity of Judicial Review: Toward Calibrated Proportionality or Scrutiny — 127
      1. Calibrating judgments about limitations on expression — 131
      2. Calibrating judgments about discrimination — 134
   E. Deference and a Legislative Action/Inaction Distinction — 140

5. Democratic Dysfunction and the Effectiveness of Responsive Review — 143
   A. Detecting Democratic Dysfunction — 145
   B. Countering Dysfunction — 151
   C. Responsive Judicial Review in Practice — 157
      1. Comparative LGBTQI + rights — 158
      2. Structural social rights — 161
      3. Unconstitutional amendment doctrine — 165
   D. Preconditions for Success — 167
      1. Judicial independence and a political tolerance interval for judicial review — 168
      2. Litigation support structure — 171
      3. Jurisdiction and remedial toolkit — 176

6. Risks to Democracy: Reverse Inertia, Democratic Backlash, and Debilitation — 181
   A. Limits on Judicial Capacity and Legitimacy — 182
   B. Reverse Burdens of Inertia — 185
   C. Democratic Backlash — 194
   D. Democratic Debilitation — 200
   E. Judicial Prudence, Principle, and Pragmatism — 201

7. Toward Strong–Weak/Weak–Strong Judicial Review and Remedies	204
A. Weakened Judicial Review	205
B. Why (and How to) Weaken Review	216
1. The democratic minimum core and the pragmatic argument for weak–strong judicial review	217
2. Blind spots and burdens of inertia: a principled and pragmatic case for weak–strong review	220
C. Toward Strong–Weak/Weak–Strong Judicial Review	228
D. Conclusion	240

PART 3 RESPONSIVE JUDGING AND COMPARATIVE CONSTITUTIONAL THEORY

8. A Responsive Judicial Voice: Building a Court's Legitimacy	245
A. Why Responsive Judging—or a Responsive Judicial Voice	246
B. Judicial Framing and Responsive Judicial Review	248
1. Authorship	248
2. Tone: Respect or comity	250
3. Narrative	252
C. Responsive Judicial Review and Judging: Building Support for LGBTQI+ Rights	254
D. Responsive Judging and the Democratic Minimum Core	261
E. Responsive Judging: Limits and Cautions	265
1. Limits on responsive judging	265
2. Democratic legitimacy versus legitimation	267
3. A responsive judicial voice beyond the bench	269
9. Conclusion: Toward a New Comparative Political Process Theory?	271
Index	281

1
Introduction

Just over forty years ago, John Hart Ely published *Democracy and Distrust*, one of the best-known works of constitutional theory of all time.[1] In it, he outlined the idea of a "representation-reinforcing" approach to judicial review, in which the role of courts was to counter various "malfunctions" in the democratic process, rather than broadly substitute for democratic decision-making by the political branches of government.[2]

Many leading scholars have questioned why Ely's ideas have had such lasting influence. Ely arguably sought to draw too sharp a distinction between constitutional "process" and "substance."[3] He had little to say about the preconditions for effective judicial representation-reinforcement. Indeed, *Democracy and Distrust* largely preceded contemporary social science understandings about the necessary political and social conditions for effective democracy protection or enhancement by courts. He also focused entirely on the United States (US): as Doreen Lustig and Joseph Weiler have noted, "in some form or another the Ely thesis underlies many current regimes of judicial review within functioning democracies."[4] Ely, however, developed his ideas solely within a US constitutional context. He purported to provide an "interpretive" account of the US Constitution, and the Warren Court's constitutional jurisprudence, and did not consider the vast comparative constitutional experience of courts seeking to protect and promote democracy.[5] And, in part because of this, Ely did not account for the full range of contemporary threats to democracy and democratic values.

Yet Ely's focus on the relationship between judicial review and democracy retains clear value: by linking the scope and intensity of judicial review to the idea of democratic dysfunction, Ely helped provide an important theoretical

[1] JOHN HART ELY, DEMOCRACY AND DISTRUST: A THEORY OF JUDICIAL REVIEW (1980).
[2] *Id.* at 103.
[3] *See, e.g.*, Laurence H. Tribe, *The Puzzling Persistence of Process-Based Constitutional Theories*, 89 YALE L.J. 1063 (1980); discussion in Chapter 2, *infra*.
[4] Doreen Lustig & Joseph H.H. Weiler, *Judicial Review in the Contemporary World: Retrospective and Prospective*, 16 INT'L J. CONST. L. 315 (2018).
[5] *Compare* Stephen Gardbaum, *Comparative Political Process Theory*, 18 INT'L J. CONST. L. 1429 (2020); Manuel José Cepeda Espinosa & David Landau, *A Broad Read of Ely: Political Process Theory for Fragile Democracies*, 19 INT'L J. CONST. L. 548 (2021).

defense of the legitimacy of judicial review in a democracy, while at the same time helping point to cases in which more restrained or deferential forms of review by courts may be appropriate. His work has also provided a common reference point for constitutional theorists worldwide as they have grappled with these same questions.

The challenge for contemporary constitutional theory, therefore, is not to move beyond the idea of judicial representation-reinforcement. It is to develop a truly comparative, sociologically informed account of judicial representation-reinforcement that both draws on comparative understandings of courts' role in democracy protection and promotion *and* acknowledges the potential limits and contestability of this role.

A. Courts and Democratic Dysfunction: Promoting Democratic Responsiveness

Several comparative constitutional scholars have begun to develop exactly this kind of modern "*comparative* political process theory" (CPPT).[6] The aim of this book is also to contribute to this emerging school of neo-Elyian thought by offering an account of judicial representation-reinforcement focused on three distinct forms of democratic dysfunction, namely the risks of:

(1) *Antidemocratic monopoly power*: political monopoly, in both an electoral and institutional sense;
(2) *Democratic blind spots*: blind spots in the adoption of democratic legislation; and
(3) *Democratic burdens of inertia*: additional blockages in the form of unjustified delay in addressing democratic demands for constitutional change.

At the heart of a theory of responsive judicial review is a commitment to ensuring democratic responsiveness through: (i) regular, free, and fair multiparty

---

[6] Gardbaum, *Process Theory, supra* note 5 SAMUEL ISSACHAROFF ET AL., THE LAW OF DEMOCRACY: LEGAL REGULATION OF THE POLITICAL PROCESS (1998); Samuel Issacharoff & Richard H. Pildes, *Politics as Markets: Partisan Lockups of the Democratic Process*, 50 STAN. L. REV. 643 (1998); NIELS PETERSEN, PROPORTIONALITY AND JUDICIAL ACTIVISM: FUNDAMENTAL RIGHTS ADJUDICATION IN CANADA, GERMANY AND SOUTH AFRICA (2017); Sujit Choudhry, *"He Had a Mandate": The South African Constitutional Court and the African National Congress in a Dominant Party Democracy*, 2 CONST. CT. REV. 1 (2009); Espinosa & Landau, *supra* note 5; David Landau, *A Dynamic Theory of Judicial Role*, 55 B.C.L. REV. 1501 (2014).

elections; (ii) political rights and freedoms; and (iii) a range of institutional checks and balances as constituting the "minimum core" of democracy.[7] And any accumulation of electoral or institutional monopoly power may threaten this commitment to democratic responsiveness. In addition, a responsive approach assumes that democracy should be understood to entail thicker commitments to rights and reasoned deliberation, but in ways informed by democratic majority attitudes and understandings, and both democratic blind spots and burdens of inertia can threaten this thicker form of democratic responsiveness.

Moreover, these various forms of political monopoly, blind spots, and inertia are all sources of democratic dysfunction that courts are relatively well placed to counter, at least under certain conditions—that is, where judges enjoy a meaningful degree of independence, political and civil society support, and remedial power.

Without these conditions being met, courts themselves may become tools for eroding rather than buttressing democratic constitutional commitments.[8] But where they are satisfied, courts can and do play a role in countering both risks of electoral and institutional monopoly and democratic blind spots and burdens of inertia. On the one hand, their role will be to slow down or deter "abusive" constitutional change of this kind,[9] and on the other, to promote democratic "dialogue."[10] But in both the cases, the underlying logic of judicial review will be the same—that is, a commitment to representation-reinforcement that involves protecting and promoting the capacity of a

---

[7] *See* Rosalind Dixon & David Landau, *Competitive Democracy and the Constitutional Minimum Core*, in Assessing Constitutional Performance 268–69 (Tom Ginsburg & Aziz Huq eds., 2016); Rosalind Dixon & David Landau, Abusive Constitutional Borrowing: Legal Globalization and the Subversion of Liberal Democracy 25 (2021).

[8] David Landau & Rosalind Dixon, *Abusive Judicial Review: Courts Against Democracy*, 53 U.C. Davis L. Rev. 1313 (2020).

[9] *Compare, e.g.*, Rosalind Dixon & David Landau, *Transnational Constitutionalism and a Limited Doctrine of Unconstitutional Constitutional Amendment*, 13 Int'l J. Const. L. 606 (2015); David Landau & Rosalind Dixon, *Constraining Constitutional Change*, 50 Wake Forest L. Rev. 859 (2015). *See also* Samuel Issacharoff, *Constitutional Courts and Democratic Hedging*, 99 Geo. L.J. 961 (2010); Choudhry, *supra* note 6.

[10] Rosalind Dixon, *Creating Dialogue about Socioeconomic Rights: Strong-Form v. Weak-Form Judicial Review Revisited*, 5 Int'l J. Const. L. 391 (2007); Kent Roach, *Dialogic Judicial Review and its Critics*, 23 S.C.L.R. (2d) 49 (2004); Barry Friedman, *Dialogue and Judicial Review*, 91 Mich. L. Rev. 577 (1993); Po Jen Yap, *Defending Dialogue*, Pub. L. 527 (2012); Po Jen Yap, *Dialogue and Subconstitutional Doctrines in Common Law Asia*, Pub. L. 779 (2013); Aileen Kavanagh, *What's So Weak About "Weak-Form Review"? The Case of the UK Human Rights Act 1998*, 13 Int'l J. Const. L. 1008 (2015); Christine Bateup, *The Dialogic Promise: Assessing the Normative Potential of Theories of Constitutional Dialogue*, 71 Brook. L. Rev. 1109 (2005); Peter W. Hogg & Allison A. Bushell, *The Charter Dialogue between Courts and Legislatures (Or Perhaps the Charter of Rights Isn't Such a Bad Thing After All)*, 35 Osgoode Hall L.J. 75 (1997); Christopher P. Manfredi & James B. Kelly, *Six Degrees of Dialogue: A Response to Hogg and Bushell*, 37 Osgoode Hall L.J. 513 (1999); Constitutional Dialogue: Rights, Democracy, Institutions 161 (Geoffrey Sigalet et al. eds., 2019).

democratic system to respond both to minority rights claims and considered majority understandings under a range of real-world, non-ideal conditions.

Domestic courts are not the only institutions that can play this role. Transnational institutions—including both courts and commissions—can often play a role in monitoring and sanctioning actions that threaten to erode democracy.[11] In most democratic constitutions, there are a range of other institutions that create "vertical" and "horizontal" checks and balances against risks of democratic erosion.[12] And even some citizen-initiated processes—such as plebiscites—may play a role in countering democratic blockages, such as burdens of inertia.

But courts often have important institutional advantages—and tools—that can allow them to counter blockages of this kind. This does not mean that they will always, or even mostly, succeed in performing this role. Courts must be structurally well placed to undertake review of this kind. Judges must also have the requisite mix of legal and political skills necessary to identify relevant democratic blockages and determine how and when they can most effectively be countered by judicial intervention. This is not a task that every judge will be capable of. The hope is that, by providing a clearer template and justification for review of this kind, this book may increase the number of judges capable of doing so successfully. But even so, it is not an approach that every judge or court will be well placed to adopt. For some courts, the lesser evil may be a more restrained or limited approach to judicial review, which has less ambition but also less scope for misjudgment or error.

Similarly, democratic representation-reinforcement will not exhaust the scope of courts' role. The foremost responsibility of courts in a democracy is to give effect to *legal* constraints and requirements. In a constitutional context, this means giving effect to the text of a written constitution. And, as Ely himself pointed out, while constitutional language itself may often be open-ended

---

[11] *See, e.g.*, Tom Gerald Daly, *Can International Organisations Help to Stem Democratic Decay?*, I-CONnect (Nov. 16, 2017), <http://www.iconnectblog.com/2017/11/can-international-organisations-help-to-stem-democratic-decay-i-connect-column/>; Kriszta Kovács & Kim Lane Scheppele, *The Fragility of an Independent Judiciary: Lessons from Hungary and Poland—And the European Union*, 51 COMMUNIST & POST-COMMUNIST STUD. 189 (2018); Lukas Zamecki & Viktor Glied, *Article 7 Process and Democratic Backsliding of Hungary and Poland: Democracy and the Rule of Law*, 34 ONLINE J. MODELLING THE NEW EUR. (2020); TOM GINSBURG, DEMOCRACIES AND INTERNATIONAL LAW (2021); Daniel R. Kelemen & Michael Blauberger, *Introducing the Debate: European Union Safeguards Against Member States' Democratic Backsliding*, 24 J. EUR. PUB. POL'Y 317 (2017); Anna M. Meyerrose, *The Unintended Consequences of Democracy Promotion: International Organizations and Democratic Backsliding*, 53 COMP. POL. STUD. 1547 (2020).

[12] Michael Pal, *Electoral Management Bodies as a Fourth Branch of Government*, 21 REV. CONST. STUD. 87 (2016); Mark Tushnet, *Institutions Protecting Constitutional Democracy: Some Conceptual and Methodological Preliminaries*, 70 U. TORONTO L.J. 95 (2020); Vicki Jackson, *Knowledge Institutions in Constitutional Democracies: Preliminary Reflections*, 7 CAN. J. COMPAR. CONST. L. 156 (2021).

and indeterminate in scope, in some cases it may have a quite clear semantic meaning.[13] Constitutional history or case law may likewise point to a specific role for a court—for example, in repudiating and overcoming a history of Nazi rule, slavery, caste, or apartheid.[14] Notions of judicial representation-reinforcement are thus relevant only in cases where formal constitutional "modalities," such as the text, history, and structure of a constitution run out—and courts are necessarily required to consider broader constitutional or political values as part of a process of constitutional constructional choice.[15]

Moreover, democracy is not the only value a constitutional court can, or should, consider in this context: other values include individual freedom, dignity (in both a Kantian and "capabilities" sense), formal and substantive equality, and a commitment to the rule of law.[16] And courts can and should play a role in enforcing these commitments—both as a necessary condition for the legitimacy of democracy, and as a constraint on majoritarian democratic decision-making.

Responsive judicial review is also predicated on courts doing exactly this, namely giving effect to both the ordinary language of a constitution and a range of constitutional values, including, but not limited to, constitutional democracy. It simply aims to offer additional guidance for courts in cases in which the scope or priority of relevant constitutional norms is unclear or the subject of reasonable democratic disagreement. In engaging in judicial review in these contexts, this book argues that courts should consider the degree to which particular constructional choices may be able to help counter all three of these risks to democratic responsiveness—that is, the risks of antidemocratic monopoly, democratic blind spots, and burdens of inertia.[17]

For example, in determining the scope of implications under a written constitution, courts should consider the degree to which making an implication may help counter blind spots, burdens of inertia, and especially forms of electoral or institutional monopoly on the part of certain political actors.

Similarly, in applying both a US-style form of tiered scrutiny and doctrine of structured proportionality, a responsive approach suggests courts should take a carefully calibrated, contextual approach—informed by the presence, or absence, of democratic blockages; that is, they should consider the degree to

---

[13] ELY, *supra* note 1, at 13.
[14] Kim Lane Scheppele, *Aspirational and Aversive Constitutionalism: The Case for Studying Cross-Constitutional Influence Through Negative Models*, 1 INT'L J. CONST. L. 296 (2003).
[15] PHILLIP BOBBITT, CONSTITUTIONAL FATE: THEORY OF THE CONSTITUTION (1982).
[16] ELY, *supra* note 1, at ch. 2. See further pp 36–38 *infra*.
[17] Lawrence B. Solum, *The Interpretation-Construction Distinction*, 27 CONST. COMMENT 95 (2010); Lawrence Solum, *Originalism and Constitutional Construction*, 82 FORDHAM L. REV. 453 (2013).

which a law threatens to undermine electoral or institutionalism pluralism or reflects potential legislative blind spots or burdens of inertia. The more a law reflects blockages of this kind, the more compelling the case will be for heightened forms of judicial scrutiny, whereas the more it preserves democratic pluralism, and reflects recent, reasoned legislative deliberation on an issue, the greater the case will be for relaxed or reduced forms of judicial scrutiny.

Underpinning this and other aspects of a responsive approach will also be a concern about the degree to which, absent judicial intervention, various sources of democratic dysfunction are likely to be reversible by future legislative or executive action. "Activist" forms of judicial review, for instance, will be more politically legitimate where they respond to irreversible threats to the democratic minimum core or individual dignity.[18] Notions of reversibility also inform the adequacy of different models of judicial remedy, and the idea of reverse democratic burdens of inertia.

Another recurrent theme in this book is the idea that the intensity and strength of judicial review should vary according to the degree of recent and reasoned legislative deliberation on an issue. Responsive judicial review is not wholly focused on prompting legislative deliberation or "democracy forcing" in the sense advocated by scholars such as Cass Sunstein; in some cases, it aims to update constitutional meaning directly, by way of judicial review itself.[19] But it also has a semi-procedural dimension: it suggests that legislatures should be encouraged to engage in, and rewarded for, good faith efforts at democratic constitutional implementation.[20]

Why call the approach developed in the book a "responsive" approach to judicial review? The key aim of doing so is to highlight the role courts can play in promoting commitments to democratic responsiveness in both at-risk and well-functioning constitutional democracies, and to explore how and when they should do so. This is also an account that is both conceptual and comparative in origin and reach: the ideas behind it are derived from attention to comparative insights and must also be applied in a manner that is responsive to the specific constitutional context.

In addition, the idea of judicial "responsiveness" has important continuities with existing theories of responsive *law* and *regulation*. In their 1978 book, *Law and Society in Transition*, Philippe Nonet and Philip Selznick famously

---

[18] *See* Chapter 4, *infra*.
[19] Cass R. Sunstein, One Case at a Time: Judicial Minimalism on the Supreme Court (2001). *See* discussion in Neal Devins, *Review: The Democracy-Forcing Constitution*, 97 Mich. L. Rev. 1971 (1999).
[20] *Compare* Ittai Bar-Siman-Tov, *Semiprocedural Judicial Review*, 6 Legisprudence 271 (2012).

argued that legal systems tend to undergo a transition between three distinct phases: phases in which law is "repressive," "autonomous," or "responsive," and that a responsive approach to law has the virtue of offering a flexible and participatory approach to regulation.[21] Nonet and Selznick further suggested that to guard against the danger of a return to repressive law, it is important for courts to guard against the dangers of political repression and non-contestation.[22]

The idea of responsive law has also been the subject of attention by a range of leading legal theorists over the last thirty years. In Germany, the idea of responsive law has been adapted and transformed as the basis of a theory of "reflexive law."[23] In the United States and Australia, the idea of responsiveness has likewise been the basis for a complex theory of regulation known as "responsive regulation," which emphasizes the idea of regulation as flexible, participatory, and multipronged—or based on a mix of "carrots and sticks" or "strong" and "weak" forms of intervention.[24] Most notably, Ian Ayers and John Braithwaite suggest that regulation should be based on a "pyramid" of sanctions, and shift from weaker to stronger forms of intervention, based on the response of regulated entities.[25] And they emphasize the importance of listening and giving voice to the perspectives of those subject to regulation, and that regulators should: "engage those who resist with fairness; [and] show them *respect* by construing the resistance as an opportunity to learn how to improve regulatory design."[26]

Similar ideas have been advanced by Michael Dorf and Charles Sabel as part of a "democratic experimentalist" approach to judicial review.[27] The idea of democratic experimentalism itself draws on theories of responsive law and regulation but proposes a distinctive evidence-based, participatory approach to legal regulation, which draws on information gained from the successes (and failures) of local democratic experiences to create "rolling" best practice standards or benchmarks for local and state democratic regulation.[28] And

---

[21] PHILIPPE NONET & PHILIP SELZNICK, LAW AND SOCIETY IN TRANSITION: TOWARD RESPONSIVE LAW 78 (1978).
[22] Id. at 95.
[23] See, e.g., Gunther Teubner, Substantive and Reflexive Elements in Modern Law, 17 L. & SOC. REV. 239 (1983); Peer Zumbansen, Law After the Welfare State: Formalism, Functionalism, and the Ironic Turn of Reflexive Law, 56 AM. J. COMP. L. 769 (2008).
[24] IAN AYRES & JOHN BRAITHWAITE, RESPONSIVE REGULATION: TRANSCENDING THE DEREGULATION DEBATE (1992).
[25] Id. at 35–100.
[26] John Braithwaite, The Essence of Responsive Regulation, 44 U.B.C. L. REV. 475, 476 (2011).
[27] See Michael C. Dorf & Charles F. Sabel, A Constitution of Democratic Experimentalism, 98 COLUM. L. REV. 267 (1998).
[28] Id. On comparative accounts of the virtues of experimentalist approaches to constitutional decision-making by courts, see also STU WOOLMAN, THE SELFLESS CONSTITUTION: EXPERIMENTALISM AND FLOURISHING AS FOUNDATIONS OF SOUTH AFRICA'S BASIC LAW (2013).

while judges have an important role to play in articulating and enforcing these benchmarks, their key role, in a democratic experimentalist paradigm, is to insist on forms of law-making that are participatory, evidence based, and consider relevant alternatives.[29]

The book also aims to provide a distinctive *adaptation* of existing ideas about legal and regulatory responsiveness to the constitutional domain. Others have made important steps in this same direction before me, including in adapting Nonet and Selznick's work to a comparative context and developing notions of responsive judging in the context of synthesis of notions of responsive and reflexive law. For example, in *The Responsive Judge: International Perspectives* (2018), Tana Sourdin and Archie Zadarski bring together global scholars to reflect on how judges across the world adapt to changing legal and political contexts. Machteld de Hoon and Suzan Verberk explore the idea of a responsive judicial approach to dispute resolution, and how this favors a contextual approach to the preferred tools and path for resolving individual disputes.[30] And most notably, in previous and forthcoming works, Malcolm Langford highlights how judges can draw on responsive and reflexive ideas to engage in democratically legitimate forms of social rights adjudication.[31]

In my own account, the focus is on promoting the responsiveness of a constitutional system as a whole to democratic majority understandings, not just to underlying social realities or institutional capacities. But it shares with responsive law, regulation and democratic experimentalism, as well as these prior accounts of responsive courts, a concern with underlying democratic realities, weak and strong form review, regulatory defaults, and respect-based forms of judicial engagement.

B. Responsiveness to Context and Limits on Judicial Capacity

Indeed, one of the benefits of the label "responsive" in this context is that it helps draw attention to the need for attention by courts to the legal and political context for judicial review, and the potential fallibility of their own

---

[29] Dorf & Sabel, *supra* note 27, at 397, 399.
[30] Machteld W. de Hoon & Suzan Verberk, *Towards a More Responsive Judge: Challenges and Opportunities*, 10 Utrecht L. Rev. 27 (2014).
[31] Malcolm Langford, *Why Judicial Review?*, 2 OSLO L. REV. 36 (2015); Malcolm Langford, Judicial Politics and Social Rights', in THE FUTURE OF ECONOMIC AND SOCIAL RIGHTS (Katherine Young eds.,, 2019), 66–109, at 69–73; MALCOLM LANGFORD, RESPONSIVE COURTS AND COMPLEX CASES (forthcoming).

judgments—both about what commitments to democratic responsiveness require and the political "tolerance interval" for attempts by courts to promote greater responsiveness.[32] Judges, for instance, may overestimate the risks to competitive democracy posed by certain legislative changes, or more often underestimate them, by failing to appreciate their cumulative or interconnected quality.[33] They may also misjudge the evolution of democratic majority opinion or the degree to which giving additional protections to constitutional rights may be compatible with the achievement of certain legislative objectives. This can mean that judicial review itself creates two distinct *democratic* risks of:

(1) *Reverse burdens of inertia*, that is, legal changes that go beyond what democratic majorities are willing to endorse or support, but which legislatures cannot effectively override or modify; and
(2) *Democratic backlash*: forms of backlash against a court, which erode a court's capacity to implement democratic constitutional requirements.

Even if courts are perfectly accurate in identifying democratic blockages, the act of countering those blockages may create a third, distinct risk to democratic responsiveness, namely the risk of:

(3) *Democratic debilitation*: dynamics whereby legislators have limited incentive actually to address constitutional questions.

In seeking to protect and promote the responsiveness of a democratic constitutional system, this book argues that courts should therefore be mindful of both the benefits to democracy of attempts at judicial representation-reinforcement *and* the potential risks—in the form of reverse burdens of inertia, democratic backlash, and democratic debilitation. It further suggests that courts should calibrate the scope and "strength" of their decisions to the nature of the blockage they are seeking to counter *and* their own institutional capacity and knowledge.

The concept of "weak review" was first introduced by Mark Tushnet as a way of describing systems of constitutional review in which courts do not

---

[32] *See, e.g.*, Lee Epstein et al., *The Role of Constitutional Courts in the Establishment and Maintenance of Democratic Systems of Government*, 35 Law & Soc'y Rev. 117 (2001); David Landau, *Substitute and Complement Theories of Judicial Review*, 92 Ind. L.J. 1283 (2017).

[33] *Compare* Dixon & Landau, *Transnational Constitutionalism*, *supra* note 9; Kim Lane Scheppele, *The Rule of Law and the Frankenstate: Why Governance Checklists Do Not Work*, 26 Governance 559 (2013).

enjoy formal legal finality.[34] Stephen Gardbaum has adopted similar terminology to describe the emergent system of judicial review in countries such as Canada, the United Kingdom (UK), New Zealand, and, more recently, various Australian states.[35] But the term has been gradually expanded to describe *any* form of judicial review that is less than final over the short to medium term—or is *de facto* as well as *de jure* revisable in nature.[36] Weakened review, in this sense, can also take numerous forms: it can involve narrow forms of judicial reasoning, the reliance on weakened remedies such as suspended declarations of invalidity, engagement remedies, or supervisory orders that leave broad scope for governments to help craft the substance of the relevant remedy, or even weakened norms of precedent or *stare decisis*.[37] A responsive approach suggests that courts should combine elements of strong and weak review, sensitive to both the nature of the blockage they are seeking to counter and concerns about the potential for reverse burdens of inertia and/or democratic backlash.

Risks of electoral and institutional monopoly, for instance, will generally require courts to engage in strong or even super-strong forms of review. Even then, they may not be effective in countering the risk of anti-democratic monopoly power because, in effect, a court is being asked to constrain the *concerted efforts* of certain political elites to erode democratic norms and structures. But any attempt to do so will likely require the use of quite strong forms of judicial review. Hence, courts should limit or weaken the immediacy or coercive force of their rulings only for pragmatic or prudential rather than principled reasons.[38]

Blind spots or burdens of inertia, in contrast, will often call, as a matter of principle, for weaker, more provisional forms of review: blockages of this kind are associated with ideas of democracy that go beyond the democratic minimum core and, to that extent, are more contestable. Courts in this context are not seeking to protect the thinnest or most minimal notions of democracy but rather thicker and more contested notions of democracy. And they

---

[34] Mark Tushnet, *Alternative Forms of Judicial Review*, 101 Mich. L. Rev. 2782 (2003).

[35] Stephen Gardbaum, The New Commonwealth Model of Constitutionalism: Theory and Practice (2013). *See also* Tom Hickey, *The Republican Virtues of the "New Commonwealth Model of Constitutionalism"*, 14 Int'l J. Const. L. 794 (2016).

[36] Tushnet himself has also welcomed this expansion and "continuization." *See* Mark Tushnet, *Weak-Form Review: An Introduction*, 17 Int'l. J. Const. L. 807 (2019); Mark Tushnet & Rosalind Dixon, *Weak-Form Review in Asia and its Constitutional Relatives: An Asian Perspective*, in Comparative Constitutional Law in Asia 102 (Rosalind Dixon & Tom Ginsburg eds., 2014).

[37] Rosalind Dixon, *The Forms, Functions, and Varieties of Weak(ened) Judicial Review*, 17 Int'l. J. Const. L. 904 (2019).

[38] *Compare* Theunis Roux, *Principle and Pragmatism on the Constitutional Court of South Africa*, 7 Int'l. J. Const. L. 106 (2009); Theunis Roux, The Politics of Principle: The First South African Constitutional Court, 1995–2005 (2013).

are engaging in judgments about evolving (considered) democratic majority opinion that, by definition, are likely to be less objective and reliable. They therefore run a greater risk of judicial over- as opposed to under-enforcement. The democratic response to court decisions of this kind can also point to whether a court has succeeded in advancing democratic responsiveness. If courts have, in fact, helped overcome democratic inertia, one could expect a democratic majority to "approve" of the decision or be grateful to courts for facilitating the expression of the popular will.[39] Conversely, if a court misreads democratic attitudes, this could be expected to lead to expressions of popular disapproval. As a matter of principle, judicial review that seeks to counter these sources of democratic dysfunction should therefore be weak–strong in approach—that is, be sufficiently strong to overcome relevant democratic blockages but weak enough to allow scope for reasonable democratic disagreement. One way to achieve this will be through a form of remedial "penalty default" structure, whereby courts give broad freedom to legislative and executive actors to help craft a constitutional remedy, but impose real and enforceable consequences for any failure to do so.[40]

This also echoes a broader theme running through the idea of responsive judicial review which is that courts should leave open meaningful scope for substantive constitutional judgments by legislators in response to court decisions: invitations to judicial-legislative dialogue should be *real not* just *rhetorical*, and hence courts should take a different approach to assessing the justifiability of practices that are a product of legislative oversight or inaction, as compared to recent and reasoned deliberation.

C. Responsive Judging: Responding to Litigants (and Disappointed Parties)

Finally, a responsive theory of judicial review suggests that judicial capacity is not necessarily something that courts must take as given, or treat as an immovable constraint on the scope for effective representation-reinforcement. Rather, it will in part be *endogenous* to how courts approach the task of judicial review, or something that courts themselves have the power to influence

---

[39] Compare ELY, *supra* note 1, at 121.
[40] Compare Ian Ayres & Robert Gertner, *Majoritarian vs. Minoritarian Defaults*, 51 STAN. L. REV. 1591–613 (1999). *See* further discussion in Chapter 7, *infra*.

through the choices they make about how to engage with civil society, and questions such as:

(1) *Authorship*, the identity of a judge who writes for the court;
(2) *Tone*, how they approach the motives of losing parties; and
(3) *Narrative*, the mix of "global" and "local" values relied on in their reasoning.

We currently have a limited understanding of how courts approach these questions, and why. At the same time, they are clearly dimensions of judicial decision-making that offer important opportunities for courts to promote the actual and perceived legitimacy of their decisions. For instance, courts can demonstrate genuine respect for losing parties, and potentially increase the willingness of those parties to abide by decisions that go against their interests, if they show: (i) a concern to ensure that the background and experience of a particular judge speaks to those disappointed by a decision; (ii) reasoning that demonstrates a posture of respect towards that party; and (iii) a narrative that combines universal and context-specific—or "global" and "local"—elements, or resonates in both localized and universal constitutional identities and commitments. This also points towards courts combining a responsive approach to judicial review with a form of responsive *judging* or responsive judicial voice.

On one level, ideas of this kind are deeply pragmatic in nature—that is, they seek to enhance the effectiveness of attempts by courts to counter electoral and institutional monopoly, democratic blind spots, and burdens of inertia.[41] There is, however, another level on which, at least if conducted in good faith, these approaches could be seen as linked to another notion of judicial responsiveness— that is, the idea that in engaging in judicial review, courts should be responsive to the distinctive nature of adjudication as a practice, and the responsibility of courts to provide citizens with a *"right to a hearing,"* and in a way that shows respect for the fundamental dignity of all parties, especially those disappointed by a decision.[42] In this sense, they involve a true mix of principle and pragmatism, or *principled* strategy, on the part of judges.[43]

---

[41] RICHARD A. POSNER, LAW, PRAGMATISM, AND DEMOCRACY (2005).

[42] Alon Harel & Adam Shinar, *The Real Case for Judicial Review*, in COMPARATIVE JUDICIAL REVIEW (Erin F. Delaney & Rosalind Dixon eds., 2018); Alon Harel & Tsvi Kahana, *The Easy Core Case for Judicial Review*, 2 J. LEGAL ANALYSIS 227 (2010). *See also* Alon Harel & Adam Shinar, *Between Judicial and Legislative Supremacy: A Cautious Defense of Constrained Judicial Review*, 10 INT'L J. CONST. L. 950 (2012).

[43] *See* Roux, *supra* note 38; ROUX, *supra* note 38. *See also* Roni Mann, *Non-ideal Theory of Constitutional Adjudication*, 7 GLOBAL CONST. 14, 38–51 (2018); Langford, *supra* note 31. Rosalind Dixon, *Strong Courts, Judicial Statecraft in Aid of Constitutional Change*, 59 COLUM. J. TRANSNAT'L L. 299 (2021).

D. A Sometimes View of the Promise of Judicial Review

Scholars often talk about "lumpers" and "splitters" in constitutional theory—the difference between those that seek to find commonalities in the face of divergence or distinction and difference in the face of apparent similarity or convergence.[44] But constitutional scholarship can also be divided into what might be described as an "everything" and "nothing" view of courts and judicial capacity. The "everything" view tends to assume a heroic conception of individual judicial skill and capacity, and even more ambitious view of what courts can achieve as institutions. This, for example, is the image of constitutional courts and judges often associated with Ronald Dworkin's hypothetical judge "Hercules,"[45] and some of the leading American constitutional theories developed during the Warren Court era.[46] Some might even suggest this was a feature of Ely's own theory of representation-reinforcing review.

In contrast, the "nothing" view posits that judges are deeply unheroic in character and inevitably shaped by the broader political context.[47] On this view, courts have little capacity to protect and promote democratic political processes or norms.[48] They are either almost entirely ineffective in creating social and political change: to use Gerry Rosenberg's famous expression, they offer a purely "hollow hope" of such change.[49] Or they tend simply to increase the difficulty of such change—by adding to the perceived legitimacy of deeply flawed existing democratic constitutional structures,[50] perhaps by acting as agents of hegemonic preservation.[51]

The reality, however, will often lie somewhere between these two poles: courts are the product of their time and political context and have limited tools for achieving social and political change. They may even be so closely aligned to a political regime that they become *instruments* of the

---

[44] *Compare* James N. Druckman & Lawrence R. Jacobs, *Lumpers and Splitters: The Public Opinion Information That Politicians Collect and Use*, 70 INT'L J. PUB. OPINION Q. 453 (2006); LEE ANNE FENNELL, SLICES AND LUMPS: DIVISION AND AGGREGATION IN LAW AND LIFE (2019).

[45] *See* RONALD DWORKIN, FREEDOM'S LAW: THE MORAL READING OF THE AMERICAN CONSTITUTION (1999).

[46] *See* discussion in MARK TUSHNET, TAKING THE CONSTITUTION AWAY FROM THE COURTS 66 (2000).

[47] Robert A. Dahl, *Decision-Making in a Democracy: The Supreme Court as a National Policy-Maker*, 6 J. PUB. L. 279 (1957).

[48] *Compare* Tom Gerald Daly, *The Alchemists: Courts as Democracy-Builders in Contemporary Thought*, 6 GLOBAL CONSTITUTIONALISM 101 (2017).

[49] GERALD N. ROSENBERG, THE HOLLOW HOPE: CAN COURTS BRING ABOUT SOCIAL CHANGE? (2008).

[50] *Compare* DUNCAN KENNEDY, A CRITIQUE OF ADJUDICATION: FIN DE SIÈCLE (1997).

[51] RAN HIRSCHL, TOWARDS JURISTOCRACY: THE ORIGINS AND CONSEQUENCES OF THE NEW CONSTITUTIONALISM (2004).

regime, and its antidemocratic aims or tendencies.[52] And they will almost certainly make errors in judging current and evolving democratic constitutional understandings and attitudes, and broader political currents. Whether they are even willing to contemplate a form of democracy-reinforcing judicial review will also depend on their own institutional role conception, which will be influenced by history and contemporary sociopolitical dynamics.[53]

But as I noted above, judges also have a distinctive institutional training and vantage point which can allow them collectively to slow down or deter certain attempts to erode the democratic minimum core and to promote attention to, or action in response to, various constitutional claims in ways that can help counter legislative blind spots and burdens of inertia. To do so, courts must meet certain minimal preconditions of at least implicit institutional realism, political independence and support, remedial power, and support within civil society. And they must engage in judicial review that is quite carefully calibrated to respond to evidence of blockages within a democratic constitutional system.

This "sometimes" view of judicial capacity, therefore, is considerably more complicated than the binary everything/nothing view. The constitutional academy also often tends to reward catchy labels and binary categories over more qualified and complex claims.[54] I am fortunate, however, to be writing this book against the backdrop of a large and growing literature on weak-form judicial review, at the heart of which is a belief in the "sometimes" view of courts and judicial capacity. Indeed, the premise of weakened models of judicial review, as Gardbaum notes, is that they "provid[e] a third alternative to either strong-form review or no judicial review that may perform many of the former's beneficial functions in the transitional context, but in a less confrontational way that reduces the risk of systematically counterproductive political attacks on judicial independence."[55]

My hope, as we embark on the collective task of developing a truly modern and comparative political process theory, is that others will come to embrace

---

[52] Landau & Dixon, *supra* note 8. *See also* Madhav Khosla, *With Freedom at Stake, Courts Are Collapsing*, N.Y. TIMES (Sept. 9, 2020), <https://www.nytimes.com/2020/09/09/opinion/hungary-turkey-india-courts.html>.

[53] *See* David Landau, *Constituent Power and Constitution Making in Latin America*, *in* COMPARATIVE CONSTITUTION MAKING 567 (David Landau & Hanna Lerner eds., 2019). For how this plays out in the post-socialist world in particular, *see* NGOC SON BUI, CONSTITUTIONAL CHANGE IN THE CONTEMPORARY SOCIALIST WORLD (2020).

[54] *Compare* Rosalind Dixon, *Toward a Realist Comparative Constitutional Studies?*, 64 AM. J. COMP. L. 193 (2016).

[55] Stephen Gardbaum, *Are Strong Courts Always a Good Thing For New Democracies?*, 53 COLUM. J. TRANSNAT'L L. 285, 290 (2014).

this same sometimes view. As constitutional scholars in the 2020s, the challenge we face is to do justice to the intellectual inheritance Ely has given us, but in a way that is fit for purpose in a truly globalized constitutional universe, where the threats to democracy are manifold and increasing by the day. In doing so, our task is also to develop a theory of judicial review that responds to both the promise of courts as potential guardians of democracy and democratic values, and the inevitable limits on courts' capacity and legitimacy in performing this role.

Getting this balance right could not be more important, and almost certainly depends on a "sometimes" view of judicial capacity. Courts worldwide also vary in their capacity to engage in successful forms of responsive review. And we are living in an era in which courts are not just the guardians of democracy but increasingly tools of democratic erosion—or agents of "abusive" as opposed to "responsive" judicial review.[56]

In part because of this, the attractiveness of a responsive approach to judicial review may itself turn out to be a "sometimes" question. But for now, my claim is that it is an account of judicial review that is almost always democratically defensible in theory, even if only sometimes achievable in practice. This book also aims to provide a roadmap for judges and scholars interested in building up the capacity for courts to engage in review of this kind. The hope is that with the benefit of this roadmap, over time more democracies may become sufficiently responsive to democratic minority and majority understandings to be worthy of public trust, and fewer will fit the label of democracies characterized by dysfunction.

A responsive approach to judicial review, however, aims to elide any sharp distinction between political and legal models of constitutionalism. Instead, it aims to adopt a realistic account of the potential institutional strengths and weakness of both legislatures and courts, and accordingly to offer an account that combines elements of weak and strong judicial review, and notions of judicial constraint and capacity building. It also envisages that some courts may promote all aspects of democratic responsiveness, while others only a subset of commitments to overcoming blind spots and/or burdens of inertia.

It is thus cautiously and qualifiedly optimistic about the idea that courts can help reinforce representation in a constitutional democracy but equally realistic about the fact that this may be possible in only a limited set of circumstances

---

[56] *See* Landau & Dixon, *supra* note 8; Rosalind Dixon & David Landau, *1989–2019: From Democratic to Abusive Constitutional Borrowing*, 17 INT'L J. CONST. L. 489 (2019); ROSALIND DIXON & DAVID LANDAU, ABUSIVE CONSTITUTIONAL BORROWING: LEGAL GLOBALIZATION AND THE SUBVERSION OF LIBERAL DEMOCRACY (2021).

16　INTRODUCTION

or cases. Just as Ely's account was in equal parts a defense and critique of US constitutional jurisprudence during the Warren Court, the idea of responsive judicial review offers both a reconstruction of, and more critical *roadmap* for, a more democracy-enhancing form of judicial review by courts on a global scale.

E. Structure of the Book

The approach of the book in this context is explicitly comparative, empirical, and sociolegal, albeit in a limited sense: it aims to *illustrate* the different democratic risks outlined at the outset of the book by reference to a close contextual reading of judicial review in a range of constitutional democracies—simply as "proof of concept," not in order to show the inevitability of any particular constitutional outcome or dynamic.[57]

The specific cases relied on reflect a mix of well-known examples of judicial review by leading constitutional courts, including courts in the United States, United Kingdom, Canada, India, South Africa, and Colombia.[58] They are, in this sense, an example of what Ran Hirschl calls a "prototypical cases" approach: they illustrate broader comparative dynamics and possibilities through examples that are broadly understood to typify certain models or dynamics in the field.[59] The South African and Colombian constitutional courts are arguably some of the leading exemplars of courts that in fact (at least at times) engage in responsive forms of judicial review. But there are also traces or intimations of a responsive approach in certain decisions of the Canadian, Indian, UK, and US supreme courts. The book further draws on well-known cases of judicial review from the United States as a "bridge" between Ely's work and comparative political process theory.

The book also canvasses a wider range of cases in less detail, including select aspects of the constitutional jurisprudence of courts in Australia, Fiji, Hong Kong, Israel, and Korea. This reflects my strong commitment to engaging with jurisdictions in the Global South, as well as Global North, and going beyond the "usual suspects" in comparative constitutional law.[60] But it also reflects the

---

[57] *Compare* Mark Tushnet, *Autochtony and Influence: The Charter's Place in Transnational Constitutional Discourse, in* CONSTITUTIONAL CROSSROADS: REFLECTIONS ON CHARTER RIGHTS, RECONCILIATION, AND CHANGE (Kate Puddister & Emmett Macfarlane eds., 2022).

[58] On the status of at least some of these courts as leading courts, *see* Rosalind Dixon, *Constitutional Design Two Ways: Constitutional Drafters as Judges*, 57 VA. J. INT'L L. 57 (2017).

[59] *Compare* RAN HIRSCHL, COMPARATIVE MATTERS: THE RENAISSANCE OF COMPARATIVE CONSTITUTIONAL LAW (2014).

[60] On the Global North critique, *see* DANIEL B. MALDONADO, CONSTITUTIONALISM OF THE GLOBAL SOUTH: THE ACTIVIST TRIBUNALS OF INDIA, SOUTH AFRICA, AND COLOMBIA (2013) and discussion in Hirschl, *supra* note 51. *See also* Philipp Dann et al., *The Southern Turn in Comparative Constitutional*

jurisdictional expertise, or limitations, of the author, as a comparative scholar working in Australia, as well as prior work (with Vicki Jackson) on "outsider" constitutional interpreters or foreign judges on national constitutional courts (e.g., as is the case in Fiji).[61] Australia is part of the economic "North" but geographic South, and has strong economic and political ties to Asia. It is also part of the Commonwealth and is strongly influenced by Anglo-American, common law legal traditions.

My own view is that this form of "local" influence is more or less inevitable in any approach to comparative constitutional studies, and we should be both open and unapologetic about this, providing that we strive to justify principles of case selection within these constraints. It simply means that for any small-n qualitative work in the field, we should be appropriately provisional and tentative about the conclusions reached, and open to those conclusions being revisited considering the work of other scholars on a broader range of jurisdictions.[62] This book is also offered in exactly this spirit—as a work of constitutional theory and constitutional comparison, which invites revision and refinement by others. And my hope is that others will take up the challenge and extend and refine the ideas offered in the context of current democratic conditions—in Latin America, Asia, Africa, and Europe. I also hope to contribute to that project through a process of ongoing scholarly dialogue and collaboration.

The aim of the book, in this context, is to draw on specific comparative examples as a means of developing "generic" constitutional principles or guidance for courts worldwide but on the understanding that guidance of this kind will inevitably need to be applied with appropriate attention to, and modification to fit, the specific constitutional context. The precise threats to democracy will vary across countries and time, and how far courts are able to go in countering them will likewise depend on a range of context-specific factors. In some dominant-party democracies, for example, courts might decide that there is little scope for countering electoral or institutional monopoly, but greater scope for countering legislative blind spots and burdens of inertia. By necessity, all judicial review in such systems might, therefore, be strong–weak or dialogic rather than strong in nature; and responsive to that—but only that—extent.[63]

Law: An Introduction, in THE GLOBAL SOUTH AND COMPARATIVE CONSTITUTIONAL LAW 1 (Philipp Dann et al. eds., 2020).

[61] Rosalind Dixon & Vicki C. Jackson, *Constitutions Inside Out: Outsider Interventions in Domestic Constitutional Contests*, 48 WAKE FOREST L. REV. 149 (2013).
[62] Dixon, *supra* note 54.
[63] *Compare, e.g.*, the characterization given by Po Jen Yap to judicial review in most countries in common law Asia: PO JEN YAP, CONSTITUTIONAL DIALOGUE IN COMMON LAW ASIA (2015).

There may also be other key roles courts must play—in resolving individual disputes, guarding against *animus* or outright breaches of individual rights, or stabilizing or enforcing the original constitutional compact, which take priority over these kinds of democracy-protecting and promoting roles in certain cases.[64]

The book provides an account that is general and global, and capable of both informing and explaining the role of constitutional judicial review in a wide range of democracies worldwide—even as it is informed by these understandings about the limits of judicial capacity, and the ideal of democracy itself. This account is itself also incomplete in a range of ways.

First, it does not explore how domestic courts can protect and promote other constitutional values, other than in so far as they intersect with or overlap with commitments to democratic responsiveness.

Second, by "constitutional court," the book means to refer to a court charged with interpreting and enforcing constitutional norms, whether as a specialized court or general court of appeal. There may be some differences between specialized and generalized courts when it comes to their ability to counter certain forms of democratic blockage. But, in principle, all courts with constitutional jurisdiction have the capacity to perform the forms of democratic protection and promotion outlined in the book. The aim here is to provide an account that is sufficiently general that it can speak to both common law and civilian systems, and systems influenced by the Anglo-American and Kelsenian constitutional tradition.[65] In doing so, the book focuses almost exclusively on domestic constitutional or appellate courts and not on the potential role that transnational courts and institutions may be able to play in countering democratic blockages.[66]

Third, it largely sidesteps the question of whether courts can effectively play a valuable role in the process of democracy *building*, as opposed to democratic preservation or enhancement. It assumes, in this context, that there is already a democratic constitutional system in place that requires courts to make choices about constitutional construction and implementation. This is a clear simplification as well as omission: many democracies face difficult questions about the balance between stabilizing an existing imperfect system and destabilization in the interests of achieving greater democratic quality or inclusion.[67] Similarly,

---

[64] Gardbaum, *supra* note 55.
[65] *Compare* Chapter 5, *infra*.
[66] For attempts to do so, see, *e.g.*, Daly, *supra* note 11; Michaela Hailbronner, Structural Reform Litigation in Domestic Courts (2022) (unpublished manuscript).
[67] *See* Licia Cianetti et al., *Rethinking "Political Monopoly" in Central and Eastern Europe: Looking Beyond Hungary and Poland*, 38 East Eur. Pol. 243 (2018).

many democracies are only partially consolidated, and may face periods of both regression and progression before achieving true democratic stability of consolidation.[68] And while many of the same principles of judicial craft and statecraft, that are identified in Chapter 8, may play a useful role in processes of constitutional democracy creation, as well as protection and promotion, the question of how and to what extent is one left for another day.[69]

Fourth, by "judicial review," the book largely means to refer to court decisions purporting to review the validity of legislation or interpret legislation in light of constitutional requirements. This is another source of limitation of the analysis provided. The ideas developed in the book certainly have potential relevance to courts' review of executive action, or the practice of judicial review as it is understood in countries such as the United Kingdom.[70] Legislative blind spots, for example, arise where legislators fail to consider the impact of legislation on concrete cases, or potential legislative alternative measures, but similar blind spots may arise in processes of administrative decision-making: for instance, where a decision-maker exceeds their power or jurisdiction by failing to take into account a relevant consideration. Burdens of inertia also generally reflect blockages in the legislative process, as opposed to processes of executive decision-making. However, some forms of inertia have a more hybrid character and reflect a failure by both the executive to take the steps necessary to implement constitutional guarantees *and* by the legislature to supervise or ensure the process of implementation. And the threat of antidemocratic monopoly power can come from the actions of a wide range of legislative and executive actors, or attempts to engage in "abusive" constitutional amendment, legislation, or executive action.[71] But the focus of the book is explicitly on legislative, and compound, as opposed to pure executive forms of blockage.

The focus of the book is thus limited on at least four levels: it is (i) on how courts can best give effect to democracy as a constitutional value, not all relevant constitutional values; (ii) on domestic rather than international or regional courts; (iii) on how courts can advance commitments to democratic preservation and enhancement, not democracy creation; and (iv) on judicial

---

[68] *Id.*

[69] For a useful attempt to address this question, in the context of two key Asian cases, *see* YVONNE TEW, CONSTITUTIONAL STATECRAFT IN ASIAN COURTS (2020).

[70] For leading accounts of judicial review in the UK, see, *e.g.*, Erin F. Delaney, *Judiciary Rising: Constitutional Change in the United Kingdom*, 108 NW. U. L. REV. 543 (2014); TOM HICKMAN, PUBLIC LAW AFTER THE HUMAN RIGHTS ACT (2010); AILEEN KAVANAGH, CONSTITUTIONAL REVIEW UNDER THE HUMAN RIGHTS ACT (2009); ALISON YOUNG, DEMOCRATIC DIALOGUE AND THE CONSTITUTION (2020).

[71] *See* Landau & Dixon, *supra* note 8; Dixon & Landau, *supra* note 54; DIXON & LANDAU, *supra* note 56.

review of legislative as opposed to executive action (alone). These are all important parts of a fully fleshed out account of responsive judicial review, but ones I leave to others, and another day.

The remainder of the book is divided into three broad parts. Part I provides an overview of the key notions of democratic dysfunction that form the core conceptual foundation for the book. Chapter 2 outlines the idea of constitutional constructional choice, and the role of constitutional values (including democracy) as potentially informing that process of choice. It discusses Ely's own understanding of these questions, as well as the limits of Ely's account, and suggests that democracy and sources of democratic dysfunction need to be understood in ways that build on but go beyond the ideas set out in *Democracy and Distrust*. Chapter 3 focuses on the three democratic risks to which a theory of responsive judicial review is directed, namely the risks of antidemocratic monopoly power, democratic blind spots, and burdens of inertia.

Part II turns to the capacity of courts to help counter these various sources of democratic dysfunction, as well as the inevitable limits on the capacity and legitimacy of courts as they engage in representation-reinforcing review of this kind. Chapter 4 explores how the ideas set out in Part I translate into potential doctrinal guidance for courts in the context of judgments about the intensity and scope of judicial review. Specifically, it explores debates about constructional choice and the making of constitutional implications, the application of doctrines of proportionality and US-style tiered review, and how attention to risks of electoral and institutional monopoly, democratic blind spots, and burdens of inertia can usefully inform the application of tests of this kind. Chapter 5 then explores the degree to which courts are able *effectively* to identify and counter the relevant three risks to democracy but also the preconditions for judicial review of this kind—that is, the necessary degree of legal authority, remedial power, judicial independence, and political support for judicial review to be responsive in nature. It also notes the additional challenges facing courts as they seek to counter the risks of electoral and institutional monopoly.

Part III turns to the potential limits on a court's actual and perceived legitimacy as it engages in responsive forms of review. Chapter 6 explores the inevitable limits to a court's actual and perceived legitimacy, and the risks this can pose to a constitutional system's overall democratic responsiveness—or the risks of reverse burdens of inertia and democratic backlash in response to court decisions. Chapter 7 considers the notion of strong versus weak judicial review as a response to these limits, and the idea of responsive judicial review as a combination of strong and weak remedies and rights-based reasoning.

Finally, Part IV explores broader questions of responsive judging, and the promise and limits to responsive review as a general account of courts' approach to constitutional construction. Chapter 8 explores the concept of a responsive judicial "voice," or how choices about judicial authorship, narrative, and tone may influence the public reaction to a court decision, and thus both its political and sociological legitimacy. Chapter 9 concludes by considering the potential global reach or relevance of the ideas contained in Parts I–III.

PART 1
DEMOCRATIC FOUNDATIONS

2
Constitutions and Constructional Choice

Constitutions contain a wide variety of provisions, some quite concrete, others highly abstract and indeterminate. For instance, the qualifications needed to run for the United States (US) Presidency are largely undisputed: Article II, Section 1 of the US Constitution provides that a person must be thirty-five years of age, a "natural born" citizen and a resident of the United States for at least fourteen years. There are some uncertainties as to the geographic boundaries of the United States for these purposes (does it extend, for example, to US military bases or certain territories?).[1] But other aspects of the Qualifications Clause are relatively clear in effect. Those running for President must have been born within the United States, at least thirty-five years ago, and resident within the United States for at least fourteen years.[2] A judge interpreting the Qualifications Clause would, therefore, be able to resolve cases and controversies before her relatively easily, simply by looking at the text or language of the Constitution.

Most constitutional provisions, both in the United States and elsewhere, however, raise numerous issues of constitutional "construction"—or choices about how best to interpret the far more open-ended language of written constitutional guarantees.[3] For instance:

(1) *Abortion, sexual privacy, and same-sex marriage*: The US Constitution guarantees a right to "liberty" and "equal protection." But what does this mean for concrete questions such as citizens' right of access to abortion, sexual privacy, or same-sex marriage? Should the US Supreme Court construe these abstract constitutional guarantees to protect concrete rights of this kind? Constitutions in most other constitutional democracies likewise recognize rights to freedom, equality, dignity, and

---

[1] *See, e.g.*, Aaron Blake, *There Was a Very Real "Birther" Debate About John McCain*, WASH. POST, Jan. 7, 2016, <https://www.washingtonpost.com/news/the-fix/wp/2016/01/07/there-was-a-very-real-birther-debate-about-john-mccain/>.

[2] Rosalind Dixon, *Updating Constitutional Rules*, 2009 SUP. CT. REV. 319 (2011).

[3] On construction, see Lawrence B. Solum, *The Interpretation-Construction Distinction*, 27 CONST. COMMENT. 95 (2010); Jeffrey Goldsworthy, *Functions, Purposes and Values in Constitutional Interpretation*, in AUSTRALIAN CONSTITUTIONAL VALUES (Rosalind Dixon ed., 2018).

security of the person. What does this mean for judicial review in these countries? Should constitutional courts elsewhere construe these provisions so as to recognize rights to abortion, sexual privacy, or same-sex marriage?

(2) *Implied speech and equality rights*: Other constitutions, such as those in Australia and Israel, recognize a far narrower range of express rights: Australia, for instance, is arguably the only constitutional democracy today that does not have a true constitutional bill of rights; and in Israel, both the 1958 *Basic Law* and 1992 *Basic Law: Human Dignity and Liberty* contain quite limited or partial guarantees of rights.[4] Courts in both countries, however, have been asked to imply a range of additional rights as protected by the constitution. Should they do so?

(3) *Structural social rights*: Still other constitutions contain both express guarantees of human dignity and obligations on the state to protect and promote the right to dignity through the realization of various social and economic rights, including rights of access to food, water, housing, and healthcare.[5] But what does this mean for courts faced with evidence of systemic violations of these rights? Should violations of this kind lead to equally systemic forms of judicial intervention, or a form of "structural" social rights enforcement?

(4) *An unconstitutional amendment doctrine*: Some constitutions contain express clauses that limit the scope of powers of formal constitutional amendment, or else create different tracks or "tiers" for different forms of constitutional change. Others, however, contain no express limits of this kind. But courts in these countries have been asked to *imply* limits on the power of amendment in order to protect the constitution's existing democratic structure. Should they have done so? The "unconstitutional constitutional amendment" (UCA) doctrine purports to immunize existing constitutional norms, and judicial constructions of those norms, from change in ways that necessarily call for strong legal and political justification.

---

[4] *See* Rosalind Dixon, *Partial Bills of Rights*, 63 Am. J. Comp. L. 403, 408 (2015). *Compare* Rosalind Dixon, *An Australian (Partial) Bill of Rights*, 14 Int'l J. Const. L. 80 (2016) (suggesting Australia has an extremely partial or narrow rather than no bill of rights). In Israel, the 1958 *Basic Law* on the Knesset guarantees a range of basic democratic norms but does not include the broader set of human rights protections later contained in the 1992 *Basic Law: Human Dignity and Liberty* (e.g., rights to life, privacy, bodily integrity, and dignity). And the 1992 *Basic Law* does not give express recognition to rights to freedom of expression, religion, or equality.

[5] David S. Law & Mila Versteeg, *The Declining Influence of the United States Constitution*, 87 N.Y.U. L. Rev. 762 (2012).

As the next section explores in more depth, these questions are far from abstract: courts around the world routinely face such questions. Yet different constitutional theories take a wide variety of views about how courts should approach these questions. And, in *Democracy and Distrust*, Ely offered just one of many different potential accounts of the role of courts in cases of this kind.

In this chapter, I explore Ely's ideas, and the answers they provide to these concrete questions of constructional choice, as well as potential criticisms and limitations of Ely's response, including the degree to which Ely's ideas downplayed the need for substantive forms of evaluative judgment about what democracy is, and requires, and failed to anticipate the full range of threats to democracy today. I also note the degree to which Ely's ideas remain relevant to contemporary contexts, and suggest that the task for contemporary constitutional theory is to build on rather than go beyond Ely's notion of democratic representation-reinforcement.

A. Judicial Review and Constructional Choice

Courts around the world have delivered numerous decisions that traverse the questions set out above; and in ways that show both the breadth and strength of judicial review worldwide.

1. Abortion, sexual privacy, and same-sex marriage

In *Roe v. Wade*, the US Supreme Court famously struck down Texas' broad legislative prohibition on access to abortion, on the basis that prohibitions of this kind were an impermissible limitation on a woman's right of access to abortion under the Fourteenth Amendment, and not justified by any compelling state interest in protecting maternal or fetal life, at least in the first two trimesters of pregnancy.[6] In *Planned Parenthood v. Casey*, the Court narrowed its prior ruling in *Roe*, but reaffirmed the "essential finding" in *Roe* that the notion of liberty in the Due Process clause includes the right of women to access an abortion, whereas in *Dobbs v. Jackson Women's Health Organization*, the Court overruled both *Roe* and *Casey* and held that rights of access to abortion were not protected under the US Constitution.[7]

---

[6] Roe v. Wade, 410 U.S. 113, 162–64 (1973).
[7] Compare *Planned Parenthood v. Casey*, 505 U.S. 833 (1992) and *Dobbs v. Jackson Women's Health Organization*, 597 U.S. ___ (2022).

So far, at least, the US Supreme Court has also progressively expanded the legal recognition of LGBTQI+ (Lesbian, Gay, Bisexual, Transgender, Queer, Intersex) rights. Starting in *Romer v. Evans*, the Court held that a Colorado state constitutional amendment purporting to prevent cities and local governments from passing ordinances protecting gays and lesbians from discrimination was inconsistent with the guarantee of Equal Protection under the Fourteenth Amendment to the US Constitution.[8] In *Lawrence v. Texas*, in 2003, the Court struck down a state law prohibiting consensual anal intercourse between adult men, as a violation of the Due Process Clause of the Fourteenth Amendment.[9] And in *Obergefell*, the Court held that the exclusion of same-sex couples from the institution of marriage was contrary to Due Process and Equal Protection requirements.[10] More recently, in *Bostock*, the Court held that the prohibition on discrimination on the grounds of sex under Title VII of the *Civil Rights Act 1964* extends to discrimination against both gays and lesbians *and* transgender Americans.[11]

Courts elsewhere have also delivered a range of decisions expanding access to abortion. In Canada, in *Morgentaler*, the Supreme Court of Canada (SCC) held that provisions of the 1970 *Criminal Code* imposing restrictions on access to abortion were inconsistent with the guarantee of freedom and security of the person in section 7 of the Canadian *Charter of Rights and Freedoms*.[12] In Colombia, the Constitutional Court has likewise held that the 1991 Constitution requires at least some form of legal access to abortion.[13] In South Korea, in 2019, the Constitutional Court of Korea found the provisions governing abortion in the 1953 *Criminal Code* "conditionally unconstitutional" or "unconformable" to the Constitution.[14] And in 2021, the Supreme Court of Mexico found unconstitutional the criminal prohibition by the state of Coahuila on access to abortion, in ways that called into question the constitutionality of similar prohibitions nationwide.[15]

---

[8] Romer v. Evans, 517 U.S. 620 (1996).
[9] Lawrence v. Texas, 539 U.S. 558 (2003).
[10] Obergefell v. Hodges, 576 U.S. 644 (2015).
[11] Bostock v. Clayton County, 590 U.S. ___ (2020).
[12] R v. Morgentaler, [1988] 1 S.C.R. 30 (Can.).
[13] *See* Decision C-355 of 2006; Decision SU-096 of 2018; Decision C-055 of 2022.
[14] *Abortion Case*, 2010 Hun-Ba402, Aug. 23, 2012, see English summary at *Abortion Case*, <http://search.ccourt.go.kr/ths/pr/eng_pr0101_E1.do?seq=1&cname=%EC%98%81%EB%AC%B8%ED%8C%90%EB%A1%80&eventNum=30803&eventNo=2010%ED%97%8C%EB%B0%94402&pubFlag=0&cId=010400>.
[15] *Mexico's Supreme Court Votes to Decriminalize Abortion*, N.Y. Times, Sept. 7, 2021, <https://www.nytimes.com/2021/09/07/world/americas/mexico-supreme-court-decriminalize-abortion.html>; Natalie Kitroeff and Oscar Lopez, *Abortion is No Longer a Crime in Mexico. But Most Women Still Can't Get One*, N.Y. Times, Sept. 8, 2021, <https://www.nytimes.com/2021/09/08/world/americas/mexico-abortion-access.html>.

Courts worldwide have played a similarly important role in recent decades in expanding the rights of LGBTQI+ citizens.[16] In Canada, between 1995 and 1998, lower courts held that a series of provincial and federal laws should be interpreted, or language read into them, to provide same-sex couples with the same access as opposite-sex couples to a range of legal benefits.[17] In 1998, in *Vriend v. Alberta*, the SCC held that sexual orientation was analogous to those grounds expressly prohibited as grounds of discrimination under section 15(1) of the Canadian *Charter of Rights and Freedoms*, and should be read into Alberta human rights legislation prohibiting discrimination in employment.[18] In *M v. H*, in 1999, the SCC held that it was no longer compatible with the *Charter* to continue to exclude gays and lesbians from statutory benefits afforded men and women in equivalent opposite-sex relationships.[19] And from 2002 to 2004, provincial courts held that the opposite-sex definition of marriage was inconsistent with the guarantee of equality in section 15(1) of the Canadian *Charter of Rights and Freedoms*.

In South Africa, in *National Coalition I*, the Constitutional Court of South Africa (CCSA) began by striking down the Apartheid-era ban on anal intercourse between men, as in violation of constitutional commitments to dignity, privacy, and equality under the 1996 Constitution, and then issued a series of decisions expanding recognition of LGBTQI+ rights in the context of statutes relating to judicial pensions, joint adoption, and the recognition of the partner of a woman who gives birth to a child by artificial insemination.[20] Then, in 2006, in *Fourie*, the CCSA held that the common law, opposite-sex definition of marriage should be declared invalid effective twelve months from the date of the decision.[21] In Colombia, in *Decision C-481 of 1998*, the Constitutional Court held that a public school teacher could not be disciplined based on their sexual identity, and that doing so constituted both a form of constitutionally impermissible discrimination and interference with the free development of personality.[22] In *Decision C-075 of 2007*, the Court held that it was

---

[16] Graeme Reid, *A Global Report Card on LGBTQ+ Rights for IDAHOBIT*, Hum. Rts. Watch (May 18, 2020, 10:47 AM), <https://www.hrw.org/news/2020/05/18/global-report-card-lgbtq-rights-idahobit>.

[17] *See* Susan B. Boyd & Claire F.L. Young, *From Same-Sex to No Sex: Trends Towards Recognition of (Same-Sex) Relationships in Canada*, 1 Seattle J. Soc. Just. 757 (2002).

[18] Vriend v. Alberta, [1998] 1 S.C.R. 493, [179] (Iaccobucci J.) (Can.).

[19] [1999] 2 S.C.R. 3.

[20] Satchwell v. President of the Republic of S. Afr., CCT 45/01 (S. Afr.) (judicial pensions); Du Toit v. Minister of Welfare and Population Dev., 2003 (2) SA 198 (CC) (S. Afr.) (joint adoption); J and B v. Dir. Gen. Dep't of Home Aff., 2003 (5) SA 198 (CC) (S. Afr.) (recognition of the partner of a woman who gives birth to a child by artificial insemination).

[21] Minister for Home Aff. v. Fourie, 2005 (3) BCLR 241 (SCA), 2006 (3) BCLR 355 (CCSA) (S. Afr.).

[22] Decision C-481 of 1998, [16]–[17], [18]–[23], [35]. See discussion in Mauricio Albarracín Caballero, *Social Movements and the Constitutional Court: Legal Recognition of the Rights of Same-Sex Couples in Colombia*, 8 Int'l J. Hum. Rts. 7, 13 (2011).

a violation of constitutional commitments to equality, dignity, and autonomy for the state to exclude same-sex partners from a regime of joint property for *de facto* couples, or those part of a "marital union in fact."[23] And from 2011 to 2016, the Court extended these prior decisions so as progressively to recognize a constitutional right of access to same-sex marriage. Similar decisions expanding access to LGBTQI+ rights have been delivered by courts in Mexico and Brazil.[24] In 2009, Mexico City's legislative assembly passed a law allowing access to same-sex marriage and, in 2010, the Supreme Court of Mexico upheld that law, and the duty of other states to recognize marriages solemnized under the law.[25] In 2016, the Court extended this reasoning to prevent states in their own laws from discriminating between opposite and same-sex marriage. And in Brazil, in 2011, the Supreme Federal Tribunal (SFT), ruled that the Brazilian Constitution required access to civil union for same-sex couples and, in 2013, the National Council of Justice (a fifteen-member council led by the Chief Justice of the SFT) held that notary publics were required to perform same-sex as well as opposite-sex marriages, and convert same-sex unions into marriages on request.[26]

In the United Kingdom (UK), in *Ghaidan v. Godin-Mendoza*, the appellate committee of the House of Lords held that Articles 8 and 14 of the European Convention on Human Rights required giving the same statutory entitlements (to protection from eviction) to same-sex couples as were enjoyed by opposite-sex couples,[27] and in *Bellinger*, the court held that the same principles required recognition of a person's post-operative transgender identity for the purposes of the law of marriage.[28] In part influenced by this, the Hong Kong Court of Final Appeal (CFA) has interpreted the 1990 *Bill of Rights Ordinance* (BORO) and 1997 *Basic Law* to require greater recognition of LGBTQI+ rights in Hong Kong.[29] In *Leung v. Secretary for Justice*, the CFA held invalid provisions of the Hong Kong *Crimes Ordinance* imposing a higher age of consent

---

[23] See Decision C-075 of 2007 in MANUEL JOSÉ CEPEDA ESPINOSA & DAVID E. LANDAU, COLOMBIAN CONSTITUTIONAL LAW: LEADING CASES 5, 87–91 (2017).

[24] *Id.*

[25] Randal C. Archibold & Paulina Villegas, *With Little Fanfare, Mexican Supreme Court Legalizes Same-Sex Marriage*, N.Y. TIMES, Jul. 31, 2016, <https://www.nytimes.com/2015/06/15/world/americas/with-little-fanfare-mexican-supreme-court-effectively-legalizes-same-sex-marriage.html>.

[26] Simon Romero, *Brazilian Court Council Removes a Barrier to Same-Sex Marriage*, N.Y. TIMES, May 14, 2013, <https://www.nytimes.com/2013/05/15/world/americas/brazilian-court-council-removes-a-barrier-to-same-sex-marriage.html>. While there were attempts to appeal and overturn this decision before the SFT, as well as in Congress, those attempts had not been successful at the time of writing.

[27] [2004] UKHL 30.

[28] [2003] UKHL 21.

[29] *See, e.g.*, Marco Wan, *Gay Visibility and the Law in Hong Kong*, 32 INT'L J. FOR THE SEMIOTICS OF LAW-REVUE 699 (2019).

for anal intercourse between men.[30] And in *W v. Registrar*, the CFA held invalid the provisions of the *Marriage Ordinance* providing for marriage between a "man" and "woman," and defining gender in ways that did not recognize post-operative transsexual identity.[31] More recently still, the CFA has upheld the rights of same-sex couples married overseas to certain statutory benefits.[32] Finally, in India over the last decade, the Supreme Court of India (SCI) has held that the Constitution requires both the recognition of transgender identity and decriminalization of consensual sexual intercourse between adults. Thus, in *National Legal Services Authority v. Union of India (NALSA)*, in 2014, the SCI held that non-recognition of gender identity by the state constituted a failure to uphold the rights to "privacy, self-identity, autonomy and personal integrity"—and, indeed, basic human dignity—under Articles 19 and 21 of the Indian Constitution, as well as the rights to equality and non-discrimination under Articles 14–16.[33] And in *Navtej Singh Johar v. Union of India*, in 2018, the SCI held that the prohibition on sodomy or consenting sexual intercourse between adults in section 377 of the Indian *Penal Code* was inconsistent with constitutional guarantees of freedom, dignity, privacy, equality, and non-discrimination.[34]

To be sure, these patterns are not universal or one-way. Even in the US, there has been a recent rollback in the constitutional right of access to abortion recognized in *Roe* and *Casey*.[35] The result has been the validation and enactment of a range of highly punitive restrictions on access to abortion in various states.[36]

---

[30] No. 317 of 2005, [49], [50]–[55].

[31] W v. Registrar of Marriages, [2013] H.K.F.C.A. 39, [25]–[39] (on the proper construction of the Marriage Ordinance). For discussion, see Marco Wan, *Queer Temporalities and Transgender Rights: Hong Kong Case Study*, 30 Soc. & Legal Stud. 563b (2020); Kelley Loper, *W v. Registrar of Marriages and the Right to Equality in Hong Kong*, 41 H.K.L.J. 89 (2011); Puja Kapai, *A Principled Approach Towards Judicial Review: Lessons from W Registrar of Marriages*, 41 H.K.L.J. 49 (2011); Howard Chiang, *Intimate Equality and Transparent Selves: Legalising Transgender Marriage in Hong Kong*, 58 Culture, Theory & Critique 166 (2017).

[32] For an analysis of the broader context for these cases, and movements toward same-sex relationship recognition in Hong Kong, see Michael Ramsden & Luke Marsh, *Same-Sex Marriage in Hong Kong: The Case for a Constitutional Right*, 19 Int'l J. Hum. Rts. 90 (2015); Kelley Loper, *Human Right and Substantive Equality: Prospects for Same-Sex Relationship Recognition in Hong Kong*, 44 N.C. J. Int'l L. 273 (2018); Joy L. Chia & Amy Barrow, *Inching Towards Equality: LGBT Rights and the Limitations of Law in Hong Kong*, 22 Wm. & Mary J. Women & L. 303 (2015); Denise Tse-Shang Tang et al., *Legal Recognition of Same-Sex Partnerships: A Comparative Study of Hong Kong, Taiwan and Japan*, 68 Soc. Rev. 192 (2020).

[33] *See* [66], [114].

[34] AIR 2018 SC 4321, [253] (2018) (India). For a useful discussion, see Pratik Dixit, *Navtej Singh Johar v. Union of India: Decriminalising India's Sodomy Law*, 24 Int'l J. Hum. Rts. 1011 (2020); Shreya Mohapatra, *Section 377 Read Down: The Way Forward*, Socio-Legal Rev. (Jul. 6, 2019), <https://www.sociolegalreview.com/post/section-377-read-down-the-way-forward>.

[35] Dobbs v. Jackson Women's Health Organization, 597 U.S. ___ (2022).

[36] *Tracking the State where Abortion is Now Banned*, N.Y. Times, Jul. 22, 2022, <https://www.nytimes.com/interactive/2022/us/abortion-laws-roe-v-wade.html>.

Courts in some countries have also consistently rejected the idea that the constitution protects rights of access to abortion and sexual privacy.[37] In Kenya, for example, the High Court has recently recognized a narrow right of access to abortion in cases where the pregnancy results from sexual assault, but rejected claims that the 2010 Constitution prevents the criminalization of same-sex intercourse.[38] In Singapore, the Supreme Court has held that a colonial-era prohibition on anal intercourse remain constitutionally valid, though the government has recently announced the intention to repeal this ban.[39] And in the Philippines, access to abortion remains prohibited in almost all circumstances and the Supreme Court has recently rejected arguments that the Constitution requires the recognition of same-sex marriage.[40]

And not all courts have been as willing to uphold constitutional claims asserting a right to same-sex marriage: for instance, both the High Court of Australia and Israel have rejected claims of this kind in the last five years, though the Supreme Court of Israel has recently recognized rights of access to surrogacy for same-sex couples.[41]

---

[37] *Homosexuality: The Countries Where It Is Illegal to be Gay*, BBC NEWS, Apr. 20, 2018, <https://www.bbc.com/news/world-43822234.amp> (noting judicial decisions striking down criminal prohibitions on consensual gay intercourse in countries such as Botswana and Trinidad and Tobago, but also the numerous countries in which this has not yet occurred).

[38] EG v. Att'y Gen., Petition 150 & 234 of 2016 (Consolidated) [2019] eK.L.R. (Aburili, Mwita, and Mativo JJ.) (Kenya);Misha Ketchell, *Homosexuality Remains Illegal in Kenya as Court Rejects LGBT Petition*, THE CONVERSATION (May. 25, 2019), <https://theconversation.com/homosexuality-remains-illegal-in-kenya-as-court-rejects-lgbt-petition-112149/>.

[39] Ong Ming Johnson v. Att'y Gen. [2020] SGHC 63 (Kee Oong J.) (Sing.). *See also Singapore Gay Sex Ban: Court Rejects Appeals to Overturn Law*, BBC NEWS, Mar. 30, 2020, <https://www.bbc.com/news/world-asia-52098362>. But see Tessa Wong, s 377A: Singapore to End Ban on Gay Sex, BBC NEWS, Aug. 22, 2022 https://www.bbc.com/news/world-asia-62545577

[40] Falcis III v. Civ. Registrar Gen., G.R. No. 217910 (2019) (Leonen J.) (Phil.), <https://perma.cc/W2F5-V24J>; Diana Chandler, *Philippines High Court Rejects Gay Marriage Appeal*, BAPTISTPRESS (Sept. 3, 2019), <https://www.baptistpress.com/resource-library/news/philippines-high-court-rejects-gay-marriage-appeal/>.

[41] In Australia, the relevant right was a quasi-constitutional or statutory right under territory law, which the HCA found was inconsistent with federal law: see Commonwealth v. Australian Capital Territory (Same-Sex Marriage Case) (2013) 250 CLR 441, 467–68, [55]–[57] (French C.J., Hayne, Crennan, Kiefel, Bell, and Keane JJ.) (Austl.). It was thus only through a popular plebiscite that Australia adopted same-sex marriage: see Nick Evershed, *Full Results of Australia's Vote for Same-Sex Marriage, Electorate by Electorate*, THE GUARDIAN, Nov. 15, 2017, <https://www.theguardian.com/australia-news/datablog/ng-interactive/2017/nov/15/same-sex-marriage-survey-how-australia-voted-electorate-by-electorate>. In Israel, the Court rejected the claim on the basis that marriage remained within the sphere of rabbinical court jurisdiction: see Israel Org. for Prot. of Individual Rts. v. Ministry of Interior (HCJ 7339/15) (2017) (Isr.); *Israel: High Court Rejects Petition to Recognize Same-Sex Marriages*, LIBRARY OF CONGRESS (Sept. 11, 2017), <https://www.loc.gov/item/global-legal-monitor/2017-09-11/israel-high-court-rejects-petition-to-recognize-same-sex-marriages/>. But the Court has held that state law regulating access to surrogacy must apply equally to same-sex couples: Claire Parker, *Israel's High Court Opens the Way for Same-Sex Couples to Have Children via Surrogacy*, WASH. POST, Jul. 12, 2021, <https://www.washingtonpost.com/world/2021/07/11/israel-lgbtq-surrogate-parents/>.

2. Implied speech and equality rights

Courts in countries such as Australia and Israel have also decided a range of cases involving the idea of "implied" rights. In Australia, for example, the High Court has held that the Constitution contains an implied principle of freedom of political communication and associated rights of association and access to the seat of government.[42] This was established in the Court's well-known decision in *Australian Capital Television Pty Ltd. v. Commonwealth*, striking down federal attempts to limit paid political advertising and replace paid advertising with a system of free airtime for all political parties in the lead up to a federal election.[43] The Court, in *Roach v. Electoral Commissioner* and *Rowe v. Electoral Commissioner*, further held that similar principles point to a guarantee of universal access to the franchise.[44] But it has rejected claims that the Constitution protects broader rights to dignity or equality. In *Leeth*, for example, the Court dismissed a challenge on these grounds to federal legislation that provided that the non-parole period for federal prisoners was to be determined by state law.[45]

The protection of rights in Israel under various Basic Laws raises interesting parallels. For instance, in 1969, in *Bergman v. Minister of Finance*,[46] the Court (sitting as the High Court of Justice (HCJ)) struck down a law providing for public funding to political parties in elections, based on their existing representation within the Knesset, on the grounds that it violated the principle of equality of political participation.[47] In 2000, in *Ka'adan*, the HCJ likewise held that a decision by the state of Israel to allocate land to the Jewish Agency for Israel, for the purpose of creating Jewish settlements, violated an implied constitutional principle of equality or non-discrimination.[48]

3. Structural social rights

For US scholars, the role of courts in protecting and promoting "social rights"—or rights such as the right of access to food, shelter, and healthcare—is less familiar. Many US states contain a right to education, and courts in some

---

[42] Australian Capital Television Pty Ltd v. Commonwealth (1992) 177 CLR 2016 (Austl.); Roach v. Electoral Comm'r (2007) 233 CLR 162 (Austl.).
[43] Australian Capital Television Pty Ltd. v. Commonwealth (1992) 177 CLR 2016 (Austl.).
[44] Roach v. Electoral Comm'r (2007) 233 CLR 162 (Austl.); Rowe v. Electoral Commissioner, (2010) 243 CLR 1 (Austl.).
[45] *Commonwealth Prisoners Act 1967* (Cth) s 4(1).
[46] HCJ 98/69 (1969).
[47] *Knesset and Local Authorities Elections (Financing, Limitation of Expenses and Audit) Law* 1969.
[48] *Id.* at 18, 29 [32]; Ka'adan v. Israel Land Administration, HCJ 6698/95 (2000).

states have taken a quite active role in enforcing this right—both via "negative" forms of judicial intervention, which prevent cuts to school funding, and more "positive" enforcement measures, which impose an affirmative obligation on the state to ensure the meaningful exercise or enjoyment of a right.[49] And the US Constitution clearly recognizes some positive rights, including the right to counsel under the Sixth Amendment. But for the most part, the US Supreme Court has rejected the idea that it should interpret the Constitution as including positive rights, such as a general right to protection from the state from violence or provision of adequate care.[50]

In many democracies, however, constitutional courts have taken an active role in protecting and promoting those rights—both through negative and positive forms of enforcement. This has also extended to structural forms of enforcement. In *Grootboom*, for example, the CCSA held that the South African government was under a constitutional obligation to take "reasonable measures ... to provide for relief for people who have no access to land, no roof over their heads, and who are living in intolerable conditions or crisis situations."[51] In the *Treatment Action Campaign Case* (TAC), the CCSA held that it was unreasonable for the government to restrict access to nevirapine aimed at preventing mother-to-child transmission of HIC, ordered the immediate lifting of restrictions on access to nevirapine in sites already able to provide testing and formula, and declared that the government was required progressively to realize universal access to testing and bottle feeding to support its roll out in other sites.[52]

A similar pattern can be seen in India. In the *Midday Meal* case, the SCI held that "every child in every Government and Government assisted Primary School be provided with a prepared mid-day meal with a minimum content of 300 calories and 8–12 grams of protein each day of school for a minimum of 200 days."[53] Similarly, in *Olga Tellis v. Bombay Municipal Corporation*,[54] the Court imposed limits on the scope for the state and city to evict pavement-dwellers, requiring that they delay such removal until after the monsoon season, and in the interim work to find suitable (i.e., relatively proximate) alternative land, and thus accommodation, for the petitioners. Courts in Brazil

---

[49] *See* EMILY ZACKIN, LOOKING FOR RIGHTS IN ALL THE WRONG PLACES: WHY STATE CONSTITUTIONS CONTAIN AMERICA'S POSITIVE RIGHTS (2013).

[50] *See, e.g.*, Castle Rock v. Gonzales, 545 U.S. 748 (2005); DeShaney v. Winnebago County, 489 U.S. 189 (1989).

[51] 2000 (11) BCLR 1169 (CC), [99] (S. Afr.).

[52] Minister of Health and Others v. Treatment Action Campaign and Others (No. 2), 2002 (5) SA 721.

[53] Order dated Nov. 28, 2001, Peoples Union for C.L. v. Union of India, Writ Petition (Civil) No. 196 of 2001.

[54] (1985) 3 SCC 545.

and Colombia have played a similar role in promoting the realization of social rights.[55] In Brazil in particular, it is often suggested that court decisions have tended to favor individual over structural relief in such cases, and thus benefit the middle class, over the poorest Brazilians.[56] But in Colombia, the Constitutional Court has relied on individual guarantees of social rights, and the *tutela* as a remedy for protecting these rights, as a basis for developing a so-called unconstitutional state of affairs doctrine, which effectively imposes a duty on the state to ensure the structural preconditions for individual rights protection.[57] The Constitutional Court has relied on the unconstitutional state of affairs doctrine nine times between 1997 and 2017.[58] However, the best known instance of reliance on the doctrine arose in the *IDP* case, where the Court held that the failure by the state to protect the social rights of several million people internally displaced as a result of the civil war constituted an "unconstitutional state of affairs."[59]

Finally, in Pakistan, the High Court has held that the Constitution supports an implied principle of climate justice.[60] Based on this, in *Leghari v. Federation of Pakistan*,[61] the Court issued an order blocking the transfer of a senior official responsive for climate policy and requiring the creation of a special "Climate Change Commission" and assignment of individuals within various state and national government departments to act as a "focal person" responsible for the implementation framework.[62]

---

[55] *See, e.g.*, Cesar Rodriguez-Garavito, *Beyond the Courtroom: The Impact of Judicial Activism on Socioeconomic Rights in Latin America*, 89 Tex. L. Rev. 1669, 1672–73 (2011); Courting Social Justice: Judicial Enforcement of Social and Economic Rights in the Developing World (Varun Gauri & Daniel M. Brinks eds., 2008).

[56] *See* Daniel M. Brinks & Varun Gauri, *The Law's Majestic Equality? The Distributive Impact of Judicializing Social and Economic Rights*, 12 Persp. Pol. 375 (2014); David Landau, *Judicial Role and the Limits of Constitutional Convergence in Latin America*, in Comparative Constitutional Law in Latin America 237 (Rosalind Dixon & Tom Ginsburg eds., 2017).

[57] *See, e.g.*, Decision T-153 of 1998; Decision T-025 of 2004.

[58] Espinosa & Landau, *supra* note 23, at 178.

[59] *Id.* at 182–83.

[60] HCJD/C-12 at 5–6.

[61] HCJD/C-121.

[62] *Id.* at 6–7. While the best-known judicial decision on climate change globally is the *Uganda* decision by the Dutch courts, that decision did not turn directly on any constitutional requirements or even human rights norms. The decision in *Leghari* is thus quite unique in its emphasis on *implied constitutional* principles of this kind: see, *e.g.*, discussion in Jacqueline Peel & Hari M. Osofsky, *A Rights Turn in Climate Change Litigation?*, 7 Transnat'l Envtl. L. 37, 38–39 (2018); Laura Bergers, *Should Judges Make Climate Change Law*, 9 Transnat'l Envtl. L. 55, 57–58 (2020); Myanna Dellinger, *See You in Court: Around the World in Eight Climate Change Lawsuits*, 42 Wm. & Mary Envt'l L. & Pol'y Rev. 525, 533–39 (2018).

4. An unconstitutional amendment doctrine

Many constitutional courts worldwide have also adopted versions of an UCA doctrine. Indeed, the UCA doctrine is now arguably one of the best-known constitutional doctrines worldwide.[63] But the "basic structure" doctrine in India remains one of the leading examples. In *Kesavananda Bharati*, in 1973, a thirteen-judge bench of the SCI held that the power of amendment in Article 368 of the Indian Constitution was subject to an important implied limitation: it could not be used so as to alter or destroy the "basic structure" of the Constitution.[64] Based on this ruling, the Court also struck down various amendments to the Constitution removing various protections for the right to property, including the Court's ability to hear constitutional challenges to land reform legislation.[65]

In Colombia, in the *Second Re-election* case, the Constitutional Court held that the power of amendment in Articles 375 and 378 could not be used to create a "substitution" of a wholly new constitution, or a form of *de facto* constitutional replacement rather than amendment.[66] And in reliance on this, the Court struck down proposed amendments to the Colombian Constitution that would have allowed the President to serve three (as opposed to two) consecutive terms.[67]

Most recently, in Kenya, in *Ndii v. Attorney-General* the High Court and Court of Appeal held that the 2010 Kenyan Constitution did not permit the President to bypass the procedures for proposing amendments under Articles 255–257 of the Constitution, and further, that these formal amendment procedures could not be used to alter the basic structure of the Constitution.[68] On this basis, both courts also struck down proposed amendments to the Constitution put forward by President Kenyatta and his "Building Bridges" Commission, which would have created a range of changes, including the expansion in the number of election districts or seats in the national parliament, and the restoration of the role of prime minister abolished in 2013.[69] The

---

[63] Yaniv Roznai, Unconstitutional Constitutional Amendments: The Limits of Amendment Powers (2017).

[64] Kesavananda Bharati v. State of Kerala, (1973) 4 SCC 225; AIR 1973 SC 1461 (India).

[65] *Id. See* Rosalind Dixon, *Constitutional Drafting and Distrust*, 13 Int'l J. Const. L. 819 (2015); Bert Neuborne, *The Supreme Court of India*, 1 Int'l J. Const. L. 476, 482–92 (2003); Colin Campbell Aikman, *The Debate on the Amendment of the Indian Constitution*, 9 Victoria U. Wellington L. Rev. 358, 366–74 (1978).

[66] Decision C-141 of 2010. *See* Espinosa & Landau, *supra* note 23, at 352–60.

[67] *Id.*

[68] Independent Electoral and Boundaries Comm'n v. David Ndii, Civil Appeal No. E291 of 2021 [2021] eKLR (Musinga P., Nambuye, Okwengu, Kiage, Gatembu, Sichale, and Tuiyott JJ.) (Kenya).

[69] *Id.*

Supreme Court of Kenya upheld this result, but on a narrower procedural basis (namely, that the President could not propose the relevant amendments).[70] In contrast to the lower courts, the Court explicitly rejected the idea of a basic structure doctrine in Kenya, thereby leaving open the possibility that these changes could be adopted in the future, via different procedures.[71]

B. Constitutional Theory and Constructional Choice

Different constitutional contexts, and theories, take different views on the desirability of these decisions. Originalist scholars, for example, argue that in construing a written constitution, courts should focus on the original intentions of those who wrote and ratified a constitution, or the public meaning of constitutional language. Originalist scholars also suggest that courts should make implications only where they are strictly *necessary* to the proper functioning of the constitutional system as a whole.[72] One reason, they suggest, is that broader approaches to judicial implication lack basic legal legitimacy— or insufficient support in recognized legal modalities of argument such as the text, history and structure of a constitution.[73] In the United States in recent decades, originalism has also gained increasing popularity as an approach to constitutional construction.[74]

Many scholars, however, reject both the *feasibility* and *desirability* of an originalist approach. Constitution makers are a "they" not an "it": they often have heterogeneous aims, in ways that make it impossible to identify any coherent intent behind constitutional language. There is, likewise, indeterminacy in the original public meaning of constitutional language or in deciding how to apply that meaning in new or unforeseen circumstances. This was the fundamental insight of the early legal realists in the United States and, as realist scholars have long argued, it points to the need for judges to consider both social and political *values* and *consequences* in the process of constitutional construction.[75] Proponents of "living" or dynamic constitutional approaches

---

[70] *Supreme Court Renders its Verdict on BBI*, REPUBLIC OF KENYA: JUDICIARY (Mar. 31, 2022).
[71] *See*, Attorney General & Others v. David Ndii & 79 Others, Petition No. 12 of 2021 (Building Bridges Initiative Case).
[72] Goldsworthy, *supra* note 3, at 43. *See also* Jeremy Kirk, *Constitutional Implications (1): Nature, Legitimacy, Classification, Examples*, 24 MELB. U. L. REV. 645 (2000).
[73] Goldsworthy, *supra* note 3.
[74] Jamal Greene, *On the Origins of Originalism*, 88 TEX. L. REV. 1, 2 (2009).
[75] *See, e.g.*, RICHARD A. POSNER, LAW, PRAGMATISM, AND DEMOCRACY (2005) .William Huhn, *The Stages of Legal Reasoning: Formalism, Analogy, and Realism*, 48 VILL. L. REV. 305, 317 (2003).

further point to the desirability from a democratic perspective of attention to contemporary community values.[76]

Moreover, many living constitutionalists argue that implications may legitimately be made by courts where they are *helpful* to the functioning of a constitutional system. And if there is some support for implications in prior precedent, or the text and structure of a constitution, these scholars argue, this can answer concerns about an implication's legal legitimacy. Justice Barak, for example, suggests that judges in the civil law tradition frequently fill "gaps" in the civil code by drawing on analogous provisions, or general legal principles.[77] Construing a constitution, he argues, requires courts to engage in similar forms of gap-filling—that is, to interpret express provisions, and imply certain other provisions, so as to advance the overall purposes of the constitution.[78]

This, however, raises the question of *what* constitutional values or purposes courts should give expression to, and when. There is often broad agreement about the importance of a range of abstract constitutional values, including the rule of law, norms of non-arbitrary government or a "culture of justification," and the protection of the "central ranges" of rights to individual dignity, equality, and freedom.[79] But there is often disagreement about what this entails in practice.

The "rule of law," for example, is a broadly shared ideal, but often a principle about which there is disagreement in practice.[80] It can be understood as a guarantee of (i) the "rule of law, not men" [sic]; (ii) legal equality; and (iii) legal predictability, or all of the above.[81] The idea of the "rule of law, not men" is that laws should reflect the collective, deliberative judgments of legislators, not the subjective judgments of individual state officials.[82] The idea of legal equality is that all government officials—including the very highest officials—should be subject to the law or live "under" law.[83] And the idea of legal certainty is that individuals should be able to know and understand the law in advance so they

---

[76] Richard H. Fallon, The Dynamic Constitution (2009).
[77] Aharon Barak, Purposive Interpretation in Law (2005). *See also* Dixon, *supra* note 65.
[78] Barak, *supra* note 77; Dixon, *supra* note 65.
[79] Etienne Mureinik, *A Bridge to Where? Introducing the Interim Bill of Rights*, 10 S. Afr. J. Hum. Rights. 31; Moshe Cohen-Eliya & Iddo Porat, *Proportionality and the Culture of Justification*, 59 Am. J. Comp. L. 463 (2011); John Rawls, Political Liberalism (2005) at 297–99 (discussing the "central range" of application of various constitutional essentials). *Compare* Frank I. Michelman, *The Question of Constitutional Fidelity: Rawls on the Reason of Constitutional Courts*, in Public Reason and Courts (Silje A. Langvatn et al. eds., 2020).
[80] *See* Richard H. Fallon, *"The Rule of Law" As a Concept in Constitutional Discourse*, 97 Harv. L. Rev. 1 (1997).
[81] Fallon, *supra* note 80.
[82] *See also* Antonin Scalia, *The Rule of Law as a Law of Rules*, 56 U. Chi. L. Rev. 1175 (1989).
[83] Fallon, *supra* note 80.

can plan their lives on this basis.[84] This can also be seen as advancing commitments to individual freedom and dignity, as well as promoting socially valuable forms of investment and cooperation.[85]

The right to privacy is a widely shared commitment among constitutional democracies worldwide. But it encompasses at least five different dimensions: (i) informational or data privacy; (ii) spatial privacy; (iii) bodily privacy; (iv) relational privacy; and (v) what the US Supreme Court has often labelled "decisional privacy," but is, in fact, closer to a form of autonomy in the making of certain fundamental decisions.[86] Not all these dimensions will be relevant in every case. In fact, sometimes they may conflict. They also point to varying degrees of overlap with other rights. The right to bodily privacy, for example, will have a close connection to the right to freedom and bodily security. And the rights to relational and decisional privacy are loosely connected to rights to individual freedom and dignity.

The right to dignity itself likewise has multiple different dimensions. It includes the right to be treated with respect by others, or to be treated by the state as an end rather than a means: this is the essence of Kantian understandings of human dignity, or the "categorical imperative."[87] But it can also be understood in a broader sense, as entailing access to a minimum degree of physical, psychological, and material security. This is the essence of the "capabilities approach" (CA), developed by Amartya Sen in economics and Martha Nussbaum in philosophy, and its approach to human dignity.[88] In a CA, especially as articulated by Nussbaum, a life worthy of human dignity requires at least a minimum threshold level of certain central capabilities, including life, bodily health, bodily integrity, senses, imagination and thought, emotions, practical reason, affiliation, play, and material and political control over one's environment.[89]

The right to equality or non-discrimination likewise encompasses multiple values or commitments: a commitment to equal opportunity and dignity for

---

[84] *See id.*

[85] *See* Jeremy Waldron, *Getting to the Rule of Law and the Importance of Procedure, in* GETTING TO THE RULE OF LAW (James E. Fleming ed., 2012); K. Martin Krygier, *What About the Rule of Law*, 5 CONST. CT. REV. 74, 88–89 (2014); Martin Krygier, *Four Puzzles About the Rule of Law: Why, What, Where? And Who Cares?*, 50 NOMOS 64 (2011).

[86] *See, e.g.*, Bernstein v. Bester, 1996 (4) BCLR 449.

[87] IMMANUEL KANT, CRITIQUE OF JUDGEMENT (1932). *See* Martha Nussbaum & Rosalind Dixon, *Abortion, Dignity, and a Capabilities Approach, in* FEMINIST CONSTITUTIONALISM: GLOBAL PERSPECTIVES (Beverly Baines et al. eds., 2012).

[88] AMARTYA SEN, DEVELOPMENT AS FREEDOM (1999); MARTHA C. NUSSBAUM, CREATING CAPABILITIES: THE HUMAN DEVELOPMENT APPROACH 33–34 (2011).

[89] NUSSBAUM, *supra* note 88 at 33–34. *See also* Nussbaum & Dixon, *supra* note 87, at 559. Nussbaum also includes in her "tentative" list "being able to live with concern for and in relation to animals, plans and the world of nature."

all individuals, and equality among groups. This also means ensuring that individuals are free from the imposition of arbitrary or unfair stereotypes about their preferences and abilities, and demeaning and inhuman forms of treatment that impair their dignity. And for (minority) groups, it means the elimination of historical forms of social, political, and economic subordination. In some cases, eliminating discrimination can also advance all these different values or objectives. Eliminating discrimination against racial minorities, for example, can help challenge racialized assumptions about individual preferences and abilities, or demeaning attitudes and treatment, and also help overcome race as a site of systematic group-based disadvantage and subordination.

But in other cases, these commitments may conflict. For example, overcoming a history of race-based subordination may require extensive forms of positive discrimination, or restitution, which conflict with individual rights to (formal) equality of opportunity.[90] Some of these measures may also pose risks to the dignity of beneficiaries.[91] Moreover, applying these criteria necessarily calls for a series of evaluative judgment by courts.

This also points to different answers to many of the questions of constructional choice raised at the outset of the chapter.

1. Abortion

A right of access to abortion, for example, is arguably a necessary corollary of a woman's right to bodily, relational, and decisional privacy, and her right to dignity, freedom, and bodily security. It implicates a woman's control over her own body, her relationship to the fetus and her doctor, and her control over the future shape of her life. In this sense, it engages a woman's right to physical and psychological security, and her freedom to make fundamental decisions about the future of her own life. This is also closely connected to her dignity—that is, her right to a life worthy of full human dignity, including a life characterized by mental and physical health, and to be treated as a subject (not object) capable of making choices about the fundamental shape of her life.[92]

---

[90] See cases in Chapter 4, *infra*.
[91] See Justice Thomas on affirmative action: *e.g.*, Tomiko Brown-Nagin, *The Transformative Racial Politics of Justice Thomas: The Grutter v. Bollinger Opinion*, 7 U. Pa. J. Const. L. 787 (2004).
[92] *See, e.g.*, Abortion I, 39 BVerfGE I (1975); Abortion II, 88 BVerfGE 203 (1993); R v. Morgentaler, [1988] 1 S.C.R. 30 at 172 (Wilson J); Columbian Constitutional Court Decision C-355 of 2006. See discussion in Nussbaum & Dixon, *supra* note 87.

Some argue, however, that the right to human dignity also extends to the fetus, and therefore imposes limits—as well as a potential lower bound—on legal rights of access to abortion.[93] In Germany, for example, the German Federal Constitutional Court (GFCC) has held that the state's duty to protect life and dignity, under the Basic Law, extends to the protection of fetal life, and as such, the Bundestag is not permitted to legalize access to abortion, without restriction.[94] The Polish Constitutional Court has made a similar finding.[95]

2. Sexual privacy and equality

Similarly, rights to sexual privacy are arguably necessary to the privacy, dignity, and equality of LGBTQI+ citizens. Sexual privacy is necessary to relational and bodily privacy for all adult citizens. It is also often closely connected to the enjoyment of spatial privacy—that is, the right to be free from state interference in the home, and especially the bedroom.[96] For gays and lesbians in particular, it is also necessary to their equality and dignity as citizens: as the CCSA noted in *National Coalition I*, laws that ban gay sex send a clear signal that in the eyes of the law, all gay men are criminals.[97] This is both a clear failure to show respect for the dignity of LGBTQI+ persons, and reinforces and perpetuates harmful stereotypes about gays and lesbians as less worthy of respect and concern.[98] Criminal prohibitions on gay sex also build into the day-to-day lives of LGBTQI+ citizens an inherent degree of physical and psychological insecurity: these prohibitions mean that they must constantly live in fear of arrest or other legal sanctions, as they go about their lives.[99] And they create clear obstacles to seeking help and protection from the police, and others, in cases where sexual intimacy goes wrong. In this way, they violate commitments to privacy, equality, and dignity.

Similarly, many countries increasingly consider laws recognizing same-sex and transgender marriage as necessary to protecting the privacy, dignity, and equality of LGBTQI+ persons. Marriage confers a range of practical benefits,

---

[93] See discussion in Nussbaum & Dixon, *supra* note 87.
[94] DONALD P. KOMMERS, THE CONSTITUTIONAL JURISPRUDENCE OF THE FEDERAL REPUBLIC OF GERMANY 339 (2d ed. 1997).
[95] Dominic Standish, *From Abortion on Demand to Its Criminalization: The Case of Poland in the 1990s*, *in* ABORTION LAW AND POLITICS TODAY 116 (Ellie Lee ed., 1998).
[96] *See, e.g.*, Lawrence v. Texas, 539 U.S. 558 (2003).
[97] National Coalition for Gay and Lesbian Equality v. Minister of Justice, 1999 (1) SA 6 (CC), 30 [28] (Ackermann J).
[98] *Id.*
[99] *Id.*

as well as responsibilities, on those who enter it—including access to immigration, tax and healthcare benefits, and shared forms of decision-making and property. It also confers important symbolic recognition to a relationship and those in it. Access to same-sex marriage, therefore, is arguably necessary to the capacity of LGBTQI+ individuals to enjoy the control over their material and physical environment necessary for a life of full human dignity,[100] and to their sense of respect and recognition for their identity.[101]

At the same time, there are opponents of same-sex marriage who suggest that their dignity requires rejecting claims to same-sex marital equality. Many arguments against recognizing same-sex marriage focus on notions of tradition and preservation of traditional forms of marriage or family life.[102] Still others focus on the relationship between marriage and child-rearing and, albeit largely unsupported, arguments about the downsides for children of same-sex as opposed to heterosexual models of parenting.[103] But some arguments against same-sex marriage are framed in explicitly rights based terms, and draw on the idea that respect for the prior marital choices of heterosexual couples, and their understanding of marriage as an (heterosexual) institution requires maintaining marriage as a solely heterosexual institution.[104]

3. Structural social rights

The same is true for social rights: some notions of democracy suggest that social rights are a matter for democratic self-government, not prerequisites for its legitimate operation, whereas other definitions emphasize that citizens cannot participate meaningfully in democratic politics without first having access to food, shelter, and housing.[105]

Social rights cases also frequently involve a clash between commitments to individual dignity and broader concerns about economic equality. In *Grootboom*, for example, the petitioners sought to gain immediate access to emergency shelter as necessary to protect their basic human dignity. But the

---

[100] NUSSBAUM, *supra* note 88.
[101] *See, e.g.*, Minister of Home Aff. v. Fourie, 2006 (1) SA 524 (CC).
[102] *See, e.g.*, discussion in Patrick Busch, *Is Same-Sex Marriage a Threat to Traditional Marriages?: How Courts Struggle with the Question*, 10 WASH. U. GLOBAL STUD. L. REV. 143 (2011).
[103] *See* Goodridge v. Dep't of Pub. Health, 440 Mass. 309, 333–36 (2003).
[104] *Id.* at 390–91.
[105] *See, e.g.*, Rawls, *supra* note 79; Cecile Fabre, *Constitutionalising Social Rights*, 6 J. POL. PHIL. 263 (1998); Suzanne B. Goldberg, *Constitutional Tipping Points: Civil Rights, Social Change, and Fact-Based Adjudication*, 106 COLUM. L. REV. 1955 (2006); Lawrence G. Sager, *Thin Constitutions and the Good Society*, 69 FORDHAM L. REV. 1989 (2001).

government opposed this relief on the grounds that it could undermine commitments to equality and the rule of law—by encouraging a form of "queue jumping" by those waiting for access to formal housing.[106] The same concerns were raised, with even greater force, in the CCSA's earlier decision in *Soobramoney*, where the Court was asked to grant immediate, individual relief to the petitioner to allow him access to dialysis, and thereby protect his health and dignity, but the Court ultimately declined this request on the grounds that to do so would endanger commitments to broader equality in the allocation of scarce public health resources.[107] And the same tension has been seen in many of the decisions of the Constitutional Court of Colombia and Supreme Court of Brazil involving the right to health.[108]

C. Why Courts? Constitutional Choice and Democracy

Even more fundamentally, the dilemma of constructional choice raises the question of why it should be *courts* and not the political branches that are trusted with resolving disputes of this kind. In striking down or invalidating legislation, courts are often acting to protect and promote commitments to the rule of law, individual freedom, dignity, equality, *and* democracy—especially in a "thick" sense.

"Thin" or competitive understandings of democracy emphasize the idea of a democracy as a system of regular free and fair elections, characterized by competition among multiple political parties. This idea was at the heart of Joseph Schumpeter's understanding of democracy as a system of competition between rival elites.[109] Democracy, for Schumpeter, was ultimately not a system that sought to empower or encourage the participation of ordinary citizens. Rather, it was a system designed to promote the accountability and effectiveness of government—by giving citizens the opportunity to remove governments that did not perform well on these criteria.[110]

---

[106] *See* Government of the Republic of South Africa v. Grootboom, 2001 (1) SA 46 (CC), at [81] (Yacoob J) (talking about the effect of any immediate relief as effectively granting a "special dispensation" to petitioners). *Compare also* Katharine G. Young, *Rights and Queues: On Distributive Contests in the Modern State*, 55 COLUM. J. TRANSNAT'L L. 65 (2016).

[107] Soobramoney v. Minister of Health, 1998 (1) SA 765 (CC), at [8], [28]–[31] (Chaskalson P.) (S. Afr.).

[108] Brinks & Gauri, *supra* note 56.

[109] JOSEPH A. SCHUMPETER, CAPITALISM, SOCIALISM AND DEMOCRACY 247–49 (1976) (originally published in 1942). See discussion in POSNER, *supra* note 75; Samuel Issacharoff, *Democracy's Deficits*, 85 U. CHI. L. REV. 485, 498–99 (2018).

[110] *Compare* POSNER, *supra* note 75; Issacharoff, *supra* note 109.

Other theories, however, insist on a "thicker" understanding of the idea of democracy, and emphasize both the value of democratic deliberation from an epistemic viewpoint, and the value of participation as itself a form of political good.[111] Deliberative democrats, such as Jürgen Habermas, Amy Gutmann, and Dennis Thompson have long pointed to the value of deliberation in promoting both more legitimate and reliable democratic decision-making.[112] A range of constitutional scholars have also pointed to the value of deliberation, and norms of public reason-giving, in promoting the political legitimacy of constitutional democratic forms of government.[113] In addition, some have pointed to the value of citizen participation in ensuring a more egalitarian form of democratic politics.[114] Roberto Gargarella, for example, emphasizes the close connection between rights-based commitments and structural provisions that "strengthen the political influence of those marginalized groups [protected by various constitutional rights]" or that "bolster their capacity to decide and control those in power."[115] A new generation of scholars in the United States have likewise pointed to citizen participation as key to ensuring that democratic processes can respond to the challenges of rising economic inequality, and its impact on both political and social life.[116]

Other scholars insist on broad forms of rights-based protections as necessary to the idea of *constitutional* democracy. Ronald Dworkin famously argued that at the heart of the idea of constitutional democracy is a commitment to treat all individuals with "equal concern and respect."[117] This, for Dworkin, further entailed a commitment on the part of the state to affording all citizens maximum freedom, dignity, and equality including, but also extending far beyond, the core political rights and freedoms emphasized by competitive democrats such as Schumpeter. Basic constitutional rights, for Dworkin, included a

---

[111] This is what Richard Posner calls "concept 2" democracy: see POSNER, *supra* note 75, at 158–78.

[112] *See, e.g.*, AMY GUTMANN & DENNIS THOMPSON, WHY DELIBERATIVE DEMOCRACY? (2009); AMY GUTMANN & DENNIS THOMSON, DEMOCRACY AND DISAGREEMENT (1996); JÜRGEN HABERMAS, BETWEEN FACTS AND NORMS: CONTRIBUTIONS TO A DISCOURSE THEORY OF LAW AND DEMOCRACY (William Rehg trans., 1996). *See also* CAROLE PATEMAN, PARTICIPATION AND DEMOCRATIC THEORY (1970). *See also* ROBERT GARGARELLA, THE LAW AS A COVERSATION AMONG EQUALS (2002).

[113] *See* Mattias Kumm, *The Idea of Socratic Contestation and the Right to Justification: The Point of Rights-Based Proportionality Review*, 4 L. & ETHICS HUM. RTS. 142 (2010); WOJCIECH SADURSKI, EQUALITY AND LEGITIMACY (2008). *See also* Joshua Cohen, *Truth and Public Reason* 37 PHIL. & PUB. AFF. 2 (2009).

[114] ROBERTO GARGARELLA, LATIN AMERICAN CONSTITUTIONALISM, 1810–2010: THE ENGINE ROOM OF THE CONSTITUTION (2013).

[115] *Id.* at 7–8.

[116] *See* K. SABEEL RAHMAN, DEMOCRACY AGAINST DOMINATION (2016); GANESH SITARAMAN, THE GREAT DEMOCRACY: HOW TO FIX OUR POLITICS, UNRIG THE ECONOMY, AND UNITE AMERICA (2019).

[117] RONALD DWORKIN, FREEDOM'S LAW: THE MORAL READING OF THE AMERICAN CONSTITUTION 17 (1999).

much broader range of personal freedoms—including notions of privacy, free movement, decisional autonomy, non-discrimination, or freedom from cruel, inhuman, and degrading treatment.[118] This echoed the arguments of leading political theorists, such as John Rawls, who argued that constitutional democracy requires that all institutions be designed so as to guarantee (i) equal basic liberties; (ii) fair value of the political liberties; and (iii) fair equal opportunity, in addition to principles of distributive justice.[119]

In protecting individual rights to freedom, and equality, courts are also often acting to promote both commitments to freedom, dignity, and equality *and* these thicker, more substantive democratic ideals. The difficulty is that, in doing so, they are also often making contested judgments about both what these ideals entail *and* how best to balance them against other, competing values.

There are arguably some "central ranges" to rights to freedom, dignity, and equality over which citizens cannot reasonably disagree if they wish to maintain a commitment to *constitutional* democracy.[120] While the content of this requirement may itself be contested, at a minimum it would seem to require that citizens treat each other with respect in processes of political debate and law-making.[121] And this would rule out the idea that legislation may be based on *animus* or hostility toward a particular minority group.[122] It would also be likely to rule out the idea of laws that reflect or create forms of status-based hierarchy, or group-based subordination. Democracy, in this sense, presumes at least some minimum degree of political and social equality as part of the minimum core.

Beyond these central ranges to the rights to freedom, dignity, and equality, however, the attempt to promote democratic values will often involve courts advancing a fundamentally contested conception of what constitutionalism and democracy require.[123] And as "political constitutionalists" such as Jeremy

---

[118] *Id.*

[119] Rawls, *supra* note 79. On the relationship between Rawls and Dworkin's thought in this context, see, *e.g.*, Frank I. Michelman, *Constitution (Written or Unwritten): Legitimacy and Legality in the Thought of John Rawls*, 4 RATIO JURIS 279 (2018).

[120] *Compare* RAWLS, *supra* note 79, at 297–99 (discussing the "central range" of application of various constitutional essentials).

[121] *See, e.g.*, JEREMY WALDRON, LAW AND DISAGREEMENT (1999). The following paragraph and the ideas in it draw heavily on Rosalind Dixon, *Constitutional "Dialogue" and Deference*, in CONSTITUTIONAL DIALOGUE: RIGHTS, DEMOCRACY, INSTITUTIONS 161 (Geoffrey Sigalet et al. eds., 2019).

[122] Richard H. Pildes, *Avoiding Balancing: The Role of Exclusionary Reasons in Constitutional Law*, 45 HASTINGS L.J. 711 (1994).

[123] In some cases, this may even be true for the central ranges of certain rights, or core constitutional textual provisions: Frank I. Michelman, *Constitutional Fidelity/Democratic Agency*, 65 FORDHAM L. REV. 1537 (1996).

Waldron have noted, this can mean that judicial review is itself *in tension* with the values of democratic self-government.[124]

Take doctrines such as implied principle of freedom of political communication, or unconstitutional amendment: the key aim of such doctrines is to protect narrow commitments to competitive democracy. They also serve to protect a wider range of commitments to participation and deliberation implicit in thicker notions of democracy. But they do so in ways that are inevitably contested. And citizens, as well as judges, may reasonably disagree about the best answer to these questions. This raises the question why courts—and not the political branches, fourth branch, independent institutions, or even the people themselves—should play a role in protecting and promoting democratic values.

Given reasonable disagreement about rights, Waldron argues, the fairest and most principled way of resolving such disagreements will generally be by reference to ordinary norms of majority decision-making among citizens. This is the only basis for resolving disagreements among citizens that fully respects norms of *equality* in the process of self-government. This, in a representative democracy, will also generally mean decision-making by ordinary legislative majority. It will *not* involve final decision-making by unelected, independent judges. "By privileging majority voting among a small number of unelected unaccountable judges," Waldron notes, judicial review of this kind "disenfranchises ordinary citizens and brushes aside cherished principles of representation and political equality in the final resolution of issues about rights."[125]

One response to this is that judicial review simply creates a "baseline" of rights protection, above which legislatures are free to decide how best to balance competing rights and interests. The difficulty with this argument, however, is that it ignores the degree to which baselines of this kind will often be contested—or themselves subject to reasonable disagreement. A key premise of this idea is that "legislative action is more likely to violate fundamental rights than is legislative inaction."[126] But as Mark Tushnet notes, "[a]sserting that governmental failures to protect do not violate fundamental rights is to take a controversial position within modern liberalism."[127] In many countries

---

[124] *See* WALDRON, LAW AND DISAGREEMENT, *supra* note 121; Jeremy Waldron, *The Core of the Case Against Judicial Review*, 115 YALE L.J. 1346 (2005). *Cf also* Adrienne Stone, *Judicial Review Without Rights: Some Problems for the Democratic Legitimacy of Structural Judicial Review*, 28 OXFORD J. LEGAL STUD. 1 (2008); Erin Delaney, *The Federal Case for Judicial Review*, 10 OXFORD J. LEGAL STUD. 1093 (2022).

[125] Waldron, *The Core of the Case, supra* note 124, at 1353.

[126] Richard H. Fallon, Jr., *The Core of an Uneasy Case for Judicial Review*, 121 HARV. L. REV. 1693, 1710 (2007).

[127] Mark Tushnet, *How Different are Waldron's and Fallon's Core Cases For and Against Judicial Review?*, 30 OXFORD J. LEGAL STUD. 49, 59 (2010).

the practice of judicial review regularly involves conflicts between rights—including between rights such as (i) rights to life, dignity, and security of the person (abortion); (ii) liberty and equality (hate speech); (iii) due process and personal security and dignity (criminal justice); and (iv) property, contract, and socioeconomic rights.[128]

The idea of judicial review as simply "an additional veto" on rights-infringing action by legislatures, therefore, simply does not hold up in most constitutional democracies worldwide. Judicial review may well do a great deal to protect and promote democratic values of deliberation and minority rights protection, but it does so in ways that are inevitably in tension with—rather than immune from—democratic objections of the kind raised by political constitutionalists.

Similarly, for democratic government to be legitimate, it must be based on a principle of equality among citizens; and this requires the elimination of all forms of social, political, and economic subordination. But legitimate forms of democratic government also depend on the consent of the governed and cannot be based on pure coercion. This creates a fundamental tension in a democracy: democratic legitimacy requires the elimination of all forms of subordination but by persuading rather than forcing those who would perpetuate subordination to make this change.[129] It also requires that while conflict or polarization persists about what subordination means, or anti-subordination requires, a court's role is to ensure that "no combatant conclusively prevails over the other"—or that both sides of a political controversy are equally happy *and* unhappy with the result of a judicial decision.[130]

D. Ely's Response

Ely's response to this problem was to argue that courts should play a role in promoting constitutional values only in a quite limited, indirect sense—that is, by seeking to counter or correct "malfunctions" in the legislative process, which might otherwise undermine the capacity for the political branches of government to engage in meaningful democratic deliberation about these questions.[131]

Ely identified two broad malfunctions of this kind: where the "ins are choking off the channels of political change to ensure that they will stay in and

---

[128] *Id.* at 55–67.
[129] ROBERT BURT, THE CONSTITUTION IN CONFLICT 31 (1992).
[130] *Id.* at 359, 368–69.
[131] JOHN HART ELY, DEMOCRACY AND DISTRUST: A THEORY OF JUDICIAL REVIEW 103 (1980).

outs will stay out"; or "though no one is actually denied a voice or a vote, representatives beholden to an effective majority are systematically disadvantaging some minority out of simple hostility or prejudiced refusal to recognize commonalities of interest, and thereby denying that minority the protection afforded other groups by a representative system."[132] That is, he pointed to both blockages to the channels of political change, and laws affecting "discrete and insular minorities," as warranting heightened forms of judicial scrutiny.[133]

This closely followed the logic of Justice Stone's opinion in *Carolene Products*, where in a famous footnote (footnote 4), Stone suggested that while most laws should be presumed constitutional and subject only to rational basis review by the Supreme Court, this presumption of constitutionality might not apply to "legislation which restricts those political processes which can ordinarily be expected to bring about repeal of undesirable legislation," or which is "directed at . . . or [reflect prejudice against] particular discrete and insular minorities."[134] And while Ely, like Justice Stone, was focused on the interpretation of the US Constitution, these ideas clearly have broader potential application.[135]

Indeed, the logic of this understanding of representation-reinforcement suggests quite clear answers to the questions of constructional choice posed at the outset of the chapter:

(1) *Abortion and LGBTQI+ rights*: The Supreme Court should *not* read the right to "liberty" and "equal protection" as encompassing a right of access to abortion or same-sex marriage. Cases of this kind directly affect women and LGBTQI+ US citizens but neither of these groups are discrete and insular minorities according to Ely. In a comparative context, courts, such as the CCSA, should give effect to clear textual requirements to eliminate discrimination based on sexual orientation, or provide access to reproductive healthcare, but absent such language, courts elsewhere should *not* interpret more open-ended constitutional guarantees to achieve the same result.

(2) *Implied speech and equality rights*: Ely's ideas would *support* doctrines designed to protect those political rights and freedoms necessary for maintaining the channels of political change, but *not* broader

---

[132] *Id.*
[133] *Id.*
[134] United States v. Carolene Prod. Co., 304 U.S. 144 (1938). See discussion in ELY, *supra* note 131, at 75–76.
[135] Rosalind Dixon & Michaela Hailbronner, *Ely in the World: The Global Legacy of Democracy and Distrust 40 Years On*, 19 INT'L J. CONST. L. 427 (2021).

implications designed to protect a broader range of personal or social rights. The only possible exception is in cases where the Supreme Court of Israel has sought to protect the rights of Arab-Israelis, as a potential discrete and insular minority within Israeli democracy.
(3) *Structural social rights*: Courts in countries such as India, South Africa, Colombia, and Brazil should give effect to the ordinary meaning of social rights provisions, but should *not* go beyond the text to develop structural responses to social rights violations (unless they affect discrete and insular minorities, such as racial minorities).
(4) *Unconstitutional constitutional amendment doctrine*: An unconstitutional amendment doctrine protects against attempts to amend a constitution, but in ways that go beyond attempts to ensure a level political playing field. They often go much further in protecting existing features of a constitutional order, including a range of institutional checks and balances not identified by Ely as part of the channels of political change. Courts, therefore, should apply such a doctrine with great *caution* or *not at all*.

Ely expressly rejected the idea that cases such as *Roe* were rightly decided. He argued that the Due Process Clauses of the Fifth and Fourteenth Amendments should be understood as requiring fair procedures to be followed, not inviting judges to assess the substantive reasonableness of limits on individual liberty.[136] And he gave *Roe* as a prime example of this kind of "substantive" as opposed to "procedural" approach.

Ely was also generally critical of judges making open-ended moral and political value judgments. "In a representative democracy," he argued, "value determinations are to be made by our elected representatives" not courts.[137] This was also a point he derived from both the specific commitment to self-government under the US Constitution *and* broader democratic principles and ideas. On this basis, Ely would also likely have opposed both decisions such as *Lawrence* and *Obergefell* and comparable decisions elsewhere recognizing rights of access to abortion and same-sex marriage.[138]

Ely did draw a distinction in this context between stronger and weaker forms of review, even within the United States. He explicitly suggested that it might *make sense* for courts to "protect the rights of the majority by

---
[136] ELY, *supra* note 131, at 21–22.
[137] *Id.* at 103.
[138] Lawrence v. Texas, 539 U.S. 558 (2003); Obergefell v. Hodges, 576 U.S. 644 (2015). *See* Chapter 4, *infra*.

ensuring that legislation truly reflect[s] popular values" in a common law or subconstitutional context, but not in the context of entrenched, strong-form constitutional adjudication.[139] What was critical for Ely was that "if the legislature [did] not approve of a court's decision" seeking to give effect to a "consensus" view of democratic values, it could "overrule" it.[140] As I explore further in Chapter 6, *Roe* purported to announce a broad and final set of rules governing access to abortion, whereas decisions such as *Casey* substantially narrowed those findings, in ways that have come closer to winning Ely's approval. And Ely might have been less opposed to courts identifying rights of access to abortion or LGBTQI+ rights in Canada, Colombia, Hong Kong, India, Korea, South Africa, or the United Kingdom than in the United States, because it is far easier to amend the constitution in these countries; and in several, there are additional powers of legislative override. And, as Chapter 7 explores in more detail, these limits all contribute to creating a far "weaker," less final model of judicial review than in the United States.

Ely also acknowledged that there were varying degrees of indeterminacy in any constitutional context, and that some constitutional questions might be answered by reference to orthodox legal sources or "modalities."[141] For instance, the requirement that the US President must be thirty-five years of age to be eligible for office was one provision Ely regarded as "so clear that a conscious reference" to constitutional purposes or values was not necessary.[142] There are also a range of comparative examples where constitutional meaning could be regarded as equally clear.

Section 9(2) of the 1996 South African Constitution, for example, expressly provides that the state may "not unfairly discriminate directly or indirectly against anyone on one or more grounds, including race, gender, sex ... [and] *sexual orientation*." Similarly, section 27(2) provides that "everyone has the right to have access to health care services, including reproductive health care." The text of the Constitution thus explicitly contemplates a role for the CCSA in ensuring legal equality between opposite and same-sex partnerships, or heterosexual and LGBTQI+ relationships, and on at least one reading of the original public meaning of section 27(2), at least minimal legal access to contraception and possibly even abortion.

---

[139] ELY, *supra* note 131, at 68–69.
[140] *Id.*
[141] Modalities is the term Philip Bobbitt, not Ely, uses in this context. *See* PHILIP BOBBITT, CONSTITUTIONAL FATE: THEORY OF THE CONSTITUTION (1982).
[142] ELY, *supra* note 131, at 13.

In general, however, Ely was skeptical of "interpretivism," or the view that constitutional history and language alone can provide concrete, determinate answers to constitutional controversies.[143] In most cases involving moral and political value judgments, for Ely, this meant that courts should adopt a quite restrained, procedurally focused role. The only exception was in cases involving equality claims brought on behalf of "discrete and insular minorities"—that is, social and political minorities unable to protect themselves politically.[144]

A further issue is how Ely would respond to an implied freedom of political communication, or an unconstitutional amendment doctrine. On one level, representation-reinforcement considerations would support implications of this kind.[145] But Ely was more concerned by leaders tilting the electoral playing field in their own favor, rather than broader threats to electoral and institutional pluralism in a democracy.

However, Ely's approach has been consistently criticized on grounds that it (i) unduly distinguishes between constitutional substance and procedure; and (ii) fails to consider judicial capacity, or dysfunction and representation-reinforcement beyond the United States.[146] While Ely adopted a *relatively thin* definition of democracy focused on the idea of free and fair elections under conditions of multiparty competition, he also included thicker commitments to equal democratic representation.[147] Hence, Ely focused on democratic failures to protect minority rights. The difficulty with Ely's approach, therefore, was its overly "proceduralized" conception of courts role in protecting democracy in both a thin and thick sense, and unduly distinguishing constitutional "process" and "substance."[148]

---

[143] *Id.* at ch 2.

[144] This could also arguably extend to groups such as Arab-Israelis, who were the petitioners in *Ka'adan v. Israel Land Admin.*, HCJ 6698/95 (2000). *See, e.g.,* Antonia Noori Farzan, *Arab Israelis Are Rising Up to Protest. Here's What You Need to Know about their Status in the Country,* WASH. POST, May. 13, 2021, <https://www.washingtonpost.com/world/2021/05/13/arab-israeli-faq/>.

[145] Rosalind Dixon & Gabrielle Appleby, *Constitutional Implications in Australia, in* THE INVISIBLE CONSTITUTION IN COMPARATIVE PERSPECTIVE 343 (Rosalind Dixon & Adrienne Stone eds., 2018). *See also* Stephen Gageler AC, *in* Rosalind Dixon & Amelia Loughland, *Comparative Constitutional Adaptation: Democracy and Distrust in the High Court of Australia,* 19 INT'L. J. CONST. L. 455 (2021).

[146] *See* Chapter 1, *supra*; Dixon & Hailbronner, *supra* note 135.

[147] See discussion in Jane S. Schachter, *Ely and the Idea of Democracy,* 57 STAN. L. REV. 737, 743 (2004).

[148] *See* Laurence H. Tribe, *The Puzzling Persistence of Process-Based Constitutional Theories,* 89 YALE L.J. 1063 (1980). *See also* Mark Tushnet, *Darkness on the Edge of Town: The Contributions of John Hart Ely to Constitutional Theory,* 89 YALE L.J. 1037 (1979); Daniel R. Ortiz, *Pursuing a Perfect Politics: The Allure and Failure of Process Theory,* 77 VA. L. REV. 721 (1991); Bruce A. Ackerman, *Beyond Carolene Products,* 98 HARV. L. REV. 713 (1984); Schachter, *Ely and the Idea of Democracy, supra* note 147.

E. Criticism of Ely's Approach

Ely suggested that the appropriate *degree* of political competition or openness in a democratic system was self-evident. However, the "optimal" number of political parties in an electoral system, or the reasonable limitation of political rights and freedoms remains unclear. Similarly, he suggested that the US Constitution promotes "adjudicative" and "representative" processes. However, as Laurence Tribe argued, which of these processes applies, when, and to what degree, depends on substantive judgments about the purposes of these processes.[149] This also prevents Ely's *Carolene Products*-style approach from avoiding the need for courts to engage in open-ended *substantive* judgments about the scope of constitutional rights, or balance between competing rights and interests.

Ely also arguably downplayed the need for evaluative judgment by courts in identifying "discrete and insular minorities" worthy of heightened judicial protection. A group's political vulnerability and social and economic may vary over time. Gays and lesbians, for example, have been subject to significant social prejudice but have gained economic and political influence in many constitutional democracies.[150] They are thus socially vulnerable, but increasingly economically and politically powerful. Women in many constitutional democracies have likewise made enormous social and economic gains but still have not achieved true economic or political parity.[151]

In addition, for some groups, there may be debate about individual fault or responsibility for membership in the group. Felons often lack economic power, are socially stigmatized, and are disenfranchised during and after their custodial sentence. But some would suggest this is caused by choices individual prisoners made, and that prisoners as a class are not a

---

[149] Tribe, *The Puzzling Persistence*, supra note 148, at 1068.

[150] *See, e.g.*, Arwen Armbrecht, *Explainer: The State of LGBT Rights Today*, WORLD ECON. F. (Jan. 4, 2016), <https://www.weforum.org/agenda/2016/01/explainer-the-state-of-lgbt-rights-today/>; M.V. Lee Badgett et al., *The Relationship Between LGBT Inclusion and Emerging Development: Emerging Economies*, UCLA SCHOOL OF LAW: WILLIAMS INSTITUTE (Nov. 2014), <https://williamsinstitute.law.ucla.edu/publications/lgbt-inclusion-economic-dev/>; Jon Miller & Lucy Parker, *Open for Business: The Economic and Business Case for Global LGB&T Inclusion*, OPEN FOR BUSINESS (2015), <https://www.wko.at/site/Charta-der-Vielfalt/Service/studien/Brunswick_Open_for_Business.pdf>; Leonore F. Carpenter, *The Next Phase: Positioning the Post-Obergefell LGBT Rights Movement to Bridge the Gap Between Formal and Lived Equality*, 13 STAN. J. C.R. & C.L. 255 (2017).

[151] *See, e.g.*, WORLD ECONOMIC FORUM, GLOBAL GENDER PAY GAP REPORT (2020); Esteban Ortiz-Ospina & Max Roser, *Economic Inequality By Gender*, OUR WORLD IN DATA (2018), <https://ourworldindata.org/economic-inequality-by-gender>; Inter-Parliamentary Union, *Women in National Parliaments* (Feb. 1, 2019), <http://archive.ipu.org/wmn-e/classif.htm>; Mark McCord, *This is How Women's Rights Have Progressed*, WORLD ECON. F. (Mar. 6, 2020), <https://www.weforum.org/agenda/2020/03/international-womens-day-equality-rights/>.

disadvantaged group. Determining group "vulnerability" depends on degree, which must be considered as part of an overarching commitment to equality and democracy.

Ely's basic notion of the courts' role in protecting rights to equality was also arguably under-inclusive from the perspective of substantive commitments to equality.[152] From this perspective, his theory ought to have pointed, but did not, to heightened forms of scrutiny of laws (such as those restricting access to abortion) that have a disparate impact on women. And it should have extended to protection for gays and lesbians—including in the form of protection for their sexual privacy and recognition of their intimate relationships, on terms equal to the recognition given to opposite-sex relationships.

For Ely, the courts' role in protecting "discrete and insular minorities" was largely designed to capture the experiences of African-American voters in the US South, where historical patterns of discrimination were closely linked to *de jure* and *de facto* patterns of vote suppression and dilution.[153] Due to this, it provided a compelling account for why discrimination against African-Americans should attract strict scrutiny under the Equal Protection Clause of the Fourteenth Amendment. It did not, however, capture the "suspect" nature of many other forms of discrimination in the United States and elsewhere from the perspective of various substantive equality values—for example, discrimination based on sex, gender, sexuality, marital status, age, or disability.[154]

All of these categories have been the focus of unfair stereotypes and assumptions, which undermine human dignity.[155] Such treatment is arguably even more fraught when one considers that all of these characteristics are "immutable," or not changeable at tolerable individual cost, or deeply personal or constitutive of individual identity.[156] The actual or *de facto* immutability of a characteristic means that discrimination on these grounds poses substantial obstacles to individuals' enjoyment of equality of opportunity.[157] And the constitutive nature of certain characteristics increases the potential harm to

---

[152] *Compare* Ackerman, *supra* note 148, at 731; Tushnet, *supra* note 148; David Landau, *A Dynamic Theory of Judicial Role*, 55 B.C.L. REV. 1501, 1533–35 (2014).
[153] *Id.*
[154] *Id.*
[155] *See* NUSSBAUM, *supra* note 88.
[156] *See* Corbière v. Canada (Minister of Indian and Northern Aff.), [1999] 2 S.C.R. 203 [13], 173 DLR (4th) 1 (McLachlin & Bastarache JJ.) (Can.); Miron v. Trudel, [1995] 2 S.C.R. 418, 124 DLR (4th) 693 (Can.); Harksen v. Lane NO (1997), [1998] 1 SA 300 [49], (CCT9/97) [1997] ZACC 1 (Goldstone J.) (S. Afr.).
[157] Rosalind Dixon, *The Supreme Court of Canada and Constitutional (Equality) Baselines*, 50 OSGOODE HALL L.J. 637 (2012).

human dignity from discrimination on these lines.[158] Women, and especially pregnant and married women, sexual minorities, young and old people, and those with mental and physical disabilities have also faced systematic economic, legal, and political disadvantage: women still earn substantially less than men and are less likely to be elected to political office, long after gaining access to the vote and the legal right to be elected. The law has historically failed to recognize—indeed, often criminalized—the identity of sexual and gender minorities. Older people and those with disabilities have also suffered social and economic marginalization, and people with mental disabilities even more profound political exclusion.

Yet few of these groups are truly "discrete and insular"—in the sense of being geographically concentrated and unable to form effective political coalitions. Men and women often live in the same household, not just same neighborhood. Older people and those with disabilities often have close connections with their families and communities and are widely geographically dispersed. And the activism of civil rights organizations and non-governmental organizations has meant that many of these groups have also been quite effective in building successful political coalitions, even though they remain disadvantaged, and subject to demeaning forms of treatment.

F. Representation-Reinforcement Beyond Ely

Moreover, as the next chapter explores more fully, Ely's account did not capture many of the most pressing contemporary threats to democracy and democratic responsiveness. While Ely focused on *deliberate* attempts by electoral majorities to burden the rights and interests of "discrete and insular" minorities, today, individual rights are often threatened by legislative inaction as much as action. And while Ely highlighted the danger of attempts by political incumbents to clog the channels of political change, as the next chapter explores in more detail, the risk to democracy today often involves the attempt to destroy—not just clog—commitments to democratic competition and accountability.

Actions of this kind have also occurred in new and established constitutional democracies—including, many would argue, in some of the world's oldest democracies, such as the United Kingdom and United States. In the United Kingdom, prior to the Supreme Court's intervention in *Miller II*, Prime Minister Boris Johnson attempted to use long-standing common law powers to prorogue parliament as a means of undermining parliamentary oversight over

[158] *Id.*

his government, and especially his attempts to exit the European Union.[159] And in the process, he misled the public and attacked the media.[160] In the United States, before losing the November 2020 election, President Donald Trump attacked federal courts, the media, and the independence of key agencies and fourth branch institutions. Following the election, and the lead up to it, Trump also encouraged distrust of the electoral process and violence directed against Congress.[161]

To be useful as a guide to constructional choice, therefore, any contemporary account of judicial representation-reinforcement must be both broader and more qualified than that offered by Ely himself: it must combine thin and thick understandings of democracy, acknowledge the inevitability of disagreement about the precise scope of these understandings, *and* take a broad view of ways in which democratic commitments of this kind may be threatened in a contemporary, comparative setting.

Modern "comparative political process theory" (CPPT) also starts from just this understanding. Gardbaum, for example, suggests that there is an important role for courts in many democracies in countering four distinct political market failures: (i) non-deliberativeness of the legislature; (ii) legislative failures to hold the executive accountable; (iii) government capture of independent institutions; and (iv) capture of the political process by special interests.[162] Niels Petersen proposes a similar taxonomy of "political market failures" as a guide to a modern theory of representation-reinforcing review. Like Ely, Petersen notes the important role for constitutional courts in protecting minorities, and courts' traditional role as "arbitrators in competency disputes."[163] But Petersen suggests that courts also have an important role to play in "safeguarding the integrity of the legislative process," protecting against "legislative capture" and "correcting [for] external effects."[164] Manuel Cepeda and David Landau likewise suggest that courts can play three broad roles in protecting and promoting democracy in addition to the functions identified by Ely: (i) guarding against democratic breakdown; (ii) improving the quality of

---

[159] *See* R. (Miller) v. The Prime Minister [2020] AC 373; Stefan Theil, *Unconstitutional Prorogation of Parliament*, Pub. L. 529 (2020); *The Supreme Court Has Laid Bare Boris Johnson's Prorogation Ruse*, Fin. Times (Sept. 25, 2019), <https://www.ft.com/content/71a691d8-dec7-11e9-b8e0-026e07cbe5b4>.

[160] Matthew Taylor & Jim Waterson, *Boris Johnson Threatens BBC With Two-Pronged Attack*, The Guardian, Dec. 16, 2019, 3:15 AM), <https://www.theguardian.com/media/2019/dec/15/boris-johnson-threatens-bbc-with-two-pronged-attack>.

[161] In Re Impeachment of President Donald J. Trump, *Trial Memorandum of the United States House of Representatives* (United States House of Representatives, Feb. 2, 2021) 2–3, 7, 14, 75, <https://judiciary.house.gov/uploadedfiles/house_trial_brief_final.pdf?utm_campaign=5706-519>.

[162] Stephen Gardbaum, *Comparative Political Process Theory*, 18 Int'l J. Const. L. 1429 (2020).

[163] Niels Petersen, Proportionality and Judicial Activism: Fundamental Rights Adjudication in Canada, Germany and South Africa 19–21 (2017).

[164] *Id.*

democratic institutions; and (iii) responding to failures of political institutions impacting majoritarian groups.[165] In earlier work, Landau also highlighted the potential role for courts in building up democratic institutions and fixing problems with political systems, and opening up alternative spaces for democratic contestation.[166]

These CPPT scholars likewise advocate combining forms of both judicial *strength* and *weakness* in response to democratic dysfunction. Sam Issacharoff, for instance, proposes a robust role for courts in maintaining the channels of political change and guarding against democratic backsliding. In this sense, he is a leading proponent of "strong" judicial review in defense of democracy, or strong forms of "democratic hedging" by courts.[167] But he also emphasizes the value of strategic forms of judicial delay, deferral, and avoidance in service of this democratic hedging function, both in our joint work and elsewhere.[168] Michaela Hailbronner is sympathetic to Charles Sabel and William Simon's notion of public law litigation as helping enforce a form of "destabilization right," or helping overcome political blockages in the form of legislative or bureaucratic inertia.[169] But she also suggests the dangers of a too weak or experimentalist an approach to judicial review in certain contexts.[170] Similarly, Landau suggests that the twin risks of ineffective government and democratic debilitation provide a rationale for courts to adopt a mix of strong and weak review, or remedies that "mine a set of tools existing somewhere on a spectrum between weak-form and strong-form review."[171] And in a social rights context, Katharine Young suggests that the particular mode of judicial review a court adopts should depend on the specific democratic blockages or pathologies present.[172] The extent to which judicial review is "peremptory" or "managerial" (i.e., strong form) versus "deferential," "conversational," or "experimentalist" (i.e., limited or weak form), she argues, should depend on whether government is "deliberately obstructively and even hostile to social and economic rights,

---

[165] Manuel José Cepeda Espinosa & David Landau, *A Broad Read of Ely: Political Process Theory for Fragile Democracies*, 19 INT'L J. CONST. L. 548 (2021).

[166] Landau, *supra* note 152.

[167] *See* SAMUEL ISSACHAROFF, FRAGILE DEMOCRACIES: CONTESTED POWER IN THE ERA OF CONSTITUTIONAL COURTS (2015).

[168] *See* Rosalind Dixon & Samuel Issacharoff, *Living to Fight Another Day: Judicial Deferral in Defense of Democracy*, WIS. L. REV. 683 (2016). *See also* Samuel Issacharoff, *The Corruption of Popular Sovereignty*, 18 INT. J. CONST. LAW. 1109 (2020).

[169] *See* Charles F. Sabel & William H. Simon, *Destabilization Rights: How Public Law Litigation Succeeds*, 117 HARV. L. REV. 1016 (2004).

[170] Michaela Hailbronner, Structural Reform Litigation in Domestic Courts (Unpublished manuscript, 2022).

[171] Landau, *supra* note 152, at 1554.

[172] Katharine Young, *A Typology of Economic and Social Rights Adjudication: Exploring the Catalytic Function of Judicial Review*, INT'L J. CONST. L. 385, 418 (2010).

whether it is advertently overriding such rights, or whether it is genuinely unable to deliver them."[173] Malcolm Langford likewise argues for a variant of CCPT, with the notion of a "responsive court," in which a judicial body is attentive to its "legally mandated social mission (which may be broad or narrow)" and its "institutional capacity and legitimacy"—including its "reflexive[e]...relationship with other actors (state organs, public opinion, non-state actors)."[174]

Most of these scholars would also answer the questions of constructional choice posed at the outset more expansively than Ely. Many CPPT scholars would support a role for courts in protecting access to abortion, or same-sex marriage, as a means of countering the role of special interests in democratic politics, overcoming "legislative capture" or "responding to failures of political institutions impacting majoritarian groups." Most would agree that the High Court of Australia (HCA) and SCI should protect implied rights to political freedom and equality, as necessary to ensure the quality of democratic debate and some (e.g., Cepeda and Landau) might also support the recognition of additional personal freedoms—again as a means of responding to failures of political institutions impacting majoritarian groups. Most (i.e., Gardbaum, Cepeda, and Landau) support broad-ranging individual and structural forms of social rights enforcement as a means of holding the executive more accountable, or again "responding to failures of political institutions impacting majoritarian groups, institutions," and as helpful to opening up "alternative spaces for democratic contestation." And almost all support the idea of courts developing and applying an UCA doctrine, in certain circumstances, as a means of preventing "the government of independent institutions," "safeguarding the integrity of the legislative process," or "guarding against democratic breakdown."[175] Indeed, this is perhaps the classic example for many CCPT scholars of courts engaging in a form of "democratic hedging."[176]

Moreover, each of these scholars suggests that these ideas represent the adaptation and extension of Elyian ideas to fit a global context. Gardbaum, for example, suggests that "Ely's central insight—that protection of a system of representative democracy against erosion or degradation by elected representatives cannot be left exclusively in their hands—remains a powerful one," but that for comparative purposes, Ely's account of erosion or degradation "is too

---

[173] *Id.* at 416, 420.
[174] Malcolm Langford, *Judicial Politics and Social Rights*, in THE FUTURE OF ECONOMIC AND SOCIAL RIGHTS 66 (Katherine Young eds., 2019), at 71–72.
[175] ESPINOSA & LANDAU, *supra* note 23.
[176] Samuel Issacharoff, *Constitutional Courts and Democratic Hedging*, 99 GEO. L.J. 961 (2010–11); ISSACHAROFF, *supra* note 167.

narrow in a variety of ways."[177] Cepeda and Landau likewise argue that their broader reading of Ely is designed to respond to the various challenges facing "legal orders around the world," especially those in the "Global South."[178]

The idea of responsive judicial review also builds on this understanding, developed both by Ely and neo-Elyian comparative scholars, about the value of connecting constitutional constructional choice to attention by judges to democratic blockages or sources of dysfunction. It simply aims to give a distinctive focus to the notion of democratic dysfunction in this context—that is, as one focused on risks of antidemocratic monopoly power, democratic blind spots, and burdens of inertia.

---

[177] Gardbaum, *supra* note 162.
[178] ESPINOSA & LANDAU, *supra* note 23, at 6.

3
Defining Democracy and Democratic Dysfunction

From 2009 to 2019, Freedom House reported that the number of countries classified as fully free and democratic fell from roughly 46 percent to 42 percent, whereas the number classified as not free rose from 24 percent to 25 percent.[1] Twenty-five out of forty-one established democracies suffered overall declines, and among countries identified as "partially free" there was a clear trend in many toward *reduced* political pluralism and openness.[2] Indeed, in some countries, there was an outright suspension of democracy in favor of authoritarian rule.[3] (Think of recent developments in Bangladesh, Fiji, Myanmar, or Thailand.) Others witnessed a series of "stealth" attacks on the democratic minimum core—or opposition leaders and political parties, the separation of parties and the state, political rights and freedoms, and "horizontal" and "vertical" constitutional checks and balances.[4]

Even in many constitutional systems in "*reasonably* good working order" today, there are also blockages that undermine the degree to which constitutional commitments are realized in practice.[5] For instance, legislative processes are often subject to "blind spots" and "burdens of inertia," which mean that the law fails to reflect evolving democratic majority understandings of both majority and minority rights.

Four decades on from the publication of *Democracy and Distrust*, it is therefore clear that Ely's own account did not exhaust the full range of malfunctions in constitutional democracies today. And as we shall see in the next chapter, courts often have an important capacity to counter each of these democratic blockages, albeit in different ways and to different degrees. The purpose of this

---

[1] Sarah Repucci, Freedom in the World 2020: A Leaderless Struggle for Democracy (Freedom House, Report booklet, n.d.).
[2] *Id.* at 10.
[3] *See, e.g.*, the coup in Myanmar: Hannah Beech, *Myanmar Coup Highlights Autocracy's Rise in Southeast Asia*, N.Y. Times, Oct. 26, 2021.
[4] On stealth authoritarianism, see Ozan A. Varol, *Stealth Authoritarianism*, 100 Iowa L. Rev. 1673 (2015).
[5] Jeremy Waldron, *The Core of the Case Against Judicial Review*, 115 Yale L.J. 1346, 1360 (2005).

chapter, however, is to outline and unpack these various blockages, before proceeding to explore in more detail how they can and should inform processes of judicial review.

To start with, this chapter explores the understanding of democracy that lies at the heart of a responsive theory of judicial review—that is, an understanding that combines thin and thick, or competitive and deliberative understandings of democracy, and emphasizes the inevitability of disagreement within democracies about what each of these ideals entail. It then goes on to discuss the range of current threats to these different dimensions to democracy posed by the risk of electoral and institutional monopoly power (i.e., antidemocratic forms of monopoly power), democratic blind spots and democratic burdens of inertia. In doing so, it draws explicitly on prior work by David Landau and myself on the idea of the "democratic minimum core," and the variety of current threats to this core that we label "abusive" constitutional in nature,[6] and more indirectly on previous work I have done on the core case for weakened or "dialogic" forms of judicial review.[7] But in each case, the focus is on how democratic processes can and do fail to live up to commitments to responsiveness, as a core part of a commitment to democratic constitutionalism.

A. Defining Democracy

As Chapter 2 notes, existing theories of democracy point to two broad understandings of democracy: "thin" notions of democracy, which emphasize the idea of democracy as a system of competition among rival political parties, based on regular, free, and fair elections, and "thick" understandings of democracy that emphasize the importance of commitments to democratic deliberation and minority rights protection.[8]

---

[6] David Landau & Rosalind Dixon, *Abusive Judicial Review: Courts Against Democracy*, 53 U.C. Davis L. Rev. 1313 (2020); Rosalind Dixon & David Landau, Abusive Constitutional Borrowing: Legal Globalization and the Subversion of Liberal Democracy (2021); Rosalind Dixon & David Landau, *Tiered Constitutional Design*, 86 Geo. Wash. L. Rev. 438 (2018); David Landau & Rosalind Dixon, *Constraining Constitutional Change*, 50 Wake Forest L. Rev. 859 (2015); David Landau & Rosalind Dixon, *Transnational Constitutionalism and a Limited Doctrine of Unconstitutional Constitutional Amendment*, 13 Int'l J. Const. L. 606 (2015). See also David Landau, *Abusive Constitutionalism*, 47 U.C. Davis L. Rev. 189 (2013).

[7] Rosalind Dixon, *Creating Dialogue about Socioeconomic Rights: Strong-Form v. Weak-Form Judicial Review Revisited*, 5 Int'l J. Const. L. 391 (2007); Rosalind Dixon, *A New Theory of Charter Dialogue: The Supreme Court of Canada, Charter Dialogue and Deference*, 47 Osgoode Hall L.J. 235 (2009); Rosalind Dixon, *The Core Case for Weak-Form Judicial Review*, 38 Cardozo L. Rev. 2193 (2016).

[8] Richard A. Posner, Law, Pragmatism, and Democracy (2005).

A responsive approach to judicial review also aims to take seriously both thin *and* thick understandings of democracy and to recognize the fact of reasonable disagreement among citizens about what these various understandings of democracy entail. This, in turn, means understanding commitments to democracy as operating at two distinct, if complementary, levels: first, as comprising a commitment to a "democratic minimum core," or a system of free and fair elections among multiple political parties, based on the accompanying protection of political rights and freedoms and a system of checks and balances—or a minimum core set of norms and institutions necessary for *electoral* and *institutional* accountability; and second, a commitment to a broader set of rights, freedoms, and institutions aimed at promoting good governance and deliberation—but in a way that recognizes room for reasonable disagreement among citizens about the scope of these rights and commitments to deliberation, and thus the need for responsiveness to democratic *majority* understandings in relation to these questions.

The first notion of democracy builds on competitive notions of democracy of the kind advanced by scholars such as Schumpeter.[9] It also extends that understanding by suggesting that for constitutional democracy to be truly competitive, it must include a commitment to: (i) free and fair multiparty elections; (ii) political rights and freedoms; and (iii) a range of institutional checks and balances.[10] Each of these prongs of a constitutional democratic system are mutually reinforcing and hence an essential part of the *democratic* minimum core. They also serve two broad purposes, namely ensuring electoral *and* institutional pluralism as a source of pressure for democratic responsiveness and accountability. Threats to the democratic minimum core, therefore, can equally be understood as threats to electoral and institutional pluralism, or as taking the form of attempts to erode that pluralism, or aggregate electoral or institutional power in a single *monopolistic entity* such as a dominant political party or dominant executive or president.

In this sense, the idea of the democratic minimum core is neither wholly procedural nor substantive in nature: it transcends the procedure and substance divide, though it is thin rather than thick, in nature.[11] It is also a "thin" account of democracy in a quite limited, or specific sense. It is not based on

---

[9] Joseph A. Schumpeter, Capitalism, Socialism and Democracy 269 (3d ed. 1950). *See also* Samuel Issacharoff, Fragile Democracies: Contested Power in the Era of Constitutional Courts (2015).

[10] In this sense, it is similar to a range of leading indices of democracy, such as V-dem. *See V-Dem: Varieties of Democracy*, <https://www.v-dem.net>. But it also places greater reliance on the notion of institutional pluralism, or institutional checks and balances.

[11] I am indebted to Adrienne Stone and Theunis Roux for pressing me on this point.

any particular political or constitutional theory but rather an overlapping consensus among democratic theorists about what democracy requires *and* extant practices among democratic systems.[12]

While the idea of democracy is fundamentally contested, there are a range of institutions that can be identified as *common* to well-functioning constitutional democracies worldwide—that is, institutions for the conduct of regular free and fair elections, guaranteeing political rights and freedoms, and ensuring the checks and balances necessary to maintain electoral accountability, integrity, and the protection of these rights and freedoms. This overlap can also help inform our intuitions about the necessary scope or content of the "minimum core" of democracy. The presumption given such overlap is that those institutions common to all (or at least the vast majority of) constitutional democracies worldwide are more or less *necessary* to the maintenance of the democratic minimum core.[13] This is what Landau and I call the notion of "transnational constitutional anchoring."[14]

This understanding also parallels the way in which various European institutions have sought to construct notions of a common human rights core, or shared democratic commitments and values necessary for membership in the Council of Europe or European Union (EU). The European Court of Human Rights (ECtHR), for instance, has adopted a variable approach to the enforcement of rights based on the degree of overlap versus divergence in member state practices (the so-called margin of appreciation doctrine).[15] The greater the consensus, or overlap in practice, among member states, the closer the scrutiny the ECtHR will apply to member state laws, whereas the greater the divergence, the wider the margin of appreciation afforded to states to make their own judgments about the best way to implement Convention rights, or about what the idea of a rights-based democracy requires.[16]

---

[12] Landau & Dixon, *Transnational Constitutionalism*, supra note 6. For the idea of an overlapping consensus as a device for generating insights about what political democracy and liberalism requires, see JOHN RAWLS, POLITICAL LIBERALISM (2005).

[13] *See* Eric A. Posner & Cass R. Sunstein, *The Law of Other States*, 59 STAN. L. REV. 131 (2006). See also discussion in Rosalind Dixon, *Democratic Theory of Constitutional Comparison*, 56 AM. J. COMP. L. 947 (2008).

[14] Landau & Dixon, *Transnational Constitutionalism*, supra note 6. *See also* Rosalind Dixon, *How to Compare Constitutionally: An Essay in Honour of Mark Tushnet* (UNSW Law Research Paper No. 21, May 17, 2020).

[15] Handyside v. United Kingdom, (1976) 1 EHRR 737. See discussion in Rosalind Dixon, *Proportionality and Comparative Constitutional Law versus Studies*, 12 LAW & ETHICS HUM. RTS. 203 (2018); Michael R. Hutchinson, *The Margin of Appreciation Doctrine in the European Court of Human Rights*, 48 INT'L & COMP. L.Q. 638, 639 (1999); George Letsas, *Two Concepts of the Margin of Appreciation*, 26 OXFORD J. LEGAL STUD. 705 (2006). For the earlier endorsement of the doctrine by the Commission, see also *Greece v. United Kingdom* (Cyprus Case), [1958–59] 2 Y.B. EUR.CONV. ON H.R. 174; Lawless v. Ireland (No 3), [1961] ECHR 2.

[16] Hutchinson, *supra* note 15, at 640.

The EU likewise requires member states to respect commitments to democracy, the rule of law, human rights, and the protection of minorities (the so-called Copenhagen principles).[17] And it has held that, among other things, democracy entails free elections with a secret ballot, the right to establish political parties without any hindrance from the state, fair, and equal access to a free press, free trade union organizations, freedom of personal opinion, and executive powers restricted by laws and allowing free access to judges independent of the executive.[18]

As this analogy suggests, the content of the "minimum core" may vary by region, or among different constitutional systems.[19] Presidential systems, for example, may differ from parliamentary systems in what they require to maintain norms of limited government, or constraints on executive power. And regional norms may point to a thicker minimum core than is generated by a purely global "least common denominator" approach.

The second understanding of democracy, however, is consistently thicker and more substantive in nature than either this kind of global or regional minimum core. Its origins lie in a commitment to a form of self-government based on norms of equality, freedom, and dignity, or norms of "equal respect and concern," among citizens.[20] And while there may be broad agreement among citizens about these ideals, there is equally clear scope for disagreement about their precise scope and content in particular concrete contexts. Disagreement of this kind is also inherently reasonable from a democratic perspective: it reflects the fact that citizens in democracy are free to make their own judgments about these questions, and often have quite different life experiences that bear on these questions.[21]

That is not to suggest that there will always be agreement about what the democratic minimum core requires, or ought reasonably to be understood to require, in practice. Even principles that are widely agreed on a relatively abstract level may invite reasonable disagreement at the level of implementation. But the fact of potential reasonable disagreement at both levels of democracy does not detract from the simple point that there is in fact some non-contestable "core" to the idea of democracy which, theoretically at least, does not permit of reasonable disagreement and ought not to be treated as up for grabs.

[17] *See* DIXON & LANDAU, ABUSIVE CONSTITUTIONAL BORROWING, *supra* note 6, at 26.
[18] *Id.*
[19] *Compare* Landau & Dixon, *Constraining Constitutional Change*, *supra* note 6.
[20] *See* RONALD DWORKIN, FREEDOM'S LAW: THE MORAL READING OF THE AMERICAN CONSTITUTION (1999).
[21] JEREMY WALDRON, LAW AND DISAGREEMENT (1999). *Compare* DIXON & LANDAU, ABUSIVE CONSTITUTIONAL BORROWING, *supra* note 6.

Further, each understanding has a somewhat different relationship to the idea of democratic "responsiveness." A minimum core understanding of democracy, for example, emphasizes the value of competition between rival political parties, or elites, in promoting accountability by such elites, *ex post*, but also encouraging policy responsiveness, or responsiveness to the views or preferences of the median voter in a democracy *ex ante*.[22] And the democratic minimum core defines the institutions necessary to guarantee structural responsiveness of this kind, within a constitutional system.

Thicker notions of democracy also emphasize the idea that a constitutional system should be responsive to the rights claims of individuals, and in some instances, the considered views of democratic majorities.[23] In some cases, commitments to majority rule may appropriately give way to other conflicting constitutional norms and values such as the rule of law, or the redress of historical disadvantage or injustice. Or they may give way to a clear, textual guarantee of certain minority rights. And where this is the case, a constitutional system may be committed to norms *other than* norms of democratic responsiveness, or even a form of democratic non-responsiveness.

In other cases, however, majority understandings may *support or align with* commitments to deliberation or minority rights protection. Minorities may make claims for the recognition of certain rights which find limited support in the constitutional text, history, structure, or prior case law, but greater support in contemporary democratic understandings. And in these cases, a commitment to democratic responsiveness would suggest that it is doubly important for a political system to reflect the views of a democratic majority.[24] There will be no principled basis in cases of this kind for refusing to recognize the relevant rights claim, and strong arguments from both thin and thick notions of democracy for doing so. Hence, the existence of democratic majority support for minority rights claims will generally be sufficient—though not always necessary—to underpin a claim for recognition of that right.

As the remainder of this chapter explores in more detail, each of these dimensions to democracy can also be threatened by a wide range of sources of democratic dysfunction.

---

[22] *See, e.g.*, POSNER, *supra* note 8, at chs 4, 5 (discussing "concept 2" democracy and its virtues).
[23] *Compare* Robert Post & Reva Siegel, *Roe Rage: Democratic Constitutionalism and Backlash*, 42 HARV. C.R.-C.L. L. REV. 373, 376 (2007).
[24] STEPHEN GARDBAUM, THE NEW COMMONWEALTH MODEL OF CONSTITUTIONALISM: THEORY AND PRACTICE 32 (2013).

B. Democratic Dysfunction: Antidemocratic Monopoly Power

Recall that the "minimum core" of a constitutional democratic system can be understood as comprising three broad elements: a commitment to (i) free and fair multiparty elections; (ii) political rights and freedoms; and (iii) a range of institutional checks and balances. For Ely, the key danger was that political incumbents might seek to tilt the electoral playing field in their own favor, in ways that undermined elections as a channel for political change.[25] But in many countries today political actors are adopting measures that go even further in undermining the democratic minimum core: They are narrowing both the formal and *de facto* scope for political protest and dissent; making highly politicized appointments to previously independent courts and fourth branch institutions, sometimes even by removing existing officeholders; shifting power from parliaments and other public institutions into party rooms and other non-public spaces, and undermining federalism and other checks and balances. Presidents in particular are also attempting to, and often succeeding in, removing or relaxing constitutional provisions limiting the number of terms they can remain in office. And they are doing so using formal and informal modes of constitutional change.[26] The result, in each case, has been a reduction in electoral and institutional pluralism, or a rise in antidemocratic monopoly power.

Take constitutional developments over the last decade across Europe, the Middle East, Latin America, Asia, and Africa. In Hungary, after gaining power in 2010 with a simple majority of votes but over two-thirds of the Parliamentary seats, the Fidesz party began amending the Constitution to undermine key institutions including the Constitutional Court.[27] It then engaged in wholesale constitutional replacement; the new Constitution weakened checking institutions designed to rein in electoral majorities and made it harder to dislodge the party from power. In Poland, in 2015, the "Law and Justice Party" (PiS) won a parliamentary majority and began passing legislation to undermine the power and independence of the Constitutional Court.[28] It then relied on the Court both to uphold and supplement its attacks on other formerly independent institutions, and political freedoms, including laws targeting civil society, freedom of assembly, and electoral rules, and the regime used its power to

---

[25] JOHN HART ELY, DEMOCRACY AND DISTRUST: A THEORY OF JUDICIAL REVIEW 106 (1980).
[26] DIXON & LANDAU, ABUSIVE CONSTITUTIONAL BORROWING, supra note 6.
[27] *Id.*
[28] WOJCIECH SADURSKI, POLAND'S CONSTITUTIONAL BREAKDOWN (2019).

pack other key institutions, such as those charged with regulating the media.[29] Similar changes have occurred in other countries in Eastern Europe, including Bulgaria, the Czech Republic, and Romania. Though these countries have not yet witnessed the same move toward competitive authoritarianism seen in Hungary and Poland, they have seen a range of quite serious and sustained attacks on norms of institutional pluralism as well as broader liberal norms of inclusivity and toleration.[30]

In the Middle East, there was a weaker ongoing commitment to constitutional democracy, but still meaningful erosion of those commitments in several leading countries within the region. In Turkey, after initial moves toward liberalization and democracy after his election in 2014, President Recep Tayyip Erdoğan has progressively attacked constitutional commitments to liberalism, secularism, and electoral and institutional pluralism by targeting journalists, lawyers, and political opponents, institutions such as the High Election Board, the civil service, and ordinary courts, and by invoking formal emergency powers and processes of constitutional amendment to expand the powers of the president and undermine checks and balances.[31] In Israel, there have been more limited but still notable signs of an erosion in commitments to institutional pluralism.[32]

---

[29] *Id.* at ch 3; Dixon & Landau, Abusive Constitutional Borrowing, supra note 6.

[30] Governments in all three countries have at various times openly attacked Muslim and gay citizens, and refugees and migrants, as threatening the national constitutional order. *See Czech Republic*, Freedom House (2021), <https://freedomhouse.org/country/czech-republic/freedom-world/2021>; *Bulgaria*, Freedom House (2021), <https://freedomhouse.org/country/bulgaria/freedom-world/2021>; *Romania*, Freedom House (2021), <https://freedomhouse.org/country/romania/freedom-world/2021>. *See also* Carlie Porterfield, *Anti-LGBTQ Rhetoric is Ramping up in Eastern Europe, Human Rights Advocates Say*, Forbes (June 10, 2020, 04:31 PM), <https://www.forbes.com/sites/carlieporterfield/2020/06/10/anti-lgbtq-rhetoric-is-ramping-up-in-eastern-europe-human-rights-advocates-say/?sh=4bbb95c3231e>.

[31] *See, e.g.*, Berk Esen & Sebnem Gumuscu, *Why Did Turkish Democracy Collapse? A Political Economy Account of AKP's Authoritarianism*, 26 Party Pol. 1 (2020); Zafer Yilmaz & Bryan S. Turner, *Turkey's Deepening Authoritarianism and the Fall of Electoral Democracy*, 46 Brit. J. Middle Eastern Stud. 691, 695 (2019). His eight years as President has also come on the back of three terms as Prime Minister, and a decade in which he used many of the same tactics in order to consolidate his electoral and institutional power: *Turkey Will Select New Prime Minister This Month to Replace Outgoing Erdogan*, The Guardian, Aug. 12, 2014, 02:46 PM, <https://www.theguardian.com/world/2014/aug/11/turkey-select-new-prime-minister-replace-recep-tayyip-erdogan>. On crackdowns on the media and media independence, see, *e.g.*, Emma Sinclair-Webb, *Turkey: Media Crackdown Amid Escalating Violence*, Hum. Rts. Watch (Sept. 11, 2015, 10:27 AM), <https://www.hrw.org/news/2015/09/11/turkey-media-crackdown-amid-escalating-violence>; Jacob Weisberg, *Capturing the News*, Slate (Oct. 9, 2014, 10:28 AM), <https://slate.com/news-and-politics/2014/10/president-erdogans-media-control-turkeys-censorship-is-less-brutal-but-more-effective.html>.

[32] *See* Nadiv Mordechay & Yaniv Roznai, *A Jewish and (Declining) Democratic State? Constitutional Retrogression in Israel*, 77 Md. L. Rev. 244 (2017); Dixon & Landau, *supra* note 6, at 166–74. *See also* Symposium, *Constitutional Capture in Israel?*, Int'l Const. L. Blog (2017); Tamara Cofman Wittes & Yaël Mizrahi-Arnaud, *Is Israel in Democratic Decline?*, Brookings (Mar. 2019), <https://www.brookings.edu/research/is-israel-in-democratic-decline/>.

A similar pattern applies in Latin America: in Venezuela, upon taking power in 1998, President Hugo Chávez used constitutional replacement to remove previous constitutional checks and balances, shut down institutions still allied with the opposition, and entrench more power in the presidency. He also subsequently used processes of constitutional and legislative amendment to increase presidential power further; for example, by eliminating term limits and passing a number of laws reorganizing the judiciary, media, and other institutions.[33] And when Nicolás Maduro took over as president in 2013, he and his allies in Congress passed new laws limiting speech and media independence, punished protesters and political opponents, and further undermined judicial independence.[34] In Nicaragua, since returning to office in 2006, President Daniel Ortega has progressively expanded his electoral and institutional dominance, relying on a range of abusive tactics: he has either imprisoned or placed under house arrest all credible opposition candidates and banned a range of civil society organizations.[35] He has appointed his wife as vice-president, and successfully bypassed constitutional limits preventing him from seeking re-election.[36]

In Brazil, the degree of electoral and institutional monopoly is arguably less severe. There is still a chance that President Jair Bolsonaro will lose the 2022 presidential election and leave office after doing so.[37] There also remain some independent checks on his power, including a Congress willing to challenge his actions.[38] But Bolsonaro has effectively attacked the independence of the Supreme Court, lower courts, and other fourth branch institutions, as well as core civil rights.[39] And conservative political elites who support Bolsonaro have relied on the Court and the impeachment process effectively to eliminate key opposition figures, including former President Lula as a presidential candidate.[40] Ecuador and Bolivia have experienced similar forms of erosion

---

[33] DIXON & LANDAU, ABUSIVE CONSTITUTIONAL BORROWING, supra note 6, at 124.
[34] *Id.* at 99–103, 126.
[35] *Opinion: Democracy Is Under Attack in Nicaragua*, WASH. POST, Aug. 5, 2021, 6:26 PM, <https://www.washingtonpost.com/opinions/2021/08/05/democracy-is-under-attack-nicaragua/>.
[36] DIXON & LANDAU, ABUSIVE CONSTITUTIONAL BORROWING, supra note 6, at 34, 134.
[37] Juliano Zaiden Benvindo, *The Historian of the Future in Brazilian Democracy: The Challenges of Interpreting and Comparing Events of Our Own Time*, INT'L J. CONST. L. BLOG (Feb. 24, 2021), <http://www.iconnectblog.com/2021/02/the-historian-of-the-future-in-brazilian-democracy-the-challenges-of-interpreting-and-comparing-events-of-our-own-time/>.
[38] Tom Phillips, *Brazil Begins Parliamentary Inquiry into Bolsonaro's Covid Response*, THE GUARDIAN, Apr. 28, 2021, 3:20 AM, <https://www.theguardian.com/world/2021/apr/27/brazil-begins-parliamentary-inquiry-into-bolsonaros-covid-response>.
[39] *See* EMILIO PELUSO NEDER MEYER, CONSTITUTIONAL EROSION IN BRAZIL (2021).
[40] *Id. See also* Payton Scott, *The Death of Brazilian Democracy, 20 Years in the Making*, DEMOCRATIC EROSION (Apr. 20, 2020), <https://www.democratic-erosion.com/2020/04/20/the-death-of-brazilian-democracy-20-years-in-the-making/>.

of the democratic minimum core, though arguably also a partial democratic restoration.[41]

In South Asia, there has been a steady decline in electoral and institutional pluralism in Bangladesh.[42] Sri Lanka has seen a "ping pong" between pro- and antidemocratic constitutional change, and continues to face major economic and political unrest.[43] And in India, the health of the democratic minimum core very much hangs in the balance. There is still some electoral opposition to the Bharatiya Janata Party (BJP), and while weakened, the Supreme Court and certain fourth branch institutions retain some degree of independence.[44] But the BJP-controlled Parliament has consistently attacked liberal commitments to secularism and inclusion, and in ways that effectively increase the power of the government's Hindu voting base.[45] Modi and the BJP have also attacked almost all the constitutional institutions charged with holding the executive to account.[46]

In South-East Asia, there have been (halting) signs of democratic renewal in some countries, such as Malaysia.[47] But other democracies have witnessed sustained attacks on their electoral and institutional architecture: in Cambodia, Prime Minister Hun Sen and the ruling Cambodian People's Party (CPP) have captured the Electoral Commission, and Supreme Court, and imposed stringent limits on electoral campaigning.[48] The Court itself has also voted to ban the major opposition party, and convict its leaders of treason, so that the country is now widely regarded as an electoral autocracy, or *de facto* one party state.[49] In the Philippines, the most overt attack on liberal democracy has

---

[41] DIXON & LANDAU, ABUSIVE CONSTITUTIONAL BORROWING, supra note 6.

[42] Arafatul Islam, *Bangladesh Turns 50 as Fears Grow Over Deteriorating Democracy*, DW (Mar. 25, 2021), <https://www.dw.com/en/bangladesh-democracy-human-rights/a-56988366>.

[43] Dinesha Samararatne, *Sri Lanka's Constitutional Ping Pong*, HIMAL MAGAZINE (Sep. 25, 2020), <https://www.himalmag.com/sri-lankas-constitutional-ping-pong-2020/>; Iqbal Athas, *Sri Lanka's Prime Minister resigns amid Protests Over Economic Crisis*, CNN, May 10, 2022, <https://edition.cnn.com/2022/05/09/asia/sri-lanka-mahinda-rajapaksa-resigns-intl/index.html>.

[44] Soutik Biswas, *Uttar Pradesh Elections: What a Historic Poll Win Says about Modi's India*, BBC NEWS, Mar. 11, 2022, <https://www.bbc.com/news/world-asia-india-60688428>; *see, e.g.*, Hari Kumar & Emily Schmall, *Covid Payments Ordered by India's Supreme Court Could Total Hundreds of Millions of Dollars*, THE N.Y. TIMES, Oct. 5, 2021, <https://www.nytimes.com/2021/10/05/world/asia/covid-india-compensation-payments.html>. But for suggestions that this is in fact no longer true, see Soutik Biswas, *"Electoral Autocracy": The Downgrading of India's Democracy*, BBC NEWS, Mar. 16, 2021, <https://www.bbc.com/news/world-asia-india-56393944>.

[45] Abigail Sklar, *Democratic Erosion in India: The World's Largest Democracy No More?*, DEMOCRATIC EROSION (Feb. 12, 2020), <https://www.democratic-erosion.com/2020/02/12/democratic-erosion-in-india-the-worlds-largest-democracy-no-more/>.

[46] *See also* Tarunabh Khaitan, *Killing a Constitution with a Thousand Cuts: Executive Aggrandizement and Party-State Fusion in India*, 14 LAW & ETHICS HUM. RTS. 49, 60, 66-67 (2020).

[47] *See* YVONNE TEW, CONSTITUTIONAL STATECRAFT IN ASIAN COURTS (2020).

[48] *Cambodia*, FREEDOM HOUSE (2020), https://freedomhouse.org/country/cambodia/freedom-world/2020.

[49] *Id. See also* David Landau & Rosalind Dixon, *Abusive Judicial Review: Courts Against Democracy*, 53 U.C. DAVIS L. REV. 1313, 1351–52 (2020).

been focused on individual rights to freedom and security of the person: since his election in 2016, President Rodrigo Duterte has led an effort to eliminate drug use and trafficking that has resulted in the death of thousands of drug dealers and users. But Duterte has also attacked aspects of the democratic minimum core: he has attacked the media and the independence of the Supreme Court (by, among other things, removing the Chief Justice on spurious charges of misconduct).[50] He has also proposed amendments to the Constitution designed to increase the devolution of power from the national level in return for a reset on presidential term limits and stronger presidential powers.[51] And while Duterte himself is no longer in power, the current President and Vice-President are close Duterte allies—that is, Bongbong Marcos (the son of former dictator Ferdinand Marcos) and Duterte's daughter, Sara Duterte.

Hong Kong has seen a series of setbacks for democratic self-government, and an autonomous democratic minimum core. Hong Kong is not a fully autonomous, competitive democracy: the "one country, two systems" principle means that it is entitled to maintain a high degree of autonomy and its own constitutional system until 2047.[52] And that system includes a Basic Law and Bill of Rights Ordinance protecting a range of civil and political rights, and system of checks and balances. But elections for the Chief Executive are limited to the professional and business community, and only twenty out of ninety seats (previously 50 percent) of the Legislative Council are popularly elected.[53] Even against this benchmark, however, there has been a recent history of democratic erosion: freedom of assembly and association have been limited, pro-democracy protests quashed, and pro-democracy candidates have been prevented from running for office and/or expelled from the Legislative Council.[54] Beijing companies have acquired various Hong Kong media outlets,

---

[50] Aries Arugay, *The Generals' Gambit: The Military and Democratic Erosion in Duterte's Philippines*, HEINRICH BÖLL STIFTUNG SOUTHEAST ASIA (Feb. 18, 2021), <https://th.boell.org/en/2021/02/18/generals-gambit-military-and-democratic-erosion-dutertes-philippines>; Sheila Coronel, *This is How Democracy Dies*, THE ATLANTIC (Jun. 17, 2020), <https://www.theatlantic.com/international/archive/2020/06/maria-ressa-rappler-philippines-democracy/613102/>.

[51] Richard Heydarian, *The Implications of Duterte's Proposed Constitutional Changes*, COUNCIL ON FOREIGN RELATIONS (Jul. 24, 2018, 4:27 PM), <https://www.cfr.org/blog/implications-dutertes-proposed-constitutional-changes>; Mong Palatino, *A Brief History of Charter Change Attempts in the Philippines*, THE DIPLOMAT (Feb. 2, 2021), <https://thediplomat.com/2021/02/a-brief-history-of-charter-change-attempts-in-the-philippines/>.

[52] Lindsay Maizland & Eleanor Albert, *Hong Kong's Freedoms: What China Promised and How It's Cracking Down*, COUNCIL ON FOREIGN RELATIONS (Feb. 17, 2021), <https://www.cfr.org/backgrounder/hong-kong-freedoms-democracy-protests-china-crackdown>. *See also* Albert H.Y. Chen, *The Hong Kong Basic Law and the Limits of Democratization Under "One Country Two Systems*, 50 THE INT'L LAW. 69 (2017).

[53] *Id. See also* SIMON YOUNG & RICHARD CULLEN, ELECTING HONG KONG'S CHIEF EXECUTIVE (2010).

[54] Maizland & Albert, *supra* note 52 Brian C.H. Fong, *Death by a Thousand Cuts: Democratic Backsliding in Hong Kong*, 15 GLOBAL ASIA 22, 24 (2020).

and other remaining local outlets have been subject to intimidation.[55] In 2020, Beijing also passed a new national security law effectively criminalizing political dissent: it made subversion, secession, and collusion a crime, and adopted a very broad definition of each.[56]

Similar patterns can be observed in Africa in Benin, Burundi, Guinea, Mali, Niger, Nigeria, Rwanda, Senegal, Tanzania, and Uganda, among other countries.[57] In Kenya and South Africa, the health of the democratic minimum core remains in the balance. Democracy in Kenya experienced a major setback in the late 2000s, with the advent of widespread ethnic and political violence. The adoption of the 2010 Constitution was, in fact, part of an effort to restore both democracy and security in the country and, to that end, created a variety of power-sharing as well as accountability mechanisms.[58] But by 2017, there were signs that this effort was stalling: there were serious allegations of electoral irregularities in the presidential election, and the Supreme Court set aside the election as a result.[59] But the (then) opposition leader, Raila Odinga, withdrew from the subsequent election, and President Uhuru Kenyatta was re-elected by a large margin. In 2018, Kenyatta proceeded further to neutralize both internal and external opposition to his power by entering into a "hand-shake" agreement to cooperate with Odinga.[60] The Supreme Court of Kenya, however, has remained largely independent of the President and willing in some cases to assert meaningful limits on his power.[61] The most recent presidential election also saw Kenyatta lose office, and a turnover in power.

---

[55] Fong, *supra* note 54, 26.
[56] Maizland & Albert, *supra* note 52.
[57] Sarah Repucci, *Freedom in the World 2020: A Leaderless Struggle for Democracy* (Report booklet, n.d.). On Burundi, see Landau & Dixon, *supra* note 49, at 88. On Benin, Mali, Guinea, and Niger, see Neil Munshi, *Democracy Erodes in Central and West Africa*, Fin. Times, Mar. 7, 2021, <https://www.ft.com/content/d7319cb8-48c3-4acf-bfcf-7aaae0e5f9fd>. On Tanzania, see Rob Ahearne, *Tanzania's New President Faces a Tough "To Do" List*, The Conversation (Mar. 27, 2021, 9:13 PM), <https://theconversation.com/tanzanias-new-president-faces-a-tough-to-do-list-157973>. On Nigeria, see Adewunmi Emoruwa, *Nigeria's Democracy Is Fading Away*, Aljazeera (Feb. 8, 2019), <https://www.aljazeera.com/opinions/2019/2/8/nigerias-democracy-is-fading-away>.
[58] Christina Murray, *Political Elites and the People: Kenya's Decade Long Constitution-Making Process*, SSRN (Mar. 22, 2018), <https://papers.ssrn.com/sol3/papers.cfm?abstract_id=3147154>.
[59] Ochieng v. Independent Electoral & Boundaries Commission [2017] eKLR 7–9. *See also* Kimiko de Freytas-Tamura, *Kenya Supreme Court Nullifies Presidential Election*, N.Y. Times, Sep. 1, 2017, <https://www.nytimes.com/2017/09/01/world/africa/kenya-election-kenyatta-odinga.html>. *Compare* Chapter 7 *infra*.
[60] Peter Muiruri, *Kenya's High Court Overturns President's Bid to Amend Constitution*, The Guardian, May 27, 2021, <https://www.theguardian.com/global-development/2021/may/27/kenyas-high-court-overturns-president-uhuru-kenyatta-bbi-bid-to-amend-constitution>; Ferdinand Omondi, *Kenya's BBI Blocked in Scathing Court Verdict for President Kenyatta*, BBC News, May 14, 2021, <https://www.bbc.com/news/world-africa-57094387>; Uhuru Kenyatta, *Kenya Government Appeals Ruling Against BBI Constitutional Changes*, Aljazeera (June 2, 2021) <https://www.aljazeera.com/news/2021/6/2/kenya-govt-appeals-ruling-against-bbi-constitutional-changes>.
[61] *See especially* Ochieng v. Independent Electoral & Boundaries Commission [2017] eKLR and UCA decisions as discussed in Chapter 2, *supra* and Chapters 5 and 7, *infra*.

In South Africa, the African National Congress (or ANC), the party that helped liberate South Africa from apartheid, remains electorally dominant twenty-five years after the transition to multiracial democracy. But its dominance is declining.[62] And the 1996 South African Constitution created a range of robust checks and balances, including a new Constitutional Court and range of fourth branch or "chapter 9 institutions."[63] The Court and fourth branch institutions, such as the Public Protector, have also played a critical role in maintaining a commitment in South Africa to institutional pluralism.[64] The key challenge to the democratic minimum core in South Africa, therefore, has so far come from those factions of the ANC (such as those allied to former President Jacob Zuma)—and splinter parties, such as the Economic Freedom Fighters—who reject the authority and importance of these independent institutions.[65] And for now, those factions do not hold the key reins of power.[66]

One important question that arises is what we should call changes of this kind: some scholars have labeled the phenomenon one of democratic "decay," "rot," or "degradation."[67] Others have labeled it a problem of democratic

---

[62] See, e.g., Joleen Steyn Kotze, *South African Elections and the Declining Dominance of the ANC*, AUSTL. INST. INT'L AFF. (May 16, 2019), <https://www.internationalaffairs.org.au/australianoutlook/south-african-elections-declining-dominance-anc-aopub/>; SUSAN BOOYSEN, DOMINANCE AND DECLINE: THE ANC IN THE TIME OF ZUMA (2015); Hakeem Onapajo & Christopher Isike, *The Decline of a Dominant African Political Party: The Case and Future of South Africa's African National Congress (ANC)*, 36 POLITEIA 1 (2017).

[63] See Heinz Klug, *Corruption, the Rule of Law and the Role of Independent Institutions*, in CONSTITUTIONAL TRIUMPHS, CONSTITUTIONAL DISAPPOINTMENTS: A CRITICAL ASSESSMENT OF THE 1996 SOUTH AFRICAN CONSTITUTION'S LOCAL AND INTERNATIONAL INFLUENCE 108 (Rosalind Dixon & Theunis Roux eds., 2018); Charles Fombad, *The Diffusion of South-African Style Institutions? A Study in Comparative Constitutionalism*, in CONSTITUTIONAL TRIUMPHS, CONSTITUTIONAL DISAPPOINTMENTS: A CRITICAL ASSESSMENT OF THE 1996 SOUTH AFRICAN CONSTITUTION'S LOCAL AND INTERNATIONAL INFLUENCE 359 (Rosalind Dixon & Theunis Roux eds., 2018).

[64] Economic Freedom Fighters v. Speaker of the Nat'l Assemb., [2016] ZACC 11. See discussion in Simon Allison, *Nklandla Verdict Shows South Africa's Democracy is Alive and Kicking*, THE GUARDIAN, Apr. 1, 2016, <https://www.theguardian.com/world/2016/mar/31/south-africa-nkandla-verdict-jacob-zuma>; Klug, *supra* note 63.

[65] See, e.g., the response to the recent order of the Constitutional Court against former President Zuma for failure to comply with the Court's order to appear before the Zondo Commission on state capture: John Eligon & Lynsey Chutel, *South African Court Orders Arrest of Ex-President Jacob Zuma for Contempt*, N.Y. TIMES, Jun. 29, 2021, <https://www.nytimes.com/2021/06/29/world/africa/jacob-zuma-prison.html>; Michael Cohen, *QuickTake: Why South Africa Just Suffered Its Worst Riots Since Apartheid*, BLOOMBERG, Jul. 13, 2021, <https://www.bloomberg.com/news/articles/2021-07-13/why-ex-leader-s-arrest-cast-south-africa-into-turmoil-quicktake>.

[66] John Eligon & Lynsey Chutel, *South African Court Orders Arrest of Ex-President Jacob Zuma for Contempt*, N.Y. TIMES, Jun. 29, 2021, <https://www.nytimes.com/2021/06/29/world/africa/jacob-zuma-prison.html>.

[67] See, e.g., AZIZ HUQ & TOM GINSBURG, HOW TO SAVE A CONSTITUTIONAL DEMOCRACY (2019); WOJCIECH SADURSKI, POLAND'S CONSTITUTIONAL BREAKDOWN 12–13 (2019); Richard Albert, *Constitutional Amendment and Dismemberment*, 43 YALE J. INT'L L. 1 (2018); CONSTITUTIONAL DEMOCRACY IN CRISIS? (Mark A. Graber et al. eds., 2018).

backsliding.[68] Landau and I call this the problem of both capital "C" and small "c" abusive constitutional change.[69] Whatever definition we adopt, however, it is important to emphasize that changes of this kind are rarely accidental or unintended. They are generally the product of quite *deliberate* attempts by political actors to entrench their own hold on power by undermining the electoral process, the viability of the political opposition, and/or the power of independent institutions.

1. Electoral monopoly

Almost all existing democratic systems are imperfectly competitive in some way or have some existing degree of partisan "tilt."[70] Constitutional norms themselves often reflect this form of partisan bias.[71] Many forms of legal and political change could thus be viewed as within this same margin of "tolerance" or deviation from a perfectly fair, competitive form of political marketplace. But at some point, those changes will be sufficient—either alone or in aggregate—to threaten the very basis of true electoral competition, or a commitment to competitive democracy.

In some cases, political actors may choose to attack the principle of free and fair elections outright: they may suspend elections, either without pretext or under the guise of a national crisis or emergency. Or they may engage in blatant forms of voter manipulation by physically preventing opposition voters from getting to the polls or engaging in forms of violence and intimidation designed to achieve the same result.

More often, however, they may attempt to undermine electoral integrity in less public ways: by enrolling ineligible voters to vote, by "stuffing" ballot boxes with additional votes for the government, or by "losing" or not counting certain ballot boxes. The same applies to attacks on the principle of free and fair *multiparty* elections.[72] Would-be authoritarians may engage in direct personal, sometimes even physical, attacks on leaders of opposition parties, or only somewhat more subtle forms of harassment in the form of the arrest

---

[68] Landau, *Abusive Constitutionalism*, supra note 6; Landau & Dixon, *Transnational Constitutionalism*, supra note 6; Landau & Dixon, *Constraining Constitutional Change*, supra note 6; Landau & Dixon, *Abusive Judicial Review*, supra note 6.

[69] Landau & Dixon, *Abusive Judicial Review*, supra note 6.

[70] Jonathan S. Gould & David E. Pozen, *Structural Biases in Structural Constitutional Law*, 97 N.Y.U. L. Rev. (2022).

[71] *Id.*

[72] *Compare* Huq & Ginsburg, *supra* note 67, 199.

and prosecution of key opposition figures.[73] Or they may target the opposition *as a party* either by banning it, deregistering it, or simply undermining its competitiveness.

From a democratic minimum core perspective, what matters most is the impact of these measures on the role of political parties, and opposition groups in civil society, in sustaining a competitive political system. Often, attacks of this kind will adversely affect individual rights and freedoms. But it is their impact on opposition organizations and *structures* that is the central concern from the perspective of the democratic minimum core.[74]

Dominant parties throughout history have often chosen to ban opposition parties or have asked courts, or other "independent" institutions, to do so. But they have also attacked opposition parties in more indirect ways designed to limit their ability to recruit and retain members, gain seats in the legislature, or maintain financial solvency. For instance, they have used a variety of tools to encourage "defection" from smaller parties to the government, and thereby weakened the strength and integrity of those parties.[75] They have manipulated electoral "thresholds" so as effectively to increase barriers to entry into the legislature, and thereby create what Sam Issacharoff and Richard Pildes call a form of "partisan lock up."[76] And they have targeted opposition parties for a form of "lawfare"—that is, legal or regulatory actions that are time-consuming and costly to defend, and often lead to fines or other financial penalties that undermine the financial competitiveness of those parties, but which serve antidemocratic rather than democratic ends.[77]

Alvin Cheung has recently noted the widespread use of defamation actions as one of the most common antidemocratic practices of this kind.[78] But there are many others: would-be authoritarians frequently adopt the legal and regulatory tools of democratic states, but then deploy them in distinctly

---

[73] It should also be noted, of course, that sometimes the opposition may be the source not subject of threats to democracy.

[74] Compare Richard H. Pildes, *Competitive Deliberative and Rights-Oriented Democracy*, 3 ELECTION L.J. 685, 687–88 (2004).

[75] *See, e.g.*, UDM v. Speaker of the Nat'l Assembly, 2017 5 SA 300 (CC).

[76] Samuel Issacharoff & Richard H. Pildes, *Politics as Markets: Partisan Lockups of the Democratic Process*, 50 STAN. L. REV. 643, 692 (1998).

[77] For the use of the term "lawfare" in this context, see, *e.g.*, Theunis Roux, *The Constitutional Court's 2018 Term: Lawfare or Window on the Struggle for Democratic Social Transformation?*, 10 CONST. CT. REV. 1 (2020); Paul R. Williams, *Lawfare: A War Worth Fighting*, 43 CASE W. RES. J. INT'L L. 43 (2010); Hugh Corder & Cora Hoexter, *"Lawfare" in South Africa and Its Effects on the Judiciary*, 10 AFR. J. LEGAL STUD. 105 (2017). Other uses of the term include the idea that warfare is becoming increasingly legalized, and either fought through or constrained by legal norms. *See, e.g., Lawfare: Hard National Security Choices*, LAWFARE, <https://www.lawfareblog.com/>.

[78] Alvin Y.H. Cheung, An Introduction to Abusive Legalism (Feb. 22, 2018) (unpublished manuscript), available at <https://osf.io/preprints/lawarxiv/w9a6r/>.

antidemocratic ways. This kind of "abusive borrowing" of liberal democratic norms also takes a wide variety of forms. It involves the superficial application of those norms, their selective or acontextual use, or a truly anti-purposive or inverted form of democratic logic.[79]

Another target for those seeking to undermine electoral competition will be political rights and freedoms, especially those freedoms likely to be exercised by critics of the government, or members of opposition parties. Incumbent governments may thus seek to ban or regulate public meetings, or all meetings of a certain size. Or they may ban or regulate the rights of certain groups to associate; for instance, the registration and regulatory requirements that political parties, non-government organizations, or civil society groups must meet in order to operate or receive funding. They may impose stringent limits on freedom of expression, both in the form of civil and criminal prohibitions on libel or defamation and various forms of "incitement." Or they may seek to undermine freedom of the press, either by banning certain kinds of publication or broadcast, or by requiring state or other media to promote the views of government.[80]

2. Institutional monopoly

A second focus for those seeking political monopoly power will be the range of institutional "checks and balances" on government provided for by democratic constitutions. Institutions of this kind include courts themselves. But they also include legislatures, and other independent agencies, or accountability institutions, sometimes known as "fourth" branch institutions.[81]

Parliaments are not simply bodies that engage in law-making and represent the views of citizens in a collective, deliberative format. They play a crucial role in supervising the exercise of executive power by a democratic government. Attacking the strength, independence, or functioning of a legislature, therefore, offers governments a powerful way to expand their power—or erode the

---

[79] Rosalind Dixon & David Landau, *1989–2019: From Democratic to Abusive Constitutional Borrowing*, 17 INT'L J. CONST. L. 489 (2019); DIXON & LANDAU, ABUSIVE CONSTITUTIONAL BORROWING, supra note 6.

[80] Issacharoff has called this the "Chavez playbook" because of the degree to which many of these techniques have been recently used and "honed in Venezuela": *see* Samuel Issacharoff, *The Corruption of Popular Sovereignty*, 18 INT'L J. CONST. L. 1109 (2020);

[81] Michael Pal, *Electoral Management Bodies as a Fourth Branch of Government*, 21 REV. CONST. STUD. 87 (2016); Mark Tushnet, *Institutions Protecting Constitutional Democracy: Some Conceptual and Methodological Preliminaries*, 70 U. TORONTO L.J. 95 (2020).

pluralism, competition, and contestation inherent in a system of democratic checks and balances.

One way in which would-be authoritarians may do this is by openly seeking to amend the constitution to give the executive greater power, compared to parliament, or "suspending" parliament for an extended period, citing emergency or other national-interest rationales. But those seeking to erode parliamentary authority, or independence, may also adopt a range of more indirect measures, including measures that effectively "subordinate" the parliamentary wing of a party to its non-parliamentary wing.[82] As Sujit Choudhry notes, there are two effective *loci* for legislative decision-making in a democracy: parliament itself or the non-parliamentary wing of those parties represented in the parliament.[83] The former locus of power promotes democratic government, whereas the latter tends to undermine the role of parliament both as a representative institution and as a check on the executive or dominant party power.[84] The same is true for presidential systems where the same party controls the legislative and executive branch: legislative power in these circumstances can either be exercised in parliament, or *de facto* by the president and/or her party in ways that undermine the diffusion and accountability of political power.

Many constitutions around the world now also include a range of "fourth branch" institutions.[85] Some of these institutions are long-standing features of constitutional democratic systems—for example, government centers for science, weather, emergency management, or disease control, or central banks. Others are newer innovations but still common in many democratic systems worldwide—for instance, human rights, equality, and electoral commissions. And others still are found only in constitutions adopted in the last few decades—for instance, integrity and accountability institutions such as a national ombudsman, or integrity office, or office of the "public protector."[86]

Institutions of this kind serve a range of purposes: they help promote "expert" or evidence-based decision-making in a range of areas, including science and macroeconomic management.[87] They play an important role in protecting

---

[82] Sujit Choudhry, *"He Had a Mandate": The South African Constitutional Court and the African National Congress in a Dominant Party Democracy*, 2 CONST. CT. REV. 1 (2009).
[83] *Id.*
[84] *Id.*
[85] *See* Pal, *Electoral Management Bodies, supra* note 81; Tushnet, *Institutions Protecting Constitutional Democracy, supra* note 81.
[86] *See, e.g.*, S. AFR. CONST., ch 9, ss 181–194 and discussion in Klug, *supra* note 63; Fombad, *supra* note 63.
[87] *See* Pal, *Electoral Management Bodies, supra* note 81; Tushnet, *Institutions Protecting Constitutional Democracy, supra* note 81; Vicki Jackson, *Knowledge Institutions in Constitutional Democracies: Preliminary Reflections*, 7 CAN. J. COMP. CONST. L. 156 (2021).

individual rights to freedom, dignity, and equality, and thereby values of constitutionalism and the rule of law. And they help protect and promote democracy itself.[88]

The most obvious example of such institutions protecting democracy are electoral commissions, which in general have broad responsibility for monitoring and ensuring electoral fairness and integrity. But human rights institutions can also play an important role in protecting and promoting political rights and freedom, and "integrity" or accountability institutions can help prevent the kind of corruption that often sustains or accelerates a dominant party's hold on power.[89] "Knowledge institutions" can likewise play a central role in ensuring both well-functioning and democratic forms of government.[90]

Would-be authoritarian actors may also attack these institutions in a range of ways. They may attempt to alter their composition in ways that undermine their true independence—thereby effectively co-opting them as more or less willing participants in the government's project of democratic erosion. Or they may accept that an institution will remain independent but seek to radically weaken the effectiveness of the institution as a check on government.

In addition to these "horizontal" checks on power, many democratic constitutions contain "vertical" checks on national government power—in the form of a federal system of government. Federal systems vary widely in design worldwide.[91] But they often share a number of common features and functions: they divide power between national and state governments in order to promote forms of government "closer to the people," "democratic experimentalism" at a state level, the accommodation of diversity across states, and *checks and balances on central government power*.[92] They may also help promote long-term democratic competition or multiparty democracy by providing a base or platform for opposition parties to develop.

National governments seeking to consolidate power may thus target federal arrangements as another way of undermining democratic checks and balances, as well as future electoral competition.[93] Again, they may do so by attempting to influence processes of appointment at the state and local government level so as to ensure state and local officials are loyal to the central government and

---

[88] *See* Huq & Ginsburg, *supra* note 67, at 192–93.
[89] *See* Choudhry, *supra* note 82, at 26.
[90] *See* Jackson, *supra* note 87.
[91] *See* Vicki C. Jackson, *Comparative Constitutional Federalism and Transnational Judicial Discourse*, 2 Int'l J. Const. L. 91 (2004).
[92] *See, e.g.,* discussion in Rosalind Dixon, *The Functional Constitution: Re-reading the 2014 High Court Constitutional Term*, 43 Fed. L. Rev. 455 (2015).
[93] *See* Choudhry, *supra* note 82, at 31.

the dominant party. A strategy of this kind is often referred to as "cadre deployment."[94] It involves deploying members of a national, dominant political party to a variety of state and local roles. Or they may seek to interfere with or influence elections at a state or local level, or else weaken the power and authority of state and local governments. Doing so will not always be straightforward, given the constitutionally entrenched role of state governments in any truly federal system, and the formal powers given to local governments under some democratic constitutions.[95] But as David Schleicher has shown in the US context, often national political parties can use the process of candidate selection in state local elections to bring state and local governments into line, and voters generally vote in a "second order" way, based on their views of the national party and not their opinions of state or local representatives.[96]

Some federal systems also make this easier than others: Article 356 of the Indian Constitution, for example, allows the federal government to assume the power of a state government where the President is satisfied that "the government of the State cannot be carried on in accordance with the provisions of th[e] Constitution." Section 139 of the South African Constitution provides for similar powers in relation to the assumption by state governments of the function of local governments.

Of course, not every use of such powers will necessarily be antidemocratic in nature: sometimes, state or local entities may be failing to deliver basic services or fulfill basic representative functions in ways that make a strong pro-democratic case for national intervention. And constructing strong, national parties can help reinforce competitive forms of democracy—and sometimes this may require deploying national party representatives at the state or local level.[97]

But some uses will be distinctly abusive or antidemocratic in their aims: in India, for example, the central government has clearly used its powers to assume power over various states both for pro-democratic reasons and in order to undermine localized democracy and dissent.[98]

---

[94] *Id.* at 16.
[95] On this as the defining feature of federal as opposed to quasi-federal systems, see, *e.g.*, ELLIOT BULMER, FEDERALISM (International IDEA Constitution-Building Primer 12, 2015); Ronald L. Watts, *Federalism, Federal Political Systems, and Federations*, 1 ANN. REV. POLIT. SCI. 117 (1998).
[96] David Schleicher, *Federalism and State Democracy*, 95 TEX. L. REV. 763 (2016).
[97] *See, e.g.*, FRANCES MCCALL ROSENBLUTH & IAN SHAPIRO, RESPONSIBLE PARTIS: SAVING DEMOCRACY FROM ITSELF 12 (2018).
[98] *See* Choudhry, *supra* note 82. *See also* Tarun Gogoi, *Indian Federalism with Party System: Changes and Continuity*, 9 INT'L J. SCI. & TECH. RES. 180 (2020).

3. Monopoly: Intent versus effect

In this sense, the attempt to create an electoral or institutional monopoly is not simply an attempt to compete effectively within the existing electoral arena— by offering policies that can appeal to voters and making clear how and why those policies are to be preferred to those of opposition parties and candidates. Nor is it simply the use of existing constitutional powers to undermine state or local governments. It is an attempt to reduce the effective opposition to or accountability of the government by changing the "rules of the [political or legal] game," or systematically skewing their implementation in favor of the incumbent electoral regime.

In some cases, it may be hard to distinguish between the two sets of practices. But conceptually there is an important difference: one set of practices could be seen as equivalent to firms engaging in competitive pricing, where price is equal to marginal cost, and consumers gain the greatest possible consumer surplus. The other is analogous to a form of predatory pricing—that is, firms using their existing market position to charge below marginal cost so as to drive out a potential competitor from the market and create or cement a form of monopoly power.[99]

One might still ask whether the creation of electoral or institutional monopoly power needs to be *intentional* in order to count as dysfunctional in nature. It is certainly logically possible to treat as "dysfunctional" any legal or constitutional change that adversely impacts the democratic minimum core. But there is also an argument that, like the idea of "abuse," the concept of dysfunction requires something more than a normal but adverse change to the stability of the democratic minimum core; indeed, that it requires some form of *deliberate* attempt by political actors to erode the democratic minimum core.[100]

On this view, the concept of electoral or institutional monopoly should also be understood in ways that require a deliberate attempt by political actors to entrench their own hold on power—through an intentional attack on the integrity of the electoral process, the viability of the political opposition, and/ or the power of independent institutions. Indeed, similar questions arise in antitrust law as to whether legal enforcement action should focus solely on business practices that have an anticompetitive purpose or also extend to conduct that is anticompetitive in effect.[101] The difficulties with any intent based

---

[99] Organisation for Economic Cooperation and Development, Predatory Pricing 7 (1989).
[100] Compare Dixon & Landau, Abusive Constitutional Borrowing, *supra* note 6.
[101] *See, e.g.*, an overview by the Federal Trade Commission: Fed. Trade Comm'n, The Antitrust Laws, <https://www.ftc.gov/tips-advice/competition-guidance/guide-antitrust-laws/antitrust-laws>.

standard are familiar: the actions in question are often those of multiple not just single actors, and this poses a conceptual difficulty for any attempt to identify intent.[102] It can also be extremely difficult to gain access to the evidentiary records necessary to show intent.

The dangers of a purely effects-based standard, however, are equally real. Often, it will be difficult to judge when a particular legislative or constitutional change will threaten the stability of the democratic minimum core. Sometimes, we may *over-estimate* the risk posed by legislative or formal constitutional changes—based on the (mistaken) view that existing national constitutional arrangements are the only possible or plausible way of realizing a commitment to the democratic minimum core, or because we are strongly opposed ideologically to a particular political actor or party.[103]

In other cases, we may *underestimate* the risk—because change occurs via a series of apparently discrete measures, which taken together have the cumulative effect of eroding minimum core norms.[104] Abusive constitutional change often has a distinctly incremental character.[105] It can involve changes adopted by way of formal constitutional amendment (or replacement) but also legislation, judicial decision, and executive order or decree.[106] And it can consist in a series of apparently disaggregated changes, which interact, and have a cumulative effect.

One helpful check against both dangers will also be to focus on legislative (or executive) intent: the intent to erode democracy may itself increase the risk that, unchecked, otherwise benign changes or reforms end up posing a threat to the stability of the democratic minimum core. And it may provide powerful evidence that more changes, of a similar kind, are likely to follow in ways that lead to incremental and cumulative threats to democracy.

For the most part, therefore, the concept of antidemocratic monopoly power should be understood as having both an effects- and intent-based dimension, or as involving the *deliberate* attempt by political actors to undermine commitments to free, fair, and regular multiparty elections, political rights and

---

[102] *See* Ernest Gellhorn, *Justice Breyer on Statutory Review and Interpretation*, 8 ADMIN. L.J. AM. U. 755 (1995).

[103] Landau & Dixon, *Transnational Constitutionalism*, *supra* note 6. I am indebted to Mark Tushnet for pressing me on this point, both in the context of this work and joint work with Landau on ABUSIVE CONSTITUTIONAL BORROWING: *see* Mark Tushnet, *Review of Dixon and Landau's Abusive Constitutional Borrowing*, 7 CAN. J. COMP. & CONTEMP. L. 23 (2021); Rosalind Dixon & David Landau, *Abusive Constitutional Borrowing: A Reply to Commentators*, 7 CAN. J. COMP. & CONTEMP. L. 49 (2021).

[104] *See* Kim Lane Scheppele, *The Rule of Law and the Frankenstate: Why Governance Checklists Do Not Work*, 26 GOVERNANCE 559 (2013); Landau & Dixon, *Transnational Constitutionalism*, *supra* note 6; Khaitan, *supra* note 46.

[105] *Compare* Scheppele, *Frankenstate*, *supra* note 104; Khaitan, *supra* note 46.

[106] DIXON & LANDAU, ABUSIVE CONSTITUTIONAL BORROWING, *supra* note 6.

freedoms, and institutional checks and balance. But the best proof of intent may still come from examining the impact of certain actions, or the procedural context in which they occur.[107] And sometimes it may make sense for a court simply to focus on effects directly as a sign that democracy is under threat.

C. Legislative Blind Spots and Burdens of Inertia

Twenty-five years after the publication of *Democracy and Distrust*, Jeremy Waldron published his "Core Case" against judicial review,[108] arguing that judicial review is neither necessary nor desirable to promote even a quite thick deliberative, rights-protective vision of constitutional democracy such as that envisaged by Ronald Dworkin or John Rawls—because often legislative processes are just as good, if not better, at achieving a form of public-regarding debate about individual rights protection.[109]

Waldron further stipulated four broad assumptions about the nature of political institutions and culture in a society, as underpinning this argument—that is, that there were:

> (1) democratic institutions in reasonably good working order, including a representative legislature elected on the basis of universal adult suffrage; (2) a set of judicial institutions, again in reasonably good order, set up on a nonrepresentative basis to hear individual lawsuits, settle disputes, and uphold the rule of law; (3) a commitment on the part of most members of the society and most of its officials to the idea of individual and minority rights; and (4) persisting, substantial and good-faith disagreement about rights (i.e., about what the commitment to rights actually amounts to and what its implications are) among the members of the society who are committed to the idea of rights.[110]

These assumptions were also deliberately designed to provide a stylized or "boiled down" account of how democratic institutions operate, not an

---

[107] *See, e.g.*, Yick Wo v. Hopkins, 118 U.S. 356 (1886); Gomillion v. Lightfoot, 364 U.S. 339 (1960). For discussion, see Landau & Dixon, *Abusive Judicial Review, supra* note 6; DIXON & LANDAU, ABUSIVE CONSTITUTIONAL BORROWING, *supra* note 6.

[108] Waldron, *The Core of the Case Against Judicial Review, supra* note 5.

[109] RONALD DWORKIN, THE MORAL READING OF THE AMERICAN CONSTITUTION 74 (1996); RAWLS, *supra* note 12, at 35–36.

[110] Waldron, *The Core of the Case Against Judicial Review, supra* note 5, at 1360. *Compare* Richard Bellamy, *Political Constitutionalism and the Human Rights Act*, 9 INT'L J. CONST. L. 86, 91 (2011).

empirically accurate picture of the actual risks to democracy in most constitutional systems today.[111]

The difficulty with this kind of "boiled down" account, however, is twofold: first, the line between "well-functioning" and "dysfunctional" democracies is often far from clear-cut, and becoming less clear with time.[112] As Waldron himself acknowledged, most well-functioning democracies have some aspects of political dysfunction. Unless we accept that, there may be no real-world democracies that in fact meet Waldron's definition of "well-functioning."[113] And less functional democracies can vary widely in their degree of political dysfunction: some may be new democracies with relatively weak democratic traditions but robust forms of political competition, others may be "dominant party" democracies with very limited forms of *de facto* political competition, and others still "hybrid" or "competitive authoritarian" systems that combine aspects of democratic and non-democratic governance.[114] And as many others have pointed out, this line has only become more porous as we have witnessed increased threats of political monopoly—and dysfunction—in some of the world's most consolidated constitutional democracies.[115]

Second, even in systems that meet Waldron's criteria of having democratic institutions in "*reasonably* good working order," there are a range of potential blockages that can undermine the capacity of the system as a whole to translate constitutional commitments into law. In the remainder of this section, I suggest that blockages of this kind can take at least two forms: *blind spots* and *burdens of inertia*, each of which has multiple forms or variants.[116]

---

[111] Waldron, *The Core of the Case Against Judicial Review*, supra note 5. See discussion in Theunis Roux, *In Defence of Empirical Entanglement: The Methodological Flaw in Waldron's Case Against Judicial Review*, in THE CAMBRIDGE HANDBOOK OF DELIBERATIVE CONSTITUTIONALISM 203 (Ron Levy et al. eds., 2018); Rosalind Dixon & Adrienne Stone, *Constitutional Amendment and Political Constitutionalism: A Philosophical and Comparative Reflection*, in PHILOSOPHICAL FOUNDATIONS OF CONSTITUTIONAL LAW 103 (David Dyzenhaus & Malcolm Thorburn eds., 2016).

[112] *Compare* Samuel Issacharoff, *Constitutional Courts and Democratic Hedging*, 99 GEO. L.J. 961 (2010–2011); Roux, *In Defence of Empirical Entanglement*, *supra* note 111.

[113] Roux, *In Defence of Empirical Entanglement*, *supra* note 111.

[114] On fragile democracies, see ISSACHAROFF, *supra* note 9. On this continuum, see Issacharoff, *Constitutional Courts and Democratic Hedging*, *supra* note 112; Roux, *In Defence of Empirical Entanglement*, *supra* note 111; David Landau, *A Dynamic Theory of Judicial Role*, 55 B.C.L. REV. 1501 (2014).

[115] *See, e.g.*, Issacharoff, *Constitutional Courts and Democratic Hedging*, *supra* note 112; Roux, *In Defence of Empirical Entanglement*, *supra* note 111; Landau, *A Dynamic Theory of Judicial Role*, *supra* note 114.

[116] *See, e.g.*, Dixon, *Charter Dialogue*, *supra* note 7; Dixon, *Creating Dialogue about Socioeconomic Rights*, *supra* note 7. Compare Guido Calabresi, *Foreword: The Supreme Court 1990 Term: Antidiscrimination and Constitutional Accountability (What the Bork-Brennan Debate Ignores)*, 105 HARV. L. REV. 80, 104 (1991); William N. Eskridge, Jr. & Philip P. Frickey, *The Supreme Court, 1993 Term—Foreword: Law as Equilibrium*, 108 HARV. L. REV. 4 (1994); Mark A. Graber, *The Nonmajoritarian Difficulty: Legislative Deference to the Judiciary*, 7 STUD. AM. POL. DEV. 35 (1993).

While blockages of this kind are often made worse by public choice dynamics, or the role of special interest groups in democratic politics, they do not depend on them; often they arise simply because of time and capacity constraints on legislators, and the ordinary workings of a well-functioning party-based system of democratic government. They can affect constitutional claims asserted by what Waldron calls "topical" minorities *and* majorities—or rights asserted by groups that are both a statistical minority and majority in demographic terms.[117] And they can extend to many areas of democratic regulation. In some constitutional settings, the regulation of constitutional rights may be the sole area in which blockages of this kind arise and are judicially cognizable. But in others, democratic blockages may have constitutional significance in a much broader range of settings—including in the context of failures to democratic liberal commitments to regulating corporate and monopoly power, addressing externalities (such as environmental damage) and promoting economic dignity and equality, or achieving appropriate constitutional "transformation."[118]

1. Legislative blind spots

Modern legislatures consider a large number of complex pieces of legislation, and as a result often lack the time to study individual pieces of legislation in detail.[119] Even if they turn their minds to the question, they may also have limited foresight about the full range of circumstances in which a law may affect the enjoyment of individual rights in the future.[120] Legislators, like all of us, can be subject to various forms of bounded rationality which mean that they do not anticipate the full range of ways in which legislation may affect rights in the future.[121] In both cases, legislators may therefore vote for a law that imposes

---

[117] Waldron, *The Core of the Case Against Judicial Review*, supra note 5, at 1397.
[118] *See, e.g.*, Richard Holden & Rosalind Dixon, From Free to Fair Markets: Liberalism After COVID-19 (2022); Karl Klare, *Legal Culture and Transformative Constitutionalism*, 14 S. Afr. J. Hum. Rts. 146 (1998); Gautam Bhatia, The Transformative Constitution: A Radical Biography in Nine Acts (2019); Transformative Constitutionalism in Latin America: The Emergence of a New Ius Commune (Armin von Bogdandy et al. eds., 2017).
[119] Lisa Burton Crawford, *The Rule of Law in the Age of Statutes*, 48 Fed. L. Rev. 59 (2020). *Compare also* Stephen Holmes's arguments in *In Case of Emergency: Misunderstanding Tradeoffs in the War on Terror*, 97 Cal. L. Rev. 301 (2009).
[120] *Compare* David Bilchitz, Poverty and Fundamental Rights: The Justification and Enforcement of Socio-economic Rights 127 (2007).
[121] On the notion of bounded rationality, see Eddie Dekel et al., *Standard State-Space Models Preclude Unawareness*, 66 Econometrica 159 (1998) (attempting to account for "unawareness" of consequences as an important aspect of bounded rationality).

unintended or unanticipated limitations on constitutional protections—or that is subject to clear "*blind spots of application.*"

Waldron himself acknowledges that "[i]t may not always be easy for legislators to see what issues of rights are embedded in a legislative proposal brought before them; it may not always be easy for them to envisage what issues of rights might arise from its subsequent application." Other scholars, such as Guido Calabresi, go further, suggesting that "[l]egislatures often act hastily or thoughtlessly with respect to fundamental rights because of panic or crises or more often [because] they are simply pressed for time."[122]

Time constraints on legislators can also mean they choose to delegate the task of considering whether laws "minimally impair" constitutional guarantees to a sub-committee of the legislature, rather than consider this question personally. And these committees may be structured in ways that emphasize certain perspectives or interests over others.[123] This can again mean that legislators overlook opportunities for the accommodation of constitutional guarantees—even forms of accommodation that could be achieved at very low cost to relevant legislative objectives, and thus which would almost certainly be supported by a democratic majority ("blind spots of accommodation").

Often an important contributor to blind spots of this kind will be the existence of a range of "blind spots of perspective," which undermine the representativeness of democratic processes. While broadly representative, legislative bodies will often fail to reflect the full range of experiences and perspectives of those subject to the law.[124] In some cases, this will be because some individuals are formally disenfranchised or barred from access to legislative office. In others, it may simply be because of how electoral districts are drawn, and the disincentives this creates for parties to select a truly diverse range of candidates. And while direct representation in the legislative process is not always necessary to ensure that various groups' interests or perspectives are considered in the design of legislation,[125] often, failures of "voice" or inclusion *will* translate into failures of accommodation in the drafting of legislation.

---

[122] *See* Calabresi, *supra* note 116. *Compare also* Malcolm Langford, *Why Judicial Review*, 2 OSLO L. REV. 36, 55 (2015).

[123] For instance, they may be staffed by those especially committed to the achievement of relevant policy objectives, as compared to countervailing interests, or major party as opposed to smaller party or independent representatives.

[124] Courts, of course, are often even less representative but provide an avenue for citizens to speak on their own behalf through constitutional litigation: *see* MARGIT COHN, A THEORY OF THE EXECUTIVE BRANCH: TENSION AND LEGALITY (2021), at 289–320; Margit Cohn, *The Role of Courts in the Public Decision-Making Sphere: A Two-Pronged Argument for Heightened Review* (article forthcoming).

[125] Waldron, *The Core of the Case Against Judicial Review*, *supra* note 5, at 1395–401.

Failures of this kind will also raise additional concerns about the legitimacy of democratic legislation itself. This is especially true if blind spots of this kind affect historically disadvantaged (minority) groups, or minorities subject to broader forms of social, economic, and political exclusion. Blind spots of perspective do not exhaust the ways in which disadvantage of this kind can play out or remove the need for attention to the broader equality claims of such groups. However, they are one way in which inequality of this kind can manifest, and thus especially troubling where they intersect with disadvantage of this kind.

2. Legislative burdens of inertia

Legislative processes may likewise be subject to a range of different forms of *inertia*. *Priority-driven burdens of inertia* will arise even in the most ideal democratic settings, simply as a result of the time-consuming nature of the law-making processes, and the limits this implies on the number of legislative changes which a legislative majority can enact within any given period.

Capacity constraints of this kind will mean that there is little reason—or space—for legislative majorities to give priority to rights-based claims which are advanced by a relatively small minority, if those claims do not command strong majority support.[126] In a competitive democracy, legislators have strong incentives to prioritize those issues which are of greatest or strongest concern to a majority of citizens. (The premise of competitive elections is that if they fail to do so, a different majority will be elected.) This need not mean that a majority of citizens would necessarily reject or oppose the recognition of a particular rights claim. They may tacitly support the recognition of rights but regard legislation that does so as having relatively low priority. Because of this, even well-functioning legislative processes can fail to respond adequately to evolving understandings of rights in the broader culture, in a way which undermines the responsiveness—and legitimacy—of the constitutional system as a whole. And as I explore further below, not all legislative processes will necessarily be well-functioning in ways that may further exacerbate this problem.

Coalition-driven forms of inertia will arise in the legislative process as a result of more real-world or second-best features of a democratic system relating

---

[126] *Compare* Michael J. Perry, *Protecting Human Rights in a Democracy: What Role for Courts*, 38 Wake Forest L. Rev. 635, 655 (2003).

to the dynamics of competition between political parties. In almost all real-world democracies, affiliation with a major political party substantially increases a candidate's chance of election. Once elected, a legislator's chance of re-election will also depend to a large degree on the broader electoral popularity of his or her political party. Legislators therefore have a strong incentive to promote both the actual and apparent coherence of the party to which they belong. If party members or factions are divided on an issue, this can mean that legislative party leaders have an interest in keeping an issue off the legislative agenda—even in the face of clear demands for legal change from the broader constitutional culture.[127]

If a party is internally divided on an issue but legal change is nevertheless to be achieved, party leaders have two options. One option is to allow a free vote among party members on the basis of their conscience, the other is to impose party discipline on members in the minority, requiring them to vote with the majority of the party. Both options can have real costs for the coherence of the party. Allowing a conscience vote can undermine the public perception of cohesion, or coherent policy, within a party, while imposing party discipline can erode the actual internal coherence of a party. If party discipline is imposed frequently enough, members of minority factions may no longer feel it is in their interests to remain part of the broad party-based coalition, and they may split-off from the party as a whole.[128] As Mark Graber has argued, party leaders are well aware of this political Catch-22, and as a result, will "do their best to avoid taking firm public stands on those matters that internally divide their coalition," and "adopt a variety of 'defensive' strategies to try and depoliticize the issue/keep it off the national agenda."[129]

Again, this need not mean that there is an absence of support for a constitutional claim in the broader culture. A majority of citizens may well support the recognition of a particular claim and even feel quite strongly about the need for legal change to give effect to that understanding. However, legislators may still decide that their medium- to long-term interests in preserving party integrity outweigh the short-term electoral gains in responding to this demand for legal change. The consequence for the broader constitutional democratic system will be that absent some breach in majority party discipline, legislators

---

[127] *See* Graber, *The Nonmajoritarian Difficulty*, *supra* note 116, at 40 (emphasis added); F.L. Morton, *Dialogue or Monologue*, *in* JUDICIAL POWER AND CANADIAN DEMOCRACY 115 (Paul Howe & Peter H. Russell eds., 2001).
[128] *See* Mark Tushnet, *New Forms of Judicial Review and the Persistence of Rights- and Democracy-Based Worries*, 38 WAKE FOREST L. REV. 813, 834 (2003).
[129] *See* Graber, *The Nonmajoritarian Difficulty*, *supra* note 116, at 40 (emphasis added).

will once again fail to respond to evolving democratic understandings of rights—but this time, in the face of even stronger support for constitutional protection.

Finally, where the realization of constitutional requirements requires sustained and complex forms of administrative action, delay or inertia in the process of legislative oversight may combine with inertia within the executive branch to produce "complex" or *compound burdens of inertia*. This is especially true for certain rights, such as social rights, which have a strong positive dimension.[130] But it is also true of a much wider range of constitutional norms, which depend on effective government action as opposed to inaction for their realization.

Dynamics of this kind will often be made worse by certain democratic pathologies. Political scientists in recent decades have highlighted the powerful role interest groups can play in shaping democratic outcomes.[131] Often, democratic political processes will be influenced by organized interest groups, not just citizens or voters; and these interest group dynamics will systematically benefit small- to medium-sized groups such as corporate or industry groups, over larger, more diffuse groups—such as consumers or democratic rights-claimants.[132]

Larger groups may have access to more resources, and a larger number of voters, but will often face significant "collective action" problems in attempting to influence democratic outcomes. The size of the group, and difficulty monitoring individual contributions to it, often mean that no individual member has any real incentive to press for legislative change benefiting the group as a whole.[133] Smaller groups, in contrast, will often be better positioned to monitor the contributions of individual members, and thus to overcome "free rider" problems of this kind. Small- to medium-sized groups, with access both to monitoring technologies and greater resources, will thus often have far greater influence over democratic outcomes than would be predicted by their size or numbers alone. And this may contribute to, or worsen, legislative inertia in

---

[130] Dixon, *Creating Dialogue about Socioeconomic Rights*, supra note 6. *See also* Rosalind Dixon & David Landau, *Defensive Social Rights*, in OXFORD HANDBOOK OF ECONOMIC AND SOCIAL RIGHTS (Malcolm Langford & Katharine G. Young eds., forthcoming).

[131] *See, e.g.*, discussion in DANIEL A. FARBER & PHILIP P. FRICKEY, LAW AND PUBLIC CHOICE: A CRITICAL INTRODUCTION (1991).

[132] *Compare* Einer R. Elhauge, *Does Interest Group Theory Justify More Intrusive Judicial Review*, 101 YALE L.J. 31 (1991); Mark Tushnet, *Darkness on the Edge of Town: The Contributions of John Hart Ely to Constitutional Theory*, 89 YALE L.J. 1037, 1054 (1980),

[133] Bengt Holmstrom, *Moral Hazard in Teams*, 13 BELL J. ECON. 324 (1982); Elhauge, *supra* note 132.

responding to the claims of larger numbers of citizens to protect various constitutional rights or values.[134]

But blockages of this kind can also arise absent this kind of public choice dynamic. They can be the product of a political system that divides power (e.g., between the executive and legislative branch) or an electoral system that provides limited incentives for policy responsiveness on the part of representatives. They may even arise in quite well-functioning systems with high levels of legislative-executive cooperation and largely non-partisan processes for drawing (competitive) electoral districts: in some cases, they may simply be the product of the time and capacity constraints on the part of legislators. Hence, they may arise even in democratic systems in "reasonably good working order" or as part of the operation of a healthy rather than dysfunctional political party system.

The same applies to potential state weakness: in many countries, especially those in the Global South, the state may lack the capacity to engage in effective service delivery, and weaknesses in the legislative branch may further undermine the kind of oversight needed to ensure effective performance of these functions. As Landau notes,

> [state] capacity ... is often weak in newer democracies just because it takes considerable time and resources to build up competent bureaucracies. Pervasive problems of corruption, which run across a large number of less mature democracies, also impact the quality of representation and the extent of accountability by weakening the links between voters and officials.[135]

Together, these dynamics can also lead to pervasive forms of compound inertia: they can mean that executive actors consistently fail to fulfill constitutional obligations but face few effective checks on their (non-)exercise of power.[136]

But again, compound inertia of this kind can arise absent any form of state failure: in systems with multiple, competing demands on government, blockages of this kind may arise simply because of time and capacity constraints on both legislators and executive actors.

---

[134] *See* Stephen Gardbuam, *Comparative Political Process Theory: A Rejoinder*, 18 INT'L J. CONST. L. (2020).
[135] Landau, *A Dynamic Theory of Judicial Role, supra* note 114, at 1512.
[136] *Id.*

D. "Deliberate" versus Interconnected Democratic Blockages

Of course, in some cases "inertia" may be a deliberate feature of a constitutional system, not a blockage or source of dysfunction. Or as Ely himself noted, "there are many things legislatures 'haven't done anything about' that should be left in precisely that condition."[137] For instance, for some constitutional norms, such as those which set out basic democratic procedural norms, it may be more important that they are "settled" than that they are settled in any particular way.[138] Unsettling them, therefore, would also be counterproductive rather than helpful to basic commitments to democracy. Similarly, federalism, bicameralism, and presidential forms of government could all be considered constitutional models designed to "slow down" ordinary forms of majoritarian democratic politics—in order to promote thicker democratic understandings, or commitments to minority rights and democratic deliberation.[139]

The idea of burdens of inertia, however, is that they involve forms of democratic delay or non-responsiveness that *do not* reflect this kind of commitment to constitutional settlement, rights-protection, or deliberation.

If the reason a democratic system does not respond to majority understandings is because it is seeking to protect the central ranges of various individual rights, this could itself be seen as pro-democratic in nature—or at least as advancing thick commitments to democracy. Similarly, if a democratic system does not respond to majority understandings because they are insufficiently well-reasoned, considered, or deliberative, this can again be seen as advancing a principled form of democratic commitment or constraint. Burdens of inertia, therefore, are not simply "inertia" in the ordinary sense but rather a specific form of a failure by democratic systems to respond to the alignment between democratic majority understandings and thicker democratic constitutional commitments. They arise where there is a good faith constitutional claim which is supported by rather than opposed by democratic majority understandings.

At the same time, some constitutional models designed to slow down majoritarian politics *may* lead to burdens of inertia. In many presidential systems, partisan polarization together with "divided" forms of government can mean that democratic politics is effectively gridlocked, and it is impossible to

---

[137] Compare ELY, supra note 25, at 117.

[138] See, e.g., Rosalind Dixon, *Updating Constitutional Rules*, 2009 SUP. CT. REV. 319 (2011).

[139] See, e.g., Adrian Vatter, *Lijphart Expanded: Three Dimensions of Democracy in Advanced OECD Countries*, 1 EUR. POL. SCI. REV. 125 (2009); AREND LIJPHART, THINKING ABOUT DEMOCRACY: POWER SHARING AND MAJORITY RULE IN THEORY AND PRACTICE (2007).

pass almost any form of legislation—including legislation that reflects thicker democratic commitments.[140] Some federal systems also face similar forms of inertia because of the inability of state and federal governments, or different houses of the legislature reflecting national and state concerns, to act in concert to address pressing social and economic challenges. Constitutional "checks and balances," therefore, may ultimately be both protections for thick forms of democracy and sources of democratic dysfunction. Which is true in any given case will inevitably be a matter of evaluative judgment. But that is true of any theory of democracy or judicial review that takes seriously the idea of reasonable democratic disagreement.

There are also potentially important connections between these various different threats to democracy. Political monopoly or degradation may undermine the responsiveness of democratic politics thereby leading to consistent blind spots and burdens of inertia. Parties with a strong electoral monopoly, for example, will generally have limited incentive to consider the claims or perspectives of electoral minorities; their hold on power will be too secure for this to be necessary. They may even have limited incentive to consider the claims or needs of the median voter. This can also lead, however, to recurrent blind spots of accommodation and perspective and priority-driven forms of inertia.

Conversely, burdens of inertia may mean that legislatures fail to adopt measures necessary to combat emerging threats to democratic functioning and integrity such as electoral laws and regulations protecting against voter suppression, or ensuring a level playing field through campaign-finance laws. And democratic systems that consistently fail to respond to majority understandings, demands, and concerns may also witness an erosion in public trust.

Democratic distrust, for Ely, was linked to the degree to which democratically elected officials engaged in self-serving forms of action—that is, actions that were aimed at self-entrenchment, or entrenchment of their own party, at the expense of true democratic competition, or representation of the interests of "discrete and insular minorities." In a responsive approach, the focus is not so much on trust or trustworthiness, but on responsiveness. There is, however, an important way in which responsiveness and trust remain linked in many democratic constitutional systems.

Democratic systems that consistently fail to respond to the needs, concerns, and perspectives of democratic majorities will often lose public support

---

[140] *See, e.g.*, Keith Krehbiel, *Institutional and Partisan Sources of Gridlock: A Theory of Divided and Unified Government*, 8 J. THEORETICAL POL. 7 (1996); Michael J. Teter, *Gridlock: Legislative Supremacy, and the Problem of Arbitrary Inaction*, 88 NOTRE DAME L. REV. 2217 (2012).

and trust.[141] The erosion of trust of this kind can also be a strong predictor or precursor of the rise of illiberal or anticonstitutional populist parties and movements, which then seek to erode democracy via a range of abusive constitutional tactics. In the United States, for instance, 57 percent of those who voted for President Donald Trump in 2016 indicated in exit polls that they were "dissatisfied" or "angry" with the performance of the federal government. As Chapter 2 noted, following his election, Trump also deployed a range of tactics amounting to a direct attack on the democratic minimum core, not just a form of partisan or constitutional "hardball."[142] He attacked individual journalists, selectively denied press access, questioned the authority of the federal judiciary, incited violence against members of Congress, and refused to acknowledge the legitimacy of President Joe Biden's election.[143]

Moreover, this kind of dynamic is not limited to right-wing or conservative parties or leaders. For instance, in Venezuela in 1999, persistent poverty and lack of access to education and healthcare for ordinary citizens was an important factor contributing to the election of President Chávez, who subsequently did some amount to address these problems but a great deal to undermine the democratic minimum core, including by undermining judicial independence and other constitutional checks and balances.[144]

Similarly, in South Africa, the perception that the ANC-led government has not done enough to respond to the economic demands of the black majority— including in the implementation of various social and economic rights under sections 25–27 of the Constitution—is an important factor contributing

---

[141] *See* Michael Dimock, *How Americans View Trust, Facts, and Democracy Today*, Pew Trusts (Feb. 19, 2010), <https://www.pewtrusts.org/en/trust/archive/winter-2020/how-americans-view-trust-facts-and-democracy-today> (noting steady decline among US voters who believe that elected officials "care what people like me think," and also decline in trust in national democratic institutions).

[142] Mark Tushnet, *Constitutional Hardball*, 37 J. Marshall L. Rev. 623 (2003).

[143] *See, e.g.*, Committee to Protect Journalists, *The Trump Administration and the Media* (Apr. 16, 2020), <https://cpj.org/reports/2020/04/trump-media-attacks-credibility-leaks/>; Peter Greste, *When Trump Attacks the Press, He Attacks the American People and Their Constitution*, The Conversation (Jun. 3, 2020), <https://theconversation.com/when-trump-attacks-the-press-he-attacks-the-american-people-and-their-constitution-139863>; *In His Own Words: The President's Attacks on the Courts*, Brennan Ctr. for Justice (Feb. 14, 2020), <https://www.brennancenter.org/our-work/research-reports/his-own-words-presidents-attacks-courts>; Kevin Liptak, *A List of the Times Trump Has Said He Won't Accept the Election Results or Leave Office If He Loses*, CNN, Sept. 24, 2020, <https://edition.cnn.com/2020/09/24/politics/trump-election-warnings-leaving-office/index.html>; *Trial Memorandum of the United States House of Representatives in the Impeachment Trial of President Donald J. Trump*, Senate of the United States, <https://judiciary.house.gov/uploadedfiles/house_trial_brief_final.pdf?utm_campaign=5706-519>.

[144] Raul A. Sanchez Urribarri, *Courts Between Democracy and Hybrid Authoritarianism: Evidence from the Venezuelan Supreme Court*, 36 Law & Soc. Inquiry 854 (2011); Dixon & Landau, Abusive Constitutional Borrowing, *supra* note 5.

to support for the far-left Economic Freedom Fighter (EFF) party and their leader, Julius Malema.[145] And while Malema is not currently in power, and thus his threats to political rights and freedoms, including the rights of journalists, and the independence of South African courts are so far just that—threats[146]—they point to potential future dangers for South African democracy, should it remain unresponsive to mainstream democratic demands for social and economic transformation. Indeed, some suggest that the ANC itself has already begun to shift toward a more illiberal populist discourse, which threatens to undermine norms of institutional pluralism, in part as a response to the electoral threat posed by the EFF.[147]

Therefore, without responsiveness, democracies become vulnerable to a high risk of erosion. Conversely, responsive democracies are capable of realizing both thin and thick versions of a commitment to self-government. The question, then, is how constitutions can best be designed and interpreted as to promote this form of responsiveness.

---

[145] Martin Plaut, *Are Malema and the EFF A Threat to Democracy*, POLITICS WEB (Sept. 15, 2014), <https://www.politicsweb.co.za/news-and-analysis/are-malema-and-the-eff-a-threat-to-democracy>; Theunis Roux, *Constitutional Populism in South Africa*, in ANTI-CONSTITUTIONAL POPULISM (Martin Krygier et al. eds, 2022).

[146] Eusebius McKaiser, *What the EFF, Malema? What About Democracy?*, MAIL & GUARDIAN, Mar. 7, 2019, <https://mg.co.za/article/2019-03-07-what-the-eff-malema-what-about-democracy/>; Bouwer van Niekerk, *Why the EFF's Threat to the Judiciary is a Threat to Our Democracy*, NEWS24, Aug. 19, 2019, <https://www.news24.com/news24/columnists/guestcolumn/opinion-why-the-effs-threat-to-the-judiciary-is-a-threat-to-our-democracy-20190819>.

[147] *See* Roux, *Constitutional Populism in South Africa*, *supra* note 145.

PART 2
COURTS AND DEMOCRATIC RESPONSIVENESS

4
The Scope and Intensity of Responsive Judicial Review

What do these understandings of democracy and dysfunction mean for the scope of judicial review, or courts' approach to questions of constructional choice? To some extent, the answer will be contextual: how courts approach the process of constitutional construction will depend on the legal and political context for judicial review. In some countries, there is a strong emphasis on "legalist" modes of interpretation, which give limited weight to notions of representation-reinforcement; whereas in others, there is much greater openness to values-based modes of reasoning that embrace a concern for democratic protection and promotion. There will likewise be important variation across countries in the degree to which there is in fact evidence of democratic blind spots, burdens of inertia, or threats of political monopoly.

A responsive theory of judicial review, however, offers general guidance for courts as they seek to construe a democratic constitution, namely that they should be guided by the presence, or absence, of various forms of democratic dysfunction both in determining the proper scope of judicial review, and calibrating its intensity. Some scholars, for example, suggest that courts should only identify constitutional implications where they are strictly necessary to the functioning of the text or structure of the constitution as a whole. A responsive approach to judicial review, however, embraces a broader approach. It suggests that judicial implications will almost always be appropriate if they help respond to an urgent and systemic threat to the democratic minimum core, and *may* be legitimate as a response to risks of democratic blind spots and burdens of inertia, but only if they enjoy stronger legal(ist) support, or there is a risk of irreversible harm to individual rights. It thus calls for courts to pay careful attention to both the legal and political context for constitutional constructional choice.

A responsive theory of review likewise suggests that attention to these same democratic blockages can usefully help guide or calibrate the application of proportionality or tiered scrutiny. In the United States (US), calibration of this kind would most likely occur implicitly, in the application of existing tiers of scrutiny, whereas elsewhere, it is more likely to involve an explicit adjustment in the intensity of judicial review. And in both contexts, it would need to occur in light of the actual evidence before a court, and the kind of evidence a court might expect to be publicly available about certain threats to constitutional norms. But the basic value of a focus on democratic dysfunction in both cases is the same: it can help provide courts with additional guideposts in the exercise of otherwise quite open-ended forms of evaluative judgment, and guidance that helps both protect and promote underlying commitments to democracy and democratic responsiveness.

Others have made similar arguments about the capacity of democracy-sensitive theories of judicial review to inform the application of doctrines of proportionality.[1] It is worth restating them here for two reasons, however: judges do not always seem to apply notions of proportionality or tiered scrutiny in ways that reflect these ideas about calibration, and this is perhaps one of the areas in which a responsive approach can provide the most clear and concrete guidance to courts. It is also an area where a clear restatement may assist lawyers, as they seek to translate the idea of responsive judicial review into arguments to courts about the need for greater judicial restraint or robust oversight of legislative or executive action. Responsive judicial review does not need to be explicitly framed by the parties as a call for courts to overcome democratic dysfunction in order to have that effect. But it can be, and arguably should be, in cases where the legal culture is such that courts are likely to be responsive to arguments in this form.[2]

A. The Legal and Political Legitimacy of Judicial Review

One of the most frequent criticisms of judicial review is that it involves an illegitimate form of "judicial activism."[3] But the charge of judicial activism can be understood to imply a range of potential conceptual claims: the idea that

---

[1] *See, e.g.*, Moshe Cohen-Eliya & Iddo Porat, *Proportionality and the Culture of Justification*, 59 AM. J. COMP. L. 463 (2011); Vicki C. Jackson, *Constitutional Law in An Age of Proportionality*, 124 YALE L.J. 3094 (2014); Aharon Barak, *Proportionality and Principles Balancing*, 4 LAW & ETHICS HUM. RTS. 1 (2010). For other useful accounts of how proportionality-style judgments might be adjusted in different contexts, *see also* MICHAELA HAILBRONNER, TRADITIONS AND TRANSFORMATIONS: THE RISE OF GERMAN CONSTITUTIONALISM 117–22 (2015); Cora Chan, *Proportionality and Invariable Baseline Intensity of Review*, 33 LEGAL STUD. 1 (2013); Julian Rivers, *Proportionality and Variable Intensity of Review*, 65 CAMBRIDGE L.J. 174 (2006).

[2] THEUNIS ROUX, THE POLITICO-LEGAL DYNAMICS OF JUDICIAL REVIEW: A COMPARATIVE ANALYSIS (2018).

[3] *See, e.g.*, discussion in Sujit Choudhry & Claire E. Hunter, *Measuring Judicial Activism on the Supreme Court of Canada: A Comment on* Newfoundland (Treasure Board) v. NAPE, 48 McGILL L.J.

courts are too willing to invalidate legislation; courts are too willing to act contrary to the will of the democratic majority; or courts are too willing to engage in creativity in the process of constitutional reasoning—or too actively seeking to *reconstruct* rather than act in accordance with existing constitutional interpretive practices.

Each of these different understandings of judicial activism suggests different ways of understanding the potential legitimacy based objections to judicial review. But what do we mean by institutional "legitimacy" in this context? The idea of legitimacy, as Richard Fallon notes, is frequently invoked but rarely defined with any precision in constitutional debate.[4] It can also be understood as operating at three different levels: as referring to "legal," "sociological," or "moral" or political forms of legitimacy.[5]

Legal legitimacy refers to the degree to which judicial decisions conform with existing legal norms or constraints: decisions that are "lawful," according to Fallon, are legally legitimate, whereas those that exceed the bounds of existing legal authority are legally illegitimate.[6] Some scholars are skeptical that legal norms establish any meaningful limit of this kind.[7] But others believe that legal modalities and professional norms do create meaningful forms of constraint.[8] And it is this notion of legal constraint that informs notions of legal (il)legitimacy.

Sociological legitimacy is closely linked to Weberian notions of legitimacy: as Fallon notes, legitimacy of this kind "signifies an active belief by citizens, whether warranted or not, that particular claims to authority deserve respect or obedience for reasons not restricted to self-interest."[9] For courts, this means a willingness by citizens to accept the decisions of a court, even when they disagree with the outcome of a specific court decision. Sociological legitimacy of this kind can admittedly be understood in stronger or weaker terms: in the strong sense it denotes actual belief in a claim to institutional authority. In a weaker sense, it simply denotes the idea of public "acquiescence in assertions of authority."[10] But in either event, if a court enjoys sufficient

---

525 (2003); Kent Roach, The Supreme Court on Trial: Judicial Activism or Democratic Dialogue (rev. ed. 2016).

[4] Richard H. Fallon, Jr., *Legitimacy and the Constitution*, 118 Harv. L. Rev. 1787.
[5] *Id.*
[6] *Id.* at 1794–95.
[7] This was the fundamental insight of the US legal realist movement, and has been further developed by critical legal studies scholars. *See, e.g.*, Duncan Kennedy, A Critique of Adjudication: Fin De Siècle (1998).
[8] *See, e.g.*, Karl Llewellyn, *The Crafts of Law Re-Valued*, 28 A.B.A. J. 801 (1942).
[9] Fallon, *supra* note 4, 1795.
[10] *Id.* at 1796.

sociological legitimacy, it is likely to see its decisions implemented, whereas if it lacks sociological legitimacy, it may expect resistance to enforcing its orders.

Moral legitimacy, in turn, is the degree to which a legal decision is "morally justifiable or respect-worthy."[11] There is broad scope for disagreement as to what counts as morally justifiable in this context. Some theories assume a relatively demanding notion of moral justifiability based on substantive political commitments—such as to individual liberty, equality, and dignity. Others focus on a more minimal definition of what is required in order to ensure the (hypothetical) consent of rational and reasonable citizens to a constitutional system: this, for example, was the basis for the theory of political liberalism advanced by John Rawls.[12] A responsive approach to judicial review also focuses on this more minimal, political conception of legitimacy: it takes seriously the idea of reasonable disagreement about questions of constitutional morality, and hence adopts a notion of moral legitimacy that is largely politically liberal in nature—that is, based on the notion of "political" legitimacy.[13]

Further, a responsive approach suggests that actual judicial legitimacy should be understood as an amalgam of legal and political sources of legitimacy, or as a cumulative concept that includes elements of both legal and political legitimacy.[14] A judicial decision may be legitimate, in this view, if it has a strong basis in formal legal sources—that is, the text, history, and structure of a constitution, or a court's prior case law.[15] Or it may be legitimate because it gives effect to powerful political commitments, or has some (lesser) degree of both legal and political legitimacy. A responsive approach to judicial review further suggests a quite particularized focus for judgments about *political* legitimacy: it suggests there will be powerful democratic arguments for courts adopting a range of constitutional implications in order to protect the minimum core of democracy, and persuasive political reasons for courts to adopt implications aimed at countering legislative blind spots or burdens of inertia. At the same time, it suggests an important difference in the degree of political legitimacy between the two sets of cases.

---

[11] *Id.* at 1796–97.

[12] John Rawls, Political Liberalism (1993). *See also* discussion in Fallon, *supra* note 4, at 1787–88.

[13] Some might still suggest it is useful to refer to this as moral legitimacy, and this is in fact more consistent with Rawls' own usage. This is also fully consistent with a responsive approach. I am indebted to Christoph Möllers for pressing me on this point.

[14] Bilyana Petkova, Towards a Discursive Model of Judicial Legitimacy for the Court of Justice of the European Union and the European Court of Human Rights (2013) (Phd Dissertation, University of Kent).

[15] *Compare* Philip Bobbitt, Constitutional Fate: Theory of the Constitution (1982).

B. The Political Legitimacy of Constitutional Implications

Any form of political monopoly power—whether electoral or institutional—poses a *systemic* and *urgent* threat to a commitment to democratic responsiveness. It involves changes to a democratic system that can undermine the entire system of political rights and freedoms, and institutional checks and balances, to ensure truly free and fair elections. And, if successful, changes of this kind can become harder and harder to reverse. They can be adopted in the form of formal constitutional amendments, or other forms of "abusive" constitutional change. They can also effectively put would-be authoritarian actors in control of all the formerly independent institutions (including courts themselves) that could be counted on to resist change of this kind. Preventing electoral or institutional monopoly, therefore, requires a resolute and timely response from institutions such as courts, and this provides a strong defense of the political legitimacy of a range of judicial implications.

Many forms of legislative blind spots or inertia, in contrast, are often far less systematic. They can pose a threat to democratic functioning and the political legitimacy of a constitutional democratic system. But they often affect one group or constitutional claimant in a specific context, not the functioning of the constitutional system as a whole, and impose harms that are capable of being addressed by future legislative or executive action. Accordingly, judicial implications designed to counter such blockages will generally enjoy a lesser degree of political legitimacy than those designed to counter the risk of anti-democratic monopoly power.

This is not always the case. Sometimes the harm posed by legislation poses an immediate risk to individuals, and no future legislative act can effectively cure that harm. This may be because the harm is practically irremediable, or because there are legal obstacles to retrospective variation of a person's rights or liability. In civil or criminal as opposed to "pure public law" cases, for example, there are often constitutional (or in common law systems, common law) limits on the capacity of the legislature to alter the rights and liabilities of the parties in a case retrospectively.[16] Countering legislative blind spots or burdens of inertia, as they affect particular individuals, is thus a matter of urgency.

---

[16] *See* Rosalind Dixon, *A Minimalist Charter of Rights for Australia: The UK or Canada as a Model?*, 37 FED. L. REV. 335 (2009). *See also* Aileen Kavanagh, *What's So Weak About "Weak-Form Review"? The Case of the UK Human Rights Act 1998*, 13 INT'L J. CONST. L. 1008 (2015); Fergal F. Davis & David Mead, *Declarations of Incompatibility, Dialogue and the Criminal Law*, 43 COMMON L. WORLD REV. 62 (2014). For the exploration of this concept of pure public law cases, see further Chapter 5, Section D(3), *infra*.

A principle of reversibility can also be understood at both a conceptual and practical level: some failures to protect human dignity may literally be impossible to reverse, whereas others may be conceptually feasible but practically extremely difficult to compensate for. The concept of reversibility should be understood in a way that acknowledges this difference in degree and is broad enough to encompass both notions of "irreversibility."[17] Some forms of democratic inertia may also be so widespread and systemic that there is little chance that they will be overcome, and basic citizen needs and demands met, without judicial intervention. And again, this will provide an additional argument for the political legitimacy of implications designed to help counter such failures.

This also suggests three broad principles governing the legitimacy of judicial implications under a written constitution:

(1) Implications that have limited legal support, and no real political justification, will be presumptively illegitimate: by definition, the idea of an "implication" suggests a limited degree of textual support for such a doctrine, and absent any real political justification, this should be sufficient to encourage a court to exercise restraint.
(2) Implications designed to protect the "minimum core" of democracy will generally be legitimate, regardless of the degree of existing legal support for such an implication (or support in the text, history, and structure of a constitution, or a court's prior case law). They will draw their legitimacy from political arguments in favor of courts seeking to respond to an urgent and systemic risk to constitutional commitments to democracy and democratic responsiveness.
(3) Implications designed to counter blind spots or burdens of inertia may also be politically legitimate, but only where they enjoy some meaningful degree of *legal* support, or are designed to counter a serious and irreversible risk to human dignity, or systemic forms of inertia or state failure.

These principles do not exhaust the scope for legitimate constitutional implications by courts. Democracy, as Chapter 3 notes, can be understood in thinner and thicker ways, as encompassing only certain political rights and freedoms (such as the right to vote and freedom of expression, assembly, and association)

---

[17] Compare in this context the notion of failures of protection of CA that involve "spiraling costs": *see* Rosalind Dixon & Martha C. Nussbaum, *Children's Rights and a Capabilities Approach: The Question of Special Priority*, 97 CORNELL L. REV. 549, 578–83 (2012).

or broader rights to dignity, equality, and freedom for all individuals. Threats to these other values may also provide a case for identifying certain constitutional implications. And even thicker understandings of democracy do not exhaust the full range of values that can inform processes of constitutional construction.

Other values may include commitments to the rule of law, ethnic and religious pluralism, or constitutional stability or unity. And threats to these commitments or values may again provide a persuasive political rationale for certain constitutional implications. In Canada, for example, one of the best-known decisions of the Supreme Court of Canada (SCC) arose in the *Secession Reference* case, where the Court identified certain implied principles governing any attempt by Québec to secede from Canada.[18] The decision also had quite weak textual or formal legal foundations.[19] But one could argue that it had far greater political justification or legitimacy: it provided a jurisprudential response to an urgent and systemic threat to the unity and stability of the Canadian constitutional compact.[20]

Overlaid with these principles will also be the need for judges to consider the evidence or facts before them that establish democratic risks of this kind. The notion of responsive judicial review emphasizes both the idea that judicial review should seek to protect and promote the capacity of a democratic constitutional system to respond to constitutional claims and democratic majority understandings *and* that courts should be responsive to their own institutional position and role.

In many constitutional systems, especially those in the Anglo-American world, one of the defining features of the judicial role is also that it involves applying the law to a given set of facts.[21] And constitutional courts play a limited role in gathering facts and making findings of fact: often, they decide constitutional questions on the basis of agreed facts, or findings made by lower courts.

---

[18] Reference Re Secession of Québec, [1998] 2 S.C.R. 217. *See further* Nathalie Des Rosiers, *From Québec Veto to Québec Secession: The Evolution of the Supreme Court of Canada on Québec-Canada Disputes*, 13 CAN. J.L. & JURIS. 171 (2000); Pierre Bienvenu, *Secession by Constitutional Means: The Decision of the Supreme Court of Canada in the Québec Secession Reference*, 23 HAMLINE J. PUB. L. & POL'Y 185 (2001); THE QUÉBEC DECISION: PERSPECTIVES ON THE SUPREME COURT RULING ON SECESSION (David Schneiderman ed., 1999).

[19] *See* THE QUÉBEC DECISION, *supra* note 18; Richard S. Kay, *The Secession Reference and the Limits of Law*, 10 OTAGO L. REV. 327 (2003); Sujit Choudhry & Robert Howse, *Constitutional Theory and the Québec Secession Reference*, 13 CAN. J.L. & JURIS. 143 (2000).

[20] For how the SCC preserved its sociological legitimacy in doing so, see also Vuk Radmilovic, *Strategic Legitimacy Cultivation at the Supreme Court of Canada: Québec References and Beyond*, 43 CAN. J. POL. SCI. 843 (2010).

[21] DAVID L. FAIGMAN, CONSTITUTIONAL FICTIONS: A UNIFIED THEORY OF CONSTITUTIONAL FACTS (2008); Malcolm Langford, *Why Judicial Review*, 2 OSLO L. REV. 36 (2015). For discussion on the difference between common law and civilian systems in this context, see Chapter 5, *infra*.

In some cases, there may also be insufficient evidence of any actual risk to democracy for a court to be justified in making implications based on the need to respond to such risks.

In general, however, these principles provide quite clear, concrete guidance to courts as they engage in the task of construing a written constitution. To begin with, they suggest that courts should give effect to the ordinary and natural language of specific constitutional guarantees, and construe more open-ended constitutional language in ways informed by a concern to overcome risks of electoral or institutional monopoly, democratic blind spots, and burdens of inertia. In addition, it suggests that courts should consider risks to the democratic minimum core, and evidence of urgent or systemic harm arising from democratic blind spots or burdens of inertia in deciding whether to make true implications under a written constitution.

C. Responsive Review in Practice

Take the questions of constructional choice set out earlier relating to abortion, LGBTQI+ rights, implied rights to freedom of speech and equality, structural social rights, and the unconstitutional amendment doctrine. In Chapter 5, I explore how and whether these decisions in fact succeeded in overcoming relevant democratic blockages. But here I note the degree to which their attempt to do so did, or did not, provide an argument for the political legitimacy of these decisions.

1. Abortion rights

Even before *Casey* and *Dobbs*, the US Supreme Court's decision in *Roe v. Wade* had been criticized as lacking both political and legal legitimacy.[22] At a political level, the Court in *Roe* helped counter inertia in the recognition of rights of access to abortion in many states. But as Chapter 6 explores, it also arguably extended rights of access to abortion beyond the point supported by a majority of Americans. This, in turn, increased the need for the Court to show strong legal justification for a finding that the Constitution recognized a "right to privacy" encompassing a right of access to abortion, and many legal scholars were not persuaded by the Court's reasoning in this context.

---

[22] *See* Chapter 6, *infra*.

The Court in *Roe* relied heavily on the doctor–patient relationship as the basis for the relevant right to privacy, and on its prior reasoning in *Griswold*, which was itself somewhat strained.[23] The Court in *Griswold* suggested that a right to privacy could be derived from "penumbras and emanations" of the First, Third, Fourth, and Fifth Amendments to the Constitution (Justice Douglas),[24] or common law rights and freedoms preserved by the Ninth Amendment (Justice Goldberg).[25] To many, this was far less persuasive than the reasoning of Justice Harlan in *Poe v. Ullman*, which suggested that "liberty ... was not an isolated pinprick" but a continuum of rights and interests deserving constitutional protection (and which arguably included rights of access to abortion).[26] Indeed, it was seen by many as a thinly disguised attempt to avoid the perception that the Court was engaged in a form of *Lochner*-style substantive due process analysis.[27]

Casey, in contrast, arguably enjoyed a higher degree of legal and political legitimacy. The Court's approach to *stare decisis* in *Casey* was clearly strained, and to that extent enjoyed quite weak legal legitimacy.[28] But as a matter of first principle, it located the right to privacy within a more compelling legal framework than the Court in *Roe*. Instead of relying on the somewhat strained logic of *Griswold*, or a notion of doctor–patient relationship as underpinning the right of access to abortion, the Court in *Casey* relied on the express guarantee of a woman's right to *liberty* in the Due Process Clause of the Fourteenth Amendment as grounding the right of access to abortion.[29]

The Court in *Casey* also narrowed its previous ruling in *Roe* so that it effectively allowed American women broad access to abortion prior to a fetus being

---

[23] Roe v. Wade, 410 U.S. 113, 153 (1973) (noting that the abortion decision is to be weighed by a "woman and her responsible physician ... in consultation"), 153–54 (noting that the "right of privacy, whether it be founded in the Fourteenth Amendment's concept of personal liberty and restrictions upon state action, as we feel it is, or, as the District Court determined, in the Ninth Amendment's reservation of rights to the people, is broad enough to encompass a woman's decision whether or not to terminate her pregnancy"), 165 (noting "the right of a physician to administer medical treatment according to his professional judgment" in this context).

[24] Griswold v. Connecticut, 381 U.S. 479, 484 (1965) (Douglas J).

[25] *Id.* at 488–89 (Goldberg J).

[26] Poe v. Ullman, 367 U.S. 497, 522 (1961) (Harlan J).

[27] *See* Joshua D. Hawley, *The Intellectual Origins of (Modern) Substantive Due Process*, 93 Tex. L. Rev. 275, 324–25 (2014); David O. Conkle, *Three Theories of Substantive Due Process*, 85 N. C. L. Rev. 63, 71–72 (2006).

[28] *See* Planned Parenthood v. Casey, 505 U.S. 833, 979-81 (1992) (Scalia J., dissenting), Dobbs v Jackson Women's Health Organization, 597 U.S. ___ 45–47 (2022) (Alito J., writing for the court), and discussion in Chapter 6, *infra*. *See also* Chris Whitman, *Looking Back on Planned Parenthood v. Casey*, 100 Mich. L. Rev. 1980 (2002); Paul Benjamin Linton & Maura Quinlan, *Does Stare Decisis Preclude Reconsideration of Roe v. Wade? A Critique of Planned Parenthood v. Casey*, 70 Case W. Res. L. Rev. 283 (2019).

[29] Planned Parenthood v. Casey, 505 U.S. 833, Pt II 846–47 (1992).

independently viable, but with the ability of legislatures to regulate access—providing they did not in the process impose an "undue burden" on the relevant constitutional right. This was arguably closer in line with democratic understandings about the scope of reproductive rights than *Roe*: a clear majority of Americans, both pre- and post-*Roe*, have suggested that they believe that abortion should be "safe, legal but rare."[30] And while this does not tell us their specific views on the questions at issue in *Casey*—that is, whether it should be constitutionally permissible to impose waiting periods, counselling requirements, or parental or spousal notification requirements as conditions of access to abortion—it does suggest democratic support for measures that can discourage access to abortion, without making it practically unavailable or unsafe. This also has important parallels with the "undue burden" approach adopted in *Casey*, and how it was applied by the Court (i.e., to uphold most of these measures, if reasonable, with the exception of spousal notification requirements).[31] And it suggests that the decision by the Court in *Dobbs*, to overrule *Casey* and *Roe*, and return decisions about access to abortion to local political majorities, lacked broader national *democratic* support and legitimacy.

Part of the premise of the Court's reasoning in *Dobbs* was that decisions such as *Roe* and *Casey* lacked legal legitimacy. But a right of access to abortion finds strong textual support in the guarantee of liberty in the Due Process Clause, and in the Court's decisions from *Roe* onwards. It also finds democratic support in national majority opinion and the fact that state legislatures routinely restrict access to abortion as a result of legislative blind spots and burdens of inertia. That is, they pass restrictions on access to abortion that fail to account for the range of ways in which those restrictions can affect young, poor, and socially vulnerable women, and decline to revisit previous restrictions in light of changing understandings about the appropriate balance between women's rights and fetal rights and/or interests.[32]

---

[30] *See Abortion*, GALLUP (2021), <https://news.gallup.com/poll/1576/abortion.aspx>; *US Public Continues to Favor Legal Abortion, Oppose Overturning Roe v. Wade*, PEW RES. CTR. (Aug. 29, 2019), <https://www.people-press.org/2019/08/29/u-s-public-continues-to-favor-legal-abortion-oppose-overturning-roe-v-wade/>.

[31] Of course, one difference could be that the undue burden test is designed to discourage access to abortion where certain conditions are not met, whereas popular opinion may favor allowing but discouraging access in a broader range of cases. But there is still meaningful overlap between the two ideas, in terms of the permission/deterrence dyad. There is also some evidence of specific democratic majority support for measures such as twenty-four-hour waiting periods: *see* Ashley Kirzinger et al., *Abortion Knowledge and Attitudes: KFF Polling and Policy Insights*, HENRY J. KAISER FAM. FOUND. (Jan. 22, 2020), <https://www.kff.org/womens-health-policy/poll-finding/abortion-knowledge-and-attitudes-kff-polling-and-policy-insights/> (showing 50 percent support among Democrats, 70 percent among Independents, and 86 percent among registered Republicans).

[32] *See* Sharon Luyre, *Exceptions to Abortion Bans May Be Hard For Women to Access*, U.S. NEWS (June 3, 2022), <https://www.usnews.com/news/best-states/articles/2022-06-03/why-exceptions-to-abort

A similar analysis could explain, or justify, the Court's insistence in cases such as *Carhart I* and *Carhart II* on the protection of women's life and health as a reason for guaranteeing a constitutional right of access to abortion. In *Carhart I*, the Supreme Court extended the reasoning in *Casey* to cover access to late-term abortion. It struck down a Nebraska statute prohibiting access to "partial birth" abortion procedures on two grounds: first, that the statute in question failed adequately to distinguish between intact (D&X) and non-intact (D&E) dilation and extraction procedures for late-term abortion, and was thus unconstitutionally vague; and second, that the state had not shown that use of D&X procedures were "never necessary to preserve the health of women."[33] And in *Carhart II*, while the Court upheld a subsequent federal law reimposing restrictions on both D&X and D&E procedures, in doing so it again affirmed the importance of protecting women's life and health in the context of post-viability abortion decisions.[34]

The text of the US Constitution, and case law prior to *Roe*, provide limited support for this insistence on the protection of a right to health. The Due Process Clause of the Fourteenth Amendment clearly protects a woman's life and liberty, and rights of this kind are closely connected to the right to health. But the right to health is more closely connected to a commitment to protecting human dignity—in the capabilities sense, of a life worthy of full human dignity.[35] And a commitment to dignity has only found recognition in more recent decisions of the Court such as *Lawrence* and *Obergefell*.[36]

---

ion-bans-may-be-hard-for-women-to-access>, David Welch & Francesca Maglione, *Overturning Roe Opens Door for Long-Dormant State Abortion Bans*, BLOOMBERG. (May 4, 2022), <https://www.bloomberg.com/news/articles/2022-05-03/overturning-roe-could-revive-long-dormant-state-abortion-bans>. This is also in addition to the fact that many state legislatures are the product of forms of political monopoly power and its exercise through extreme forms of partisan gerrymandering: *see* Jonathan Weisman & Jazmine Ulloa, *Supreme Court Throws Abortion to an Unlevel State Playing Field*, N.Y. TIMES (June 25, 2022), <https://www.nytimes.com/2022/06/25/us/politics/abortion-ruling-states.html?action=click&pgtype=Article&state=default&module=styln-abortion-us&variant=show&region=BELOW_MAIN_CONTENT&block=storyline_flex_guide_recirc>. See also discussion in Rosalind Dixon & David Landau, 'Dobbs, Democracy and Dysfunction' (Working Paper, 2022).

[33] Stenberg v. Carhart, 530 U.S. 914 (2000).
[34] Gonzales v. Carhart, 550 U.S. 124 (2007). For the failure by the Court adequately to recognize a life/health exception to the general prohibition on D&X procedures, *see* 550 U.S. 124, 161–68 (2007) (Ginsburg J., dissenting); Vicki C. Jackson, *Thayer, Holmes, Brandeis: Conceptions of Judicial Review, Factfinding and Proportionality*, 130 HARV. L. REV. 2348, 2380–83 (2017).
[35] Martha Nussbaum & Rosalind Dixon, *Abortion, Dignity and a Capabilities Approach*, *in* FEMINIST CONSTITUTIONALISM: GLOBAL PERSPECTIVES (Beverly Baines et al. eds., 2012).
[36] Lawrence v. Texas, 539 U.S. 558 (2003); Obergefell v. Hodges, 576 U.S. 644 (2015). *See* Mark Strasser, *Obergefell, Dignity, and the Family*, 19 J. GENDER RACE & JUST. 317 (2016); Autumn L. Bernhardt, *The Profound and Intimate Power of the Obergefell Decision: Equal Dignity as a Suspect Class*, 1 TULANE J.L. & SEXUALITY 25 (2016).

The decisions in *Carhart I* and *II*, however, had a strong claim to political legitimacy: while democratic support for access to much lower in the third as opposed to first trimester of pregnancy, 75 percent of Americans support the idea that there should be access to a third trimester abortion in order to protect a woman's life from a serious threat.[37] And the failure by Congress clearly to authorize access to medically necessary D&E procedures was an arguable blind spot of application. Blind spots of this kind can also never be cured by the legislature in time to benefit the plaintiffs in a case of this kind. The urgency of the democratic blockage in question, therefore, provided a strong political justification for the Court in both *Carhart I* and *II* to insist on health- and life-based limitations on Congress' power to limit access to late-term abortion.

The decisions of the SCC and the Colombian and Korean constitutional courts broadening access to abortion could likewise be seen as responding to burdens of inertia in the recognition of reproductive rights. In Canada, there was growing support for liberalizing access to legal abortion from the 1960s onwards, and a sustained effort in the 1970s by groups such as the Canadian Medical Association and the Canadian Bar Association to achieve this. In 1977, an independent, federally appointed committee (the Badgley Committee) also recommended major legal change in the area. The political process, however, was extremely slow to respond.[38] In 1986, Parliament made minor changes to the Canadian *Criminal Code* to allow broader access to therapeutic abortions, in accredited hospitals, but failed to address the broader issues raised by the Badgley Committee, or the fact that the existing system imposed significant restrictions on access to abortion in many parts of Canada.[39] Therefore, in striking down the relevant provisions of the *Criminal Code* in *Morgentaler*, the SCC arguably helped counter persistent legislative inertia affecting the progress of national abortion law reform in Canada.[40]

The decision in *Morgentaler* also arguably helped counter blind spots of application on the part of the Parliament about the effect of the Code in rural and regional areas in Canada: while the provisions allowed some access to abortion in major urban centers, in some rural parts of Canada there was simply not the necessary number of doctors available to form a committee and then perform the procedure, and a range of provincial regulations existed discouraging

---

[37] Lydia Saad, *Trimesters Still Key to U.S. Abortion Views*, GALLUP (Jun. 13, 2018), <https://news.gallup.com/poll/235469/trimesters-key-abortion-views.aspx>.
[38] Mollie Dunsmuir, *Abortion: Constitutional and Legal Developments* (Report, Aug. 18, 1998), <https://publications.gc.ca/Collection-R/LoPBdP/CIR/8910-e.htm>.
[39] *Id.*
[40] For the complexity to this, and the fact that it arguably also led to reverse burdens of inertia, see Chapter 6, *infra*.

hospitals from gaining the relevant specialization.[41] This was also an effect of the law seemingly unforeseen by legislators seeking to create *controlled access* to abortion, under section 251 of the *Criminal Code*. And while access today remains uneven, it is much broader and more consistent across Canada than it was prior to the SCC's intervention in *Morgentaler*.

In Colombia, constitutional litigation over access to abortion has likewise helped overcome legislative burdens of inertia. Public support for access to abortion is substantially weaker in Colombia, compared to the United States and Canada, but has been progressively increasing, at least in certain cases.[42] Yet legislators have been unwilling to introduce legislation giving effect to these changing attitudes. In striking down the criminal prohibition on access to abortion, and granting direct access to abortion where continuing a pregnancy threatened a woman's life, physical or mental health, was the result of rape, incest, or another crime, or involved "medically certified malformations of the fetus," the Court thus helped counter a clear form of democratic blockage.[43]

In South Korea, in finding provisions of the *Criminal Code* prohibiting access to abortion conditionally unconstitutional, the Court likewise helped counter democratic burdens of inertia. Prior to the Court's decision, access to abortion in Korea was governed by provisions of the *Criminal Code* enacted in 1953, which made it a crime to perform or obtain an abortion—except in cases of rape, incest, or where continuing the pregnancy posed a threat to a woman's life or health. These provisions were enacted at a time where abortion was discouraged, in part because of a concern about sex-selective abortion.[44] But over time, there was a gradual shift toward increased social and political acceptance of abortion. In the 1970s and 1980s, Korean governments moved toward greater acceptance of abortion as a means of limiting population growth, whereas in the 1990s they discouraged it, as part of an attempt to reverse a declining birthdate.[45] Among the public, however, there was a steady

---

[41] R. v. Morgentaler, [1998] 1 S.C.R. 30, 33.

[42] *See Only 20% Would Agree that Women Who Get An Abortion Should Go to Jail*, EL ESPECTADOR (Jun. 18, 2021, 5:22 AM), <https://www.elespectador.com/actualidad/solo-el-20-estaria-de-acuerdo-con-que-las-mujeres-que-aborten-en-colombia-vayan-a-la-carcel/>.

[43] MANUEL JOSÉ CEPEDA ESPINOSA & DAVID E. LANDAU, COLOMBIAN CONSTITUTIONAL LAW: LEADING CASES 5, 77–78 (2017). As Chapter 7 explores in more detail, the decision was later codified in guidelines issues by the Colombian Ministry for Health (Decree 4444), but those guidelines were struck down by the Council of State, in ways that forced petitions to fall back on direct reliance on the Court's decision in this context: Alba Ruibal, *Movement and Counter-Movement: A History of Abortion Law Reform and the Backlash in Colombia 2006–2014*, 22 REPROD. HEALTH MATTERS 42, 44 (2014).

[44] Jeong-In Yun, *Recent Abortion Decision of Korean Constitutional Court*, IACL BLOG (Jul. 31, 2019), <https://blog-iacl-aidc.org/2019-posts/2019/7/31/recent-abortion-decision-of-korean-constitutional-court>.

[45] Choe Sang-Hun, *South Korea Rules Anti-Abortion Law Unconstitutional*, N.Y. TIMES, Apr. 11, 2019, <https://www.nytimes.com/2019/04/11/world/asia/south-korea-abortion-ban-ruling.html>.

increase in support for a legal right of access to abortion. In 2019, for example, a government survey showed 75 percent support for increased access to abortion among Korean women aged between fifteen and forty-four.[46] When the Court's decision ultimately decriminalized access to abortion in 2021, after further failed attempts by the National Assembly to address the issue, the result was therefore arguably both a more rights-protective and democracy-respecting legal position on abortion.[47]

2. LGBTQI+ rights

Court decisions expanding access to LGBTQI+ rights can likewise be seen as responding to complex forms of legislative inertia. Most of these decisions are best understood as involving the construction of express but open-ended guarantees of freedom, privacy, dignity, and equality—not the "implication" of freestanding guarantees distinct from these rights. But they have nonetheless involved a degree of constructional choice that can be assessed through the same lens of a concern about the legal and political legitimacy of judicial review.

Part of their claim to legitimacy, in this context, is also that they have combined a strong textual basis (i.e., legal legitimacy) with the political legitimacy that comes from helping to counter urgent threats to human dignity, and persistent legislative burdens of inertia. And in many cases the two sources of legitimacy have overlapped: the text of the relevant constitutions explicitly protects rights to dignity and equality, and courts' role has been to realize those commitments by overcoming blind spots and burdens of inertia.

In Canada, for instance, in the late 1990s and early 2000s there was growing support for the recognition of LGBTQI+ rights at a national level, but arguable coalition-driven forms of inertia in the passage of laws reflecting this shift in attitudes. Within the national government, as Canadian political scientist Miriam Smith notes, there was real "opposition to lesbian and gay rights from a small group of pro-family MPs," and the rise of the Reform Party and the Bloc Québecois made the government "highly sensitive to the opposition to lesbian and gay rights from within their own party."[48] Similar dynamics were at play at

---

[46] Id.

[47] *South Korea: Abortion Decriminalized Since January 1, 2021*, US LIBRARY OF CONGRESS (Mar. 18, 2021), <https://www.loc.gov/item/global-legal-monitor/2021-03-18/south-korea-abortion-decriminalized-since-january-1-2021/>.

[48] Miriam Smith, *Social Movements and Judicial Empowerment: Courts, Public Policy, and Lesbian and Gay Organizing in Canada*, 33 POL. & SOC. 327 (2005).

a provincial level. The result was that from the mid-1990s onwards, there was very little legislation passed in Canada expanding LGBTQI+ rights, other than as a direct response to litigation before Canadian courts.

In South Africa, from the 1990s onwards a clear gap emerged between the dominant faction and more left-wing faction of the African National Congress (ANC) government on issues of sexuality. And while this gap was most visible in the context of issues relating to HIV/AIDS, it extended to the issue of gay and lesbian rights. The left-wing of the party supported broad recognition and respect for LGBTQI+ rights, whereas the right-wing of the party raised questions about the consistency of gay and lesbian sexuality with "African values."[49] The result was that the National Assembly made no independent move to promote LGBTQI+ rights. Indeed, for the first two years following the transition to democracy, the Apartheid-era ban on sodomy in the *Sexual Offences Act* of 1957 remained on the books, despite the express prohibition in the 1993 South African Constitution of discrimination on the grounds of sexual orientation. The Assembly also made no move to give broader recognition to same-sex relationships, absent direct prompting from the courts.

In Colombia, there was likewise growing popular and elite support from the early 2000s onwards for the recognition of LGBTQI+ rights. Gay Pride parades began to be held in Bogotá and other major cities, and there were increasing numbers of openly gay media personalities.[50] Popular support for same-sex marriage also progressively increased: In 2010, 34 percent of Colombians expressed support for same-sex marriage, and by 2016 that number had risen to 40 percent.[51] In the 2006 presidential election, President Uribe supported extending property and other economic rights to same-sex couples, and in 2014, President Santos came out in favor of same-sex marriage.[52] At the same time, there was powerful opposition from within both the government and the Catholic Church, which effectively blocked successive legislative attempts

---

[49] *Id. See* National Coalition for Gay and Lesbian Equality v. Minister of Justice, 1999 (1) SA 6 (CC).

[50] José Fernando Serrano-Amaya, *Modernities in Dispute: the Debates on Marriage Equality in Colombia* (Paper presented at the Cultural Studies Association of Australasia Conference, Adelaide, Nov. 22–24, 2011); Mauricio Albarracín Caballero, *Social Movements and the Constitutional Court: Legal Recognition of the Rights of Same-Sex Couples in Colombia*, 8 INT'L J. HUM. RTS. 7, 12–13 (2011).

[51] *See* Adriana Piatti-Crocker & Jason Pierceson, *Unpacking the Backlash to Marriage Equality in Latin America* 11 (Paper presented at the Western Political Science Association Annual Meeting, San Francisco, Mar. 29–31, 2018).

[52] *See* Caballero, *supra* note 50, at 20; Chris Herlinger, *In Catholic Colombia, LGBT People Find Growing Acceptance*, WASH. POST (Aug. 24, 2005), <https://www.washingtonpost.com/national/religion/in-catholic-colombia-lgbt-people-find-growing-acceptance/2015/08/24/9a23ec08-4a99-11e5-9f53-d1e3ddfd0cda_story.html>.

to broaden recognition of same-sex relationships.[53] From 2009 to 2016, the National Inspector General, Alejandro Ordóñez, was a conservative Catholic who used the considerable powers of his office to block attempts to expand same-sex rights—including through public opposition and threats to discipline governmental officials who supported gay rights.[54] And the Church consistently opposed proposals to expand same-sex rights, so that legislative attempts to change the law in this direction were invariably defeated, or failed to reach a vote on the floor, in Congress.[55]

In the United Kingdom (UK), the Blair Labour government initially took decisive steps to expand legal recognition of LGBTQI+ rights by introducing legislation to equalize the legal age of consent to sexual intercourse for same-sex and opposite-sex intercourse and by repealing the provisions of the *Local Government Act 1988* (UK) introduced by the Thatcher government, prohibiting local authorities from "intentionally promot[ing] homosexuality or publish[ing] material with the intention of promoting homosexuality" or "promot[ing] the teaching in any maintained school of homosexuality as a presented family relationship."[56] Thereafter, however, divisions emerged within the Labour Party as to how far it should go in implementing campaign promises to eliminate various forms of discrimination against gays and lesbians. In 2000, the Home Secretary sought to introduce legislation which would have repealed the criminal prohibition of sexual intercourse between adult males where more than two people were present, but the prime minister blocked the move out of concern for the party's electoral support.[57] In 2002, when the government introduced legislation designed to allow same-sex couples access to adoption, major division within the party forced the party leadership to allow a free vote on the issue, and the legislation was ultimately defeated by the decision of twenty Labour Members of the House of Lords to vote with the Conservatives in opposing the Bill.[58] No further legislative change in this area therefore occurred until 2013, absent direct prompting from British and European courts.

---

[53] *See, e.g., Colombian Court Says Congress Must Decide on Gay Marriage*, CNN, Jul. 27, 2011, <http://edition.cnn.com/2011/WORLD/americas/07/27/colombia.gay.marriage/index.html> (noting opposition from several Colombian churches).

[54] Mauricio Albarracin & Julieta Lemaitre, *The Crusade Against Same-Sex Marriage in Colombia*, 8 RELIGION & GENDER 32, 36 (2018).

[55] GERMÁN LODOLA & MARGARITA CORRAL, SUPPORT FOR SAME SEX MARRIAGE IN LATIN AMERICA 1 (2010); Albarracin & Lemaitre, *supra* note 54.

[56] Philip Britton, *Gay and Lesbian Rights in the United Kingdom: The Story Continued*, 10 IND. INT'L & COMP. L. REV. 207 (2000).

[57] *Id.*

[58] *Adoption and Children Act 2002* (UK).

In Hong Kong, political support for LGBTQI+ rights has been more limited still.[59] But the "rainbow community" in Hong Kong has been growing in size and visibility, and in its calls for changes to outlaw discrimination on the grounds of sexual orientation and transgender identity.[60] There has also been an increasing willingness by key institutions—including both Chinese and English-language newspapers, such as the *South China Morning Post*—to support these calls, and a series of private member bills and working groups calling for legal change.[61] The Chief of the Executive Council and various pro-business law-makers have expressed support for LGBTQI+ rights.[62] But the government has been slow to act, largely out of a concern to be seen to go too far ahead of Hong Kong citizens' and their conservative views on family norms, and to encourage forms of LGBTQI+ activism that have (too) close ties to the pro-democracy Umbrella movement.[63] Decisions such as *Leung* and *W v. Registrar*, therefore, could arguably be seen as either classic instances of Ely-style minority rights protection *or* decisions that help promote both minority rights and evolving majority understandings by countering legislative burdens of inertia.

In India, while there remains significant discrimination against the transgender community, there has been a growing consensus about the need for legislative reform to recognize transgender status, or a "third gender."[64] In 2015, Prime Minister Narendra Modi stated publicly that the government "need[ed] to amend and make new laws for transgenders [sic]."[65] This did not occur, however, until after the decision in *NALSA* and the passage of several more

---

[59] Craig Hoyle, *An Uphill Battle for Hong Kong's Rainbow Community*, SAMESAME.COM (Nov. 30, 2015); Phil C. Chan, *Same-Sex Marriage/Constitutionalism and their Centrality to Equality Rights in Hong Kong: A Comparative-Socio-Legal Appraisal*, 11 INT'L J. HUM. RTS. 33 (2007); Phil W. Chan, *The Lack of Sexual Orientation Anti-Discrimination Legislation in Hong Kong Breach of International and Domestic Legal Obligations*, 9 INT'L J. HUM. RTS. 69 (2005).

[60] Craig Hoyle, *An Uphill Battle for Hong Kong's Rainbow Community*, Samesame.com (Nov. 30, 2015).

[61] Nigel Collett, *Ms W v. The Hong Kong Registrar of Marriages*, FRIDAE CONNECTING GAY ASIA (Aug. 19, 2010), <https://www.fridae.asia/gay-news/2010/08/19/10235.ms-w-vs-the-hong-kong-registrar-of-marriages>; Chan, *Same-Sex Marriage/Constitutionalism and their Centrality to Equality Rights in Hong Kong*, supra note 59, at 44–45.

[62] Chris Lau & Lilian Cheng, *Hong Kong Leader Carrie Lam Says City Will Support Gay Games, and Calls Lawmaker's Hate-Filled Outburst "Unnecessarily Divisive,"* S. CHINA MORNING POST (Jun. 15, 2021), <https://www.scmp.com/news/hong-kong/politics/article/3137333/hong-kong-leader-carrie-lam-says-city-will-support-gay>.

[63] Hoyle, *An Uphill Battle for Hong Kong's Rainbow Community*, supra note 59.

[64] Satya Prakash, *The Law is Not Moved: SC Puts Decriminalising Homosexuality on Backburner*, HINDUSTAN TIMES (Jun. 30, 2016) <https://www.hindustantimes.com/editorials/the-law-is-not-moved-sc-puts-decriminalising-homosexuality-on-backburner/story-OYppBrGLPeHBFi1iIQwxJI.html>; Padmapriya Govindarajan, *Beyond Section 377: Where Does India's LGBT Movement Stand*, THE DIPLOMAT (Jun. 7, 2016), <https://thediplomat.com/2016/07/beyond-section-377-where-does-indias-lgbt-movement-stand/>.

[65] Prakash, *supra* note 64.

years—suggesting the existence of quite powerful priority-driven forms of inertia in the recognition of transgender rights.[66]

Democratic support for gay and lesbian rights in India remains more limited. While results vary, some opinion polls show that a democratic majority recently opposed the recognition of LGBTQI+ identity.[67] If true, this would also suggest that decisions such as *Johar* have largely been counter- rather than pro-majoritarian in nature. A decision of this kind could be still justified as necessary to effect to basic liberal democratic commitments to equality, mutual respect, and non-domination among citizens.[68] But in this case, *Johar* could not properly be treated as an example of the Supreme Court of India promoting greater democratic responsiveness to LGBTQI+ rights, as opposed to constitutional commitments to equality. As elsewhere, however, there is also evidence of increasing democratic support for the recognition of LGBTQI+ rights in India. Many public opinion polls do not particularize the kind of recognition involved—so they may, for example, overstate the degree of opposition to decriminalizing sodomy, as opposed to recognizing same-sex relationships. There is also growing support for LGBTQI+ rights among younger Indian voters, in civil society, Bollywood, and in Gay Pride parades in major Indian cities.[69] The 172nd Law Commission of India recommended the repeal of section 377.[70] And an increased number of Indian elected representatives—engaged in norms of democratic constitutional deliberation—have suggested that section 377 of the *Criminal Code* is inconsistent with constitutional commitments to dignity and equality and should be repealed.

Prior to *Johar*, for example, there were two decisions on the constitutionality of section 377 of the *Criminal Code*—a decision of the High Court of Delhi, *Naz Foundation v. Government of India* (*Naz*), striking down section

---

[66] *Transgender Persons (Protection of Rights) Act 2019* (India).

[67] Ira Trivedi, *The Indian in the Closet: New Delhi's Wrong Turn on Gay Rights*, FOREIGN AFF. Mar./Apr. 2014, at 21 (reporting the results of a nationwide CNN-IBN poll); Sadanand Dhume, *The Politics of Gay Rights in India*, WALL ST. J. (Jul. 2, 2015), <https://www.wsj.com/articles/the-politicsl-of-gay-rights-in-india-1435854890> (reporting results of Pew Research Center poll); Siddharth Narrain, *Lost in Appeal: The Downward Spiral from Naz to Koushal*, 6 NUJS L. REV. 4 (2013); Vikram Chandrasekhar, *The Denial of LGBT Rights and Civil Liberties in India: A Comprehensive Critique*, NUALS L.J. (Mar. 24, 2020) <https://nualslawjournal.com/2020/03/24/the-denial-of-lgbt-rights-and-civil-liberties-in-india-a-comprehensive-critique/>.

[68] *See, e.g.*, Robert Wintemute, *Lesbian, Gay, Bisexual and Transgender Human Rights in India: From Naz Foundation to Navtej Singh Johar and Beyond*, 12 NUJS L. REV. 3 (2019).

[69] Raghu Karnad, *Hope for LGBT Rights in India*, N.Y. TIMES, Jan. 19, 2016, <https://www.nytimes.com/2016/01/20/opinion/hope-for-lgbt-rights-in-india.html>; *Refusing to be Criminals (Again): Struggle for Equality Continues in India*, UMBC I3B: INITIATIVES FOR IDENTITY, INCLUSION AND BELONGING (Dec. 13, 2013), <https://i3b.umbc.edu/?id=39459>; Trivedi, *supra* note 67; Danish Sheikh, *The Road to Decriminalisation: Litigating India's Anti-Sodomy Law*, 16 YALE HUM. RTS. & DEV. L.J. 104, 116–18 (2013).

[70] Navtej Singh Johar v. Union of India, AIR 2018 SC 4321 at 111 [92].

377, and a subsequent decision of the Supreme Court of India (SCI) in *Suresh Kumar Koushal v. Naz Foundation* reversing *Naz*, and reinstating the criminal prohibition on sodomy.[71] Beginning with *Naz*, key government and political actors also began to express public support for the repeal of section 377. In *Naz* itself, the Home Ministry sought to defend section 377 of the *Penal Code* against constitutional challenge, whereas the Ministry of Health supported the challenge.[72] The government chose not to appeal the decision, and in *Koushal* and *Johar*, did not seek to defend the constitutionality of section 377.[73] And after the SCI's decision in *Koushal*, the Congress Party, Aam Admi Party, and Communist Party all continued to express support for the repeal of section 377.[74] But both Congress and the Bharatiya Janata Party (BJP) declined to put the issue on the legislative agenda in the lead-up to national elections.[75] There was also evidence of division on the issue within the BJP itself. While the party initially supported the decision in *Koushal*, it subsequently endorsed the approach of the Delhi High Court in *Naz*.[76] BJP government ministers have also split on the issue. For example, in 2016, the national Finance Minister expressed support for the repeal of section 377, while the Home Minister opposed it—suggesting that a national "consensus" was required before change was adopted.[77]

The decision in *Johar* also arguably enjoyed a high degree of legal legitimacy. In adopting a narrow reading of section 377 of the *Penal Code*, which excluded consensual sexual intercourse, the Court in *Johar* was required to overrule the decision of the three-judge bench in *Koushal*.[78] But the decision in *Koushal* had obvious flaws: it adopted a formalist view of equality, rejected the relevance of

---

[71] (NCT) 160 DLT 277; (2014) 1 SCC 1.

[72] *Supreme Court Pulls up Centre for Flip-Flop on Homosexuality*, INDIAN EXPRESS (Oct. 31, 2016), <https://indianexpress.com/article/news-archive/latest-news/supreme-court-pulls-up-centre-for-flipflop-on-homosexuality/>.

[73] *Johar*, *supra* note 70 at 103 [80]. *See* discussion in Tarunabh Khaitan, *Koushal v. Naz: Judges Vote to Recriminalise Homosexuality*, 78 MOD. L. REV. 672, 677 (2015).

[74] Satya Prakash, *SC Haring on Gay Sex: All You Need to Know About Section 377*, HINDUSTAN TIMES (Feb. 2, 2016), <https://www.hindustantimes.com/india/sc-hearing-on-gay-sex-today-india-s-struggle-with-sec-377-explained/story-PH22Ogrrwgsw9mtNTBKXTM.html>; Trivedi, *supra* note 67; Dhume, *supra* note 67.

[75] Bhanu Bhatnagar, *India's LGBT Community Celebrates a Small Victory*, AL JAZEERA (Feb. 5, 2016), <https://www.aljazeera.com/features/2016/2/5/indias-lgbt-community-celebrates-a-small-victory> ("Just months before a general election, no political party was willing to champion LGBT rights for fear of alienating mainstream voters").

[76] K.C. Archana, *As SC Refers Section 377 Appeal to Chief Justice, Here's a Look at its History*, INDIATODAY (Jun. 29, 2016) <https://www.indiatoday.in/fyi/story/tracing-the-history-of-the-section-377-scs-final-call-to-cast-aside-the-punitive-law-11698-2016-06-29>.

[77] *Id. See also* Dean Nelson, *India's Top Court Upholds Law Criminalising Gay Sex*, THE TELEGRAPH (Dec. 22, 2013) <https://www.telegraph.co.uk/news/worldnews/asia/india/10509952/Indias-top-court-upholds-law-criminalising-gay-sex.html>; Prakash, *supra* note 64; Dhume, *supra* note 67.

[78] *Johar*, *supra* note 70, at 110 [89].

comparative law reasoning, and suggested that the degree of judicial protection for minority rights should be *positively* (rather than negatively) correlated to the size of the relevant minority—so that small minorities, which the *Koushal* Court identified as including LGBTQI+ Indians, were entitled to lesser rather than greater judicial protection than larger minorities.[79] This reasoning had also been effectively overruled by decisions of the SCI, such as *NALSA* and *Puttaswamy*, recognizing the rights of transgender citizens to legal recognition of their identity, and a general right under the Constitution to protection of privacy.[80] India also has a long tradition of larger constitutional benches reconsidering the reasoning of smaller benches, and the bench in *Johar* comprised five compared to three justices.

Even compared to *Naz*, the decision in *Johar* enjoyed important affirmative support in recent decisions of the SCI, such as *NALSA* and *Puttaswamy*.[81] A majority of the Court in *Johar* held that discrimination based on sexual orientation should attract heightened scrutiny under Articles 15 and 16 of the Constitution, analogous to the scrutiny applied to forms of discrimination based on sex. The justices likewise emphasized the idea that the petitioners' claim was supported by a right to sexual freedom and privacy, and that the right to life in Article 21 of the Constitution included the right to live with dignity, and that dignity required both respect for LGBTQI+ identity and freedom from psychological stress and fear for gays and lesbians.[82] All these ideas also found support in *NALSA* and *Puttaswamy*. *NALSA* held that Article 15 prohibited discrimination based on sex, gender identity, and sexual orientation.[83] And *Puttaswamy* recognized an implied right to privacy under the Constitution, connected to the right to dignity, and including sexual and decisional as well as spatial forms of privacy.[84] Other decisions on the right to die, such as *Common*

---

[79] *See* discussion in *Johar*, *supra* note 70, at 112 [95] (criticizing numerical minority reasoning), 129 [59] (criticizing formalism). For popular criticism, see Suhrith Parthasarathy, *To be Equal Before the Law*, The Hindu (Oct. 31, 2016), <https://www.thehindu.com/opinion/lead/To-be-equal-before-the-law/article14479752.ece>. For academic criticism, see M.P. Singh, *Constitutionality of Section 377, Indian Penal Code: A Case of Misplaced Hope in Courts*, 6 NUJS L. Rev. 567 (2013); Sujitha Subramanian, *The Indian Supreme Court Ruling in Koushal v. Naz: Judicial Deference or Judicial Abdication?*, 47 Geo. Wash. Int'l L. Rev. 711 (2015); Narrain, *Lost in Appeal*, *supra* note 67; Khaitan, *Koushal v. Naz*, *supra* note 73; Shreya Mohapatra, *Section 377 Read Down: the Way Forward*, Soc.-Legal Rev. (Jul. 6, 2019), https://www.sociolegalreview.com/post/section-377-read-down-the-way-forward.

[80] *See, e.g.*, discussion in *Johar*, *supra* note 70, at 42 [160] (Misra C.J.). *See also* Jayna Kothari, *Section 377 and Beyond: A New Era for Transgender Equality?*, in How Liberal is India? The Quest for Freedom in the Biggest Democracy on Earth 190–91 (Ronald Meinardus ed., 2019).

[81] *See* Ankit Srivastava & Vivek Kumar, *Section 377 and LGBT Activism in India*, 6 Int'l J. Res. & Analytical Rev. 30 (2019).

[82] *Johar*, *supra* note 70, at 99 [69] (Misra C.J.) (on dignity and psychological harm).

[83] (2014) 5 SCC 438.

[84] (2017) 10 SCC 1. *See* discussion in *Johar*, *supra* note 70, at 102 [79] (Misra C.J.). For discussion, see Mayur Suresh, *The Right to be Public: India's LGBT Movement Builds an Argument About Privacy*, 20 Austl. J. Asian L. 1 (2019).

Cause v. Union of India, provided additional support for the centrality of rights to autonomy and dignity under the Constitution.[85]

3. Implied rights to freedom of expression and equality

This same lens can help explain why the High Court of Australia could legitimately have chosen to imply a principle of freedom of political of communication, in *ACTV*, while later rejecting a principle of implied equality under the Constitution, in *Leeth*. *ACTV* was later criticized as lacking sufficient grounding in the text of the Constitution.[86] And in *Lange*, the Court revisited its prior reasoning, and suggested that the implied freedom of political communication identified in *ACTV* should be seen as directly grounded in the text of sections 7 and 24 of the Constitution, and their provision for members of the House of Representatives and Senate to be "directly chosen" by the people, as well as section 128 of the Constitution and its provision for approval of constitutional amendment by voters at a national referendum.[87]

From the perspective of a responsive approach to judicial review, however, additional legal or political justification of this kind was potentially helpful, but not necessary.[88] The Court's decision in *ACTV* was sufficiently "necessary" for the preservation of a system of representative and responsible government—one of the key structural commitments found in the Australian Constitution—that additional arguments from the text of the Constitution were helpful but not essential to justifying the implication identified by the Court.

The difficulty with the scheme under challenge, in *ACTV*, was that free airtime was allocated based on prior electoral success and therefore disproportionately favored existing political parties.[89] This posed a direct threat to the competitiveness of the Australian political system. While it still preserved scope for competition among existing parties—or effective two-party competition—it reduced the scope for entry by new parties. The possibility, or threat, of entry is generally viewed as a key requirement for competitive

---

[85] *Johar*, supra note 70, at 94 [62]–[63] (Misra C.J.), citing *Common Cause v. Union of India*, (2018) 5 SCC 1 (Chandrachud J).

[86] *See* Theophanous v. Herald & Weekly Times Ltd. (1994) 182 CLR 104 (McHugh J.).

[87] *Australian Constitution* ss 7, 24. *See* Lange v. Australian Broad. Corp. (1997) 189 CLR 520 (referring to ss 7, 24, and 128 of the Constitution).

[88] For an excellent analysis of whether *Lange*, in fact, added such legal legitimacy, see, *e.g.*, Adrienne Stone, *The Limits of Constitutional Text and Structure: Standards of Review and the Freedom of Political Communication*, 23 MELB. U. L. REV. 668 (1999).

[89] *Political Broadcasts and Political Disclosures Act 1991* (Cth), Pt. IIID (Austl.). *See* discussion in *Australian Capital Television Pty Ltd. v. Commonwealth* (1992) 177 CLR 2016.

markets.[90] The threat to the democratic minimum core in *ACTV* was thus real and potentially systemic.[91]

Leeth, in contrast, arguably involved a claim that had both relatively weak legal and political justification. While the text of the Australian Constitution contains a range of specific prohibitions against discrimination, those prohibitions largely relate to the protection of federal economic or political unity.[92] They do not prohibit discrimination against individuals, or seek to protect individual dignity or equality of opportunity, or prevent group-based subordination. Existing approaches to interpretation in Australia also favor reading those specific provisions as undermining, rather than strengthening, the argument for a general constitutional non-discrimination principle.[93]

Leeth also ultimately involved a concern about legislative burdens of inertia. The Australian Law Reform Commission had repeatedly recommended change to the law.[94] And by 1990 the law had been repealed.[95] *Leeth*, decided by the Court in 1992, was therefore ultimately about how prior burdens of inertia affected a relatively small group of individuals (federal prisoners sentenced under the previous law), not about ongoing legislative inertia. And while additional time in prison inevitably has real human costs, these prisoners could be expected to be released within a defined period, according to state law. The democratic blockages at issue, therefore, were neither urgent nor systemic.

In Israel, this same analysis suggests a more mixed view of the legitimacy of decisions such as *Bergman* and *Ka'adan*. *Bergman* like *ACTV* had a clear political justification: it responded to the same risk of political monopoly, or reduction in electoral competition confronted by the High Court of Australia in *ACTV*. And if anything, the exclusion of new parties could have been viewed by the Israeli High Court of Justice (HCJ) as more dangerous to democratic stability in Israel than Australia: new parties in Israel are often a response to new social cleavages which may otherwise threaten broader social and political stability in ways far less likely to arise in Australia. But the Court's reasoning

---

[90] M.A. Porter, *How Competitive Forces Shape Strategy*, HARV. BUS. REV. 137 (1979b).

[91] Gerald N. Rosenberg & John M. Williams, *Do Not Go Gently into that Good Right: The First Amendment in the High Court of Australia*, 11 SUP. CT. REV. 439, 456–58 (1997) (arguing for a tension between the decision and deliberative conceptions of democracy).

[92] *See, e.g.*, Constitution ss 92, 99, 117. *See* discussion in *Leeth v. Commonwealth* (1992) 174 CLR 455; *Kirk v. Industrial Relations Comm'n (NSW)* (2010) 239 CLR 531; Amelia Simpson, *Equal Treatment and Non-discrimination Through the Functionalist Lens*, in AUSTRALIAN CONSTITUTIONAL VALUES 195 (Rosalind Dixon ed., 2018).

[93] Jeremy Kirk, *Constitutional Guarantees, Characterisation and the Concept of Proportionality*, 21 MELB. U. L. REV. 1 (1997).

[94] *Sentencing of Federal Offenders (1978–88)*, AUSTL. L. REFORM COMM'N (Mar. 9, 1998), <https://www.alrc.gov.au/inquiry/sentencing-of-federal-offenders-1978-88/>.

[95] *Crimes Legislation Amendment Act (No. 2) 1989* (Cth) (Austl.).

also raised the same logical difficulties confronted by the petitioners in *Leeth*. It treated specific principles as evidence of a more general principle, when in some cases it may be evidence of an intention on the part of the framers to reject such a principle, at least as one enforceable by courts.[96]

Similarly, the decision in *Ka'adan* had a strong political justification, but a less powerful one than for cases such as *Bergman*, and thus the degree of legal support for the decision had greater importance. The decision arguably helped respond to a powerful blind spot of perspective in Israeli political decision-making: Arab-Israelis represent approximately 20 percent of the Israeli population, but have historically been represented at significantly lower levels in the Knesset.[97] Only in 2020 did Arab-Israeli representation in the Knesset reach 14 percent—the highest-ever level of non-Jewish representation.[98] But especially in a case involving the grant of land, blind spots of this kind can often be corrected by later political actions, or subsequent equalizing actions.[99]

4. Structural social rights

As to structural social rights, almost all these decisions had some basis in the text of the Constitution or prior case law. In South Africa, for example, cases such as *Grootboom* and *TAC* gave direct effect to the language in sections 26(2) and 27(2) of the Constitution, requiring governments to take "reasonable measures" toward the progressive realization of rights of access to housing and healthcare. They were also decided against the backdrop of both democratic blind spots and a clear pattern of democratic inertia.

In *Grootboom*, the South African government pledged in 1997 to build 1 million new homes within two years, to redress the lack of access to formal housing among Black South Africans. But this plan was subject to a clear blind spot: it made no provision for access to emergency housing (e.g., tents, running water, and sewage) for those who lacked access to both informal and formal

---

[96] *See* discussion of this argument in Rosalind Dixon, *Constitutional Carve-outs*, 37 Oxford J. Legal Stud. 276 (2017).

[97] Khader Sawaed, *The Arab Minority in Israel and the Knesset Elections*, The Wash. Inst. (Apr. 9, 2019), <https://www.washingtoninstitute.org/fikraforum/view/the-arab-minority-in-israel-and-the-knesset-elections>. *See also* Ahmed Asmar, *Israel's Population Hits 9.2M Including 1.93M Arabs*, AA (Apr. 27, 2020), <https://www.aa.com.tr/en/middle-east/israels-population-hits-92m-including-193m-arabs/1820022>.

[98] Oliver Holmes, *Israel's Arab Parties Make Historic Gains as Election Support Surges*, The Guardian, Mar. 4, 2020, <https://www.theguardian.com/world/2020/mar/04/israel-arab-parties-make-historic-gains-election-support-surges>.

[99] For discussion, but fair criticism of the realism of this claim, see H.C. 6698/95 at 25.

housing or who were rendered homeless as a result of a natural disaster or eviction from formal housing.[100]

There were also continual delays in realizing commitments to build more formal housing. At a national level, the government built only 250,000 homes in the first year of its housing plan, and in the next year fell 300,000 homes short of its target.[101] In the Cape area, the Cape municipality announced a plan to provide formal public housing to the thousands of people living in informal settlements between the center of Cape Town and the airport around the same time the proceedings in *Grootboom* were commenced, but thereafter made almost no progress in implementing that plan for more than four years after the *Grootboom* decision.[102] Similar patterns of delay were also evident in other provinces, such as Gauteng, around the time the decision was heard.[103]

Similarly, in the *TAC* case, even prior to the case, there was some progress by the government in providing access to nevirapine in certain "trial sites" as a means of preventing mother-to-child transmission of HIV. But this pilot program was subject to clear blind spots: it did not consider, or extend to, the needs of poor women in many rural areas.[104]

There was also ongoing coalition-driven inertia surrounding the further roll-out of access to antiretrovirals. Until 2003, President Thabo Mbeki and his supporters consistently questioned the link between HIV and AIDS, and opposed the use of antiretrovirals on that basis, whereas more left-wing factions of the ANC strongly supported the government taking urgent measures to combat the HIV/AIDS epidemic, including via the provision of universal access to antiretrovirals.[105] This also led to powerful coalition-driven forms of inertia in the government's response to the HIV/AIDS epidemic.

---

[100] Government of the Republic of South Africa v. Grootboom 2001 (1) SA 46 (CC); Rosalind Dixon, *Creating Dialogue about Socioeconomic Rights: Strong-Form Versus Weak-Form Judicial Review Revisited*, 5 INT'L J. CONST. L. 391 (2007).

[101] Marcia Klein, *Development: SA Govt Builds on Housing Promise*, BUS. TIMES (S. AFR.) (Jul. 6, 1997), 3; Sven Lunsche, *ANC Good Deeds Come to Grief at Local Level*, BUS. TIMES (S. AFR.) (May. 30, 1999) 10.

[102] *See* Ilse Fredericks, *The Promise No-one Keeps*, SUNDAY TIMES (S. AFR.) (May 6, 2004) 12 (noting the announcement of the plan, "Operation Shack Attack," in 2001, but lack of any progress in implementation by May 2004).

[103] In Gauteng, in the Diepsloot area, the local and provincial governments announced a plan in 2001 to provide water, sewerage, and electricity to all of the residents living in the area within two years, and a plan to provide housing for the 6,000 people who had recently been relocated from Alexandria to Diepsloot within one year, but by July 2004 (namely three years later), no new housing had been provided, and little progress had been made in providing basic water, sewerage, and electricity: *see* Dominic Mahlangu, *A Place Where Promises Come to Die*, SUNDAY TIMES (S. AFR.) (Jul. 11, 2004) 13.

[104] Minister of Health v. Treatment Action Campaign (2002) 5 SA 721 (CC); Dixon, *Creating Dialogue about Socioeconomic Rights*, *supra* note 100.

[105] *See* Claire Bisseker, *Aids, Medicine, Drugs, State President*, FIN. MAIL (S. AFR.) (Sept. 22, 2000) 35.

In India, the Court's orders in the *Midday Meal* case had some support in Article 47 of the Directive Principles of state policy which requires the state to work toward "the raising of the level of nutrition and the standard of living of its people and the improvement of public health as among its primary duties,"[106] and prior decisions such as *Maneka Gandhi v. Union of India*[107] and *Olga Tellis v. Bombay Municipal Corporation*,[108] which held that the right to life in Article 21 of the Constitution encompassed the right to a dignified life, including the right not to be deprived of access to shelter without due process.[109]

In Pakistan, the implication of a principle of climate justice likewise had some degree of textual support in the guarantees of life, human dignity, property, and information in Articles 9, 13, 23, and 19A of the Pakistan Constitution, and prior case law in Pakistan supported the notion of "environmental justice."

In Colombia, decisions such as the *IDP* case were based on the express guarantee under the 1991 Colombian Constitution of rights to health, housing, and social security, and constitutional principles of respect for human dignity and a "social state."[110] They also followed earlier decisions finding that, under these provisions, individuals enjoyed a right to a minimum level of subsistence (*derecho al mínimo vital*),[111] and that it was open to the Court to find an "unconstitutional state of affairs" in respect of the realization of this vital minimum, as well as other constitutional requirements.[112] In the *IDP* case, the Court also further developed these principles to emphasize, among other factors: (i) the seriousness of the relevant rights violation; (ii) the dispersed nature of authority for protecting relevant rights; and (iii) the degree to which structural causes included an insufficient budgetary allocation.[113] And it noted the importance of considering the degree to which the relevant violations were leading to large numbers of individual petitions or *tutelas*.

At the same time, all these decisions also involved some form of "gloss" on the express language of the relevant constitution in ways that have at times attracted criticism. In India, for example, decisions such as the *Midday Meal* decision and *Olga Tellis* ignored express language purporting to make Article 47

---

[106] *Constitution of India* art 47.
[107] AIR 1978 SC 597.
[108] (1985) 3 SCC 545.
[109] *See* Rosalind Dixon & Rishad Chowdhury, *A Case for Qualified Hope? The Supreme Court of India and the Midday Meal Decision*, *in* A QUALIFIED HOPE: THE INDIAN SUPREME COURT AND PROGRESSIVE SOCIAL CHANGE (Gerald N. Rosenberg et al. eds., 2019).
[110] *Compare* ESPINOSA & LANDAU, *supra* note 43, at 150.
[111] *See, e.g.*, Decision T-426 of 1992, in ESPINOSA & LANDAU, *supra* note 43.
[112] ESPINOSA & LANDAU, *supra* note 43, at 182.
[113] *Id.* at 183. Other factors included the existence of unconstitutional practices, and failure to pass legislative, administrative, or budgetary measures necessary to avoid the problem.

non-justiciable, and the constitutional history indicating that Article 21 was not intended to have this effect. In Pakistan, in *Leghari*, the High Court made a significant conceptual leap in connecting individual rights to life, dignity, property, and information to a general, structural principle of "climate justice." The same was true in Colombia, albeit to a lesser degree. The Court's decision in the *IDP* case again involved a degree of judicial creativity in connecting *express* guarantees of human dignity to *implied structural* principles defined by the notion of a vital minimum and an "unconstitutional state of affairs."

In a responsive approach, however, judges must consider the degree to which decisions of this kind responded to blind spots or burdens of inertia *and* a serious and *irreversible* harm to individual dignity. An application of these criteria also suggests support for decisions such as the *Grootboom, TAC, Midday Meal, IDP*, and *Leghari* cases, but for reasons that are narrower and more qualified than those that are often provided by proponents of structural social rights enforcement. In India, for example, the midday meal program is aimed at countering a serious and irreversible risk to children's physical and educational development resulting from malnutrition, and inertia in state action designed to counter that threat.[114]

In Pakistan, the decision in *Leghari* was a response to systemic inertia in the development of a national climate-change mitigation and adaptation policy. The Pakistani government in 2012 adopted a national climate change policy containing 734 action items, and in 2014 a "framework for implementation."[115] But in 2015, there had been little response from national departments about how to implement relevant action items; indeed the Court noted a history of "delay and lethargy" on the part of key state actors in the implementation of the relevant policy.[116] The decision itself, however, effectively encouraged much greater state coordination and responsiveness in the development of a national climate policy.

And in Colombia, the *IDP* case was arguably a response both to a serious risk of harm to individual health and dignity—in the form of the non-treatment of curable diseases, or non-protection against preventable harms—a prolonged and systemic pattern of state non-responsiveness.[117] The Constitutional Court itself underlined that the legislature had acknowledged the "seriousness" of the

---

[114] Dixon & Nussbaum, *supra* note 18.
[115] HCJD/C-121 at 2.
[116] *Id.* at 6.
[117] *See* David Landau, *Aggressive Weak Form Remedies*, 5 CONST. CT. REV. (S. AFR.) 244, 260–61 (2013); ESPINOSA AND LANDAU, *supra* note 43, at 178–79; Varun Gauri & Daniel M. Brinks, *Human Rights as Demands for Communicative Action*, 20 J. POL. PHIL. 407 (2012). *Compare also* Dixon & Nussbaum, *supra* note 18.

violation of rights facing internally displaced persons (IDPs), including rights to dignity, healthcare, housing, and education, but that equally there was clear evidence of "problems regarding coordination, lack of resources, administrative obstacles, unnecessary paper work and procedures, deficient design of some policy instruments, as well as prolonged omission by authorities to adopt necessary corrective measures."[118]

All of these decisions can thus be seen as a response to a serious and conceptually or practically irreversible threat to human dignity. One could argue that threats to individual health and bodily integrity are harder to reverse than climate change. Some impacts on health and development may be literally impossible to reverse, whereas climate change may be reversible at a later point, with increased investment or new technologies. There is, however, clear scientific consensus that delays in addressing climate change are extremely difficult and costly to address—in part because the costs of current inaction are likely to compound over time so that it becomes *exponentially* more difficult and costly to achieve the same levels of temperature reduction.[119] Many forms of malnutrition, or lack of access to preventive healthcare, could also be seen to have a similar impact; they may be reversible but only at substantially higher cost to the state than the cost of earlier forms of rights-protection or intervention.[120] And both climate and health risks may at some point reach a tipping point whereby it becomes impossible to reverse relevant forms of harm.

There was still, however, some potential differences in the degree of political legitimacy of these various decisions, and especially the degree to which they accommodated a concern about reverse democratic inertia. In Colombia, the Constitutional Court relied on prior legal precedents developing an unconstitutional state of affairs doctrine, and stated the relevant implication at a very high level of generality: it suggested that the existing state of affairs was unconstitutional, not that any particular new set of state responses or arrangements was required in order to respond to this constitutional breach.[121] And in doing so, the Court largely avoided the risk of creating reverse democratic inertia explored in Chapter 6. In Pakistan, the High Court was likewise quite vague about the exact scope and content of the principle of "climate justice" under the Constitution. In subsequent litigation, this also allowed the Court to

---

[118] ESPINOSA & LANDAU, *supra* note 43, at 183.

[119] *The Cost of Delaying Action to Stem Climate Change*, Executive Office of the President of the United States (Research Report, Jul. 2014), <https://scholar.harvard.edu/files/stock/files/cost_of_delaying_action.pdf>.

[120] Dixon & Nussbaum, *supra* note 18, at 581.

[121] Decision T-025 of 2004, translated in ESPINOSA & LANDAU, *supra* note 43, at 183; T-760 of 2008, as translated in ESPINOSA & LANDAU, *supra* note 43, at 172.

respond to evidence of decreased bureaucratic inertia and adapt its remedy to involve less intensive judicial oversight of the implementation of national climate change policy.[122]

In India, in contrast, the Supreme Court was highly prescriptive as to the exact kind and mode of delivery for the midday meal program.[123] This has also arguably made it more difficult for some states to refine and improve the delivery of adequate nutrition for school children, and for the Court itself to adjust its approach to the oversight of its orders—so as to be both more limited and effective in scope.[124] That is, it created a much greater risk of ongoing compound and reverse burdens of inertia.

The fact that *some* form of constitutional implication may be justified as a means of protecting human dignity does not mean that any and all implications designed to do so will be justified. Implications themselves must be drawn with a view to responding to the dangers of both compound and reverse burdens of inertia, and the broader legal and political context. And in this respect, the Court's decision in the *Midday Meal* case may have been broadly justifiable on democratic grounds, but too specific or prescriptive in the precise order it involved.

But the lessons from Latin America and South Asia in this context are still potentially important and wide-ranging in scope. In principle they suggest that courts elsewhere might be justified in developing constitutional implications designed to respond to some of the most pressing threats facing democracies today—including unaddressed threats of climate change, inequality, gun violence, and containment of the COVID-19 pandemic. Whether that is the case will depend, in part, on the text of the relevant constitution, and prior constitutional case law of a country, and the degree of legal legitimacy it provides for such an approach.

5. Unconstitutional amendment doctrine

Finally, consider the "unconstitutional constitutional amendment" (UCA) doctrine, as it was announced in cases such as *Kesavanada* in India and

---

[122] HCJDA38, Case No. WP 22501/2015.
[123] Order dated Nov. 28, 2001, Peoples Union for Civil Liberties v. Union of India, Writ Petition (Civil) No. 196 of 2001.
[124] *Compare* Dixon & Chowdhury, *supra* note 109; Alyssa Brierly, *PUCL v. Union of India: Political Mobilization and the Right to Food*, *in* A QUALIFIED HOPE: THE INDIAN SUPREME COURT AND PROGRESSIVE SOCIAL CHANGE (Gerald N. Rosenberg et al. eds., 2019).

Second Re-election case in Colombia. The decision in *Kesavananda* was prefigured by earlier decisions such as *Golak Nath*, which found very broad implied limits on the power of amendment under Article 368 of the Constitution.[125] The Court in *Golak Nath* held that any amendment to the Constitution had to be consistent with existing provisions of the Constitution. The basis for this, the Court held, was that amendments were themselves "laws" subject to the Constitution.

In Colombia, the limits applied by the Court in the *Second Re-election* case were likewise foreshadowed in earlier reasoning of the Court in *Decision C-551 of 2003* and the *First Re-election* case (*Decision C-1040 of 2005*), when the Court suggested that while amendments to allow a second presidential term might be permissible, creating a third term was likely beyond the scope of Congress power under Articles 375 and 378.[126]

This also was likely to have helped increase the perceived legitimacy of the decisions in *Kesavananda* and the *Second Re-election* case, at least among lawyers and certain political elites.[127] For instance in India, when the decision in *Golak Nath* was handed down, "few jurists supported it, as there was little in Anglo-American constitutional theory [from] which they drew intellectual nourishment to sustain the doctrine."[128] But a decade or two later, according to Ramaswamy Sudarshan, it was "a well-recognized and established doctrine" with "widespread support from intellectuals, lawyers, and even politicians."[129]

A UCA doctrine, however, can still be legitimate where it is developed afresh by a court, without prior doctrinal support—providing it responds to an urgent and systemic threat to democracy in the form of a credible risk of electoral or institutional monopoly. In Kenya, for example, the decisions of the High Court and Court of Appeal in *Ndii v. Attorney General* had some support in prior reasoning of members of the High Court, but the basic structure doctrine had not previously been applied so as to limit the power of amendment under Articles 255–257 of the 2010 Constitution.[130] The Supreme Court also

---

[125] I.C. Golaknath and Ors. vs State of Punjab and Anrs (1967) SCR (2) 762.
[126] Espinosa & Landau, *supra* note 43, at 340–51.
[127] Rosalind Dixon & Samuel Issacharoff, *Living to Fight Another Day: Judicial Deferral in Defense of Democracy*, Wis. L. Rev. 683 (2016).
[128] *Id.*
[129] R. Sudarshan, *In Quest of State: Politics and the Judiciary in India*, 28 J. Commonwealth & Comp. Pol. 44, 57 (1990). *See* Dixon & Issacharoff, *supra* note 127.
[130] [2020] High Court of Kenya E282, [454]–[460]. For the relevant support in obiter, see, *e.g.*, Njoya v. Att'y Gen. [2013] eKLR (Lenaola J.); Commission for the Implementation of the Const. v. Nat'l Assembly of Kenya [2013] eKLR (Lenaola, Ngugi, and Majanja JJ.); Kivuitu v. Att'y Gen. [2015] eKLR. *See* discussion in *Ndii* per Okwengu J.A. at 290–91 and Kairu J.A. at [45]–[49].

emphasized this, together with the *expressio unius* principle (that specific limits on amendment exclude more general, implied limits).[131]

But in holding that the Constitution did *not* allow these amendment procedures to be used to alter the basic structure of the Constitution, both the High Court and Court of Appeal arguably responded to an emerging threat of electoral monopoly. In proposing a significant increase in the number of seats in Parliament, many observers suggest President Uhuru Kenyatta was effectively seeking to dilute the electoral support of his deputy, William Ruto, and therefore Ruto's ability to challenge Kenyatta's institutional power and authority— and also his future electoral dominance. And while that may not have posed an obvious threat to the democratic minimum core, and Ruto himself may pose risks to constitutionalism, the broader context suggested that the threat was real. In 2018, Kenyatta entered into a "hand-shake" agreement with his former rival, and leader of the opposition, Raila Odinga, which was touted as an attempt to end ongoing civil unrest and violence, but it also simultaneously undermined the most immediate prospect of a challenge to the President's power.[132]

Moreover, attempts to increase the *legal* legitimacy of the UCA doctrine may not always increase the overall legitimacy of doctrines of this kind—especially if they come at the expense of a focus on the risk of electoral or institutional monopoly, or increase the risk of reverse democratic inertia. For instance, in India, in *Golak Nath*, the SCI attempted to give the UCA doctrine a quite strong textual basis, linked to the status of constitutional amendments as laws within the meaning of Article 368. But the result was a doctrine that lacked basic political legitimacy. As articulated in *Golak Nath*, the doctrine was much broader than a doctrine focused on protecting the "basic structure" or "democratic minimum core" of the Indian Constitution. It protected all aspects of the Constitution, including the Court's own existing interpretation of those

---

[131] *See*, Attorney General & Others v. David Ndii & 79 Others, Petition No. 12 of 2021 (Building Bridges Initiative Case), [180]–[227] (Koome CJ), [371]–[476] (Mwilu P), [1039]–[1061] (Wanjala SCJ), [1158]–[1171] (Njoki SCJ), [1385]–[1482] (Lenaola SCJ), [1809]–[1813] (Ouko SCJ), (Ibrahim SCJ dissenting).

[132] Peter Muiruri, *Kenya's High Court Overturns President's Bid to Amend Constitution*, The Guardian, May 27, 2021, <https://www.theguardian.com/global-development/2021/may/27/kenyas-high-court-overturns-president-uhuru-kenyatta-bbi-bid-to-amend-constitution>; Ferdinand Omondi, *Kenya's BBI Blocked in Scathing Court Verdict for President Kenyatta*, BBC News, May. 14, 2021, <https://www.bbc.com/news/world-africa-57094387>; Uhuru Kenyatta, *Kenya Government Appeals Ruling Against BBI Constitutional Changes*, Al Jazeera, Jun. 2, 2021, <https://www.aljazeera.com/news/2021/6/2/kenya-govt-appeals-ruling-against-bbi-constitutional-changes>. Of course, Odinga may still be a long-term source of opposition for Kenyatta. See also, *Kenya's William Ruto's Case Dismissed by ICC*, BBC News, Apr. 5, 2016, available at <https://www.bbc.com/news/world-africa-35965760>.

provisions. As a result, it also had a real capacity to contribute to reverse burdens of inertia or create an unduly strong form of judicial review.

A similar critique could be made of recent decisions in India such as *Supreme Court Advocates on Record Association v. Union of India* (*NJAC*) regarding the validity of attempts by the Indian Parliament to alter the model of judicial appointment in India. While at a general level the *NJAC* decision had some basis in prior precedent (i.e., *Kesavananda Bharati*), it lacked any direct support in the constitutional text.[133] And it arguably sought to protect a vision of the "basic structure" that went substantially beyond the democratic minimum core. Judicial independence, as the SCI itself held, is clearly part of the basic structure in India. But the question the SCI faced in *NJAC* was whether judicial independence requires the consultation or concurrence of the judiciary in the appointment process. The position in most countries is that consultation is sufficient, whereas in India (and Japan) the understanding (in India, at least since the *Second Judges* case in 1993) has been a requirement of concurrence.[134] The Indian Parliament was also seeking to remove this judicial veto as part of the changes enacted by the Twenty-Ninth Amendment to the Constitution and National Judicial *Appointments Commission Act* of 2014. In effect, the relevant changes shifted the power of appointment from "the collegium" or a body comprising the Chief Justice and other senior judges, to a Commission comprising three judges, the Attorney General, and two other "eminent persons" from civil society or the political branches of government.[135] The Court, however, struck down these changes as inconsistent with the basic structure doctrine.

This does not mean that the decision lacked any legitimate basis. As Chapter 2 noted, there is currently a very real threat to electoral and institutional pluralism in India, and this extends to attempts to undermine the independence of a range of institutions, including courts.[136] This also suggests a quite plausible basis for the Court's decision to invalidate attempts to undermine that independence as contrary to the existing basic structure of the Constitution. But in finding that a model of judicial concurrence was part of the basic structure, or necessary to maintaining judicial independence, the Court ignored both dominant global practices and the potential for judges' own institutional position and behavioral biases (in favor of the institutional *status quo*) to affect the

---

[133] Rehan Abeyratne, *Upholding Judicial Supremacy in India: The NJAC Judgment in Comparative Perspective*, 49 Geo. Wash. Int'l L. Rev. 569, 570 (2016).
[134] *See* Supreme Court Advocates-on-Record Association v Union of India (1993) 4 SCC 441 (Second Judges Case).
[135] Abeyratne, *supra* note 133.
[136] *See, e.g.*, Tarunabh Khaitan, *Killing a Constitution with a Thousand Cuts: Executive Aggrandizement and Party-State Fusion in India*, 14 Law & Ethics Hum. Rts. 49 (2020).

assessment of these questions. It therefore enforced as essential to democratic constitutionalism a model of court-controlled judicial appointment that has been long-standing in India, but which is extremely unusual in global terms—and thus presumptively unnecessary to maintaining judicial independence, or protecting the democratic minimum core.[137] The Court also overlooked the broad degree of cross-party support for the proposed changes to the existing model of judicial appointment.[138]

A more politically legitimate approach, therefore, would probably have involved the Court focusing on the motive behind the relevant amendments—as impermissibly designed to create antidemocratic forms of monopoly power, or else striking down the amendments, but on the proviso that some more modest adjustment in the existing model of judicial appointment would be constitutionally permissible.

Similarly, in Colombia the Constitutional Court has applied the substitution doctrine in several cases besides the *Second Re-election* case that are far harder to defend from a responsive perspective. In *Decision C-588 of 2009*, for example, the Court relied on the doctrine to invalidate a constitutional amendment creating a new constitutionally mandated civil service system, but exempting current office-holders from the new system of competitive exams and applications, as in violation of the substitution doctrine.[139] Two years later, in *Decision C-574 of 2011*, the Court relied on the doctrine to strike down a constitutional amendment seeking to recriminalize the possession of marijuana (in response to a court decision decriminalizing it).[140] And while these decisions had the same basis in precedent as the *Second Re-election* case, they were far less closely calibrated to responding to a risk of political monopoly, or even democratic blind spots or burdens of inertia than the *Second Re-election* case.

While some form of independent and professional civil service is surely necessary to the minimum core of democracy, global practice suggests a wide range of ways in which the civil service may be organized, consistent with maintaining a commitment to independence and professionalism.[141] And while the criminalization of marijuana may be the result of blind spots of perspective, or accommodation, this is a matter of reasonable disagreement.[142]

---

[137] No. 13 of 2015, at 142–57. *Compare* Bangalore Principles of Judicial Conduct.
[138] Abeyaratne, *supra* note 133.
[139] Espinosa & Landau, *supra* note 43, at 368–69. *See also* discussion David Landau & Rosalind Dixon, *Transnational Constitutionalism and a Limited Doctrine of Unconstitutional Constitutional Amendment*, 13 Int'l J. Const. L. 606 (2015).
[140] Espinosa & Landau, *supra* note 43, at 52–59. *See also* discussion Landau & Dixon, *Transnational Constitutionalism, supra* note 139.
[141] Landau & Dixon, *Transnational Constitutionalism, supra* note 139.
[142] *Id.*

And even if one accepts the existence of blind spots of this kind, they clearly do not pose as urgent and systemic a risk to democracy as the risks considered in the *Second Re-election* case.

D. The Intensity of Judicial Review: Toward Calibrated Proportionality or Scrutiny

In the United States, the Supreme Court has developed three "tiers" or levels of scrutiny for assessing the constitutionality of legislation limiting or impacting on constitutional guarantees: strict scrutiny, intermediate scrutiny, and rational basis review.[143] For strict scrutiny, it asks whether a law is "strictly narrowly tailored" to advancing a "compelling government interest."[144] For intermediate scrutiny, it asks whether a law is "substantially narrowly tailored" to advancing "an important government interest."[145] And for rational basis review, it asks simply whether the law is rationally related to a legitimate government interest.[146] (Sometimes, the Court has found that the relevant objective is not valid because it reflects a form of hatred or *animus* toward a group of citizens.)[147]

The Court also applies these various tiers of scrutiny to different categories of case. Under the First Amendment, for example, the Court applies strict scrutiny to any content-based regulation of protected speech; intermediate scrutiny to time, manner, and place regulations, and the regulation of the secondary effects of speech and historically, to the broadcast media and commercial speech; and rational basis review to the regulation of "low value" speech—that is, libel, true threats, fighting words, and obscenity.[148] The Court also treats any law that

---

[143] For a thoughtful exploration of the relative benefits of proportionality compared to this kind of more US-style "categorical" approach, see, *e.g.*, Stone, *The Limits of Constitutional Text and Structure*, supra note 88. Compare also The Hon. Sir Anthony Mason, *The Use of Proportionality in Australian Constitutional Law*, 27 Pub. L. Rev. 109 (2016).

[144] Richard H. Fallon, Jr., The Dynamic Constitution: An Introduction to American Constitutional Law and Practice 1268 (2013).

[145] *Id.* at 1273.

[146] *Id.*

[147] *See, e.g.*, Romer v. Evans, 517 U.S. 620 (1996). Compare Department of Agriculture v. Moreno, 413 U.S. 528 (1973). On *animus* grounds, see Barbara J. Flagg, *Animus and Moral Disapproval: A Comment on Romer v. Evans*, 82 Minn. L. Rev. 833 (1997); Susannah W. Pollcock, *Unconstitutional Animus*, 81 Fordham L. Rev. 887 (2012).

[148] For this rule and the important exceptions to it, see, *e.g.*, RAV v. St Paul, 505 U.S. 377 (1992). *See also, e.g.*, Ashutosh Bhagwat, *The Test That Ate Everything: Intermediate Scrutiny in the First Amendment Jurisprudence*, 2007 U. Ill. L. Rev. 783 (2007); Fallon, Jr., The Dynamic Constitution, *supra* note 144; Calvin Massey, *The New Formalism: Requiem for Tiered Scrutiny*, 6 U. Pa. J. Const. L. 945 (2003).

discriminates based on the viewpoint of the speaker as *per se* unconstitutional, unless the government itself is the speaker.[149]

In the context of Equal Protection cases, the Supreme Court generally applies a test of strict scrutiny to classifications based on race or laws that affect fundamental interests under the Equal Protection Clause. It applies a form of heightened or intermediate scrutiny to classifications based on gender. And, theoretically, it applies a rational basis review or a form of quite deferential scrutiny to all other classifications, including those based on age, disability, and sexuality. In practice, it has applied a more demanding form of scrutiny—or a rational basis review "with bite"—to some of these classifications, such as sexuality.[150] In effect, therefore, it applies four tiers of scrutiny: rational basis review, rational basis review with bite, intermediate scrutiny, and strict scrutiny.

Ely largely defended this framework. Putting aside cases in which there was a clear violation of constitutional norms, Ely suggested that strict judicial scrutiny should apply in two sets of cases—where "the ins are choking off the channels of political change to ensure that they will stay in and outs will stay out," or where legislation affected "discrete and insular minorities."[151] In other cases, he suggested, courts should adopt a far more deferential approach to legislative constitutional judgments, and apply something like a test of "rational basis review."[152]

Most constitutional democracies, in contrast, apply a test of structured "proportionality" to determine the permissibility of limits on constitutional guarantees. Indeed, proportionality has been a defining feature of democratic constitutionalism in Europe, following the Second World War.[153] It is also an increasingly common feature of rights-based judicial review in most other constitutional democracies worldwide. It is the basis of judicial review in Canada, under section 1 of the Canadian *Charter of Rights and Freedoms*; in South Africa, under section 36 of the 1996 Constitution; in Israel, under section 8 of the 1992 *Basic Law*; in Hong Kong under the *Basic Law*;[154] in Taiwan, under

---

[149] *See, e.g.,* Leslie Gielow Jacobs, *Clarifying the Content-Based/Content Neutral and Content/Viewpoint Determinations,* 34 McGeorge L. Rev. 595 (2002); Joseph Blocher, *Viewpoint Neutrality and Government Speech,* 52 B.C.L. Rev. 695 (2011).

[150] *See, e.g.,* Romer v. Evans, 517 U.S. 620 (1996), and discussion in Flagg, *Animus and Moral Disapproval, supra* note 147.

[151] John Hart Ely, Democracy and Distrust 103 (1980).

[152] *Id.* at 73–77, citing *United States v. Carolene Products Company,* 304 U.S. 144 (1938).

[153] Mattias Kumm, *Institutionalizing Socratic Contestation: The Rationalist Human Rights Paradigm, Legitimate Authority and the Point of Judicial Review,* 1 Eur. J. Legal Stud. 153 (2007).

[154] R v. Sin Yau Ming, CACC No. 289 (1990). *See also* P.J. Yap, Constitutional Dialogue in Common Law Asia (2015).

Article 23 of the Constitution of the Republic of China;[155] in South Korea, under Article 37 of the 1987 Constitution;[156] and in Latin America, as part of the "new constitutionalism" endorsed by courts such as the Constitutional Court of Columbia[157] and Supreme Court of Brazil.[158]

The doctrine of proportionality also involves four basic stages, whereby courts ask whether: (i) the impugned law has a legitimate purpose; (ii) there is a "rational connection" between the legislature's purpose and the means it has selected to pursue that objective ("suitability"); (iii) the law is "narrowly tailored" to its purpose ("minimal impairment"); and (iv) the law is truly proportionate, in the sense that it achieves greater benefits in terms of its objective than costs to other constitutional commitments (true proportionality, or proportionality *stricto sensu*).[159]

In countries such as Canada and South Africa, the SCC and Constitutional Court of South Africa have also applied constitutional guarantees of equality in ways that closely resemble a form of proportionality analysis. In both countries, the first step in any assessing any claim to discrimination is to ask whether either in law or fact an individual has been subject to differential treatment. Next courts ask whether that treatment was "based on" a prohibited ground of discrimination—that is, a ground expressly listed in section 15(1) of the Canadian *Charter* or section 9(2) of the South African Constitution, or that is sufficiently analogous to count as a prohibited ground.[160] The key question in both countries, however, is ultimately whether any differentiation of this kind is discriminatory, or (in South Africa) unfairly discriminatory. And while courts in both countries have recognized the possibility that discrimination may be justified or proportionate in some limited circumstances,[161] the notion of discrimination—and especially unfair discrimination—carries strong negative connotations. Both courts, therefore, have tended to build in

---

[155] Interpretation No. 476 (1999).
[156] Constitutional Court, 92 Hun-Ga 8, Dec 24, 1992 (S. Kor.).
[157] Case T-406/92 (1992) at [11].
[158] *See* Juliano Zaiden Benvindo, On the Limits of Constitutional Adjudication: Deconstructing Balancing and Judicial Activism, ch 3 (2010).
[159] *See, e.g.*, Moshe Cohen-Eliya & Iddo Porat, Proportionality and Constitutional Culture (2013); Jackson, *Constitutional Law in An Age of Proportionality, supra* note 1; Alec Stone Sweet & Jud Mathews, *Proportionality Balancing and Global Constitutionalism*, 46 Colum. J. Transnat'l L. 72 (2008); David M. Beatty, The Ultimate Rule of Law (2004).
[160] *See* R v. Kapp, 2008 SCC 41. *See* discussion in Rosalind Dixon, *The Supreme Court of Canada and Constitutional (Equality) Baselines*, 50 Osgoode Hall L.J. 637 (2012).
[161] *See* R v. Kapp, 2008 SCC 41; Harksen v. Lane NO, 1998 (1) SA 300 (per O'Regan, Madala, and Mokgoro JJ., dissenting).

proportionality-like considerations into the question of whether differentiation amounts to discrimination, or unfair discrimination.[162]

Proportionality analysis of this kind is also substantially more standard-like than the US Court's current model of tiered scrutiny, in ways in which scholars such as Ely would have been likely to have found fault.[163] It invites courts to consider the ultimate costs and benefits of a law, albeit through a constitutional lens, in ways that necessarily call for a form of judicial evaluative judgment. And it invites a form of "floating" standard of scrutiny that will inevitably vary in intensity, depending on how a court perceives the competing balance of interests in a case.

In practice, however, doctrines of proportionality *and* US-style tiered forms of scrutiny are both applied in ways that vary with context. The US Supreme Court is constantly required to adapt its existing categories to fit new contexts, and often varies their application based on the context.[164] Most courts also *apply* a doctrine of proportionality in a way that is sensitive to different contexts. There are thus important similarities between the two approaches.[165] Both also leave ample scope for courts to "calibrate" the ultimate intensity of review in light of a concern about representation-reinforcement.[166]

Consider a potential *continuum* of different intensities of scrutiny, whereby a court would apply something like "reduced," "ordinary," "heightened," and especially "close" scrutiny.[167] This continuum is largely hypothetical, but arguably approximates the actual approach of at least some judges in applying a tiered approach to judicial scrutiny and a test of structured proportionality: A court in each case will not simply engage in a curtailed inquiry akin to a form of US-style "rational basis review." Instead, it will inquire into the compatibility,

---

[162] *See, e.g.*, Andrews v. Law Society of British Columbia, [1989] 1 S.C.R. 143; R v. Kapp, 2008 SCC 41; Harksen v. Lane NO, 1998 (1) SA 300 (CCSA); President of the Republic of South Africa v. Hugo, 1997 (4) SA 1 (CCSA).

[163] *See, e.g.*, Jackson, *Constitutional Law in an Age of Proportionality, supra* note 1; Adrienne Stone, *Proportionality and its Alternatives*, 48 Fed. L. Rev. 123 (2020).

[164] *See* discussion in Evelyn Douek, *All Out of Proportion: The Ongoing Disagreement about Structured Proportionality in Australia*, 47 Fed. L. Rev. 551 (2019).

[165] *See* Jackson, *Constitutional Law in An Age of Proportionality, supra* note 1; Jamal Greene, *Rights as Trumps*, 132 Harv. L. Rev. 28 (2018).

[166] On this idea of calibrated proportionality, see, *e.g.,* decisions of the Constitutional Court of Colombia such as Decision C673 of 2001; Decision CC-345 of 2019. *See also* Rosalind Dixon, *Calibrated Proportionality*, 48 Fed. L. Rev. 92 (2020); Chan, *Proportionality and Invariable Baseline Intensity of Review, supra* note 1.

[167] *Contrast* Cora Chan, *A Preliminary Framework for Measuring Deference in Rights Reasoning*, 14 Int'l J. Const. L. 851, 861 (2016) (proposing for empirical purposes a triadic scale of not deferential, moderately deferential and highly deferential); Chan, *Proportionality and Invariable Baseline Intensity of Review, supra* note 1 (proposing from a more normative standpoint a "minimum baseline" of review, and variation from that only above the threshold).

suitability, necessity, and (at least outside the United States) true proportionality of a law. But it will do so in a way that involves *variable intensity* in the degree of judicial scrutiny given to legislative judgments about necessity and adequacy in the balance.

A responsive approach both supports this kind of standard-like approach to assessing the constitutionality of limitations on constitutional norms and suggests that is application should be informed by attention to relevant *constitutional values* and *circumstances* and the presence (or absence) of *democratic blockages*.

Any approach of this kind will itself need to be calibrated to the specific constitutional context, including the degree to which the test is being applied in a system of tiered versus proportionality-style review, or by a large number of judges in a system of diffuse review, as opposed to a smaller number of judges in a constitutional or appellate court.[168] But it offers a general framework for thinking about the relevance of democratic dysfunction to the intensity of judicial review, which can potentially inform this more context-specific approach to calibration.

1. Calibrating judgments about limitations on expression

Take a guarantee of freedom of expression. A guarantee of this kind helps promote three broad constitutional values: a commitment to individual self-realization or expression; the pursuit of truth or a "marketplace for ideas"; and a system of political democracy.[169] Each of these values may also usefully inform how a court applies or implements a guarantee of freedom of expression. For instance, if a law is non-content based and imposes a limited burden on expression—for example, because it contains important limits or exceptions, or leaves open a range of *adequate* alternative channels of communication—this would suggest that concerns about both self-expression and the market-place for ideas are similarly reduced, and hence reduced forms of scrutiny should apply. Conversely, if a law imposes a substantial burden on expression and is content-based, this may pose a significant risk to a well-functioning market-place for ideas. This also suggests that a court should apply heightened scrutiny to laws of this kind.

---

[168] *See* Mark Tushnet, *The Possibilities of Comparative Constitutional Law*, 108 YALE L.J. 1225 (1999).
[169] *See, e.g.*, Irwin Toy Ltd. v. Québec (Att'y Gen.) [1989] 1 SCR 927; R v. Keegstra [1990] 3 SCR 697.

But a focus on democracy, and the democratic minimum core, suggests that even closer scrutiny should apply to certain laws which discriminate against certain viewpoints or classes of speaker. Laws that discriminate by viewpoint can undermine the functioning of the marketplace for ideas but also the scope for *criticism* of government in ways that raise special risks from the perspective of a concern about antidemocracy forms of monopoly power. Discrimination against certain *political actors* can likewise be especially troubling because of its impact on political competition. It has the capacity to impose a competitive disadvantage on one or another side of politics, where one of the key requirements for democratic responsiveness—highlighted by Ely himself—is the exercise of electoral choice against a background of meaningful political competition.[170] This also suggests that extremely close scrutiny should apply where there is a close connection between the expression regulated and the political process, and/or discrimination against a particular political viewpoint or class of speaker.

In addition, a responsive approach suggests that a focus on democratic blind spots and burdens of inertia can further help calibrate the application of a test of heightened, close, or even strict scrutiny. One important question for a court under both US-style tests of intermediate and strict scrutiny and structured proportionality is whether there were any plausible alternatives open to the legislature in seeking to achieve its objective. The first stage of this inquiry is also relatively straightforward: it requires a court to identify whether other jurisdictions have adopted a "less restrictive" approach to an issue, or experts have proposed such an approach. The inquiry is largely empirical or conceptual in nature. The second stage, however, is more complex. It calls on a court to assess the degree to which plausible legislative alternatives are likely to be *effective* in achieving a given legislative objective. And this will require an assessment of relevant social scientific and expert evidence, which can often be inconclusive.[171]

---

[170] There may, of course, be cases where legislation appears on its face to discriminate but is in fact not relevantly discriminatory: for example, it may draw a distinction between groups but that difference in treatment may correspond to an actual difference in the capacity of various groups to undermine the fairness or integrity of the political process, or the realization of other legislative objectives. But absent some persuasive justification of this kind, any differential burden on freedom of expression carries clear dangers from the perspective of a concern about political monopoly, or protection of the democratic minimum core.

[171] Chan, *A Preliminary Framework*, supra note 167. See also, SHIPRA CHORDIA, PROPORTIONALITY IN AUSTRALIAN CONSTITUTIONAL LAW (2020).

A focus on legislative blind spots, however, can provide courts with additional "guideposts" in making complex evaluative judgments of this kind. Where there is evidence of legislative blind spots, for example, a commitment to democratic responsiveness implies that courts should *not* defer to legislative judgments about narrow tailoring. Conversely, where there is evidence that legislators have actively considered the impact of a law on constitutional guarantees, and turned their mind to potential legislative alternative approaches, there will be a far stronger democratic case for deferring to legislative constitutional judgments about narrow tailoring.[172]

Attention to democratic blockages can likewise help a court calibrate the intensity of judgments about "true" proportionality or proportionality *stricto sensu*. In applying this test, courts must first assess the *cost* a law imposes on the enjoyment of constitutional rights and values. This includes the cost to constitutional democracy, and a responsive approach suggests that a key focus, in this context, should be on the degree to which a law threatens to undermine the democratic minimum core.

In addition, a court must determine the constitutional "benefits" of a law—or the degree to which legislation advances a compelling or important government objective. This requires considering the degree to which particular legislative objectives are underpinned by a range of constitutional values and may also be informed by the degree to which democratic majorities view certain objectives as important or compelling. The existence of burdens of inertia will also point against a conclusion that a particular legislative objective should be viewed as important: it suggests that current democratic majorities do not support the objective of a law, whereas in other cases, there may be quite recent democratic debate showing support for the legislature's objective.

All else being equal, a responsive approach would thus suggest that heightened scrutiny will be appropriate where there is evidence of apparent legislative blind spots—and especially blind spots of perspective—in debating or enacting such laws, or the operation of legislative burdens of inertia. And reduced scrutiny will be justified if, and only if, there was evidence of recent and reasonable deliberation by the legislature on an issue.

---

[172] Katharine Young suggests a similar approach in the context of a catalytic approach to judicial review. *See, e.g.*, Katharine Young, *A Typology of Economic and Social Rights Adjudication: Exploring the Catalytic Function of Judicial Review*, 8 INT'L J. CONST. L. 385, 416–17 (2010). And some scholars have highlighted similar ideas or approaches in the context of the ECtHR's "margin of appreciation" doctrine: *see* Thomas Kleinlein, *The Procedural Approach of the European Court of Human Rights: Between Subsidiarity and Dynamic Evolution*, 68 INT'L & COMP. L.Q. 91, 93–97 (2019).

Table 4.1 Calibrating Judgments about Proportionality in the Context of Guarantees of Freedom of Expression

Reduced scrutiny ↔	Ordinary scrutiny ↔	Heightened scrutiny ↔	"Close" or the most demanding scrutiny
Non-content-based regulation *and* Minimal burden on expression *and* Recent, reasoned deliberation	Content-based regulation *but* Moderate burden on expression— i.e., leaves open adequate alternative channels of communication	Content-based regulation *and* Significant burden on expression, including via potential "deterrent" effects *or/and* Evidence of legislative blind spots or burdens of inertia	Factors attracting ordinary/heightened scrutiny *and* Close nexus between expression and elections *or/and* Regulation discriminates by viewpoint, targets criticism against government or one or other political party/side of electoral politics

2. Calibrating judgments about discrimination

A similar analysis applies to the standard of scrutiny applied to laws engaging a constitutional equality clause. A guarantee of equality, as Chapter 2 notes, can be understood as advancing three broad commitments: a commitment to equality of opportunity, equal dignity, and the eradication of group based forms of subordination. These commitments can also be understood in more or less substantive terms: formal understandings of equality emphasize the notion of equality as "like treatment," whereas substantive approaches emphasize the "like treatment of those who are relevantly like," and "different treatment of those who are relevantly unlike."[173] And these different understandings will also affect how we understand equality-based values. A commitment to eradicating subordination is also inherently substantive in nature. It takes as its starting point the notion of differences in power between different groups. But commitments to equality of opportunity and equal dignity can be understood in both formal and substantive terms—or in ways that overlook, versus incorporate, differences in the starting point of individuals in encountering obstacles

---

[173] ARISTOTLE, ETHICA NICOMACHEA 112–17, 1131a–1131b (J.L. Ackrill & J.O. Urmson eds., W. Ross trans., 1980); ARISTOTLE, THE POLITICS 307 (Benjamin Jowett trans., 1943). *See* useful discussion in Catharine A. MacKinnon, *Sex Equality Under the Constitution of India: Problems, Prospects, and "Personal Law"*, 4 INT'L J. CONST. L. 181 (2006).

to their individual progress, messages of exclusion or disfavor, or enjoyment of certain capabilities.

A responsive approach also assumes both a values-based and substantive approach to these questions. That is, it suggests that an equality clause—or the kind of continuum set out above—should be applied in a manner sensitive to substantive commitments freedom, dignity, and the eradication of all forms of subordination, as well as to the presence or absence of democratic blockages. Reduced scrutiny will thus be justified, in a responsive approach, if a law does not have any direct or significant impact on a historically vulnerable group or individual dignity interests. Ordinary scrutiny will be appropriate where there is a greater impact on historically vulnerable or disadvantaged groups, the potential to create new forms of disadvantage, or greater impact on human dignity.[174] And the closest, most searching, scrutiny will be reserved for laws with the potential to disadvantage historically vulnerable groups and adversely affect human dignity.

Unlike Ely's own approach to the protection of "discrete and insular minorities," a responsive approach openly acknowledges the potential for reasonable disagreement about what counts as a "historically vulnerable group" for these purposes.[175] As Chapter 2 notes, historical vulnerability will be a product of a group's social, economic, and political power; and these may vary over time, or point in different directions. And this suggests that disadvantage itself must be seen through the lens of evolving democratic understandings of a group's social, economic, and political power(lessness), and the moral or political valence to that lack of power.

In addition, a responsive approach suggests that any values-based approach should be complemented by attention to the risk of democratic dysfunction. Some forms of unequal treatment, for example, have a close relationship to the electoral process: they involve issues of voter suppression, unequal access to the ballot box, or the meaning of principles such as "one person, one vote." Like laws that burden freedom of expression with a close nexus to the political process, a responsive approach to judicial review would therefore suggest that laws of this kind should attract the closest or most demanding form of scrutiny. Similarly, some laws impinging on individual dignity are largely the product of legislative blind spots of application, accommodation, or perspective, whereas others are the result of more recent, reasoned debate. Some laws that affect historically vulnerable groups are likewise the pure product of legislative inertia,

---

[174] On the relevance of new potential disadvantage, see, *e.g.*, Pretoria (City of) v. Walker [1998] 3 B Const LR 257.
[175] *Compare* discussion in Chapter 2, *supra*.

whereas others reflect more recent, reasoned attempts to overcome that disadvantage. And a responsive approach suggests that the calibration of both tiered forms of scrutiny and proportionality-style doctrines should be informed by this degree of a recent, reasoned deliberation on a question.

Consider laws discriminating *in favor of* historically disadvantaged groups. In the United States, the Supreme Court has held that for state actors, affirmative action will only be constitutionally permissible (i.e., withstand a test of strict scrutiny) where it seeks to remedy institution-specific forms of past discrimination, or promote broader diversity goals.[176] Such measures cannot aim simply to provide compensation or restitution for societal-level forms of past discrimination or disadvantage.[177] But in many other countries, the dominant understanding of constitutional equality guarantees is that they emphatically allow—and may even require—measures of this kind.

In Canada, for example, section 15(2) of the Canadian *Charter* provides that the general guarantee of equality in section 15(1) "does not preclude any law, program or activity that has as its object the amelioration of conditions of disadvantaged individuals or groups including those that are disadvantaged because of race, national or ethnic origin, color, religion, sex, age or mental or physical disability." In South Africa, section 9(3) of the 1996 Constitution provides that: "To promote the achievement of equality, legislative and other measures designed to protect or advance persons, or categories of persons, disadvantaged, by unfair discrimination may be taken." And in India, Articles 15(4) and 16(4) provide that nothing in those articles, or Article 29, prevent "the State from making any special provision for the advancement of any socially and educationally backward classes of citizens or for the Scheduled Castes [i.e., Dalits] and the Scheduled Tribes."

There are a variety of ways in which courts may approach constitutional "carve-outs" of this kind.[178] One approach to such carve-outs is that they simply provide valuable textual evidence that constitutional drafters intend to endorse a *substantive* approach to equality, which includes a commitment to eradicating group-based forms of subordination, and to taking into account these differences in position or starting point. That is, they could be seen as purely "confirmatory" of the kind of calibrated approach to equality doctrine set out above, or as simply an additional source of guidance for courts

---

[176] Regents of the University of California v. Bakke, 438 U.S. 265 (1978); Grutter v. Bollinger, 539 U.S. 306 (2003); Gratz v. Bollinger, 539 U.S. 244 (2003).
[177] Regents of the University of California v. Bakke, 438 U.S. 265 (1978); Grutter v. Bollinger, 539 U.S. 306 (2003); Gratz v. Bollinger, 539 U.S. 244 (2003).
[178] Dixon, *Constitutional Carve-outs, supra* note 96.

in interpreting general prohibitions on inequality.[179] Another approach, however, is to treat provisions of this kind as having some (additional) independent operation—or as providing either an exception to a general (quite formalist) prohibition on discrimination, or as creating a special *safe harbor* for certain forms of positive discrimination.[180]

One potential objection to this safe harbor-based approach is that it *assumes* that, rather than tests whether, a law that aims to benefit a particular group will in fact do so.[181] This is a question on which there is scope for reasonable disagreement: some measures designed to benefit a historically disadvantaged group, for example, may end up having an adverse impact—because they tend to provide limited meaningful opportunities, but perpetuate damaging stereotypes and stigma.[182] This is also one reason a majority of the modern US Supreme Court has held that race-based affirmative action measures should attract the same form of strict scrutiny as all other forms of race-based classification.[183]

But a safe harbor-based approach assumes that an assessment of these risks can legitimately be made by legislators, as well as judges. And it seeks to encourage legislators to adopt measures of this kind—by reducing the degree to which they are subject to costly and time-consuming forms of legal challenge.[184] In this sense, they could be seen as a proactive attempt by

---

[179] *See, e.g.*, Minister of Finance v. Van Heerden, 2004 (6) SA 121 (Sachs J); Lovelace v. Ontario, 2000 SCC 37, [108] (Iacobucci J.). *See also* discussion in Dixon, *Constitutional Carve-outs*, *supra* note 96.

[180] Dixon, *Constitutional Carve-outs*, *supra* note 96.

[181] *See, e.g.*, Richmond v. Croson, 488 U.S. 469 (1989) (O'Connor J.) (finding that, "absent searching judicial inquiry," there is no way of knowing whether a classification is "benign" or motivated by illegitimate notions of racial inferiority or racial politics); Grutter v. Bollinger, 539 U.S. 306 (2003) (O'Connor J.) (holding that strict scrutiny of affirmative action measures necessary to "smoke out" illegitimate uses of race).

[182] *See* Grutter v. Bollinger, 539 U.S. 306 (2003) (Thomas J); Gratz v. Bollinger, 539 U.S. 244 (2003); Fisher v. University of Texas, 570 U.S. 297 (2013) (*Fisher I*); Fisher v. University of Texas, 579 U.S. 365 (2016) (*Fisher II*).

[183] *See, e.g.*, Grutter v. Bollinger, 539 U.S. 306 (2003); Gratz v. Bollinger, 539 U.S. 244 (2003); Fisher v. University of Texas, 570 U.S. 297 (2013) (*Fisher I*); Fisher v. University of Texas, 579 U.S. 365 (2016) (*Fisher II*). In practice, there is of course debate about whether the standard applied was closer to intermediate or heightened rather than true strict scrutiny: *see, e.g.*, Evan Gerstmann & Christopher Shortell, *The Many Faces of Strict Scrutiny: How the Supreme Court Changes the Rules in Race Cases*, 72 U. PITT. L. REV. 1 (2010). And the deeper reason is that the Court has tended to embrace a quite formalistic rather than substantive approach to equality. *See, e.g.*, Catharine A. MacKinnon, *Substantive Equality: A Perspective*, 1 MINN. L. REV. 96 (2011); Catharine A. MacKinnon, *Substantive Equality Revisited: A Reply to Sandra Fredman*, 14 INT'L J. CONST. L. 739 (2016); Kimberlé Crenshaw, *Demarginalizing the Intersection of Race and Sex: A Black Feminist Critique of Antidiscrimination Doctrine, Feminist Theory and Antiracist Politics*, 1989 U. CHI. LEGAL F. 139 (1989).

[184] *See, e.g.*, Minister of Finance v. Van Heerden, [2004] (6) SA 121, [42] (Moseneke J.) (suggesting that without such a gateway such measures could be "stillborn"); [86] (Mokgoro J.) (arguing that a similar, if somewhat more demanding approach, helped reduce the "burden" on the state in taking such measures); R v. Kapp, [2008] 2 SCR 483, [40] (suggesting that such an approached helped remove the "fear of challenge" or reduce the potential political costs to legislators).

constitutional drafters, and judges, to overcome the risk of legislative inertia in the achievement of substantive commitments to equality.

This is also entirely consistent with a responsive approach to judicial review, subject to one important requirement—that there is in fact a history of recent, reasoned deliberation on the merits of policies of this kind, and no immediate threat of democratic backsliding. Some affirmative action measures may simply be the product of burdens of inertia—or a failure to revisit past policies or assumptions about how (best) to achieve racial, gender or religious equality. Or they may be the product of blind spots of perspective. Rather than attracting minimal scrutiny, provisions of this kind should also be subject to more ordinary forms of scrutiny, which encourage reconsideration of the true necessity and proportionality of such measures.

In the United States, for instance, Congress voted in 1982 and 2006 to reauthorize the 1965 *Voting Rights Act* (VRA), in ways that reflected a clear commitment to protecting minority voting rights,[185] but the original coverage formula Congress adopted in section 5 of the VRA remained unchanged, in ways many observers suggest were linked to coalition-driven forms of inertia.[186] In applying relevant federalism or federal equality doctrines, in *Shelby County v. Holder*, a responsive approach would therefore suggest that the Court was correct to apply ordinary rather than minimal scrutiny to the constitutionality of the pre-clearance procedures established by section 5 of the VRA.[187] But equally, it would suggest that the Court was wrong not to place greater weight on the *past* as well as ongoing political disadvantage of African-Americans, and to do nothing to help counter that inertia—for example, by issuing a form of weak-strong remedy, such as a suspended declaration of invalidity.[188]

In some cases, so-called affirmative action measures may even pose a risk of democratic backsliding. Clearly, one important way in which to realize a commitment to substantive equality is to provide for reserved seats, or special quotas, for historically disadvantaged groups in parliamentary elections. Doing so can have powerful symbolic benefits.[189] And in some cases it can

---

[185] *Shelby County v. Holder*, 570 U.S. 529, 530, 534–47 (2013) (Roberts C.J.). Richard Pildes, *Political Avoidance, Constitutional Theory, and the VRA*, 117 YALE L.J. POCKET PART 148 (2007).

[186] *See*, Nathaniel Persily, *The Promise and Pitfalls of the New Voting Rights Act*, 117 YALE. L.J. 174 (2007); Pildes, *supra* note 185.

[187] *Shelby County v. Holder*, 570 U.S. 529, 553 (2013) (Roberts C.J.).

[188] *Id. See* Chapter 7, *infra*, for further discussion.

[189] *See, e.g.*, Jennie E. Burnet, *Women Have Found Respect: Gender Quotas, Symbolic Representation, and Female Empowerment in Rwanda*, 7 POL. & GENDER 303 (2011); Christina Isabel Zuber, *Reserved Seats, Political Parties, and Minority Representation*, 14 ETHNOPOLITICS 390 (2015); Gretchen Bauer & Jennie E. Burnet, *Gender Quotas, Democracy, and Women's Representation in Africa: Some Insights from Democratic Botswana and Autocratic Rwanda*, 41 WOMEN'S STUD. INT'L FOR. 103 (2013).

translate into substantive gains in representation.[190] But electoral quotas of this kind also invite the possibility of manipulation by would-be authoritarians: they may introduce such quotas with a view to ensuring they are filled by party loyalists.[191] Or they may use them to gain the support of an electoral minority for a form of hybrid regime that is essentially competitive authoritarian, or electoral-autocratic, rather than truly democratic in nature.[192] Rather than effectively upholding all true "affirmative action programs," a responsive approach therefore suggests that constitutional equality doctrines should be calibrated to account for this danger. They should allow governments to defend the constitutionality of such action as necessary to achieving true political equality and redressing the past political disadvantage of a group, but under a test of heightened or close scrutiny.

In this sense, a responsive approach could be understood as "splitting the difference" between US and comparative approaches to affirmative action. Like most courts worldwide, it suggests that positive forms of discrimination should attract lower or more deferential forms of scrutiny than equivalent forms of negative discrimination—that is, something less demanding than true "strict" scrutiny in the United States. But equally, it suggests that reduced forms of scrutiny should themselves be variable in application: minimal or reduced scrutiny should apply only in cases where such measures have been openly and recently debated in a reasoned and inclusive way, and do not involve any direct threat to the democratic minimum core. More ordinary forms of scrutiny should apply to measures that have not been the subject of deliberation of this kind and involve a meaningful threat to individual dignity, and heightened scrutiny to those that involve a real risk of eroding the democratic minimum core.

---

[190] *See* HANNA FENICHEL PITKIN, THE CONCEPT OF REPRESENTATION (1972). *See, e.g.*, on Rwanda, Claire Devlin & Robert Elgie, *The Effect of Increased Women's Representation in Parliament: The Case of Rwanda*, 51 PARLIAMENTARY AFF. 237 (2008); Bauer & Burnet, *supra* note 189; Kathleen A. King, *Representation of Women: Constitutional Legislative Quotas in Rwanda and Uganda*, 1 CHARLESTON L. REV. 217 (2006).

[191] This, for example, is one way of viewing the role of gender quotas in Rwanda. *See* ROSALIND DIXON & DAVID LANDAU, ABUSIVE CONSTITUTIONAL BORROWING: LEGAL GLOBALIZATION & THE SUBVERSION OF LIBERAL DEMOCRACY 71–74 (2021).

[192] Mikael Wigell, *Mapping "Hybrid Regimes": Regime Types and Concepts in Comparative Politics*, 15 DEMOCRATIZATION 230 (2008). This could be one way to view the expanded rights to communal representation for indigenous Fijians proposed by 2000 coup leader, George Speight, and his interim Prime Minister, Laisenia Qarase. While indigenous Fijians have clearly suffered historical disadvantage, the aim of such policies seemed to be to secure support for the Speight-Qarase government. See, *e.g.*, discussion in Rosalind Dixon, *Constitutional Rights as Bribes*, 50 CONN. L. REV. 767, 802–03 (2018); Sina Emde, *Feared Rumours and Rumours of Fear: The Politicisation of Ethnicity During the Fiji Coup in May 2000*, 75 OCEANIA 387, 388, 392, 396 (2005).

Table 4.2 Calibrating Judgments about (Positive) Discrimination

Minimal scrutiny ↔	Reduced scrutiny ↔	Ordinary scrutiny ↔	Heightened/close scrutiny
Aims to and is rationally related to advancing position of historically advantaged group *and* Recent, reasoned, legislative deliberation on the topic	Minimal burden on historically disadvantaged group and individual dignity/opportunity	Adversely affects historically disadvantaged group *or/and* Moderate to significant burden on human dignity/individual opportunity *or/and* Evidence of legislative blind spots *or* burdens of inertia	Factors attracting ordinary/heightened scrutiny *and* Close nexus between unequal treatment and elections/electoral politics

A responsive approach also suggests a variable approach to questions of legislative intent. In the United States, the Supreme Court has held that only intentional discrimination is sufficient to attract heightened scrutiny, whereas in most countries, the test is one of discriminatory or disparate impact.[193] In a responsive approach, intent will also be a relevant touchstone in some but not all cases. In cases involving threats to the democratic minimum core, as Chapter 3 outlined, intent is a key indicator of whether relevant changes are likely to do long-term damage to electoral and institutional pluralism. Hence, it is also relevant to determining the applicability of a test of close or heightened scrutiny. But in cases involving blind spots and burdens of inertia, intent does not have the same significance: indeed, it is often legislation inattention not intentional harm that is the source of democratic dysfunction. Ordinary or reduced, as opposed to minimal, scrutiny will thus depend on the impact rather than intent of a law.

E. Deference and a Legislative Action/Inaction Distinction

A responsive approach could thus be seen as embracing a form of legislative action/inaction distinction in the application of a test of tiered scrutiny or structured proportionality. It rejects the idea of across-the-board or absolute deference by courts to legislative constitutional judgments but suggests

---

[193] Washington v. Davis, 426 U.S. 229 (1976). See also, TARUNABH KHAITAN, A THEORY OF DISCRIMINATION LAW (2015).

that recent, reasoned legislative deliberation on a question will be one factor pointing toward greater judicial deference to certain legislative constitutional judgments.

Some scholars suggest that any form of deference by courts to legislative (or executive) constitutional judgments is antithetical to constitutionalism and constitutional commitments to judicial independence and the rule of law.[194] Others suggest that judicial deference should be restricted to judgments about policy as opposed to constitutional principle, or about how particular legislative objectives are best achieved, rather than the scope or meaning of constitutional principles and requirements.[195] But at the core of any truly dialogic theory is the idea that courts and legislators (and in some cases executive actors) should *share* responsibility for interpreting and implementing constitutional principles and show appropriate deference to the institutional strengths of each in this process.[196]

Similar ideas underpin other democracy-sensitive theories of judicial review. Matthias Kumm, for example, suggests that where there has been "a serious, extended and mutually respectful parliamentary debate" this provides a "good reason for a court to be deferential to the outcome reached."[197] Other theories have a less idealized conception of legislative debate and deliberation, but emphasize the degree to which democratic processes are well-functioning. Theunis Roux suggests that "judges should be thinking about the quality of democracy in the society in which they are operating and adapting their role to changing democratic pathologies [or blockages] or downgrading that role to the extent that the democratic system begins to function better."[198] And Michael Dorf and Charles Sabel argue that in a "democratic experimentalist" approach the intensity of judicial review of both administrative action and legislation should be calibrated to the degree to which an administrative agency or legislative body has "under[taken] the kind of information and coordination effort necessary to generate rolling best-practice standards," or a legislative body has "canvass[ed]" alternative means of achieving a given objective,

---

[194] *See, e.g.*, Luc Tremblay, *The Legitimacy of Judicial Review: The Limits of Dialogue Between Courts and Legislatures*, 3 INT. J. CONST. L. 617 (2005).
[195] *See, e.g.*, TOM HICKMAN, PUBLIC LAW AFTER THE HUMAN RIGHTS ACT (2010).
[196] Jeremy Waldron, *Some Models of Dialogue Between Judges and Legislators*, 23 SUP. CT. L. REV. (2D) 7 (2004); Rosalind Dixon, *The Supreme Court of Canada and Constitutional (Equality) Baselines*, 50 OSGOODE HALL LAW J. 637 (2009); Rosalind Dixon, *Constitutional "Dialogue" and "Deference"*, in CONSTITUTIONAL DIALOGUE: RIGHTS, DEMOCRACY, INSTITUTIONS 1 (Geoffrey Sigalet et al. eds., 2019).
[197] Kumm, *supra* note 153, at 167 (emphasis added).
[198] Theunis Roux, *In Defence of Empirical Entanglement: The Methodological Flaw in Waldron's Case Against Judicial Review*, in The Cambridge Handbook of Deliberative Constitutionalism (Ron Levy et al. eds., 2016); David Landau, *A Dynamic Theory of Judicial Role*, 55 B.C. L. REV. 1501 (2014).

"given reasons" for its choice, "rooted in the particular of local experience and reflecting the diversity of local views".[199]

All these approaches—including responsive judicial review—can be seen as closely related to, if not an actual species of, "semi-procedural review."[200] While they differ in their vision of what democracy or democratic deliberation entails, they fuse a substantive approach to the scope and definition of constitutional guarantees with at least a *partially* proceduralized approach to determining the justifiability of limits on those guarantees.[201]

---

[199] Michael C. Dorf & Charles F. Sabel, *A Constitution of Democratic Experimentalism*, 98 COLUM. L. REV. 267, 399 (1998).

[200] *See* Ittai Bar-Siman-Tov, *Semiprocedural Judicial Review*, 6 LEGISPRUDENCE 271 (2012).

[201] *Id.* at 273.

5
Democratic Dysfunction and the Effectiveness of Responsive Review

One of the criticisms of Ely's own version of process-based judicial review is that it did not take seriously the challenge of judicial *capacity*. In *Democracy and Distrust*, Ely focused largely on issues of judicial legitimacy and gave limited attention to the actual capacity of courts to effectively protect the democratic process. One potential reason for this was that Ely was writing about the Warren Court, a court that was widely seen as extremely strong and powerful—indeed potentially too powerful. He was not writing with attention to the experiences of weaker, more fragile courts, with more incipient forms of legal and political authority.

Democracy and Distrust largely preceded the modern social science of judging. Since 1980, political scientists, economists, and empirically oriented constitutional comparativists have all contributed to a much more fine-grained understanding of the necessary preconditions for effective forms of judicial democracy promotion. Any modern theory of representation-reinforcement, therefore, must also take account of these understandings and explain both how and when we might expect judges actually to be successful in overcoming democratic dysfunction.

The aim of this chapter is to address these questions of judicial capacity at three levels: first, by considering how judges can go about identifying risks of antidemocratic monopoly power and democratic blind spots and burdens of inertia; second, by examining how courts can succeed in countering these sources of democratic dysfunction; and third, by considering the necessary legal and political preconditions for courts to do so.

The conceptual framework for answering these questions is relatively straightforward. Courts can identify risks of antidemocratic monopoly by focusing on changes that, either separately or in aggregate, have the capacity to have broad-ranging effects on electoral or institutional pluralism, and by considering the likely visibility and reversibility of relevant changes. For legislative blind spots, they can look at the actual legislative history behind a law, or lessons from other jurisdictions about potential less rights restrictive policy alternatives, and for burdens of inertia, at a range of democratic sources—including public opinion polls, legislative deliberation, comparative sources, and even legislative patterns within a federal system. They can also counter these risks through a combination of coercive and communicative forms of intervention. Both these tools can help courts counter blind spots and burdens of inertia. And they can help raise the political costs of undertaking measures that contribute to monopoly, in ways that contribute a form of "*speed bump*" or deterrent against such action.[1]

The more difficult question is determining when judges will have both the institutional capital and skills necessary for this logic to apply. Courts will be aided in performing this task by the parties before them, and in some cases *amicus curiae*, and need not rely on all of these sources in order to engage in effective representation-reinforcement. But even still, not all courts or judges will be equally well placed or equipped to engage in review of this kind. To do so, courts must have the necessary degree of political independence, remedial tools, and the political and litigation support structure to undertake the task.[2] And as we will see in subsequent chapters, individual judges must be skilled in orthodox forms of legal reasoning but equally capable of adopting a sensitive and responsive judicial voice.

In arguing that courts can play a valuable role in countering democratic blockages, therefore, I do not suggest that courts can or should seek to do so in all cases. The idea of responsive judicial review is that courts should seek to counter democratic blockages where they have the necessary capacity and legitimacy to do so—not that they should attempt to do so in ways that are insensitive to the specific legal and political context, and especially limits on their own capacity or legitimacy. And of course, judges themselves may disagree about when these conditions are present, so that even judges that are generally open to the idea of democratic representation-reinforcement may disagree about when and how they should go about this task. But that does not detract

---

[1] Rosalind Dixon & David Landau, *Transnational Constitutionalism and a Limited Doctrine of Unconstitutional Constitutional Amendment*, 13 INT'L J. CONST. L. 606 (2015). For discussion of these ideas, see also Yaniv Roznai, *Who Will Save the Redheads? Towards an Anti-Bully Theory of Judicial Review and Protection of Democracy*, 29 WM. & MARY BILL RTS. J. 1 (2019); TOM GINSBURG & AZIZ Z. HUQ, HOW TO SAVE A CONSTITUTIONAL DEMOCRACY 186–89 (2018); Bojan Bugaric, *Can Law Protect Democracy? Legal Institutions as "Speed Bumps"*, 11 HAGUE J. RULE L. 447, 448–50 (2019).

[2] Compare Marta Cartabia, *COVID-19 and I-CON*, I-CONNECT (May 21, 2020), <http://www.iconnectblog.com/2020/05/icon-volume-18-issue-1-editorial/> (arguing the need for a more relational account of courts' role and capacity to perform various constitutional functions); Varun Gauri & Daniel M. Brinks, *Human Rights as Demands for Communicative Action*, 20 J. POL. PHIL. 407 (2012) (on demand and supply-side variables necessary for effective judicial social rights protection).

from the value of responsive judicial review as a guiding idea for courts in a range of real-world constitutional democracies.

A. Detecting Democratic Dysfunction

How do courts determine whether democratic dysfunction exists? For the most part, they will be required to make these judgments based on the evidence presented to them by the parties and their lawyers. But in some cases, they may also be able to rely on evidence and argument from *amicus curiae*, or *elicit* information from government and civil society, by having special hearings on a question, or making interim orders designed to prompt government and civil society to provide this information.[3]

Amicus curiae can present arguments of law or contribute evidence about social facts.[4] The model for this in the United States (US) was the lengthy brief submitted by Justice Louis Brandeis, as a lawyer, in *Muller v. Oregon* documenting the health impacts of long working hours on women, hence briefs of this kind are often referred to as "Brandeis briefs."[5] While not all briefs of this kind will necessarily be reliable, they can often provide useful information about the broad contours of democratic opinion on a question.[6] And in some cases, the mere fact of various briefs being filed may itself provide information to a court about democratic opinion: if the civil society actors involved are large and significant enough, who files for what side can itself give a court important information about the attitudes of these actors on constitutional questions.

---

[3] *See, e.g.*, Allison Orr Larsen & Neal Devins, *The Amicus Machine*, 102 VA. L. REV. 1901 (2016); Anthony J. Franze & R. Reeves Anderson, *Record Breaking Term for Amicus Curiae in the Supreme Court Reflects New Norm*, NAT'L L.J. (Aug. 19, 2015), <https://www.arnoldporter.com/~/media/files/persp ectives/publications/2015/08/record-breaking-term-for-amicus-curiae-in-suprem__/files/publicat ion/fileattachment/recordbreakingtermforamicuscuriaeinsupremecourtr__.pdf;> .Evan Caminker, *A Glimpse Behind and Beyond Grutter*, 48 ST. LOUIS U. L.J. 889 (2004); Allison Orr Larsen, *The Trouble with Amicus Facts*, 100 VA. L. REV. 1757 (2014); Stevan Kochevar, *Amici Curiae in Civil Law Jurisdictions*, 122 YALE L.J. 1653 (2013); Christina Murray, *Litigating in the Public Interest: Intervention and the Amicus Curiae*, 10 S. AFR. J. HUM. RTS. 240 (1994).

[4] *See, e.g.*, Larsen & Devins, *The Amicus Machine*, supra note 3; Franze & Reeves Anderson, *Record Breaking Term for Amicus Curiae in the Supreme Court Reflects New Norm*, supra note 3; Caminker, *A Glimpse Behind and Beyond Grutter*, supra note 3; Larsen, *The Trouble with Amicus Facts*, supra note 3; Kochevar, *Amici Curiae in Civil Law Jurisdictions*, supra note 3; Murray, *Litigating in the Public Interest: Intervention and the Amicus Curiae*, supra note 3.

[5] 208 U.S. 412 (1908). *See* David E. Bernstein, *Brandeis Brief Myths*, 15 GREEN BAG 2D 9 (2011).

[6] This is especially true if they are uncontested: *see* Rosalind Dixon, *The Functional Constitution: Re-reading the 2014 High Court Constitutional Term*, 43 FED. L. REV. 455, 471 (2015).

Assessing this evidence, however, will inevitably call for a series of evaluative judgments by courts. For instance, when will threats to electoral and institutional pluralism be sufficient to warrant a judicial response? And when will it be too late for courts effectively to counter the risk of electoral or institutional monopoly?

The key yardstick for courts in answering this question will be the concept of the democratic minimum core. And both the concept, and its application, can be informed by attention to comparative constitutional practices.[7] Courts, for example, may look to countries facing similar risks of democratic backsliding, or countries that have already experienced more dramatic forms of erosion, in order to understand the path that democratic erosion may take. Or they may engage in a form of "transnational anchoring" and consider whether proposed legal changes are to laws or practices adopted by a wide range of other constitutional democracies or else to more historically contingent national constitutional arrangements.[8] If there was no meaningful support elsewhere for the proposed changes, this would make these changes presumptively suspect from a democratic constitutional perspective and call for special justification by the state as to why those changes were a necessary response to a distinctive national problem, or a new and pressing global problem, whereas if there was such support, this would suggest a lower risk to the democratic minimum core.

At the same time, one of the challenges facing courts is that it will not always be clear what the impact will be of proposed constitutional changes on the democratic minimum core. Sometimes, what appears to be a process of democratic erosion may in fact be the beginning of a process of democratic transformation—or the transition from one model of democratic constitutionalism to another quite different variant or specification of those ideas. Or it may be the beginnings of a major reform within an existing democratic constitutional tradition or order.

This is one reason a process of "transnational anchoring" cannot be treated as conclusive of whether constitutional change is legitimate, or illegitimate, in nature. If it were, it could become a major obstacle to democratic constitutional transformation.

Conversely, courts may sometimes be too slow to identify changes as posing a risk of electoral or institutional monopoly. One of the hallmarks of abusive constitutional change is that it often involves changes that, by themselves, do

---

[7] Whether this is something courts are open to will, of course, vary by country and context.
[8] Dixon & Landau, *Transnational Constitutionalism*, *supra* note 1; David Landau & Rosalind Dixon, *Constraining Constitutional Change*, 50 WAKE FOREST L. REV. 859 (2015).

not pose an obvious or immediate threat to the minimum core—yet together, do so quite clearly.[9] This can also make it difficult for courts to assess, at any given time, whether to invalidate specific measures as posing a threat to the democratic minimum core. Courts must, first, determine what counts as sufficient evidence to establish a risk of electoral or institutional monopoly. And second, they must determine the threshold level of risk to the democratic minimum core necessary to justify judicial intervention. Both questions will also require courts to make a series of complex, context-dependent judgments.

Judgments of this kind, however, can usefully be informed by courts considering several factors, including the degree to which specific legal changes are likely to have (i) enduring or irreversible legal and political consequences, and (ii) effects that are visible or observable, over the short-term.

Again, one important guiding principle will be a principle of political reversibility.[10] The key question here will not be formal legal reversibility—though that may be one factor a court considers in assessing the overall effect of a proposed legal change. Rather, it will be the degree to which there are likely to be popular or elite pressures to continue, as opposed to reverse, those changes. Pressures of this kind may arise for a number of reasons. Democratic citizens may become used to new arrangements in ways that create a form of *status quo* bias. The independent institutions they rely on to call out, or publicize, democratic harms may be effectively silenced or deprived of power. Or political elites may gain power and privileges that they are reluctant to relinquish, and that create exactly the kind of problem of self-entrenchment identified by Ely himself—that is, barriers to successful competition and entry into the political market by opponents.

Another consideration will be the degree to which evidence pointing to a risk to the democratic minimum core is likely to be publicly available. If it is, it will make sense for courts to apply a demanding standard in assessing the evidence needed to establish such a risk. But if that evidence is classified or confidential, or not readily accessed by "outsiders" to an institution, it will make much greater sense for courts to apply a more relaxed standard to assessing

---

[9] The changes to floor-crossing, under challenge in the *UDM* case in South Africa, could be considered an example. On their face, they did not pose an obvious threat to the democratic minimum core, but over time, and in the context of other changes, there was a much greater risk to political pluralism: *see* Rosalind Dixon & Theunis Roux, *Marking Constitutional Transitions: The Law and Politics of Constitutional Implementation in South Africa*, in From Parchment to Practice: Challenges of Implementing New Constitutions (Tom Ginsburg & Aziz Huq eds., 2020). *Compare also* Sujit Choudhry, *"He Had a Mandate": The South African Constitutional Court and the African National Congress in a Dominant Party Democracy*, 2 Const. Ct. Rev. 1 (2009).

[10] *Compare* Chapter 4, *supra* on implications and reversibility.

relevant evidence. The same is true for evidence that is only likely to be publicly available or observable in the long-term.

Take attempts by a government to erode the independence of two different "fourth" branch institutions—that is, an anticorruption commission and a central bank. Attacks on an anticorruption body may lead to a substantial increase in government corruption. But the public often has very little knowledge of, or information about, corruption of this kind. This is not to say that *attacks* on anticorruption bodies will necessarily be non-public or hard to detect. But the *effects* of corruption on the democratic minimum core will often be delayed, and thus hard to detect within a reasonable political time frame: a systematic increase in corruption might deter pro-democratic actors from running for office, or serving in government, but these effects are only likely to occur after current officer-holders leave office. And an increase in corruption may open the door to broader forms of political patronage and clientelism that undermine true democratic competition, but again, these effects will only be felt after one to two election cycles.

Attacks on a central bank, in contrast, will often occur in public and have more immediate economic effects.[11] True central bank independence prevents governments directly meeting or communicating with members of the bank. Hence, attacks on the bank's independence will often need to occur *publicly*, in speeches and through the media. The effect of any perceived attack on central bank independence will also tend to be felt in the short- as well as longer-term: capital and currency markets are extremely sensitive to perceived attacks of this kind and will often react within minutes or hours, rather than months and years. These market reactions are also both visible and harmful to the public—often leading to an increase in government bond rates which flow through into private and business lending. A government that attacks its central bank, therefore, may create publicly identifiable and immediate short-run economic harms, in ways that generate at least some socio-political support for continued central bank independence. Accordingly, there will also be less need for judicial protection of central bank independence than for institutions such as an anticorruption commission.

---

[11] *See, e.g.*, attacks on the Reserve Bank of India (RBI) and its governor: Tarunabh Khaitan, *Killing a Constitution with a Thousand Cuts: Executive Aggrandizement and Party-state Fusion in India*, 14 Law & Ethics Hum. Rts. 49, 83–84 (2020). *See also*, Eswar Prasad, *Commentary: Warning, India's Central Bank is Under Attack*, Channel News Asia (Nov. 23, 2018), <https://headtopics.com/sg/commentary-warning-india-s-central-bank-is-under-attack-2672282> (on attacks against both the RBI and US Federal Reserve).

In the case of democratic blind spots, the most logical starting point for courts seeking to identify these blockages will be the legislative debate or record for particular legislation. Blind spots of application arise where the legislature, as a whole, fails to consider the impact of laws on the enjoyment of constitutional rights, or other guarantees, and the most obvious place to start in determining whether that is true is to look at the relevant legislative history.

For blind spots of accommodation, the question will have a more evaluative quality. It will require courts to identify the full range of regulatory measures that could have been adopted by the legislature, and then whether those measures would be likely to have done more to protect constitutional rights, without imposing a significant cost on the relevant legislative objective. This will also require identifying both the range of plausible regulatory alternatives and some understanding of their likely impact. But in making these judgments, courts can often rely on expert evidence, or evidence of social scientists and other experts on regulation. Another potential source of information for courts will be comparative in nature and focused on the actual practices and experiences of other jurisdictions in regulating a particular area.

For burdens of inertia, the task facing courts will be at once both simpler and more challenging. Courts must seek to ascertain the actual contours of democratic opinion, and the evolution or change in that opinion, specifically as it relates to constitutional commitments. One important source of evidence or information for courts in this context will therefore be public opinion data or polling.[12] But it will also be a source with clear limitations: polling of this kind is subject to a range of familiar limitations, including the potential for it to be insufficiently representative of a broad cross-section of voters and influenced by "framing effects," or how questions are framed or asked.[13] But for courts, they have a key additional limitation: they are not sources judges are accustomed to assessing or engaging with, and are indications of opinion that are disconnected from thicker democratic commitments to rights and deliberation.

A second source of information will be legislative change in an area, or related areas. This will not always be the case. For example, it would be dangerous to rely on particular legislation under challenge as a guide to the democratic understandings that should inform that challenge. Doing so involves a form of circular logic and does not account for the possibility of democratic burdens

---

[12] *Compare* Rosalind Dixon, *A Democratic Theory of Constitutional Comparison*, 56 AM. J. COMP. L. 947 (2008).

[13] *See, e.g.*, Dennis Chong & James N. Druckman, *Framing Public Opinion in Competitive Democracies*, 101 AM. POL. SCI. REV. 637 (2007); Thomas E. Nelson et al., *Toward a Psychology of Framing Effects*, 19 POL. BEHAV. 221 (1997).

of inertia. But broader legislative trends across time in an area can be a useful guide to the scope of democratic opinion that is both responsive and deliberative in nature. Information of this kind will also be especially rich in a federal system, where there are many different legislatures that can act on an issue, and regional or transnational systems where national-level developments can help inform both the application of a "margin of appreciation" doctrine and the identification of evolving moral-political attitudes on the part of a regional democratic majority.[14]

Third and finally, courts may again be able to rely on processes of constitutional comparison, and specifically on a form of comparison that is reflective and dynamic in nature.[15] The logic of reflective comparison generally is simple: it is that encountering others makes us understand ourselves better, or to "engage in a discussion of what our constitutional character is, rather than leaving us to take it for granted."[16] In some cases, this may highlight the need for change or critical reflection on those practices. In others, it may help clarify what is distinctive about national values and practices. Some forms of reflective comparison, however, will have a more dynamic focus. They will seek to understand how changes in the practices of countries with sufficient ongoing general and "topical" similarity may cast light on potential changes in democratic constitutional understandings domestically.[17]

Of course, one difficult question for courts is how they should approach cases in which there is no clear or discernible majority position on a question. In many countries, public opinion on key questions has become increasingly polarized.[18] And polarization of this kind can mean there is no actual majority viewpoint on a question but at best, a plurality view, or a series of competing viewpoints. In fact, this may be closer to the norm than the exception in democratic decision-making; as Kenneth Arrow, a Nobel laureate, showed in his pathbreaking work on social choice theory, it is generally impossible for collective processes of decision-making to respect even quite a minimal set of principled democratic requirements (i.e., non-dictatorship, unrestricted

---

[14] *See, e.g.,* Thomas A. O'Donnell, *The Margin of Appreciation Doctrine: Standards in the Jurisprudence of the European Court of Human Rights*, 4 HUM. RTS. Q. 474 (1982); Jeffrey A. Brauch, *The Margin of Appreciation and the Jurisprudence of the European Court of Human Rights: Threat to the Rule of Law*, 11 COLUM. J. EUR. L. 113 (2004); George Letsas, *Two Concepts of the Margin of Appreciation*, 26 OXFORD J. LEGAL STUD. 705 (2006). *See also* Rosalind Dixon, *Proportionality and Comparative Constitutional Law versus Studies*, 12 LAW & ETHICS HUM. RTS. 203 (2018).

[15] Dixon, *A Democratic Theory of Constitutional Law, supra* note 12. One might raise questions, of course, about how well-equipped courts are to engage in comparison of this kind. But this is closely related to broader questions of judicial capacity of a kind I address in Chapter 9, *infra*.

[16] Mark Tushnet, *The Possibilities of Comparative Constitutional Law*, 108 YALE L.J. 1225, 1281 (1999).

[17] *Compare* Dixon, *A Democratic Theory of Constitutional Comparison, supra* note 12.

[18] *See, e.g.,* NOLAN MCCARTY ET AL., POLARIZED AMERICA (2006).

domain, Pareto efficiency, and independence of irrelevant alternatives).[19] Principled, stable social choices are possible only if there is sufficient consensus among voters, certain choices are ruled out *ex ante*, or there is some democratic mechanism (such as political parties) that can effectively structure social choices along a single dimension, such as a left-right policy axis (so-called single-peaked preferences).[20]

There are, however, two potential responses to this situation: one is to treat it as an instance that requires ongoing democratic deliberation, with a view to reaching increased agreement or consensus—and therefore a form of abstention or avoidance by constitutional courts.[21] The other is for courts to attempt to identify an *emerging* if still nascent democratic majority position. In doing so, a court will inevitably exercise an important form of evaluative judgment—both about the most normatively desirable direction of constitutional change and the likely evolution of democratic opinion. This form of evaluative judgment also inevitably carries with it an increased risk of "error" compared to more restrained forms of judicial review.

But in some cases, a court's intervention may foreshadow increasing democratic support for a particular constitutional claim or understanding, or even help galvanize change in popular attitudes, which then mean that there is actual democratic majority—not just plurality—support for certain forms of constitutional change. This is also an argument for courts seeking to counter both actual and emerging forms of legislative inertia. Indeed, this was the argument by Ely's teacher and colleague at Yale, Alexander Bickel, who suggested that courts should "declare as law ... such principles as will—in time, but in a rather foreseeable future—gain general assent."[22]

B. Countering Dysfunction

Constitutional—or ultimate appellate—courts worldwide have a range of different institutional features and powers. Some courts enjoy *abstract* powers of review—or powers to review legislation *ex ante* before it is enacted and not

---

[19] Kenneth J. Arrow, *A Difficulty in the Concept of Social Welfare*, 58 J. POL. ECON. 328 (1950).
[20] *See* discussion in DANIEL A. FARBER & PHILIP P. FRICKEY, LAW AND PUBLIC CHOICE: A CRITICAL INTRODUCTION (1991).
[21] *Compare* ALEXANDER M. BICKEL, THE LEAST DANGEROUS BRANCH: THE SUPREME COURT AT THE BAR OF POLITICS 181, 216 (1986); Erin F. Delaney, *Analyzing Avoidance: Judicial Strategy in Comparative Perspective*, 66 DUKE L.J. 1 (2016).
[22] BICKEL, *supra* note 21, at 239. *See* discussion in ROBERT BURT, THE CONSTITUTION IN CONFLICT 21–22 (1992).

to consider its application or validity after enactment. This, for example, was the model of judicial review advocated by Hans Kelsen and then adopted in Austria in 1920.[23] It also had important precursors in Latin America, in the *actio popularis* introduced in Colombia in 1910, and in Venezuela prior to 1920.[24] And it was common in many European countries for much of the twentieth century.[25] France only moved to adopt a mix of abstract and concrete review in 2008.[26]

Other courts conduct judicial review of legislation on a concrete or *a posteriori* basis. This is the dominant tradition of judicial review in the Anglo-American world and means that courts conduct processes of judicial review at the instigation of specific parties and in a way that involves the consideration of legislation as applied to particular concrete cases. An increasing number of courts worldwide also exercise both forms of review—often through a combination of different procedures, or procedures that allow direct access by petitioners as well as access by way of a referral or appeal. In Colombia, for example, the Constitutional Court hears a mix of both constitutional appeals and individual *"tutela"* petitions brought directly by individuals.[27] Similar forms of *"amparo"* procedure also exist in Argentina, Brazil, Mexico, and several other Latin American jurisdictions.[28]

Another of Kelsen's influences is that courts vary in the degree to which they are "specialized" versus "general" courts of appeal. Many countries now have some form of specialized constitutional court, with jurisdiction only in respect of constitutional matters.[29] Others, however, have a general appeals court with

---

[23] Victor Ferreres Comella, *The European Model of Constitutional Review of Legislation: Toward Decentralization*, 2 Int'l J. Const. L. 461 (2004).

[24] Manuel José Cepeda-Espinosa, *Judicial Activism in a Violent Context: The Origin, Role, and Impact of the Colombian Constitutional Court*, 3 Wash. U. Global Stud. L. Rev. 529 (2004); Mario Alberto Cajas Sarria, *The Colombian Model of Judicial Review of Legislation: A Predecessor to the Austrian Constitutional Court of 1920*, I-CONnect (Nov. 19, 2020), <http://www.iconnectblog.com/2020/11/the-colombian-model-of-judicial-review-of-legislation-a-predecessor-to-the-austrian-constitutional-court-of-1920/>; Vicente F. Benítez-R, *With a Little Help from the People:* Actio Popularis *and the Politics of Judicial Review of Constitutional Amendments in Colombia 1955–1990*, 19(3) Int'l J. Const. L. 1020 (2021).

[25] *Id.*

[26] *See* Otto Pfersmann, *Concrete Review as Indirect Constitutional Complaint in French Constitutional Law: A Comparative Perspective*, 6 Eur. Const. L. Rev. 223 (2010) for the broader history of judicial review in France; *see also* Alec Stone Sweet, The Birth of Judicial Politics in France: The Constitutional Council in Comparative Perspective (1992).

[27] *See* Manuel José Cepeda & David Landau, *A Broad Read of Ely: Political Process Theory for Fragile Democracies*, 19(2) Int'l J. Const. L. 548 (2021).

[28] Gloria Orrego Hoyos, *The Amparo Context in Latin American Jurisdiction: An Approach to an Empowering Action*, GlobaLex (Apr. 2013), <https://www.nyulawglobal.org/globalex/Amparo.html>. In Chile, the procedure is known as *Recurso de protección*. An amparo is closer to a writ of habeas corpus. *Id.*

[29] *See* Victor Ferreres Comella, *The Rise of Specialized Constitutional Courts*, in Comparative Constitutional Law 265 (Tom Ginsburg & Rosalind Dixon eds., 2011).

jurisdiction in constitutional matters. There may be important differences in the training and background of judges on the two kinds of court. Judges on specialized courts may have a variety of backgrounds, including legislative and academic backgrounds, whereas judges in ordinary courts will tend to be former practicing lawyers or lower court judges.

This may also mean there are differences among courts in their ability to identify and counter different kinds of democratic pathology or blockage; the composition and caseload of specialized courts, for example, may make them better equipped to identify currents in democratic opinion that point to legislative burdens of inertia, whereas the background and jurisdiction of judges on ordinary courts may mean they are better positioned to identify certain kinds of legislative blind spot. Whether this is true will depend on whether the caseload of a constitutional court gives it a broad view of issues and attitudes within civil society without overwhelming its capacity to give the necessary careful and detailed attention to specific cases.

Similarly, courts exercising abstract forms of review may have the capacity to counter legislative inertia but more limited capacity than courts with concrete powers of review to assess the law in action—as it applies to specific contexts and individuals—in ways that allow them effectively to identify and counter legislative blind spots. Typically, in systems of concrete review, for example, as former lawyers or lower court judges, most judges will have the benefit of significant experience in *applying* laws to particular concrete cases, and considering whether there are relevant procedural protections, or substantive exceptions, that apply in a particular case. At an appellate level, they are accustomed to judging the constitutionality of legislation by reference to a standard of scrutiny that invites attention to the question of whether laws are in fact narrowly tailored to the achievement of their objectives. This also often gives judges both the expertise and institutional framework necessary for identifying blind spots of accommodation—or ways in which particular laws could be more narrowly tailored to protect individual rights either at the level of statutory (re)interpretation or redrafting. But this will not always be true, especially in a constitutional system in which judicial review is conducted on a largely or exclusively abstract basis.[30]

Judges within different systems will also vary in their capacity to engage in successful representation-reinforcement. Some judges may have the necessary legal skills to do so, but lack broader political, prudential skills, and judgment.

---

[30] Malcolm Langford, *Why Judicial Review*, 2 OSLO L. REV. 36, 47–51 (2015).

Others may have stronger pragmatic, political skills but be too inclined to approach questions politically—without attention to the specific legal and institutional limitations that apply to courts as agents of democracy protection or promotion.

But constitutional—or ultimate appellate—courts also have a range of features in common that often do give them the institutional capacity to counter various sources of democratic dysfunction. Almost all courts conduct their proceedings largely, if not exclusively, in public, and they generally provide reasons for their decisions.[31] They are also often the subject of significant media scrutiny and attention.[32] In addition, at an ultimate appellate level, they generally have a caseload that allows them to give careful consideration to each case, and to deliberate in a way that is not strictly time-limited. In addition, those courts with a larger caseload generally have large staff of legally trained assistants who function as deputy or quasi-justices.[33]

Unlike legislators, judges also generally enjoy a long period of tenure, are protected from removal from office, and have limited incentives to respond to electoral demands and pressures (e.g., they are generally also protected from reductions in pay). They also face less of a direct trade-off between addressing issues of concern to electoral minorities and majorities. As Fred Schauer has shown, even courts such as the US Supreme Court generally play a limited role compared to legislatures in deciding the issues of greatest importance to democratic majorities.[34] In selecting cases of concern only to small minorities, therefore, courts will do less to displace attention to issues of importance to democratic majorities. Even where courts do face this trade-off, they may have greater scope than many modern legislatures to expand the number of issues they consider within a given time frame; they simply have more scope within

---

[31] *Compare* Langford, *Why Judicial Review*, *supra* note 30, at 57–58. On whether or not courts have a duty to do so, *compare also* Michael Taggart, *Should Canadian Judges Be Legally Required to Give Reasoned Decisions in Civil Cases?*, 33 U. Toronto L.J. 1 (1983); B.V. Harris, *The Continuing Struggle with the Nuanced Obligation on Judges to Provide Reasons for Their Decisions*, 132 Law Q. Rev. 216 (2016); Mathilde Cohen, *When Judges Have Reasons Not to Give Reasons: A Comparative Law Approach*, 72 Wash. & Lee L. Rev. 483 (2015); Frederick Schauer, *Giving Reasons*, 47 Stan. L. Rev. 633 (1995); Luke Beck, *The Constitutional Duty to Give Reasons*, 40 UNSW L.J. 92 (2017).

[32] *Cf.* Kent Roach, *Dialogic Review and its Critics*, 23 Sup. Ct. L. Rev. (2d) 49, 54 (2004). *See also* Roy B. Flemming et al., *Attention to Issues in a System of Separated Powers: The Macrodynamics of American Policy Agendas*, 61 J. Pol. 76, 84 (1999) (providing compelling empirical evidence of the link between judicial and media attention that has been demonstrated most definitively in the US context).

[33] *See, e.g.*, Latin American courts, especially the Colombian Court. An important exception is arguably the Supreme of India: *see, e.g.*, Rishad Chowdhury, Missing the Wood for the Trees: A Critical Exploration of the Supreme Court of India's Chronic Struggle with Its Docket (2016).

[34] Frederick Schauer, *The Supreme Court 2005 Term—Foreword: The Court's Agenda—and the Nation's*, 120 Harv. L. Rev. 5 (2006).

existing institutional constraints to expand their effective "docket," by agreeing to grant leave to hear more petitions or appeals.

This gives courts a range of tools with which to counter legislative blind spots and burdens of inertia. They can do so by using both coercive remedial tools to impose new legal solutions or outcomes and communicative tools that allow them to draw broader public attention to certain legal issues or options. Indeed, sometimes the mere fact that a court hears a case may be sufficient to attract media or public attention in ways that help overcome blind spots or burdens of inertia.[35] It may create pressure on legislators to revisit an issue in line with evolving democratic majority understandings in ways that can overcome both blind spots and burdens of inertia.

Court decisions can also have important *indirect* effects on democratic blockages.[36] Rights-based decisions in particular can encourage the development of a new rights consciousness on the part of previously disadvantaged or marginalized groups, and thereby their willingness to make claims for recognition and justice. It can also increase the chances that those claims are heard, and understood, by elite actors, who come to understand those claims as valid, and legitimate, in part because of how they are framed by courts.

Courts can also often raise the political costs of undertaking measures that contribute to sources of electoral or institutional monopoly.[37] Courts cannot literally "prevent" instances of antidemocratic monopoly power. If would-be authoritarian actors are determined to achieve antidemocratic forms of change, they will have a range of ways in which to achieve this. They can act legally or extra-legally, or at the border of existing legality, by engaging in various forms of constitutional "workaround."[38] And even if the existing democratic constitution prevents them taking certain actions, they almost always have the option of repealing the existing constitution and replacing it with a wholly new (ostensibly but in fact far less) democratic constitution.[39]

---

[35] This is particularly true in the United States, given the Supreme Court's central role in national public life, but is also increasingly true in many other constitutional democracies, including those with systems of weak-form review. *See, e.g.,* Flemming et al., *supra* note 32; Roach, *supra* note 32.

[36] César Rodríguez-Garavito, *Beyond the Courtroom: The Impact of Judicial Activism on Socioeconomic Rights in Latin America*, 89 Tex. L. Rev. 1669, 1684–85 (2011); Langford, *Why Judicial Review, supra* note 30, at 76.

[37] Dixon & Landau, *Transnational Constitutionalism, supra* note 1. *See also* Roznai, *Who Will Save the Redheads?, supra* note 1; Ginsburg & Huq, *supra* note 1, at 186–89; Bugaric, *supra* note 1.

[38] Mark Tushnet, *Constitutional Workarounds*, 87 Tex. L. Rev. 1499 (2008).

[39] Mark Tushnet, *Peasants with Pitchforks, and Toilers with Twitter: Constitutional Revolutions and the Constituent Power*, 13 Int'l J. Const. L. 639 (2015). I say "almost always" because of potential formal legal constraints on replacement, as for example in South Africa in 1993 and Bolivia more recently: *see* Landau & Dixon, *Constraining Constitutional Change, supra* note 8.

Ultimately, the authority of any democratic constitution depends on the "consent" of the people. And the people are free to remake a constitution through the exercise of their "constituent power."[40] The idea of constituent power is also hard to define with any precision and it is one of the democratic concepts most readily abused by would-be authoritarian actors. It is frequently invoked by those seeking to create antidemocratic forms of change and in a way that is highly selective and decontextualized. This is the essence of what David Landau and I call "abusive constitutional borrowing."[41] Courts, however, can often act as an important *"speed bump"* or deterrent against such action.[42]

Court decisions, for example, that strike down antidemocratic legislation will generally deprive that legislation of immediate effect. To achieve their objective, legislators must therefore re-enact similar legislation and hope for a change in judicial approach. Similarly, if courts strike down an antidemocratic constitutional amendment, legislators must re-enact the amendment in similar form. In each case, legislators are required to incur additional costs in terms of the time and political capital necessary to achieve a desired outcome. This form of delay, or increased political cost, can also have a significant impact.[43] It can give time for economic conditions to change, or evidence of official misconduct or ineffective governance to emerge, so that a would-be authoritarian leader no longer enjoys the same degree of popular support. Or it can allow time for the political opposition to organize and mobilize, so as to counter relevant forms of change.

In some cases, increasing the costs of antidemocratic action can also serve as a useful *deterrent* against such action. Knowing that such action is unlikely to succeed, at least within a given time frame, can make it much less attractive to would-be authoritarians. If may even mean that the time and political capital needed to pursue such changes no longer seem worthwhile.

For judicial review to have this effect, it must be quite carefully (or fortuitously) timed. If courts wait too long to intervene in the face of such a threat, it will often be too late for judicial review to play any role in protecting democracy. Courts themselves may be captured by the regime, or else severely weakened in

---

[40] *Compare* Joel I. COLÓN-RÍOS, WEAK CONSTITUTIONALISM: DEMOCRATIC LEGITIMACY AND THE QUESTION OF CONSTITUENT POWER (2012); Landau & Dixon, *Constraining Constitutional Change*, *supra* note 8.

[41] ROSALIND DIXON & DAVID LANDAU, ABUSIVE CONSTITUTIONAL BORROWING: LEGAL GLOBALIZATION AND THE SUBVERSION OF LIBERAL DEMOCRACY (2021).

[42] Dixon & Landau, *Transnational Constitutionalism*, *supra* note 1. *See also* Roznai, *Who Will Save the Redheads?*, *supra* note 1; GINSBURG & HUQ, *supra* note 1, at 186–89; Bugaric, *supra* note 1.

[43] *Compare* Dixon & Landau, *Transnational Constitutionalism*, *supra* note 1; Rosalind Dixon & Samuel Issacharoff, *Living to Fight Another Day: Judicial Deferral in Defense of Democracy*, WIS. L. REV. 683 (2016).

their power and independence. Often, potential allies in the effort to protect democracy—for example, civil society and the political opposition—may be destroyed or go into hiding or exile. But conversely, if courts act too early— when support for a would-be authoritarian actor is at its peak—political support for judicial review may be quite limited.[44] Both elites and the public may support the relevant president or prime minister in ways that mean that efforts to limit or constrain their power are met with strong public *disapproval*. And without elite or public support, courts cannot effectively hope to enforce constitutional constraints.[45]

Courts, therefore, face a narrow window in which to engage in effective representation-reinforcement of this kind. It may also be a window that is quite difficult for courts to identify at the time, with any confidence. But it is still a window that can offer important opportunities to slow down attempts to create antidemocratic forms of monopoly power, or deter future attempts to create such power. And it is one that courts are more likely to identify successfully if they are guided by the logic of responsive judicial review—that is, a concern to preserve the minimum core of constitutional democracy, to consider the degree of risk to democratic pluralism posed by specific constitutional changes, from both a national and comparative perspective, and to assess this in the context of the likely visibility and reversibility of the effects of such changes on open, competitive forms of democratic contestation.

C. Responsive Judicial Review in Practice

For cases involving legislative blind spots and burdens of inertia, one measure of "judicial success" will be quite straightforward. It will simply involve showing that there has been actual legislative change in an area or acceptance of a court order granting additional forms of rights protection. Beyond this, gauging the success of judicial intervention will often be more complex. It will require assessing whether legislative change has in fact led to change on the ground *and* whether court decisions have been causal or instrumental in achieving that change.

---

[44] *Compare* Section D, *infra*.
[45] *Compare* Varun Gauri & Daniel Brinks, Introduction: The Elements of Legalization and the Triangular Shape of Social and Economic Rights, in COURTING SOCIAL JUSTICE: JUDICIAL ENFORCEMENT OF SOCIAL AND ECONOMIC RIGHTS IN THE DEVELOPING WORLD 1 (Varun Gauri & Daniel Brinks eds., 2009).

Formal legal changes do not always equal changes in access to services on the ground. In the context of abortion law changes, for example, social scientists have shown that legislative change has not always equated to actual changes in access to abortion services. In the United States, for instance, following *Roe*, state and local officials generally ceased to enforce criminal prohibitions on access to abortion but many continued to enforce a range of practical, *de facto* restrictions on access—in part because a significant portion of relevant state or local publics disagreed with it.[46]

The first question thus requires complex empirical judgments about the law "in action," not just on the books. The second is even more difficult to address: any definitive answer will depend on sophisticated forms of large-n comparison, or even synthetic forms of "matching."[47] Most small-n forms of comparison, however, can provide some tentative answers—largely by highlighting patterns of change following court rulings, and explaining how and why those patterns may be causal in nature.

Take the impact of court decisions involving LGBTQI + rights, structural social rights, or the "unconstitutional constitutional amendment" (UCA) doctrine.

1. Comparative LGBTQI + rights

In Canada, the decision in *M v. H* led the Ontario legislature to amend relevant provisions of the *Family Law Act*, and prompted the national legislature and other provincial legislatures to amend a range of legislation so as to give the same general recognition to same-sex relationships as that given to opposite-sex *de facto* relationships.[48] National and provincial political leaders also responded to provincial court decisions, such as *Hendricks v. Québec*, *Halpern v. Canada*, and *Egale Canada Inc. v. Canada* finding the common law opposite definition of marriage inconsistent with the *Charter*, by moving to adopt same-sex marriage. The Québec attorney-general did not seek to appeal the decision of the Québec superior court in *Hendricks*, and the federal attorney-general discontinued his appeal of the decision in July 2003. Thereafter, the provincial

---

[46] Gerald N. Rosenberg, The Hollow Hope (1991); Gerald N. Rosenberg, *Courting Disaster: Looking for Change in All the Wrong Places*, 54 Drake L. Rev. 795, 811 (2005).

[47] *See* Rosalind Dixon & Richard Holden, *Comparative Constitutional Matching: From Most Similar Cases to Synthetic Control?*, U. Chi. L. Rev. (Online) (Apr. 5, 2021), <https://lawreviewblog.uchicago.edu/2021/04/05/cv-dixon-holden/>.

[48] M v. H, [1999] 2 S.C.R. 3.

and federal attorneys-general also consented to the judgments of the Ontario and British Columbia courts of appeal in *Halpern* or *Egale*. After referring several questions to the Supreme Court of Canada (SCC) regarding the recognition of same-sex marriage, the federal government also introduced federal legislation giving comprehensive recognition to same-sex marriage.[49]

In South Africa, the government did not seek to oppose any of the constitutional arguments for expanded access to a range of statutory benefits for gays and lesbians. And following the Constitutional Court of South Africa's (CCSA) decision in *Fourie*, declaring the common law definition of marriage invalid,[50] there were reports of a protracted debate within the government about the best way of responding to the decision.[51] But the National Assembly passed a *Civil Unions Act*, which effectively recognized same-sex marriage in all but the name of the act itself.[52]

In Colombia, the Court was required to play an even more active role in guaranteeing access to same-sex marriage. While the Court in *Decision C-577 of 2011* gave Congress two years to remedy the "deficit of protection" it identified in respect of same-sex relationships, that deadline passed without the successful passage of legislation by Congress.[53] The 2011 decision itself, however, provided for judges and notary publics to provide formal recognition to same-sex relationships (i.e., to "*solemnizar y formalizar su vínculo contractual*"), failing legislation of this kind.[54] Some judges also chose to exercise the authority to do so, even while others declined, or were prevented from doing so by the Office of the Inspector General.[55] And in 2016, the Court voted to uphold these decisions granting access to same-sex marriage and held that the Constitution required access to civil marriage for same-sex couples.[56] While these decisions did not prevent ongoing violence against LGBTQI+ Colombians, or attempts to defeat both gay rights and the ongoing peace process as somehow linked and "anti-family" in approach, they did succeed in

---

[49] *See, e.g., Civil Marriage Act 2005* (Canada).
[50] Minister of Home Affairs v. Fourie; Lesbian and Gay Equality Project v. Minister for Home Affairs 2006 (1) SALR 524 (CC).
[51] *See* discussion in Dixon & Issacharoff, *supra* note 43, at 705.
[52] *Civil Unions Act 2006*. For the relationship between the Court's decision and this legislation, see discussion in Dixon & Issachaaroff, *supra* note 43; Chapter 7, *infra*.
[53] Manuel José Cepeda Espinosa & David E. Landau, Colombian Constitutional Law: Leading Cases 91–97 (2017); Mauricio Albarracin & Julieta Lemaitre, *The Crusade Against Same-Sex Marriage in Colombia*, 8 Religion & Gender 32, 36 (2018).
[54] Espinosa & Landau, *supra* note 53, at 97–100; Albarracin & Lemaitre, *The Crusade Against Same-Sex Marriage in Colombia*, *supra* note 53, at 35.
[55] Albarracin & Lemaitre, *The Crusade Against Same-Sex Marriage in Colombia*, *supra* note 53, at 36–42.
[56] Sibylla Brodzinsky, *Colombia's Highest Court Paves Way for Marriage Equality*, The Guardian, Apr. 8, 2016, <https://www.theguardian.com/world/2016/apr/07/colombia-court-gay-marriage-ruling>.

creating substantial and enduring legal change in the treatment of LGBTQI+ relationships in Colombia.[57]

In the United Kingdom (UK), courts have played a more limited role in promoting legal change. Same-sex marriage became legal in the United Kingdom in 2014 with the passage of the *Marriage (Same-Sex Couples) Act* 2013, which did not immediately follow any court challenge. But both *Ghaidan* and *Bellinger* led to important changes to *facto* same-sex relationship recognition, and the recognition of transgender identity in marriage. Five months after *Ghaidan v. Godin-Mendoza*, the Westminster Parliament passed the *Civil Partnerships Act 2004* (UK) giving comprehensive recognition to same-sex and opposite-sex civil partnerships.

Similarly, following the decision of the English Court of Appeal in *Bellinger*, and a subsequent decision by the European Court of Human Rights (ECtHR) on the issue, the UK Lord Chancellor reconvened the previous interdepartmental working group on transgender issues, and then announced an intention to bring forward legislation to allow for the registration of transgender identity by the end of 2003.[58] Following the decision of the appellate committee in April 2003, the government also accelerated this schedule, publishing a draft *Gender Recognition Bill* in July of the same year, and introducing it into parliament in November. The Bill was then passed less than a year later.[59]

In India, the change created by the Supreme Court of India (SCI) has been more limited still. In *NALSA*, the Court held that the state was obliged to adopt measures to recognize transgender identity, and five years later, the Indian Parliament passed the *Transgender Persons (Protection of Rights) Act* 2019. The Act has been criticized for being too narrow and not going far enough to recognize transgender and nonbinary identities. It focuses on post-operative gender identity and does not include protections for nonbinary and transgender persons who have not undergone surgery or other medical forms of intervention.[60] There are also signs that discrimination against transgender persons continues, especially outside major urban areas.[61]

---

[57] On ongoing violence and threats of violence, see Albarracin & Lemaitre, *The Crusade Against Same-Sex Marriage in Colombia*, supra note 53, at 42–47. On the linking of gay rights and the peace protest, and in a critical way, see also Nicholas Carey, Colombian Opposition to Peace Deal Feeds off Gay Rights Backlash, N.Y. TIMES, Oct. 8, 2016, <https://www.nytimes.com/2016/10/09/world/americas/colombian-opposition-to-peace-deal-feeds-off-gay-rights-backlash.html>.

[58] *See,* Joint Committee on Human Rights, *Submission from Press for Change* (UK Parliament, Dec. 4, 2003), <https://publications.parliament.uk/pa/jt200203/jtselect/jtrights/188/188we18.htm>.

[59] *See, Gender Recognition Act 2004* (UK).

[60] Shreya Mohapatra, *Section 377 Read Down: The Way Forward*, SOCIO-LEGAL REV. 1, 7 (2019); Jayna Kothari, *Section 377 and Beyond: A New Era for Transgender Equality?* in HOW LIBERAL IS INDIA? THE QUEST FOR FREEDOM IN THE BIGGEST DEMOCRACY ON EARTH 192–93 (Ronald Meinardus ed., 2019).

[61] *Two Years Since Art 377 Annulment, LGBTQ Community Still Battling Challenges*, THE HINDU (Sept. 6, 2020), <https://www.thehindu.com/news/national/two-years-since-article-377-annulm

But the legal change is still important—both for its direct effect on transgender legal rights, and indirect effects on the broader LGBTQI+ rights movement, and its subsequent litigation success in cases such as *Johar*. As Jayna Kothari notes, the judgment "became a catalyst for the organization of the transgender movement in the country," "led to several government authorities providing an additional gender option in government documents such as passports, driving licenses [and] PAN cards," and "gave new grounds and indeed new hope to revive the Section 377 challenge."[62]

And in *Johar* itself, the SCI ultimately held that section 377 of the *Criminal Code* was inconsistent with the guarantee of equality, freedom, dignity, and privacy in Articles 14, 15, 19, and 21 of the Constitution.[63] Based on this, the Court also read down the scope of section 377 so as not to apply to consensual intercourse between adults—thereby taking the first step toward the legal recognition of gay and lesbian identity at a national level in India.[64] And while this has not eliminated broader sources of legal discrimination, or social prejudice, observers suggest that "LGBT people [in India] are now more confident to express themselves ... and own their relationships without the fear of discrimination and harassment."[65]

2. Structural social rights

Similarly, for social rights, there is evidence of real—if sometimes limited—change on the ground following various court decisions. In *Grootboom*, for example, the CCSA's intervention arguably had only a modest impact on inertia in the provision of basic emergency shelter. It led to national policy changes in this area, but only three years after the CCSA's decision.[66] And while some

---

ent-lgbtq-community-still-battling-prejudice/article32534479.ece> (citing Shubhankar Chakravorty, a Bengalaru-based writer).

[62] Kothari, *Section 377 and Beyond*, supra note 60, at 189.
[63] Navtej Singh Johar v. Union of India, AIR 2018 SC 4321 (India).
[64] For earlier steps by the High Court of Delhi, see *Naz Foundation v. Government of India*, WP(C) No. 7455/2001 (2009), though note that the decision was overturned on appeal to the SCI in *Suresh Kumar Koushal v. Naz Foundation* (2014) 1 SCC 1.
[65] *Two Years Since Art 377 Annulment, LGBTQ Community Still Battling Challenges*, supra note 61.
[66] Rosalind Dixon, *Creating Dialogue about Socioeconomic Rights: Strong-Form Versus Weak-Form Judicial Review Revisited*, 5 INT'L J. CONST. L. 391 (2007); David Landau, *The Reality of Social Rights Enforcement*, 53 HARV. INT'L L.J. 189 (2021). *See also* Kameshni Pillay, *Implementation of Grootboom: Implications for the Enforcement of Socio-Economic Rights*, 6 AF. J. ONLINE 255 (2002); DAVID BILCHITZ, POVERTY AND FUNDAMENTAL RIGHTS: THE JUSTIFICATION AND ENFORCEMENT OF SOCIO-ECONOMIC RIGHTS 151 (2007).

critics suggest this was far too long to count as meaningful, others suggest that this was nonetheless an importance advance in developing a comprehensive response to the severe national housing shortages in South Africa at the time.[67]

In *TAC*, both the CCSA and various high courts had an even greater impact on inertia in the realization of the right to health. In April 2002, less than a month after the Gauteng High Court's decision in the case, the government announced its decision to reverse its prior policy of restricting access to nevirapine to certain pilot sites. And in July 2002, following the CCSA's decision, it announced its intention immediately to comply with the direction to remove restrictions on government hospitals providing access to nevirapine where they were equipped to do so.[68] And when there were further delays in rolling out testing facilities, the Treatment Action Campaign (TAC) brought follow-up litigation in various high courts, thereby effectively overcoming inertia in provinces such as Mpumalanga where the provincial government had been slowest to act in response to the HIV epidemic.[69]

Cases such as *Olivia Road*,[70] *Joe Slovo*,[71] and *Jaftha v. Schoeman*[72] also played a decisive role in effectively countering a range of *legislative* and *executive blind spots*.[73] In *Port Elizabeth Municipality v. Various Occupiers*, the CCSA held that in seeking the order for eviction, the municipality did not appear to have considered "the lengthy period during which the occupiers ha[d] lived on the land in question," and the fact that they represented a "relatively small group of people who appear[ed] to be genuinely homeless and in need."[74] The Court also drew the city's attention to the impact of forced eviction on vulnerable populations, noting that

> a home is more than just a shelter from the elements. It is a zone of personal intimacy and family security. Often it will be the only relatively secure space

---

[67] *Id.* For a more favorable assessment of the progress this represented, and the relevant time frame, see VARUN GAURI & DANIEL BRINKS, COURTING SOCIAL JUSTICE: JUDICIAL ENFORCEMENT OF SOCIAL AND ECONOMIC RIGHTS IN THE DEVELOPING WORLD (2009).

[68] *See* Mark Heywood, *Contempt or Compliance? The TAC Case After the Constitutional Court Judgment*, 4 ESR Rev. 7, 9 (2003).

[69] *Id.*

[70] Occupiers of 51 Olivia Road, Berea Township v. City of Johannesburg, 2008 (3) SA 208 (CCSA).

[71] Residents of Joe Slovo Community, Western Cape v. Thubelisha Homes and Others 2010 (3) SA 454 (CCSA).

[72] Jaftha v. Schoeman, 2005 (2) SA 140 (CCSA).

[73] *See* Chapter 7, *infra. See also* Sandra Liebenberg & Katharine Young, *Adjudicating Social and Economic Rights: Can Democratic Experimentalism Help? in* SOCIAL RIGHTS IN THEORY AND PRACTICE: CRITICAL INQUIRIES (Helena Alviar García et al. eds., 2015); BRIAN RAY, ENGAGING WITH SOCIAL RIGHTS: PROCEDURE, PARTICIPATION AND DEMOCRACY IN SOUTH AFRICA'S SECOND WAVE (2016).

[74] Port Elizabeth Municipality v. Various Occupiers, 2005 (1) SA 217 (CCSA), [59] (Sachs J.).

of privacy and tranquility in what (for poor people in particular) is a turbulent and hostile world. Forced removal is a shock for any family, the more so for one that has established itself on a site that has become its familiar habitat.[75]

Similarly, in *Olivia Road*, the CCSA noted that it was "common cause that the City in making the decision to evict the people concerned took no account whatsoever of the fact that the people concerned would be rendered homeless."[76] Implicitly, in making the order for engagement, the CCSA further suggested that the city had not previously considered the full range of ways of engaging residents to help upgrade existing health and safety on the relevant site.[77] And in *Jaftha*, the CCSA likewise suggested that the National Assembly had not given adequate consideration to the potential impact of such actions on those in poverty, owing very small debts, and especially those living in a home purchased with state aid, where a forced sale had the effect of permanently disqualifying a person from access to such aid.[78]

The Court further held any relevant order for forced sale could only be made by "a court, after consideration of all relevant circumstances," including the financial position of both the debtor and creditor, the size of the debt both in absolute terms and relative to the value of the property, any capacity and efforts made by the debtor to make repayment by other means, and the debtor's knowledge and intent at the time of assuming the debt.[79] The National Assembly did not seek to overturn that gloss on the operation of the relevant legislation.

A similar pattern can be seen in India. The *Midday Meal* case was decided against the backdrop of persistent and complex forms of inertia in the implementation of the right to food, and especially supplemental nutrition programs, in Indian schools. The case was brought following severe drought and food shortages in Rajasthan, accompanied by a failure by national and state governments to respond by releasing surplus grain in storage, as required by the terms of the national famine code.[80] A midday meal program for school children in India was implemented in some states as early as the 1950s and 1960s (and

---

[75] *Id.* at [17].
[76] *See* Occupiers of 51 Olivia Road, Berea Township v. City of Johannesburg, 2008 (3) SA 208 (CCSA), [44] (Yacoob J.).
[77] *Id.* at [5(2)] (Yacoob J.).
[78] The Court framed this as a finding that the limitation on rights was not justifiable given these considerations: *see Jaftha v. Schoeman*, 2005 (2) SA 140 (CCSA), [43], [55]–[59] (Mokgoro J.).
[79] *Id.*
[80] Varun Gauri & Daniel M. Brinks, *Human Rights as Demands for Communicative Action, supra* note 2, at 18–19; Alyssa Brierley, *PUCL v. Union of India: Political Mobilization and the Right to Food, in* A QUALIFIED HOPE: THE INDIAN SUPREME COURT AND PROGRESSIVE SOCIAL CHANGE 212, 213–14 (Gerald N. Rosenberg et al. eds., 2019).

in Tamil Nadu prior to independence).[81] The Union government also adopted a nationwide midday meal program in 1995.[82] However, there was enormous delay and variation in implementation of the program across the country.[83] The decision itself could thus be viewed as aimed at countering both a form of compound democratic inertia and serious and irreversible risk to children's physical and educational development resulting from malnutrition. It has also had a powerful impact: it has arguably helped catalyze the nation-wide rollout of a program that now feeds more than 110 million school children a day.[84]

Similarly, in *Olga Tellis v. Bombay Municipal Corporation*,[85] the SCI imposed limits on the scope for the state and city to evict pavement dwellers, requiring that they delay such removal until after the monsoon season, and work in the interim to find suitable (i.e., relatively proximate) alternative land, and thus accommodation. In doing so, the Court implicitly suggested that its orders were aimed at countering clear blind spots on the part of the state and city (of Bombay) to evict "pavement dwellers". Their actions, the Court suggested, did not appear to take full account of the impact of such actions on access to work for informal occupiers. There was a clear lack of work in rural areas of India, which informed the pressure for individuals to move to cities to find work. Yet in seeking orders for eviction, the state and city did not appear to have considered that this would deprive people of access to work and their livelihood, and thus in the long-run prove unsustainable. The fact that the search for work necessarily encouraged people to *return* to the city to find work, the Court suggested, meant that forced removal was likely to be "an ineffective remedy" for urban overcrowding, and simply a source of short-term "misery and degradation" for informal occupiers.[86]

In Colombia, the impact of decisions such as the *IDP* case has been mixed. Critics suggest that significant gaps remain in ensuring access to key services for internally displaced persons (IDPs).[87] But most observers agree that it has

---

[81] Rosalind Dixon & Rishad Chowdhury, *A Case for Qualified Hope? The Supreme Court of India and the Midday Meal Decision, in* A QUALIFIED HOPE: THE INDIAN SUPREME COURT AND PROGRESSIVE SOCIAL CHANGE (Gerald N. Rosenberg et al. eds., 2019).

[82] *Id.*

[83] *Id.*

[84] Dixon & Chowdhury, *supra* note 81; Brierley, *PUCL v. Union of India: Political Mobilization and the Right to Food, supra* note 80. On the concept of a catalytic function for judicial review, see Katharine G. Young, *A Typology of Economic and Social Rights Adjudication: Exploring the Catalytic Function of Judicial Review*, 8 INT'L J. CONST. L. 385 (2010). It is also important to note, however, that there were a range of other factors supporting this broader roll-out within India, including strong economic growth and a supportive government and political narrative.

[85] (1985) 3 SCC 545.

[86] *Id.* At [16] (Chandrachud CJ).

[87] *See, e.g.*, Rodríguez-Garavito, *supra* note 36, at 1686–87 (discussing this criticism and the evidence supporting it); Gauri & Brinks, *Human Rights as Demands for Communicative Action, supra* note 2, at 17–18 (noting limits on implementation).

led to meaningful improvements in access in certain areas, in ways that have involved tackling long-standing and complex forms of state incapacity and inertia.[88] It has also led to a substantial increase in government spending on the needs of IDPs; the relevant state budget increased by a factor of four between 2004 and 2009.[89] And many commentators suggest it contributed to the development and recognition of a broader rights consciousness and political mobilization on the part of IDPs.[90]

3. Unconstitutional amendment doctrine

Finally, consider the impact of two variants of the UCA doctrine in India and Colombia—the basic structure and substitution doctrines—in deterring, or slowing down, attempts by Prime Minister Indira Gandhi and President Álvaro Uribe Vélez to undermine electoral and institutional pluralism. In an immediate sense, the decision in *Kesavanada Bharati* was about the scope of the Indian Parliament's power to engage in land reform and, as part of that, to insulate certain legislation from judicial review. But the decision also had far broader-ranging effects. The basic structure doctrine it announced imposed clear limits on the power of the Indian Parliament to limit or remove the Supreme Court's jurisdiction, and this became especially important in later cases, as Prime Minister Indira Gandhi sought to pursue a range of antidemocratic or *monopolistic* tactics in order to remain in office.

In 1975, in India, a High Court judge found Gandhi guilty of various (criminal) breaches of Indian election law, thereby putting pressure on Gandhi to resign. Gandhi's response, however, was to have the Parliament pass the *Elections Laws (Amendment) Act* (1975), retrospectively removing the relevant offence from the electoral code, and placing all electoral laws in the Ninth Schedule to the Constitution (exempting laws from judicial review).[91]

In the *Elections* case, however, the SCI held that these measures were in violation of the basic structure doctrine. While the Court set aside Gandhi's prior conviction for lack of supporting evidence, it simultaneously signaled

---

[88] See, e.g., Landau, *The Reality of Social Rights Enforcement, supra* note 66; ESPINOSA & LANDAU, *supra* note 53, at 188–89. Gauri & Brinks, *Human Rights as Demands for Communicative Action, supra* note 2, at 17–18.

[89] Gauri & Brinks, *Human Rights as Demands for Communicative Action, supra* note 2, at 17; Rodríguez-Garavito, *supra* note 36, at 1685.

[90] Rodríguez-Garavito, *supra* note 36, at 1678–87.

[91] Dixon & Landau, *Transnational Constitutionalism, supra* note 1, at 617.

to Gandhi the likely *future* limits on her capacity to immunize electoral manipulation or misconduct through constitutional amendment. Doing so, the SCI suggested, would run into obstacles under the basic structure doctrine. When Gandhi called fresh elections in 1977, against this backdrop, the evidence also suggests she decided to run a relatively clean and fair electoral campaign.[92] The result was that, for the first time in India's history, a non-Congress Party government (a government led by the Janata Party) was elected.[93]

In Colombia, in the *Second Re-election* case, the threat to the democratic minimum core was more immediate. The case involved a challenge to the attempt by President Uribe to seek a third term in office, having previously succeeded in obtaining an amendment to the Constitution to allow re-election to a second presidential term. A third term would also have given Uribe the power to exercise effective appointment power over a range of independent institutions.[94] And it would have allowed him to "dominate the media landscape ... and use clientelism to amass a large amount of power."[95] Instead, however, the Court held that an amendment to allow this result would create an effective substitution of the Constitution and was thus beyond the power of Congress, or could only be authorized by a Constituent Assembly convened for that purpose.[96] This also helped avoid an urgent and systemic threat to the health of Colombian democracy. Uribe complied with the decision and stepped down at the end of his second term, ceding power to his Minister of Defense, Juan Manuel Santos.[97] Santos, in turn, developed his own distinctive political agenda, and Uribe ultimately joined the political opposition, thereby creating a true turnover in political power.[98]

Thus, while the *Second Re-election* case did not "prevent" Uribe from running for a third term, as he could always have attempted to ignore or override

---

[92] *Id.* at 619–20. *See also* Dixon & Issacharoff, *supra* note 43, at 29–30; GRANVILLE AUSTIN, WORKING A DEMOCRATIC CONSTITUTION: THE INDIAN EXPERIENCE 394–95 (1999); R.V.R. Chandrasekhara Rao, *Mrs Indira Gandhi and India's Constitutional Structures: An Era of Erosion*, 22 J. ASIAN & AFR. STUD. 156, 173 (1987).

[93] Dixon & Landau, *Transnational Constitutionalism*, *supra* note 1 at 620.

[94] *Id.* at 617.

[95] *Id.* at 617–18.

[96] I am indebted to Vicente Fabián Benítez-Rojas for helpful clarification on this point.

[97] Dixon & Landau, *Transnational Constitutionalism*, *supra* note 1 at 617; SAMUEL ISSACHAROFF, FRAGILE DEMOCRACIES: CONTESTED POWER IN THE ERA OF CONSTITUTIONAL COURTS (2015); Dixon & Issacharoff, *supra* note 43, at 32–34.

[98] Dixon & Landau, *Transnational Constitutionalism*, *supra* note 1, at 617; Dixon & Issacharoff, *supra* note 43, at 33. *See also* ISSACHAROFF, FRAGILE DEMOCRACIES, *supra* note 97.

the decision, it raised the political cost of him doing so, and gave a close ally, but nascent potential opposition leader (i.e., Santos), the necessary political window or opportunity to assert his own leadership—and desire to chart a more democratic path.[99] And while Santos was ultimately replaced by another, even closer Uribe ally, Iván Duque Márquez, as president, the rotation in power itself served to preserve an important degree of institutional pluralism within Colombia.[100]

In Kenya, it is too early to judge the effects of the decisions in *Ndii*.[101] But so far, there have been some promising signs: the government chose to appeal rather than ignore the decision of the High Court striking down its proposed constitutional changes. And the government ultimately complied with the narrower decision of the Supreme Court to set aside the proposed amendment process, on procedural grounds. Moreover, the 2022 presidential election saw the defeat of President Kenyatta, and election of his vice president and rival, William Ruto, who many saw as the target of several elements of the earlier proposed amendments.[102]

D. Preconditions for Success

For courts successfully to play this role, it is important to note that a number of other preconditions must be present, and that there may be significant variation worldwide in the degree to which they are met in practice.

---

[99] Dixon & Landau, *Transnational Constitutionalism*, supra note 1; Dixon & Issacharoff, *supra* note 43; GINSBURG & HUQ, *supra* note 1, at 186–89; Samuel Issacharoff et al., *Judicial Review of Presidential Re-Election Amendments in Colombia*, in MAX PLANCK ENCYCLOPEDIA OF COMPARATIVE CONSTITUTIONAL LAW (Rainer Grote et al. eds., 2020).

[100] On the possibility that Duque himself also subsequently lost office to a left-wing challenger: see, e.g. <https://www.npr.org/2022/06/19/1106118791/tight-colombian-runoff-pits-former-rebel-mill ionaire>; Carlos Tejada & Julie Turkewitz, *Colombia's Troubles Put a President's Legacy on the Line*, N.Y. TIMES, Aug. 30, 2021, <https://www.nytimes.com/2021/08/30/world/americas/colombia-president-duque.html>.

[101] Attorney General & Others v. David Ndii & 79 Others, Petition No. 12 of 2021 (Building Bridges Initiative Case); Independent Electoral and Boundaries Commission & Ors v. David Ndii & Ors, Civil Appeal No E291 of 2021 [2021] eKLR. On the reaction, see e.g., Jacinta Matura, *Secretariat to Join AG in BBI Appeal at Apex Court*, THE SUNDAY STANDARD (Aug. 27, 2021), <https://www.standardmedia.co.ke/national/article/2001421902/secretariat-to-join-ag-in-bbi-appeal-at-apex-court>; Sharon Maombo, *Mixed Reactions After Appeals Court Halts BBI Reggae*, THE STAR (Aug. 20, 2021), <https://www.the-star.co.ke/news/2021-08-20-mixed-reactions-after-appeals-court-halts-bbi-reggae/>.

[102] Declan Walsh, *With Tears and Steel, Kenya's 'Hustler' President Vanquishes His Foe*, N.Y. TIMES (Sep. 10, 2022), <https://www.nytimes.com/2022/09/10/world/africa/kenya-president-william-ruto.html>.

1. Judicial independence and a political tolerance interval for judicial review

One of the challenges for courts, in the context of any representation-reinforcing role, is that this role depends for its success on a mix of both political support *and* independence. Courts, as Alexander Hamilton noted in the *Federalist Papers*, have "neither the power of the purse nor the sword."[103] To have their decisions implemented, courts must therefore enjoy some degree of *support* from political actors.[104]

Or at the very least, there must be some political "tolerance" for independent judicial review.[105] While political scientists—such as Lee Epstein, Jack Knight, and Olga Shvetsova—define the "political tolerance interval" for judicial review in terms of the specific policy preference of elites, in a given context, the same broad principles apply to the attitudes of elites toward constitutional judicial review generally.[106] Public support for a court may mean that political elites have good reason to respect court orders, whether or not they agree with them. Political elites may support a court decision because it is "friendly" to their aims or objectives.[107] National political elites, for example, may benefit from limits on the actions of executive officials, or sub-national actors, which effectively reduce agency costs for these actors,[108] or they may do so because disobeying those orders will attract public disapproval and criticism.

Alternatively, political actors may be close to indifferent toward attacking a decision or acquiescing to it.[109] For example, if courts intervene to counter

---

[103] ALEXANDER HAMILTON, THE FEDERALIST PAPERS 78 (Lawrence Goldman ed., 2008) (originally published 1787–88).

[104] *See* Robert Cover, *Violence and the Word*, 95 YALE L.J. 1601 (1985–1986).

[105] Lee Epstein et al., *The Role of Constitutional Courts in the Establishment and Maintenance of Democratic Systems of Government*, 35 LAW & SOC'Y REV. 117 (2001).

[106] *Id.* For other influential "strategic" accounts of judicial power, see also James Gibson et al., *On the Legitimacy of National High Courts*, 92 AM. POL. SCI. REV. 343 (1998); GRETCHEN HELMKE, COURTS UNDER CONSTRAINS: JUDGES, GENERALS AND PRESIDENTS IN ARGENTINA (2005); GEORG VANBERG, THE POLITICS OF CONSTITUTIONAL REVIEW IN GERMANY (2005); James Gibson, *Challenges to the Impartiality of State Supreme Courts*, 10 AM. POL. SCI. REV. 59 (2008); Vuk Radmilovic, *Strategic Legitimacy Cultivation at the Supreme Court of Canada: Quebec References and Beyond*, 43 CAN. J. POL. SCI. 843 (2010).

[107] *See* Keith E. Whittington, *"Interpose Your Friendly Hand": Political Supports for the Exercise of Judicial Review by the United States Supreme Court*, 99 AM. POL. SCI. REV. 583 (2005). *See also* Howard Gillman, *How Political Parties Can Use the Courts to Advance Their Agendas: Federal Courts in the United States, 1875–1891*, 96 AM. POL. SCI. REV. 511 (2002). *Compare* Michael J. Klarman, *Majoritarian Judicial Review: The Entrenchment Problem*, 85 GEO L.J. 491 (1996)); David A. Strauss, *The Modernizing Mission of Judicial Review*, 76 U. CHI. L. REV. 859 (2009).

[108] *See* Erin F. Delaney & Barry Friedman, *Becoming Supreme: The Federal Foundations of Judicial Supremacy*, 111 COLUM. L. REV. 1137 (2011). On constitutions and agency costs, see, *e.g.*, Tom Ginsburg & Eric A. Posner, *Subconstitutionalism*, 62 STAN. L. REV. 1583 (2010).

[109] Epstein et al., *supra* note 105, at 130.

true legislative blind spots or burdens of inertia, political actors may see little benefit to attacking a court—even if as individuals they disagree with a court's approach.[110]

Conversely, political actors may be unified in their approach to an issue, in which case the tolerance interval for judicial review may be quite small. This can pose especially significant challenges for a court seeking to counter the risk of antidemocratic monopoly. A risk of this kind is most likely to arise where a party or leader has widespread public and legislative support and hence, where the tolerance interval for judicial review is especially small.[111]

At the same time, to engage in responsive forms of review, courts must enjoy some degree of political *independence*. Without it, courts themselves may simply end up undermining rather than protecting the democratic minimum core—or contributing to rather than constraining a process of abusive constitutional change. This is what Landau and I have called the problem of "abusive judicial review."[112]

Abusive judicial review of this kind can take two broad forms: it can be weak or strong, or passive versus active in nature. By purporting to "validate" antidemocratic measures, passive forms of judicial review can add to the perceived legitimacy of those measures in the eyes of domestic or international actors. And by purporting to invalidate *pro-democratic* constitutional constraints, more active forms of review can actively facilitate abusive or antidemocratic forms of constitutional change. Both forms of review can contribute to the erosion of the democratic minimum core. And both can arise where courts knowingly or consciously construe a constitution in ways that advance antidemocratic ends. For this to occur, however, generally courts will need to be coerced or captured by a would-be authoritarian regime.

Where courts *unintentionally* erode the democratic minimum core, this will generally be because of a mistaken belief that the constitution or judicial prudence requires a particular decision, or miscalculation about the likely effect of a judicial decision.[113] Some forms of antidemocratic judicial decisions, therefore, may be consistent with some degree of judicial independence. But

---

[110] *See* Dixon, *Creating Dialogue About Socioeconomic Rights, supra* note 66; Rosalind Dixon, *The Supreme Court of Canada, Charter Dialogue, and Deference*, 47 Osgoode Hall L.J. 235 (2009). *Compare also* Guido Calabresi, A Common Law for the Age of Statues (1982); William N. Eskridge, Jr., *The Marriage Cases—Reversing the Burden of Inertia in a Pluralist Constitutional Democracy*, 97 Cal. L. Rev. 1785 (2009); William N. Eksridge, Jr., *Pluralism and Distrust: How Courts Can Support Democracy by Lowering the Stakes of Politics*, 114 Yale L.J. 1279 (2004).
[111] *Compare* David Landau, *A Dynamic Theory of Judicial Role*, 55 B.C.L. Rev. 1501 (2014).
[112] *Compare* David Landau & Rosalind Dixon, *Abusive Judicial Review: Courts Against Democracy*, 53 U.C. Davis L. Rev. 1313 (2020). *See also* Ginsburg & Huq, *supra* note 1, at 186–90.
[113] Landau & Dixon, *Abusive Judicial Review, supra* note 112, at 1326–28.

knowing or intentional forms of abusive judicial review depend on some meaningful degree of judicial non-independence—that is, direct or indirect judicial coercion or "capture," or judicial appointments that create an ideologically or politically sympathetic bench that is not functionally independent of the executive.

There is also significant variation in the degree to which courts worldwide enjoy true formal and functional independence. Courts around the world have greater or less control over their own budget and staff and be more or less strongly protected from adverse changes to their budget, salary, and terms of office. There are also a wide variety of norms governing judicial appointment. Judicial appointments processes may be classified along three broad axes: one- versus two-stage appointment processes; processes that involve political versus "technocratic" forms of judgment; and those that involve a unified or divided appointment authority. This variation will also affect both the degree to which judicial appointments are subject to partisan influences, and the influence of a single (dominant) political actor or party.

This, in turn, suggests quite stringent conditions for the practice of responsive judicial review—that is, a combination of both political support and independence or courts, which in most cases will translate into a mix of popular and elite support, or at least indifference, and structural and conventional guarantees of judicial independence.

One clear illustration involves the decisions of certain courts in the context of proposed changes to presidential term-limits. In Colombia, as earlier chapters note, the Constitutional Court relied on the UCA doctrine in order to prevent attempts to amend presidential term-limits in ways that would have threatened the democratic minimum core in Colombia.[114] And there have been numerous challenges that take a similar form—that is, ask courts to strike down attempts to alter presidential term-limits, based on some combination of a procedural or substantive UCA doctrine.[115] Most of these challenges, however, have failed—in large part because the court in question has been captured by the regime, or made quiescent by the threat of capture or other forms of attack on its independence.[116]

---

[114] *See* Chapter 4, *supra*.

[115] On the differences and similarities between the two, see: Rosalind Dixon and Vicki C. Jackson, *Constitutions Inside Out: Outsider Interventions in Domestic Constitutional Contests*, 48 WAKE FOREST L. REV. 149 (2013).

[116] *See* Landau & Dixon, *Abusive Judicial Review*, *supra* note 112, at 1346–47 (discussing decisions of courts in Ecuador, Venezuela, Nicaragua, Bolivia, Burundi, and Senegal).

2. Litigation support structure

Another key precondition for successful judicial representation-reinforcement is a support structure for constitutional litigation, or parties willing and able to bring cases before constitutional courts, and to present the arguments and evidence necessary for courts to establish threats of monopoly, indications of blind spots, or burdens of inertia.

Some courts do not rely on individual litigants to bring cases. But many do, including courts influenced by the continental tradition of abstract review, but which allow some form of direct access to the court via individual petitions. Any form of concrete review of this kind also relies on *individuals* to bring cases before a court. In some cases, individuals may have the means and willingness to bring constitutional claims of this kind. This may be supported by the availability of legal aid or pro bono legal presentation, or by court-led procedural reforms aimed at reducing the cost and complexity of filing individual complaints. In Colombia, for example, the *tutela* system has been refined over time to allow broad and simple direct forms of access by citizens to the Constitutional Court.[117] In India, the Supreme Court has even accepted complaints as constitutional complaints, without any formal legal complaint being lodged under its so-called epistolary jurisdiction.[118]

But in many countries, there remain substantial obstacles to ordinary citizens bringing a constitutional challenge. Doing so will simply be too costly and complex, both economically and practically. And this means that constitutional litigation will depend on the existence of a broader "support structure" in civil society. Indeed, as scholars such as Charles Epp have argued, non-governmental actors, or civil society groups, often provide a crucial support structure for constitutional litigation.[119] They help organize and fund individuals to bring a constitutional case or complaint, and amass the social and political evidence necessary to support their constitutional claim. And they support

---

[117] See David Landau, *Courts and Support Structures: Beyond the Classic Narrative*, in COMPARATIVE JUDICIAL REVIEW (Erin F. Delaney & Rosalind Dixon eds., 2018).

[118] See, e.g., Nick Robinson, *Structure Matters: The Impact of Court Structure on the Indian and US Supreme Courts*, 61 AM. J. COMP. L. 173 (2013); VARUN GAURI, PUBLIC INTEREST LITIGATION IN INDIA: OVERREACHING OR UNDERACHIEVING (2009); Nick Robinson, *Expanding Judiciaries: India and the Rise of the Good Governance Court*, 8 WASH. U. GLOBAL STUD. L. REV. 1 (2009).

[119] CHARLES EPP, THE RIGHTS REVOLUTION: LAWYERS, ACTIVISTS, AND SUPREME COURTS IN COMPARATIVE PERSPECTIVES (1998). Compare MICHAEL W. MCCANN, HOW DOES LAW MATTER FOR SOCIAL MOVEMENTS? (1998). See also discussion in Brierley, *PUCL v. Union of India: Political Mobilization and the Right to Food*, supra note 80; Dixon & Chowdhury, *A Case for Qualified Hope? The Supreme Court of India and the Midday Meal Decision*, supra note 81, at 212.

the implementation of a court decision by continuing to press for political attention to and action on a question.

In some cases, there may be room for debate about the line between social activism of this kind and public choice, or interest group dynamics, of the kind that can undermine democratic responsiveness. One difference is that social movement activism of this kind is generally aimed at promoting the rights and interests of historically marginalized or disadvantaged, rather than powerful or advantaged, groups. It also mostly aims to encourage positive state action to protect these groups rights or interests, as opposed to state inaction. The question, however, is one of degree, and one that may be open to reasonable disagreement at least in certain cases.

Inevitably, there will also be variation across countries in the degree to which a true support structure of this kind exists. In some countries, there are a large number of groups that consistently engage in constitutional litigation as part of a broader movement for social change, whereas in others, there is almost no tradition of social movement activism. The political culture may not support or encourage social movement activism of this kind, or the jurisdiction may be too small or economically stressed to support effective social movement mobilization.[120] And without some support structure for litigation, courts will have little capacity to engage in the kind of constitutional construction that can protect or promote democratic constitutional values.[121]

Consider the difference between social rights decisions such as *Grootboom* and *TAC*. *Grootboom* was brought with the support of the Legal Resources Centre, a leading public interest litigation center in South Africa, but it lacked any broader social movement backing or support. The *TAC* case, in contrast, was part of a well-organized legal and political social movement campaign to expand access to antiretrovirals in South Africa. This made a major difference to the capacity to enforce the court's orders in the two cases, both politically and through subsequent litigation.[122]

As critics of the CCSA's judgment in *Grootboom* have pointed out, almost four years elapsed between the date of the CCSA's decision and the adoption of a housing plan by the national government, which included provisions designed to provide temporary shelter to those in urgent need.[123] Individuals

---

[120] *See* Dixon, *A Democratic Theory of Constitutional Comparison*, *supra* note 12.
[121] *Id.*
[122] Jackie Dugard, *Testing the Transformative Premise of the South African Constitutional Court: A Comparison of High Courts, Supreme Court of Appeal and Constitutional Court Socio-Economic Rights Decisions, 1994–2015*, 20 INT'L J. HUM. RTS. 1132 (2016).
[123] BILCHITZ, *supra* note 66, at 162–66; Dixon, *Creating Dialogue about Socioeconomic Rights*, *supra* note 66; JAMES FOWKES, BUILDING THE CONSTITUTION: THE PRACTICE OF CONSTITUTIONAL INTERPRETATION IN POST-APARTHEID SOUTH AFRICA (2016); Ilse Fredericks, *The Promise No One*

outside the Cape Town area in urgent need of temporary shelter therefore obtained almost no additional protection as a result of the Court's decision in the case. This delay at the national level also had very direct consequences for the *Grootboom* plaintiffs themselves. It meant there was no government policy in place to support the ongoing provision and maintenance of amenities such as taps and portable toilets, of the kind initially provided by the Cape Town municipality in response to the high court's decision. Those facilities thus increasingly fell into disrepair over the relevant four-year period.[124]

There was an uneven response to the CCSA's decision in *TAC*, when it came to the roll-out of the testing and counseling services necessary to support nevirapine provision.[125] While some delay in this roll-out was to be expected, several provinces began this process almost immediately following the Constitutional Court's decision, whereas others took no immediate steps to implement the decision. In the Eastern Cape, for example, the legislature took no steps to allocate the funding necessary to establish necessary training and counseling services.[126] And in provinces such as Mpumalanga, the health minister continued to oppose any form of roll-out. The Treatment Action Campaign, however, organized both legally and politically to overcome this ongoing inertia. It mounted a further constitutional challenge to the actions of provincial health ministers, such as those in Mpumalanga, which led to the province reversing its position and announcing a plan to expand the roll-out of nevirapine within the province. And the Campaign pressured the national government to establish a taskforce to implement the CCSA's decision, which played a major role in ensuring truly national implementation.[127]

These differences can also be observed across a range of countries and contexts. Individuals such as Irene Grootboom can sometimes be the ones to bring a successful constitutional challenge, and thus one of the key preconditions for responsive judicial review is a litigation system in which individuals have access to paid or pro bono legal representation, or direct and low-cost access to constitutional courts. But more often, successful constitutional change will depend on a broader form of litigation support structure, or the existence of civil society or social movement actors both willing to bring cases before courts and

---

Keeps, SUNDAY TIMES (S. AFR.) (May 6, 2014) at 12; Sasha Planting, *Housing: A Boost to Transform Informal Settlements*, FIN. MAIL (S. AFR.) (Feb. 25, 2005) at 32.

[124] *Id.*
[125] BILCHITZ, *supra* note 66, at 162–66; Dixon, *Creating Dialogue about Socioeconomic Rights*, *supra* note 66; FOWKES, *supra* note 123; Heywood, *Contempt or Compliance?*, *supra* note 68.
[126] Heywood, *Contempt or Compliance?*, *supra* note 68.
[127] *Id.*

able to engage in legal and political advocacy designed to ensure the implementation of favorable court rulings.[128]

Of course, courts can play a role in shaping this kind of support structure—both in who they allow to appear before them, and in how they shape their remedies. First, they can allow a broad range of actors to join constitutional litigation either as interveners or parties, or *amicus curiae* or "friends of the court."[129] This includes other levels of government, or government actors, and a wide range of civil society or nongovernment actors.[130] Second, they can issue orders and remedies that either explicitly or implicitly engage with—and seek to build up—social movements as partners in the process of constitutional implementation.[131]

In Colombia, for instance, in the *IDP* case the Constitutional Court ordered a range of state institutions, including the National Ombudsman and Attorney-General, to play a role in monitoring the implementation of its decision. It also created a Monitoring Commission comprising senior state officials, former members of the Court, and civil society groups such as the National Indigenous Organization of Colombia (ONIC) representing IDPs.[132] In addition, it held a series of public hearings designed to monitor and encourage implementation, and included in these public hearings a wide range of grass-roots civil society groups representing IDPs—including ONIC, but also the National Association of Displaced Afro-Colombians (AFRODES), the Corporation Women's House (*Casa de La Mujer*), the Indigenous Authorities of Colombia (AICO), and representations from local and regional roundtables.[133] These hearings ran from 2004 to 2010 and gave these groups a direct role in setting standards for evaluating progress, but also "media attention and ... opportunities to make their voices heard" more widely.[134] They

---

[128] *See* Order dated November 28, 2001, Peoples Union for Civil Liberties v. Union of India, Writ Petition (Civil) No. 196 of 2001; Decision T-025 of 2004 in Espinosa & Landau, *supra* note 53, at 179–86, and discussion therein.

[129] *See, e.g.*, Larsen & Devins, *The Amicus Machine*, *supra* note 3; Franze & Reeves Anderson, *Record Breaking Term for Amicus Curiae in the Supreme Court Reflects New Norm*, *supra* note 3; Caminker, *A Glimpse Behind and Beyond Grutter*, *supra* note 3; Larsen, *The Trouble with Amicus Facts*, *supra* note 3; Kochevar, *Amici Curiae in Civil Law Jurisdictions*, *supra* note 3; Murray, *Litigating in the Public Interest: Intervention and the Amicus Curiae*, *supra* note 3.

[130] *See, e.g.*, Larsen & Devins, *supra* note 3.

[131] *See* David Landau, Beyond Judicial Independence: Construction of Judicial Power in Colombia (2015) (Doctoral dissertation, Harvard University, Graduate School of Arts & Sciences) (on file with author); Landau, *Courts and Support Structures*, *supra* note 117, at 226; Allan R. Brewer-Carías, Constitutional Courts as Positive Legislators: A Comparative Law Study (2017).

[132] David Landau, *Aggressive Weak Form Remedies*, 5 Const. Ct. Rev. (S. Afr.) 244, 260–61 (2013); Landau, *A Dynamic Theory of Judicial Role*, *supra* note 111, at 1524.

[133] Landau, *Aggressive Weak Form Remedies*, *supra* note 132, at 227–28.

[134] Landau, *A Dynamic Theory of Judicial Role*, *supra* note 111, at 227.

thus strengthened both the coherence and visibility of these groups *and* their capacity to engage in the kind of political advocacy necessary to support the implementation of the Court's decision.[135]

Similarly, in the *Midday Meal* case, the Supreme Court of India created a special bench responsible for monitoring compliance with the decision, and appointed national and state commissioners to gather information about implementation of the Court's orders, and to make recommendations to the states and the Court about implementation, and follow-up orders.[136] These monitoring commissions also consistently included members of civil society, especially the "right to food" campaign, and relied on information gathered by the campaign in their reports and recommendations.[137] In this sense, the commissioners "created an unofficial, yet legitimate, channel for civil society's perspective in both the court and interventions with the government."[138] Moreover, this triangular relationship, between the Court, the various commissions, and the Right to Food campaign, played a central role in "catalyzing" the campaign itself.[139] Before the *Midday Meal* case, Alyssa Brierley suggests, there was no nationally organized right to food campaign. "The RTF Campaign emerged from and became organized around the case."[140]

A support structure for successful litigation is therefore more or less a fixed requirement for responsive forms of judicial review, though its shape and development may vary. Courts themselves can play a role in building the support needed to sustain a responsive approach to judicial review in ways that make the success of a responsive approach self-generating.[141] And the degree to which a structure of this kind is necessary to counter democratic dysfunction will depend on the nature of the dysfunction itself, and how complex the legal-political change is that courts seeking to create.

---

[135] Landau, *Aggressive Weak Form Remedies*, supra note 132, at 260–61; Landau, *A Dynamic Theory of Judicial Role*, supra note 111, at 227–29.

[136] Nick Robinson, *Closing the Implementation Gap: Grievance Redress and India's Social Welfare Programs*, 53 COLUM. J. TRANSNAT'L L. 351 fn 73 (2015); Brierley, *PUCL v. Union of India: Political Mobilization and the Right to Food*, supra note 80, at 6–13; Dixon & Chowdhury, supra note 81.

[137] Robinson, *Closing the Implementation Gap*, supra note 136, at fn 73. Brierley, *PUCL v. Union of India: Political Mobilization and the Right to Food*, supra note 80, at 6–13; Dixon & Chowdury, supra note 81.

[138] Brierley, *PUCL v. Union of India: Political Mobilization and the Right to Food*, supra note 80, at 16.

[139] *Compare* KATHARINE G. YOUNG, THE FUTURE OF ECONOMIC AND SOCIAL RIGHTS (2019); Landau, *A Dynamic Theory of Judicial Role*, supra note 111, at 208–09.

[140] Brierley, *PUCL v. Union of India: Political Mobilization and the Right to Food*, supra note 80, at 2.

[141] Landau, *Judicial Power*, supra note 131; Landau, *Courts and Support Structures*, supra note 117, at 226.

3. Jurisdiction and remedial toolkit

Finally, courts must have the remedial tools necessary to counter democratic blockages. This can also mean a combination of weak and *strong* remedies, or remedies that are both timely and coercive in nature.

In crafting judicial orders, courts generally have a choice between two broad styles of remedy: "declaratory" and "coercive" remedies. Declaratory orders simply state what the law is, whereas coercive orders generally direct individual government actors to take specific actions to implement the law. Government actors can therefore act contrary to the requirements of a declaration without breaching an order, whereas if they act contrary to coercive orders, they may be subject to a range of penalties, including (criminal) penalties for contempt of court. Declaratory orders are thus generally viewed as weaker than more coercive remedies such as injunctions, or structural edits, or orders for mandamus (the making of a specific decision) or certiorari (setting aside or quashing of a decision).

Further, declarations themselves can take a stronger or weaker form.[142] One of the defining features of the "new Commonwealth" constitutional model, in countries such as the United Kingdom, New Zealand, and several Australian states and territories, is that they adopt a distinctive model of weak declaratory remedies. Courts in each of these jurisdictions have much broader power, compared to their powers at common law, to read down or re-interpret statutes to align with their interpretation of rights, provided the terms of the statute are linguistically open to such reinterpretation (an extended power of reading down).[143] They can also declare legislation to be incompatible with the substantive provisions of the bill of rights.

In the United Kingdom, for instance, section 3 of the *Human Rights Act* 1998 (UKHRA) provides that "[s]o far as it is possible to do so ... legislation must be read and given effect in a way which is compatible with the Convention rights." Where a statute cannot be interpreted consistently with protected rights, section 4 of the UKHRA further gives courts power to make a declaration of incompatibility. In New Zealand, section 6 of the New Zealand *Bill of Rights*

---

[142] *Compare* Chapter 7, *infra*.
[143] *See* STEPHEN GARDBAUM, THE NEW COMMONWEALTH MODEL OF CONSTITUTIONALISM: THEORY AND PRACTICE (2013). In the United Kingdom, see, *e.g.*, *Ghaidan v. Godin-Mendoza* [2004] UKHL 30; in Australia, see, *e.g.*, *Momcilovic v. The Queen* (2011) 245 CLR 1, 92 [170] (Gummow J.), 250 [684] (Bell J.), 123 [280] (Hayne J.). For application of this plurality test by lower courts, see also *Taha v. Broadmeadows Magistrates' Court* [2011] VSCA 642; and for discussion, see Bruce Chen, *The Principle of Legality and Section 32(1) of the Charter: Same or Different?*, AUSTL. PUB. L. (Oct. 26, 2016), <https://auspublaw.org/2016/10/same-same-or-different/>. In New Zealand, see, *e.g.*, *R v. Hansen* [2007] NZSC 7.

1990 provides that "[w]herever an enactment can be given a meaning that is consistent with the rights and freedoms contained in this Bill of Rights, that meaning shall be preferred to any other meaning." Where that is not possible, the Supreme Court has held that it has an implied power to make a declaration of inconsistency similar to section 4 of the UKHRA, and the New Zealand Parliament is currently legislating to require such declarations to be brought to the attention of Parliament by the Attorney-General.[144]

In Australia, section 30 of the ACT *Human Rights Act* 2004 provides that "[s]o far as it is possible to do so consistently with its purpose, a Territory law must be interpreted in a way that is compatible with human rights," and section 32 provides that if the territory supreme court is satisfied that a law "is not consistent with the human right, the court may declare that the law is not consistent with the human right."[145] And section 32 of the Victorian *Charter of Rights and Responsibilities* 2006 provides that "[s]o far as it is possible to do so consistently with their purpose, all statutory provisions must be interpreted in a way that is compatible with human rights," while section 36 provides that "[s]ubject to any relevant override declaration" if a provision cannot in the view of the state Supreme Court "be interpreted consistently with a human right, the Court may make a declaration to that effect."

At the same time, the judiciary in these countries is expressly *denied* the power to strike down legislation, or otherwise deprive it of effect, on the grounds of such incompatibility or inconsistency. A declaration of incompatibility, or inconsistency, is deemed to have no effect on the ongoing validity or operation of relevant legislation.[146] It thus also has no effect on the legal rights or duties of parties before a court. It simply signals to the legislature the need to revise legislation in order to bring it in line with rights-based commitments. This is in sharp contrast to the effect of declarations of inconsistency under more traditional "strong" models of remedial power. In the United States, for example, the Supreme Court is clearly understood to have power to strike down federal and state laws which it finds to be inconsistent with the Bill of Rights. The same position applies in almost all other countries that have entrenched structural constitutional provisions.

---

[144] *See, e.g., Moonen v. Film and Literature Board of Review* [2000] 2 NZLR 9 (CA). See also discussion in Claudia Geringer, *On a Road to Nowhere: Implied Declarations of Inconsistency and the New Zealand Bill of Rights*, 40 Vic. U. Well. L. Rev. 613 (2009).

[145] *Human Rights Act 2004* (ACT) ss 30, 32(2) (Austl.).

[146] *Human Rights Act 1998* (UK) s 4; *Human Rights Act 2004* (ACT) s 32(3); *Charter of Human Rights and Responsibilities Act 2006* (Vic) s 36(5).

This can have an important impact on the capacity of courts to counter certain forms of democratic blockage, especially in cases that are not "pure public law" in character. As Chapter 4 notes, in pure public law cases, most petitioners will be seeking relief in respect of ongoing rights and liabilities (e.g., to remain in administrative detention, to pay tax, or to comply with various administrative regulations). In most constitutional systems, legislatures will also have broad power to vary the effect of the law *prospectively*. In criminal or civil law cases, in contrast, most constitutional petitioners will be seeking relief from a past finding of liability. Legislatures in most systems will also have limited power *retrospectively* to remove the liability of a particular individual, or to alter the effect of a court order. They can remove liability only prospectively, in ways that do little to provide redress to individuals subject to liability as a result of blind spots or burdens of inertia. Judicial remedies, therefore, will often need to be both coercive and immediate in effect in order to overcome legislative blind spots or burdens of inertia. Otherwise, parties seeking relief from courts will be unable to benefit from that relief—or benefit only if they can persuade the executive to provide some form of discretionary relief.[147] This, in effect, means that if courts do not grant some form of strong remedy, there may be serious and irreversible harm to individual rights, including rights to human dignity.[148]

Consider the role of the UK courts, in *Bellinger* and *Ghaidan*, in the recognition of transgender and same-sex relationships. In both cases, the UK courts upheld the substance of the petitioners' claims that failure to recognize transgender and/or same-sex relationships was in breach of Articles 8 and 14 of the European Convention on Human Rights, as incorporated into the *Human Rights Act 1998* (UK) (HRA). And both issued a *form* of weak remedy, but in *Ghaidan* the remedy was much stronger than in *Bellinger*. In *Ghaidan*, the appellate committee relied on section 3 of the HRA as supporting a decision to read the definition of legal and de facto "spouse" under the *Rent Act 1977* (UK) to include same-sex couples living "as *if they were* [their] wife or husband." This also arguably reflected a key difference between the two sets of cases: one was a case that turned solely on public law rights and duties, whereas the other

---

[147] Stephen Gardbaum suggests such a scheme, for example, as one way of increasing the effectiveness of the new Commonwealth constitutional model: *see* Gardbaum, *supra* note 143. This is also the basis of Kent Roach's proposed two-track remedial model: *see* KENT ROACH, REMEDIES FOR HUMAN RIGHTS VIOLATIONS: A TWO-TRACK APPROACH TO SUPRA-NATIONAL AND NATIONAL LAW (2021).

[148] Rosalind Dixon, *A Minimalist Charter of Rights for Australia?*, 37 FED. L. REV. 335 (2009); Fergal F. Davis & David Mead, *Declarations of Incompatibility, Dialogue and the Criminal Law*, 43 COMMON L. WORLD REV. 62 (2014).

involved both public law rights and duties and potential private law (i.e., property) rights claims.

The plaintiff in *Bellinger* was already married to a man who recognized her transgender identity and did not face any immediate obstacle to enjoying the legal rights associated with marriage. Therefore, the fact that in response to her claim the UK courts issued a weak remedy (i.e., a declaration of incompatibility) did not prevent her gaining the ultimate relief she sought. It took some time, but the plaintiff suffered no irreversible harm in the interim. In *Ghaidan*, in contrast, the petitioner was seeking to remain in the home he had shared with his same-sex partner under the terms of existing legislation giving such rights to surviving "spouses." No future legislation could achieve this result.[149] In *Bellinger*, a weak declaratory remedy (i.e., declaration of incompatibility) was therefore logically sufficient to provide effective relief for the petitioner, whereas in *Ghaidan*, a far stronger remedy was required to protect the petitioner's rights. In fact, to provide effective relief to Mr. Godin-Mendoza as an individual, the Court was required to issue a form of de facto or "backdoor" strong remedy—in the form of reliance on section 3 of the HRA.

Backdoor strong remedies of this kind can also create their own potential democratic difficulties. One frequent objection to such remedies is that they involve judges impermissibly blurring the line between the acts of "interpreting" and "legislating."[150] Indeed, this is one reason why, even in *Ghaidan*, the House of Lords insisted that there are limits to section 3 of the HRA as a remedy.[151] But in a responsive approach, this objection has limited force. Judges must always seek to ensure the legal and political legitimacy of their decisions, and this means respecting commitments to the constitutional separation of powers. But separation of powers ideas are themselves understood through a functionalist lens, and with an appreciation of the promise and limits of both judicial and legislative decision-making in practice.[152]

The primary concern is instead democratic in origin, namely that an approach of this kind may reduce scope for legislatures to engage in both formal

---

[149] If legislation of this kind had purely prospective effect, it would not provide relevant protection, but if it purported to have *retrospective* effect, it could infringe a landlord's right to *"peaceful enjoyment"* of their possessions under the European Convention on Human Rights (ECtHR). *See* Dixon, *A Minimalist Charter of Rights for Australia?*, *supra* note 148. This may also explain why the *Civil Partnerships Act 2004* (UK) had only prospective effect.

[150] This critique was even more pointed in relation to cases such as *R v. A* (No. 2) [2002] 1 AC 45.

[151] Aileen Kavanagh, *What's So Weak About "Weak-Form Review"? The Case of the UK Human Rights Act 1998*, 13 INT'L J. CONST. L. 1008 (2015).

[152] *Compare* David Landau & David Bilchitz, *Introduction: The Evolution of the Separation of Powers in the Global South and Global North*, in THE EVOLUTION OF THE SEPARATION OF POWERS 1 (David Landau & David Bilchitz eds., 2018).

and informal "dialogue" with courts about the relationship between constitutional requirements and democratic understandings.[153]

Why? In constitutional systems such as the United Kingdom, legislatures have four broad means of engaging in dialogue with courts. They can amend constitutional norms. They can expressly or impliedly repeal the operation of those norms in a given case. They can choose not to respond to a declaratory remedy, such as a declaration of incompatibility. Or they can pass legislation that aims to narrow rather than wholly displace the effect of a prior court ruling. *All* of these mechanisms also depend for their effectiveness on the passage of "ordinary" legislation, and the willingness of courts to give effect to such legislation. This means that if courts stretch the bounds of statutory interpretation and read in language under the guise of "interpretation" or "reading down," they undermine the capacity for legislative language to serve as an effective means by which legislators can express disagreement with courts.

---

[153] Dixon, *A Minimalist Charter of Rights for Australia?*, supra note 148, at 343–51. *Compare* AILEEN KAVANAGH, CONSTITUTIONAL REVIEW UNDER THE UK HUMAN RIGHTS ACT 130, 132 (2009); Kent Roach, *Dialogic Remedies*, 17 INT'L J. CONST. L. 860, 870 (2019).

6
Risks to Democracy

Reverse Inertia, Democratic Backlash, and Debilitation

Even courts that have the *capacity* to engage in representation-reinforcing review will inevitably face limitations as they seek to engage in review of this kind. Even the most skilled and powerful courts may lack access to relevant information, or perspectives, or make errors in judging the contours of democratic opinion—or the degree of threat posed by a specific legislative measure to broader democratic constitutional values. Judicial review that aims to be democratically responsive, therefore, may in some cases end up creating new and distinct forms of "*reverse*" democratic inertia or the related but distinct problem of "*democratic backlash*."

Three basic conditions must be satisfied for reverse burdens of inertia to arise: (i) widespread disagreement with a court decision; (ii) disagreement that is *reasonable*; and (iii) an inability for legislators to give voice to that disagreement or engage in "dialogue" with a court. They may also pose a risk to a court's own legitimacy. If one of the aims of judicial review is to promote democratic responsiveness, one could expect that many judicial decisions would enjoy quite high degrees of public support or perceived legitimacy. Democratic majorities may recognize that courts have helped promote responsiveness to their (considered) views, and accordingly be grateful to the court for playing this role. But if courts over-reach, and over-enforce certain constitutional values from a democratic perspective, this may lead to significant public disapproval or disappointment. And from a principled perspective, if a decision elicits clear disagreement, this might be seen as a sign that a court has in fact erred in performing its representation-reinforcing function.

Democratic backlash is a closely related, but slightly different danger for courts attempting to engage in responsive judicial review. It too depends on disagreement with a court that is deep and widely felt. But it need not be reasonable in nature. And instead of being focused on differing interpretations of the constitution, or a project of democratic dialogue and reinterpretation,

Responsive Judicial Review. Rosalind Dixon, Oxford University Press. © Rosalind Dixon 2023.
DOI: 10.1093/oso/9780192865779.003.0006

backlash is focused on a form of democratic retaliation—that is, an attack on the court itself as an institution.

Even if courts correctly identify democratic majority understandings on constitutional questions, they may create risks to democratic responsiveness in the form democratic "debilitation."[1] Courts that *too* effectively and consistently update laws and policies in line with majority understandings reduce the incentive for legislators themselves to undertake this role. And while judicial updating may be just as legitimate and effective as legislative updating in any given case, it is almost always less systematic and wide-ranging. This also poses a distinct risk to overall democratic responsiveness.

Courts, in a responsive approach, should be mindful of all these risks as part of a commitment to representation-reinforcement. The extent to which they do so may depend on how reasonable that disagreement is, and their existing stock of perceived legitimacy and authority. But some degree of response will be important in order to promote both a legitimate and stable form of representation-reinforcing review.

To illustrate these arguments, this chapter draws on some of the best-known instances of constitutional judicial review worldwide—court decisions involving the constitutional regulation of access to abortion, and especially the US experience from *Roe v. Wade* to *Dobbs v Jackson Women's Health Organization*.[2] Attention to these cases shows the potential value of judicial review in helping counter legislative burdens of inertia and blind spots, but also the danger of judicial over-enforcement of democratic constitutional commitments—in ways that lead to "reverse burdens of inertia" rather than a lessening in overall democratic inertia, and potentially damaging forms of democratic backlash.

A. Limits on Judicial Capacity and Legitimacy

Courts, as the previous chapter noted, have a range of institutional strengths or advantages. They are often politically independent, and are not subject to immediate electoral pressures. They have the time and scope to engage in careful deliberation on constitutional questions—both in the abstract and in the context of specific case and controversies. And they are staffed by judges

---

[1] Mark Tushnet, Taking the Constitution Away from the Courts (1999).
[2] 410 U.S. 113 (1973), 597 U.S. ___ (2022),

with significant skill and experience in processes of constitutional and statutory construction.

But courts are also limited in their capacity in various ways. Many judges lack direct knowledge or experience of electoral processes, and some may lack understanding of popular constitutional attitudes. Some courts may thus issue decisions they expect to be quite controversial but find that public opinion evolves in ways that lead to rapid acceptance of the decision.[3] Others may make decisions that seem relatively uncontroversial at the time, but which then become focal points for broader political mobilization against certain ideas or changes.[4]

Courts likewise generally lack access to detailed information about state budgets and financial capacity. And courts are often confined to considering the facts and arguments before them, when those arguments may not always include a focus on the *systemic* consequences of a particular decision.

As the previous chapter notes, courts can broaden the information they have access to in a range of ways—including by expanding the range of parties they hear from.[5] While the traditional model of litigation involves a contest between two parties about past events, a more contemporary, public interest litigation model often involves a party structure that is "not rigidly bilateral but sprawling and amorphous," relief that is "forward-looking" rather than retrospective, and a process of active judicial management of the process.[6] Often, this can give courts a much broader opportunity to consider the systemic consequences of issues, and access to relevant information about those consequences.[7]

No amount of additional argument, however, can ever fully overcome the limits on judicial capacity in this context. For one, the arguments made to courts will never be perfectly representative of majority opinion on constitutional questions. The same dynamics that underpin interest group influence over legislatures will inevitably have some, even if somewhat lesser, impact on the arguments made before courts. Smaller, better-resourced groups will have a greater capacity and incentive to make their voices heard before a court than larger or more moderate-sized groups with more diffuse interests and fewer resources. And while courts may have greater capacity to adjust for this

---

[3] This, for example, is arguably what occurred in some countries in relation to the recognition of same-sex marriage. *See* further discussion in Chapter 5, *infra*.
[4] This, for example, is arguably what occurred in the context of *Roe v. Wade*, 410 U.S. 113 (1973) in the United States (US).
[5] *See* Chapter 3, *supra*.
[6] Abram Chayes, *The Role of the Judge in Public Law Litigation*, 89 HARV. L. REV. 1281, 1302 (1976).
[7] *Id.* at 1308.

skew, and less direct electoral incentive to respond to it than legislatures, they may still be disproportionately influenced by the voices actually represented before them.

For another, like all of us, judges can be subject to a range of *cognitive biases* in assessing the information and arguments before them. One of the major advances in social science understandings in the last few decades has been towards an understanding of the limits of individuals as fully rational, "Bayesian" decision-makers. Instead, social psychologists and behavioral economists have shown that individuals tend to process information in ways that are subject to a range of biases.[8] One of the key dangers for judges is that they will also process information in ways that "confirm" the correctness of their prior decisions, or that effectively bolster their view about the appropriateness of existing judicial institutional arrangements.[9]

And this can lead to a range of errors in the process of constitutional construction and implementation. Judges may both under- *or* over-estimate the degree to which proposed legislative or constitutional changes in fact raise a risk of electoral or political monopoly—as opposed to simply a move towards a different but equally reasonable specification of democratic constitutional arrangements. Judges may misread the degree of democratic support among citizens for certain constitutional claims. They may fail to perceive the extent of evolving democratic support for certain claims. Or they may over-read the degree of that support, compared to ongoing support for the *status quo* or the degree of opposition to those claims.

Finally, judges may underestimate the consequences of their decisions for the enjoyment of *other* constitutional rights or guarantees, or other socially and economically valuable interests. As Lon Fuller noted, many constitutional questions have a "polycentric" character.[10] The enjoyment of one right can affect the legal scope for the enjoyment of a range of conflicting or overlapping rights. And the resources allocated to protect one right can either detract from or complement the resources available for the protection of other rights. And while this may not be a valid objection to the practice of judicial review, it will strain courts' capacity, or create possibilities for judicial error.[11]

---

[8] *See* Christine Jolls et al., *A Behavioural Approach to Law and Economics*, 50 STAN. L. REV. 1471 (1997–1998).
[9] *Id.*
[10] *See* Lon L. Fuller, *The Forms and Limits of Adjudication*, 92 HARV. L. REV. 353 (1978). *See also* discussion in Jeff King, *The Pervasiveness of Polycentricity*, PUB. L. 101 (2008).
[11] *Compare* King, *supra* note 10; Rosalind Dixon, *Creating Dialogue about Socioeconomic Rights: Strong-Form Versus Weak-Form Judicial Review Revisited*, 5 INT'L J. CONST. L. 391 (2007).

Objections of these kind are often raised with particular force in the context of judicial decisions protecting socioeconomic rights.[12] But they can apply to a much broader range of cases and contexts.[13] One of the core ideas behind a responsive approach is that courts can help prompt legislative and executive action in response to legitimate democratic constitutional demands. This idea of action-forcing review also has important continuities with the idea that courts can serve as guarantors or protectors of social rights, as positive as well as negative rights. And in both contexts, courts have a clear capacity for error—based on lack of expertise, information, and capacity to predict the consequences of their decisions.

These limitations can also lead courts to make both "type 1" and "type 2" errors. In seeking to counter risks of antidemocratic monopoly power, democratic blind spots, and burdens of inertia, courts will inevitably *under*-enforce commitments to democratic promotion and protection (type 1 errors) and *over*-enforce those commitments (type 2 errors). Where judges over-enforce commitments to democracy or democratic responsiveness, this may also lead to forms of both *reverse inertia* and/or *democratic backlash* that threaten a court's legal, political, and sociological legitimacy.

B. Reverse Burdens of Inertia

Not everyone in a democracy will agree with every court decision. Part of the rationale for judicial review in a constitutional democracy is to promote deliberation, and protect minority rights, in ways that mean we should *not* expect court decisions to be met with universal public approval. Disagreement with court decisions is thus not, by itself, a sign of judicial over-reach. Often it may be a sign that courts are in fact fulfilling their constitutionally mandated role.

Some forms of disagreement, however, *will* raise greater questions about the political legitimacy of judicial review. Many constitutional provisions permit of multiple different possible constructions. Citizens in a democracy are also free to make up their own minds on these questions, based on their own life experiences and perspectives.[14] In a diverse society, the answers they reach to these

---

[12] *See* Jeff King, *Rights and the Rule of Law in Third Way Constitutionalism*, 30 CONST. COMM. 101, (2015); DAVID BILCHITZ, POVERTY AND FUNDAMENTAL RIGHTS: THE JUSTIFICATION AND ENFORCEMENT OF SOCIO-ECONOMIC RIGHTS 151 (2007); BRIAN RAY, ENGAGING WITH SOCIAL RIGHTS: PROCEDURE, PARTICIPATION AND DEMOCRACY IN SOUTH AFRICA'S SECOND WAVE (2016); Dixon, *Creating Dialogue about Socioeconomic Rights*, *supra* note 11.
[13] *See* CASS R. SUNSTEIN, THE PARTIAL CONSTITUTION (1998).
[14] JOHN RAWLS, POLITICAL LIBERALISM 56–58 (1993) (explaining the idea of burdens of judgment).

questions are likely to be correspondingly diverse. This, in turn, suggests the need for some mechanism for resolving disagreements about questions of constitutional construction; and courts clearly provide such a mechanism. There are also good reasons in a democracy, however, to insist that the mechanisms chosen should respect *majority* constitutional understandings—or constitutional understandings or values that command the widest, or clearest majority or plurality, support in the broader "constitutional culture."[15] As political constitutionalists such as Jeremy Waldron have argued, this approach most directly advances a commitment to equality among democratic citizens.[16] It also respects democratic principles of "equal concern and respect" for all citizens.[17]

Judicial review that goes beyond what democratic majorities could reasonably be expected to endorse, or support, will thus raise obvious democratic difficulties. As a range of scholars have suggested, it effectively gives "an electorally unaccountable committee of experts unreviewable power to decide many important and weighty normative issues that virtually all democratic political systems face, even though it turns out that these issues are not ones for which the committee's expertise is especially or uniquely relevant."[18] And for voters, as Waldron notes, it effectively "disenfranchises ordinary citizens and brushes aside cherished principles of representation and political equality in the final resolution of issues about rights."[19]

This is also the essence of the idea of "reverse burdens of inertia"—that is, the idea that if there is widespread disagreement with a court decision that is reasonable and cannot readily be expressed through legislative "dialogue" with a court, this raises serious difficulties for the political legitimacy of judicial review.

The idea of dialogue can itself be understood in a variety of ways. For instance, it could refer to *any* legislative response to a court decision, or else only

---

[15] On the concept of "constitutional culture," see Robert Post, *Foreword—The Supreme Court 2002 Term: Fashioning the Legal Constitution: Culture, Courts and Law*, 117 HARV. L. REV. 4, 107 (2003).

[16] JEREMY WALDRON, LAW AND DISAGREEMENT (1999).

[17] RONALD DWORKIN, FREEDOM'S LAW: THE MORAL READING OF THE AMERICAN CONSTITUTION (1999).

[18] STEPHEN GARDBAUM, THE NEW COMMONWEALTH MODEL OF CONSTITUTIONALISM: THEORY AND PRACTICE 60 (2013). See also MARK TUSHNET, WEAK COURTS, STRONG RIGHTS: JUDICIAL REVIEW AND SOCIAL WELFARE RIGHTS IN COMPARATIVE CONSTITUTIONAL LAW (2009); Rosalind Dixon, *The Core Case for Weak-Form Judicial Review*, 38 CARDOZO L. REV. 2193 (2016); Rosalind Dixon, *The Forms, Functions and Varieties of Weak(ened) Judicial Review*, 17 INT'L. J. CONST. L. 904 (2019). The same point is made by leading political constitutionalists: *see, e.g.*, Richard Bellamy, *The Republican Core of the Case for Judicial Review: A Reply to Tom Hickey. Why Political Constitutionalism Requires Equality of Power and Weak Review*, 17 INT'L. J. CONST. L. 317 (2019); Adam Tomkins, *In Defence of the Political Constitution*, 22 OXFORD. J. LEGAL STUD. 157 (2002); Adam Tomkins, *The Role of Courts in the Political Constitution*, 60 U. TORONTO L.J. 1 (2010). See also Chapter 2, *supra*, Chapter 7, *infra*.

[19] JEREMY WALDRON, POLITICAL THEORY 199 (2009).

responses that embody certain forms of disagreement. In Canada, early dialogue scholars such as Peter Hogg and Alison Bushell (née Thornton) often used the term "dialogue" to describe all "legislative sequels" to decisions of the Supreme Court of Canada (SCC), and on this basis found a very high rate of legislative dialogue with the SCC.[20] In later highly regarded work on dialogue in Canada, Kent Roach used the concept in the same broad sense.[21] He simply distinguished between more compliant and "in your face" legislative sequels, and their relationship to ideas of dialogue.[22]

Other Canadian scholars, however, criticized this approach as both too broad and formalistic. Political scientists Christopher Manfredi and James Kelly, for instance, have argued that the idea of dialogue is only meaningful if it involves the expression of some form of legislative *disagreement* with a court decision.[23] It cannot simply mean that legislators take *some action* in response to a court decision—or enact amendments designed to implement or comply with a court decision. If this were true, dialogue would be a ubiquitous feature of democratic constitutional systems, not something that distinguished the Canadian (or any other) system of judicial review, and do little if anything to contribute to the political legitimacy of judicial review.[24]

The most useful understandings of constitutional dialogue, therefore, emphasize the idea of a form of "give and take" between courts and legislators on constitutional questions.[25] In the long run, as Robert Post and Reva Siegel note, all constitutional meaning is ultimately produced in a dialogue between courts, legislatures, and the broader constitutional culture.[26] And that dialogue can occur without any direct judicial opening or accommodation. It is the inevitable product of how constitutional meaning is shaped and produced in a democratic constitutional context in which citizens make conflicting claims and counterclaims on the constitution.[27]

---

[20] Peter W. Hogg & Allison A. Bushell, *The Charter Dialogue Between Courts and Legislatures (Or Perhaps the Charter of Rights Isn't Such a Bad Thing After All)*, 35 Osgoode Hall L.J. 75 (1997).
[21] Kent Roach, The Supreme Court on Trial: Judicial Activism or Democratic Dialogue (rev. ed. 2016).
[22] *Id.*
[23] Christopher P. Manfredi & James B. Kelly, *Six Degrees of Dialogue: A Response to Hogg and Bushell*, 37 Osgoode Hall L.J. 513 (1999). *See also* Rosalind Dixon, *Constitutional "Dialogue" and Deference*, in Constitutional Dialogue: Rights, Democracy, Institutions 171 (Geoffrey Sigalet et al. eds., 2019).
[24] Dixon, *Constitutional "Dialogue" and Deference*, *supra* note 23.
[25] Rosalind Dixon, *A New Theory of Charter Dialogue: The Supreme Court of Canada, Charter Dialogue and Deference*, 47 Osgoode Hall L.J. 235 (2009); Charles-Maxime Panaccio, *Professor Waldron Goes to Canada (One More Time): The Canadian Charter and the Counter-Majoritarian Difficulty*, 39 Common L. World Rev. 100 (2010).
[26] Reva B. Siegel, *Community in Conflict: Same-Sex Marriage and Backlash*, 64 UCLA L. Rev. 1728 (2017).
[27] *Id.*

But, in the short to medium term, the success of constitutional dialogue will be far more contingent. It will depend on both the willingness and capacity of *legislators* to express reasoned and reasonable forms of disagreement with courts and of *courts* to uphold legislation that gives effect to disagreement of this kind. This, in turn, will depend on the degree to which the same pressures towards democratic inertia that arose prior to a court decision (e.g., time, capacity, and political constraints together with interest group pressures) persist after it, despite attempts by courts to overcome it. And it will depend on the degree to which courts themselves are willing to show some measure of deference, at any point, to reasonable legislative sequels.[28]

Consider a case such as *Roe v. Wade*.[29] The US Supreme Court in *Roe* struck down Texas' broad legislative prohibition on access to abortion. Prohibitions of this kind, the Court held, were an impermissible limitation on a woman's right of access to abortion, and were not justified by any state interest in protecting maternal or fetal life, at least in the first two trimesters of pregnancy.[30] Limits on abortion were only permissible in the interests of maternal health, according to Justice Blackmun, in the second trimester of pregnancy, and in the interests of fetal life, after the end of the second trimester—or the point of fetal "viability."[31]

On one view, this helped overcome democratic burdens of inertia in the reform of state abortion law.[32] (That is, at least, if one assumes a national baseline for judgments about democratic constitutional requirements, not a purely state-level conception of the relevant democratic majority).[33] Most of the evidence suggests that *Roe* reflected clear public support for broadened access to abortion at the time it was decided. Gallup opinion polls prior to the decision showed broad public support for access to legalized abortion. Indeed, Linda Greenhouse has shown that Justice Blackmun himself considered these surveys in the course of drafting his opinion in *Roe*.[34] A National Opinion Research survey two months after the decision also found a consistent increase in support for the liberalization of access to abortion among all groups of respondents, and in 1976, that 67 percent of respondents agreed with the statement that

---

[28] Dixon, *A New Theory of Charter Dialogue*, supra note 25; Dixon, *Constitutional "Dialogue" and Deference*, supra note 23, at 171.
[29] 410 U.S. 113 (1973).
[30] *Id.* at 162–64.
[31] *Id.*
[32] *See, e.g.*, David A. Strauss, *The Modernizing Mission of Judicial Review*, 76 U. Chi. L. Rev. 859, 906–07 (2009).
[33] *Id. See also* Erin F. Delaney, *The Federal Case for Judicial Review*, 42 Oxford. J. Legal Stud. (2022).
[34] *See* Reva Siegel & Linda Greenhouse, *The Unfinished Story of Roe v. Wade* 61, 69 (Yale Law School Public Research Paper No. 643, 2019).

"the right of a woman to have an abortion should be left entirely up to a woman and her doctor."[35] Support for access to abortion on the grounds of maternal health was also especially strong; even some evangelical Christian churches supporting access to abortion on health-based grounds.[36]

Over time, however, evidence emerged suggesting that *Roe* went beyond longer-term public support in the United States for access to abortion *without restriction* in the first trimester of pregnancy. In 1975, only 21 percent of respondents in a Gallup poll indicated support for the idea that abortion should be "legal under any circumstances."[37] An almost equal number (i.e., 22 percent) supported a ban on abortion in all circumstances, while as already noted, 54 percent of respondents indicated support for abortion being legal "in some circumstances." This breakdown of opinion has remained largely stable over time.[38]

On one view, therefore, there were significant reverse burdens of inertia in the United States between 1975 and 1992 (i.e., until the Court modified its approach in *Casey*) toward the regulation of access to abortion, prior to viability. In striking down the relevant Texas law prohibiting access to abortion in *Roe*, Justice Blackmun went far beyond the narrow question of whether the Constitution in some way protects a woman's right to obtain an abortion, or whether a state can permissibly limit access to abortion in cases of rape.[39] Instead, he laid out a broad framework, based on the relevant stage (or trimester) of a woman's pregnancy and also the particular state interest asserted, for when a state could impose limits on a woman's constitutional right to access an abortion.[40] Abortion could not be prohibited, according to this framework, prior to the end of the second trimester of pregnancy when, according to medical understandings of the time, the fetus became viable (and only then, if the prohibition in question was directed towards protecting fetal life and contained an exception in cases where a pregnancy threatened a woman's life or health). It could also be regulated only after the end of the first trimester, and only with a view to protecting women's health—and not protecting fetal life.

Following *Roe*, many states nonetheless attempted to enact legislation regulating and limiting access to abortions prior to viability, for example, by

---

[35] *Id.*
[36] *Id.*
[37] Gallup Organisation, *Gallup Poll: Abortion*, available at <http://www.gallup.com/poll/1576/abortion.aspx>.
[38] *Id.*
[39] *See, e.g.*, discussion in Cass R. Sunstein, One Case at a Time: Judicial Minimalism on the Supreme Court 37 (2001).
[40] For the characterization of the decision as broad, see *id.* at 18 ("the decision as wide in that it settled a range of issues relating to the abortion question").

requiring parental or spousal consent/notification,[41] imposing mandatory waiting periods before abortions, and restricting the locations in which abortions could be performed.[42] But many of these measures were struck down by the Court in subsequent cases, based on the application of the trimester framework set out in *Roe*.[43]

For instance, in *Akron v. Akron Center for Reproductive Health*, the Court both struck down various requirements relating to "informed consent," waiting periods, parental consent, and hospitalization for second-trimester abortions, and held that "rule of law" considerations favored reaffirming, rather than reconsidering, the finding in *Roe* that the state's interest in protecting maternal health and potential life respectively became compelling only after the first and second trimesters of pregnancy.[44] In *Thornburgh v. American College of Obstetricians*, the Court again struck down various counseling and waiting-period requirements and also emphasized that, in its view, the vitality of the principles announced in *Roe* "[could not] be allowed to yield simply because of disagreement with them."[45]

Even in *Webster v. Reproductive Health Services*,[46] where the Court began to relax the application of the framework set out in *Roe*, the Court formally declined to reconsider the merits of this framework, this time on the grounds of mootness.[47] And it was not until 1992 and the Court's decision in *Planned Parenthood of Pennsylvania v. Casey*[48] that the Court began to give greater effect to these kinds of understandings about the need for abortion to be "safe, legal but rare" (i.e., legal but discouraged). And even in doing so, the Court purported to reject rather than give effect to democratic majority opinion on these questions.[49]

That is not to say that the *way* in which state legislatures sought to limit the effect of *Roe* was necessarily in line with national majority opinion. For

---

[41] *See* Planned Parenthood of Central Missouri v. Danforth, 428 U.S. 52 (1976) (finding unconstitutional a Missouri statute requiring parental and spousal consent for abortions).

[42] *See* City of Akron v. Akron Ctr. for Reprod. Health, 462 U.S. 416 (1983) (finding unconstitutional an Ohio law requiring all abortions after the first trimester be performed at a hospital, a twenty-four-hour waiting period and parental consent for girls younger than fifteen years of age).

[43] This text is taken from Rosalind Dixon, *Partial Constitutional Amendment*, 13 INT'L J. CONST. L. 391 (2011).

[44] City of Akron v. Akron Center for Reproductive Health, 462 U.S. 416 (1983).

[45] 476 U.S. 747, 759 (1986), quoting *Brown v. Board of Education*, 349 U.S. 294, 300 (1955).

[46] Webster v. Reprod. Health Serv., 492 U.S. 490 (1989).

[47] *Id.* at 520–21.

[48] Planned Parenthood of Pa. v. Casey, 50 U.S. 833 (1992).

[49] *Id. See* JAMAL GREENE, HOW RIGHTS WENT WRONG: WHY OUR OBSESSION WITH RIGHTS IS TEARING AMERICA APART 136 (2021); Rosalind Dixon & Jade Bond, *Constitutions and Reproductive Rights: Convergence and Non-Convergence*, in CONSTITUTIONS AND GENDER 438 (Helen Irving ed., 2017).

example, the idea that access to abortion should be limited or discouraged could be linked to a concern to encourage access to contraception and a greater emphasis on fetal life, and in no way supportive of measures that either endanger female physical or mental health (e.g., additional waiting periods) or reflect patriarchal notions of women's decision-making (e.g., waiting periods and/or spousal notification requirements). But at some level of generality, the attempt by state legislatures to impose greater limits on access to abortion in the first trimester was supported by democratic majority understandings.

Much of this form of democratic disagreement—or legislative dialogue—was inherently reasonable from a democratic perspective.[50] There are powerful arguments in favor of recognizing a constitutional right of access to abortion. Access to abortion is often necessary to protect women's physical and psychological health, and thus basic human dignity or security of the person. Access to abortion is critical to ensuring women have control over their bodies and the shape and course of their lives. And it helps promote women's social, political, and economic equality.[51]

But many reasonable people also view the fetus as entitled to some degree of legal or constitutional protection. This may stem from a view that the fetus is actual human life, entitled to protection from the state. Or it may simply reflect the view that the fetus represents potential human life. In each case, protecting the life and *dignity* of the fetus will clearly require some limits on access to abortion.

How one balances these competing understandings is itself also a matter on which there may be reasonable disagreement. There are certainly some limits to the reasonableness of attempts to balance these competing values. As Martha Nussbaum and I have shown, the fact that commitments to dignity are on both sides provides a helpful way of calibrating the strength of these different claims—or giving them some degree of commensurability.[52] And when dignity is on both sides, it will clearly be unreasonable to give *complete priority* to the dignity of the fetus—for instance, by banning all access to abortion, including in circumstances where a pregnancy threatens a woman's physical and psychological health, or life, or is the result of sexual assault.[53] It will likewise

---

[50] *Compare* discussion in Chapter 2, *supra*.

[51] For a compelling account of the relationship between limits on access to abortion and structural gender inequality, see JULIE C. SUK, AFTER MISOGYNY: LAW AND FEMINISM IN THE TWENTY-FIRST CENTURY (forthcoming 2022).

[52] Martha Nussbaum & Rosalind Dixon, *Abortion, Dignity and a Capabilities Approach*, *in* FEMINIST CONSTITUTIONALISM: GLOBAL PERSPECTIVES (Beverly Baines et al. eds., 2012).

[53] This, for example, would suggest that the recent laws passed in Texas seeking to prohibit access to abortion after six weeks of pregnancy, with only narrow exceptions for the life and health of the mother, would be unreasonable from a democratic perspective. *See* Maggie Astor, *Here's What the Texas Abortion Law Says*, N.Y. TIMES, Sept. 9, 2021, https://www.nytimes.com/article/abortion-law-texas.html.

be unreasonable *wholly* to deny women's claims to dignity and autonomy—in the form of the capacity to control their bodies and their destiny. This also has direct implications for the reasonableness of the Court's decision in *Dobbs* to overrule prior decisions recognizing constitutional rights of access to abortion; the decision not only ignored longstanding precedent from *Roe* to *Casey* onwards. It arguably ignored the fact that any reasonable democratic constitutional order must recognize some minimum rights of access to abortion as a part of a commitment to equal dignity for all citizens—that is, a guarantee of access to abortion in cases where it is necessary to preserve women's life and health, or where carrying a pregnancy to term would impose an unreasonable degree of psychological suffering or burden on a women's control over her own life path.

But equally, this same understanding suggests that it may be entirely reasonable to demand *some* sacrifice from women in order to protect and promote fetal life and dignity. In Germany, for instance, the Constitutional Court has held that it is not reasonable to ask women to carry a pregnancy to term where it would interfere with their life, health, or impose an undue burden on their life plans. It has, however, upheld a range of limits on the capacity of the Bundestag to fund, and allow unregulated, access to abortion—on the theory that is reasonable to ask women to pay for "non-indicated" abortions (i.e., those that are not based on health or some criminological indication), when abortion is otherwise covered by the state health insurance system, and to undergo explicitly pro-life forms of counselling in such circumstances.[54]

Even canonical decisions, such as *Roe*, that helped overcome persistent legislative inertia, therefore, arguably created new forms of reverse democratic inertia up until 1992. While the Court in *Roe* helped strike down overly broad criminal prohibitions on access to abortion, in doing so it created a trimester framework that was itself over-broad from the perspective of an ongoing democratic dialogue on abortion. And thus, at least until this framework was revisited in *Casey*, it imposed a clear obstacle to reasonable attempts by state legislatures to (re)define the balance between reproductive rights and fetal protection.

This also shows how mistaken exercises of responsive judicial review, though they might be revisable over time, can be costly for democracy in the shorter term. And in a responsive approach, these are costs that must be taken into account in a court's own approach to constitutional construction,

---

[54] *See* Abortion I Opinion, 39 BVerfGE I (1975), discussed *supra*; Mary Anne Case, *Perfectionism and Fundamentalism in the Application of the German Abortion Laws*, 11 FIU L. Rev. 149 (2015).

as well as in any overall evaluation of the value of responsive judicial review as a practice.

The same could be said for decisions such as *Morgentaler*, even though for different reasons, and with a result that could be viewed as closer in line with (Canadian) public opinion. The SCC in its decision in *Morgentaler* reasoned in quite narrow or minimalist terms. In finding a violation of section 7, Chief Justice Dickson and Justice Lamer, for example, simply stressed the irrationality of the Canadian Parliament formally permitting access to abortion on therapeutic (or health-based) grounds, while at the same time imposing procedural requirements that then significantly increased "the trauma, expense and inconvenience" of such access. Justices Beetz and Estey likewise stressed this same form of irrationality, while noting, in addition, only that Parliament could not "completely remove" all access to abortion, consistent with section 7 of the *Charter*. And even Justice Wilson, who authored a far more maximalist concurrence, attempted to limit the breadth of her ruling under section 2(b) by holding that "the complete" nature of the denial of access to abortion was the reason that the law could not withstand constitutional scrutiny. This form of narrowness was also in deliberate contrast to the breadth of the US Supreme Court's reasoning in *Roe*, and the result was that it was *clearly open* to the Parliament of Canada to respond by passing legislation re-criminalizing abortion, providing such a new law did not have these same procedural irrationalities or flaws.

But in the final result, the Parliament did not do so—in part because there was disagreement among MPs as to whether to impose moderate, strict, or no further restrictions on access to abortion. Attempts to impose moderate restrictions, for example, were consistently defeated by those seeking more stringent limits and no limits at all.[55] And while this *could* be seen as consistent with public support for legal access to abortion in Canada, many Canadian elected officials and citizens have continued to express opposition to a complete lack of federal legal regulation of the abortion decision.[56]

Inertia of this kind also raises serious questions about the overall political legitimacy of judicial review that aims to protect and promote democracy, as

---

[55] *See, e.g., 1988 R. v Morgentaler Supreme Court Decision*, McGILL BLOGS (Apr. 6, 2018), <https://blogs.mcgill.ca/hist203momentsthatmatter/2018/04/06/1988-r-v-morgentaler-supreme-court-decision/>; Manfredi & Kelly, *supra* note 23.

[56] Linda Long, *Abortion in Canada*, THE CANADIAN ENCYCLOPEDIA (Feb. 26, 2006), <https://www.thecanadianencyclopedia.ca/en/article/abortion> (noting that 52 percent of Canadians identify as pro-choice but the rest as pro-life or undecided, and continued controversy over the issue). On provincial efforts to regulate, see Dixon & Bond, *Constitutions and Reproductive Rights: Convergence and Non-Convergence*, *supra* note 50.

in some cases it may involve disagreement that is relatively minor, or not reasonable in nature, and therefore of limited significance from a democratic perspective; but in others, it may preclude the expression of disagreement that is wide-ranging and reasonable in scope, and therefore of much greater democratic significance.

C. Democratic Backlash

Some forms of disagreement with court decisions may also raise distinct challenges to a court's *sociological* legitimacy or capacity to enforce constitutional requirements.

Some forms of disagreement with a court may again be relatively inconsequential in nature. The relative *insignificance* of the constitutional issues at stake may mean that even if a majority of citizens disagrees with the court on an issue, the fact of this disagreement does little to undermine a court's claim to sociological legitimacy. The decision itself may have quite limited practical and symbolic consequences, or it may have broader effects, but other political issues may be seen by the public as more pressing in nature.[57]

Other forms of disagreement, as section B notes, may represent a form of democratic *dialogue* as opposed to backlash.[58] By encouraging citizens both to attack and defend a court using a common language and set of commitments (i.e., "the constitution"), dialogue may actually increase citizens' shared sense of a discursive community or set of commitments.[59] And in some cases, this shared sense may increase support for courts, and democratic constitutions, as institutions.[60] Dialogue between judges and legislators can also help "maintain the democratic responsiveness of constitutional meaning,"[61] or allow courts to "recalibrate [their] decision-making—taking social and political forces into account."[62]

Democratic backlash, in contrast, involves disagreement that is widespread, deeply felt, but *not* necessarily reasonable in nature. Instead of focusing on

---

[57] *Compare* Frederick Schauer, *The Supreme Court, 2005 Term—Foreword: The Court's Agenda—and the Nation's*, 120 Harv. L. Rev. 4 (2006).

[58] *See, e.g.*, Barry Friedman, *Dialogue and Judicial Review*, 91 Mich. L. Rev. 577 (1993). *Contrast* Robert Post & Reva Siegel, *Roe Rage: Democratic Constitutionalism and Backlash*, 42 Harv. C.R.-C.L. L. Rev. 373 (2007) (ascribing this function to backlash).

[59] Post & Siegel, *supra* note 59. *See also* Siegel, *Community in Conflict*, *supra* note 26.

[60] Post & Siegel, *supra* note 59, at 375.

[61] *See, e.g.*, Friedman, *supra* note 59. *Contrast* Post & Siegel, *supra* note 59 (ascribing this function to backlash).

[62] *See* Neal Devins & Louis Fisher, The Democratic Constitution 224 (2015).

encouraging constitutional reinterpretation by courts, it focuses on a project of democratic retaliation—or an attack on courts as institutions.[63]

The relevant time horizon for measuring democratic backlash of this kind should always be identified with care. In the short run, popular opposition to a decision may mean there is little willingness on the part of political actors to implement the decision. Yet over time, a decision may help reshape popular attitudes, or priorities, in ways that lead to long-term change. This is especially true for decisions with important expressive effects, that is, those which affirm the equal worth and dignity of previously excluded or vulnerable groups. But it may be true of any decision that helps create a focal point for new forms of political activism by such groups. Conversely, some decisions might lead to short-term compliance but a longer-term backlash against a court or particular set of constitutional requirements, which means there is a gradual erosion in support for implementation of a court decision, and the constitutional mandate it seeks to enforce.

It is likewise important to distinguish between different forms of backlash. Some forms of backlash may focus on a particular constitutional claim or cause. And "issue-specific" forms of backlash of this kind may have broad-ranging effects on the achievement of certain political aims and objectives. As Michael Klarman notes, backlash of this kind can arise following a court decision because a decision "raise[s] the salience of an issue," incites "anger over 'outside interference' and alters the order in which social change would otherwise have occurred."[64] It can apply to the issue decided by a court but also issues seen by the public as interconnected in terms of partisan or political valence.[65] It can also lead to a range of short- and long-term electoral consequences—including the increased election of opponents of particular constitutional change, or the passage of initiatives (i.e., popular amendments) or constitutional measures designed to block or override previous constitutional "gains."[66] But in general, it will not directly threaten a court's own standing or independence.

---

[63] *Compare* Karen J. Alter & Michael Zürn, *Backlash Politics: Introduction to a Symposium on Backlash Politics in Comparison*, 22 BRIT. J. INT'L REL. 563 (2020) (defining backlash as involving "taboo breaking" actions, and also political mobilization: (i) with a retrograde objective; (ii) with extraordinary goals and tactics; and (iii) that reaches a threshold level within public discourse).

[64] Michael J. Klarman, *Brown and Lawrence (and Goodridge)*, 104 MICH. L. REV. 431, 473 (2005).

[65] In Colombia, for example, the decisions of the Constitutional Court expanding rights of access to abortion and gay rights have been linked to each other, and the subsequent peace process, by opponents, in ways that have arguably led to a form of backlash against both—though not one sufficient to defeat either form of change (at least in their entirety): *see* Nicholas Carey, *Colombian Opposition to Peace Deal Feeds off Gay Rights Backlash*, N.Y. TIMES, Oct. 8, 2016, <https://www.nytimes.com/2016/10/09/world/americas/colombian-opposition-to-peace-deal-feeds-off-gay-rights-backlash.html>; Adriana Piatti-Crocker & Jason Pierceson, *Unpacking the Backlash to Marriage Equality in Latin America* (Paper presented at the Western Political Science Association Annual Meeting, San Francisco, Mar. 29–31, 2018).

[66] Klarman, *supra* note 65 at 452–72.

"Institutionally focused" forms of backlash, in contrast, can pose a direct threat to a court's own *sociological legitimacy*, and therefore capacity to enforce constitutional requirements.[67] They may threaten public support for the implementation of a specific court decision, or even constitutional requirements generally, in ways that have a far more corrosive effect on the stability and implementation of democratic constitutional requirements. If the public is opposed to a court decision, political actors may simply refuse to implement a court decision. They too may disagree with a decision. And the lack of public support for a decision may mean that refusing to follow a court order carries few political costs. It may even offer electoral benefits. This may also do long-term damage to the capacity of a court to uphold constitutional requirements: It could encourage or embolden political actors to engage in systemic attacks on judicial independence, or the scope of judicial review as an institution.

There are multiple tools political actors can use to undermine a court's independence and authority.[68] Some of these tools focus on undermining a court's *independence* or co-opting the institution of judicial review so that it is no longer an instrument that can effectively promote rather than constrain anti-democratic or "abusive" forms of constitutional change. Others focus on weakening or limiting a court's institutional role and authority, or its independent capacity to determine its own norms of procedure, deliberation, voting, or publication of its decisions. Moreover, those seeking to undermine courts need not necessarily *use* any of these tactics in order to curb a court's power or authority. In some cases, the mere threat of taking actions of this kind may be sufficient to cause a court to lose the capacity, or willingness, to engage in robust forms of review.[69]

Responses of this kind are sometimes defended by "departmentalist" scholars as expressing reasonable disagreement with a court decision.[70] There may also be cases in which tools of this kind are used for dialogic purposes, or to express reasonable disagreement with prior court decisions, and a legitimate democratic demand for greater judicial responsiveness and accountability.[71] Jurisdiction-stripping measures, for example, may be part of a backlash against

---

[67] *Cf.* Scott Stephenson, *Are Political "Attacks" on the Judiciary Ever Justifiable? The Relationship between Unfair Criticism and Public Accountability*, AM. J. COMP. L. (forthcoming 2022).

[68] David Landau & Rosalind Dixon, *Abusive Judicial Review: Courts Against Democracy*, 53 U.C. DAVIS L. REV. 1313, 1346–47 (2020).

[69] *Compare id. See also* TOM S. CLARK, THE LIMITS OF JUDICIAL INDEPENDENCE (2010).

[70] *See, e.g.*, Michael Stokes Paulsen, *The Most Dangerous Branch: Executive Power to Say What the Law Is*, 83 GEO. L.J. 217 (1994); Mark Tushnet, *Alternative Forms of Judicial Review*, 101 MICH. L. REV. 2781 (2003); Keith E. Whittington, *Extrajudicial Constitutional Interpretation: Three Objections and Responses*, 80 N.C.L. Rev. 773, 783 (2002); Dixon, *A New Theory of Charter Dialogue*, *supra* note 25.

[71] *Compare* discussion in Roach, *supra* note 21.

a court, or used for abusive ends, but are also a means of weakening the finality of judicial review in cases where courts might otherwise refuse to uphold a reasonable legislative "sequel."[72] The difference will largely turn on the extent of attempts to oust a court's jurisdiction (backlash will generally involve much broader attempts to limit jurisdiction than true attempts at legislative dialogue), and the broader context for the interaction between courts and legislatures.

There is likewise a potential difference between measures that involve "stacking," "packing," or shrinking a court's size and composition.[73] In most cases, the "stacking" of a court will simply involve the appointment of new ideologically or politically sympathetic judges. *Some* consideration of a judge's political ideology is also a necessary and desirable part of any process of judicial appointment informed by notions of legal merit *and* democratic accountability. In most cases, therefore, the practice of court stacking will simply lead to an amplification in the role of partisan or ideological factors in the process of judicial appointment, not any long-term threat to the underlying constitutional system of checks and balances.

Court packing, in contrast, necessarily involves an increase in the size of a court, in order to clear the path for the appointment of new ideologically or politically sympathetic judges. And while this may be defensible in some cases as necessary to establish or restore norms of democratic responsiveness and accountability, it involves a significant change to the previous constitutional architecture for partisan ends, and therefore the specter of a long-term "tit-for-tat" battle among different political parties for control over a court's composition, using tools of expansion and stacking.[74] Repeated packing of this kind is also likely to do significant damage to the public perception of a court as independent and impartial. And while in some cases this may be justified as helping to diminish the perceived legitimacy of a fundamentally illegitimate court, in others it will have much clearer adverse consequences for commitments to democratic constitutionalism. It may undermine the capacity of courts to enforce constitutional commitments to individual rights, the rule of law, and democracy, both in a specific case and more broadly.

---

[72] *See* Chapter 8, *infra*. *Compare* Landau & Dixon, *Abusive Judicial Review*, *supra* note 69.

[73] David Kosar and Katarina Sipulova call this the difference between judicial "expansion" and "swapping" versus "emptying" strategies: *see* David Kosar & Katarina Sipulova, *How to Fight Court-Packing?*, 6 Const. Stud. 133, 133 (2020).

[74] Tom Gerald Daly, *'Good' Court-Packing? The Paradoxes of Democratic Restoration in Contexts of Democratic Decay*, Ger. Law J. (forthcoming) (noting risk of repetition).

Let's assume, as some believe, that disagreement with the decision in *Roe* was unreasonable. If so, the subsequent events illustrate the argument here. It is often suggested that "*Roe v. Wade* generated a politically potent right-to-life movement that helped elect Ronald Reagan president in 1980 and has significantly influenced national politics ever since."[75] But there is good evidence that conservative opposition to abortion began well before *Roe*, in the context of state-level changes to abortion law, and that conservative political movements arose as much in response to proposed changes such as the Equal Rights Amendment, and mobilization for LGBTQI+ rights.[76] What is clear, however, is that in the years after *Roe*, those who opposed the decision adopted a number of different measures designed to influence—or "encourage," or place pressure on—the Supreme Court to overrule or limit the effect of its prior decision.[77]

One measure was a proposed "right to life" amendment that would have altered the scope of the text of the Constitution.[78] But many other measures aimed specifically to limit the independence or jurisdiction of the Court: opponents of *Roe* sought to ensure that nominees to the federal judiciary opposed any recognition of a constitutional right to privacy that included access to abortion. Defenders of *Roe* responded by mobilizing to ensure that nominees publicly committed to upholding and applying *Roe* and the doctrine of *stare decisis*. But the result was that for twenty years "the judicial confirmation process [in the US became] a single-issue debate over nominees' attitudes towards abortion."[79] And the Court's decision in *Dobbs* suggests that those efforts were not fully effective. While previously professing respect for *Roe* and/or the doctrine of *stare decisis* in their confirmation hearings, in *Dobbs* almost all of the justices who voted to overrule *Roe* and *Casey* were appointed by Republican presidents in the era of conservative efforts to "stack" the federal bench with pro-life/anti-abortion justices.[80] And these justices have been willing to question a much broader range of rights-protective constitutional precedents.

---

[75] *See* Michael Klarman, quoted in Ariane De Vogue, *Roe v. Wage: Abortion Backlash Persists 40 Years Later*, ABC News (Jan. 21, 2013), at <https://abcnews.go.com/Politics/OTUS/roe-wade-abortion-backlash-persists-40-years/story?id=18271433>.

[76] Linda Greenhouse & Reva B. Siegel, Before Roe v. Wade: Voices That Shaped the Abortion Debate Before the Supreme Court Ruling 72–73 (2012).

[77] *See* Hatch-Eagleton Amendment (1983). For discussion, see, *e.g.*, Clarke D. Forsythe & Stephen B. Presser, *Restoring Self-Government on Abortion: A Federalism Amendment*, 10 Tex. Rev. L. & Pol. 301 (2005).

[78] *Id.*

[79] Anthony Dutra, *Men Come and Go, But Roe Abides: Why Roe v. Wade Will Not Be Overruled*, 90 B.U. L. Rev. 1261, 1290–91 (2010).

[80] Mariana Alfaro, What Conservative Justices Said About Roe in their Confirmation Hearings, Washington Post, June 24, 2022 <>https://www.washingtonpost.com/politics/2022/06/24/justices-roe-confirmation-hearings/ (noting statements to this effect by Justices Gorsuch, Kavanagh, Coney Barrett, and Alito, and Chief Justice Roberts, though not by Justice Thomas)

Similarly, opponents of *Roe* in Congress successfully sponsored legislation removing all federal funding for abortions through the Medicaid program (which provides free healthcare for the extreme poor or indigent Americans)—the so-called Hyde Amendment—and limiting the capacity of any federally funded family planning clinic to provide abortion services.[81] They also introduced hundreds of bills seeking to remove jurisdiction from the Supreme Court and lower federal courts to consider cases involving abortion: 433 such measures were introduced into Congress between 1973 and 1980, representing 70 percent of all attempts to limit the Court's jurisdiction during the relevant period.[82] And several of these measures had the potential to undermine the Court's broader independence and functioning.[83]

At a state level, as Gerald Rosenberg and others have shown, state legislatures also consistently passed legislation that effectively ignored *Roe*, not just sought to narrow or limit its effect.[84] And many state and local officials continued to enforce laws limiting access to abortion, which *Roe* had clearly ruled unconstitutional. Indeed, many existing institutions "simply ignored the law" on abortion, because both they and a large portion of relevant (especially state or local) publics disagreed with it.[85]

Democratic backlash, therefore, can be a threat to a court's capacity to protect and promote democratic responsiveness in a wide a variety of contexts. It will not simply threaten a court's capacity to counter the most pressing threats to the democratic minimum core. It will also affect the capacity of courts to create meaningful constitutional change, in the face of perceived democratic blind spots and burdens of inertia.

---

[81] *See* Sandra Berenknopf, *Judicial and Congressional Back-Door Methods that Limit the Effect of Roe v. Wade: There is No Choice if There is No Access*, 70 TEMP. L. REV. 653, 655–57 (1997); Lisa J. Allegrucci & Paul E. Knuz, *The Future of Roe v. Wade in the Supreme Court: Devolution of the Right of Abortion and Resurgence of State Control*, 7 JOHN'S J. LEGAL COMMENT 295, 301, 303 (1991) (noting amendments to Title X). Family Planning Program, Title X of the Public Health Service Act (42 U.S.C. §§300–300a-6).

[82] Dave Bridge & Curt Nichols, *Congressional Attacks on the Supreme Court: A Mechanism to Maintain, Build, and Consolidate*, 41 LAW & SOC. INQUIRY 100 (2016) (noting 233 on abortion and 230 on abortion/non-prayer out of a total of 612 proposed measures of this kind during this period).

[83] Stuart Taylor, Jr., *The Congress vs. The Courts*, N.Y. TIMES, Mar. 16, 1981, at <https://www.nytimes.com/1981/03/16/us/the-congress-vs-the-courts-news-analysis.html>. *See* discussion of the issues and constitutional limits and significance in Tara Leigh Grove, *The Article II Safeguards of Federal Jurisdiction*, 112 COLUM. L. REV. 250 (2012); Richard H. Fallon, Jr., *Jurisdiction-Stripping Reconsidered*, 96 VA. L. REV. 1043 (2010).

[84] GERALD N. ROSENBERG, THE HOLLOW HOPE: CAN COURTS BRING ABOUT SOCIAL CHANGE? (2008); Gerald N. Rosenberg, *Courting Disaster: Looking for Change in All the Wrong Places*, 54 DRAKE L. REV. 795 (2005). *See also* MICHAEL J. KLARMAN, FROM THE CLOSET TO THE ALTAR: COURTS, BACKLASH, AND THE STRUGGLE FOR SAME-SEX MARRIAGE (2013).

[85] Rosenberg, *Courting Disaster*, *supra* note 84, at 811.

D. Democratic Debilitation

Even if courts act consistently *in line with* democratic majority opinion, they may risk undermining commitments to democratic responsiveness by creating problems of "democratic debilitation."[86]

There are a range of reasons in a democracy to encourage legislative and executive actors to take an active role in the process of constitutional implementation. Some laws that raise constitutional questions may never come before courts.[87] In most systems, there are a range of constitutional norms that, by definition, call for legislative and executive forms of implementation. And political actors bring a distinctive perspective and set of experiences to questions of constitutional construction that engage both the judicial and political branches.

There are thus clear dangers to forms of judicial review that displace, rather than encourage, processes of constitutional implementation outside the courts. As Mark Tushnet notes, it is quite likely that "neither the people nor their representatives [will] take the Constitution seriously [if] they know—or believe—that the courts will."[88] Doing so inevitably involves the expenditure of time and political capital, and the necessity to do so may be far less if courts are in any event likely to fill gaps in legislation. This can also mean that if courts are *too* consistent in responding to sources of democratic dysfunction, judicial review will actually discourage legislators from taking appropriate responsibility for their own role in constitutional implementation—or create new forms of democratic "debilitation" or inertia.[89]

For some constitutional theorists, there is a qualitative difference between judicial and legislative attention to a constitutional question. Judicial review in this account involves an exercise of legal authority, by non-elected judges, whereas the process of legislation represents the direct exercise of political authority by representatives of "the people." There is thus inherent benefit to encouraging legislative as opposed to judicial deliberation on constitutional questions.[90]

---

[86] A court that is often seen as encountering this danger is the Supreme Court of India, especially in its public interest litigation jurisdiction: VARUN GAURI, PUBLIC INTEREST LITIGATION IN INDIA: OVERREACHING OR UNDERACHIEVING (2009).

[87] GARDBAUM, *supra* note 18, at 59.

[88] TUSHNET, *supra* note 1, at 66.

[89] *Id.*

[90] *Cf.* SUNSTEIN, *supra* note 39 (on the virtues of democracy-forcing review and its deliberative benefits).

In a responsive approach to judicial review, the distinction between legal and political authority and processes is more blurred. The process of constitutional construction ultimately involves an exercise of both legal and political judgment. And a key focus of judicial review is democratic representation-reinforcement—that is, the promotion of an appropriately deliberative, inclusive, and responsive form of democratic politics. Both legislatures and courts also have certain institutional advantages when it comes to these aims.

Legislatures tend to be better informed about democratic constitutional opinion and constraints and have better incentives to engage with information of this kind. But courts tend to be more responsive to the constitutional claims of individuals and certain minorities and have greater opportunity and experience in crafting certain forms of accommodation for constitutional rights. As Aileen Kavanagh notes, the process of legislation and judicial review are therefore best understood as "collaborative" or interconnected in nature, rather than following any strict separation between legal and political authority.[91] The costs of democratic "debilitation," therefore, are not *per se* the loss of an opportunity for legislators to contribute to debating and deciding on a question. Rather, they are a loss in the breadth of attention to constitutional claims.

The whole idea of democratic blockages—or legislative blind spots or burdens of inertia—is that legislators do not always take this opportunity. But reducing their incentive to do so will necessarily increase the chances that some forms of democratic legislation are subject to legislative blind spots or burdens.

E. Judicial Prudence, Principle, and Pragmatism

How should courts respond to the dangers of reverse inertia and democratic backlash of this kind? In the next chapter, I argue that courts should respond by weakening the scope or finality of judicial review. This is also arguably exactly what the US Supreme Court did, if not what it said it did, in *Casey* in response to evidence of reverse democratic inertia and backlash in response to decisions such as *Roe*. (And for that reason, the further retreat by the Court from the protection of abortion rights, in *Dobbs*, was both unnecessary and undesirable from a democratic constitutional perspective.)

---

[91] AILEEN KAVANAGH, THE COLLABORATIVE CONSTITUTION (forthcoming 2023). *See also* Eoin Carolan, *Dialogue isn't Working: The Case for Collaboration as a Model of Legislative-Judicial Relations*, 36 LEGAL STUD. 209 (2016).

The Court in *Casey* preserved a minimalist reading of *Roe* (in terms of the scope of women's right to seek an abortion pre-viability), but then overruled *Roe* in so far as it was out of step with contemporary democratic constitutional attitudes. The plurality in *Casey* ostensibly identified a change from 1973 to 1992 in the relative safety of abortions compared to childbirth in later stages of pregnancy, and in the point of fetal viability, as reasons to revisit the precedential force of its decision in *Roe*.[92] Neither of these changes, however, was seemingly sufficient to justify overruling (rather than adjusting) the trimester framework endorsed by Justice Blackmun in *Roe*, or the finding that protecting fetal life became a compelling state interest after viability, yet the Court did both of these things in its opinion in *Casey*. Partly for this reason, the plurality's judgment was also widely criticized, including by Justice Scalia who argued in dissent that the plurality in this context was relying on what was a clearly "revised version" of *Roe*, rather than the "real *Roe v. Wade*," and a "contrived" version of *stare decisis*.[93] This criticism was likewise echoed in the opinion of the Court *in Dobbs* purporting to overrule *Roe* and *Casey*.[94]

At the same time, the Court's approach *was* consistent with a norm of deference to reasonable legislative disagreement, or a willingness to narrow aspects of a prior judicial ruling in the face of (reasonable) legislative disagreement.

A similar analysis can be applied to *Carhart v. Gonzales (Carhart II)*, and the decision by the Court in that case to uphold the *Partial-Birth Abortion Ban Act* of 2003. The Court in *Carhart I* struck down a Nebraska statute prohibiting access to "partial birth" abortion procedures on two grounds: first, that the statute in question failed adequately to distinguish between intact (D&X) and non-intact (D&E) dilation and extraction procedures for late-term abortion, and was thus unconstitutionally vague; and second, that the state had not shown that use of D&X procedures were "never necessary to preserve the health of women."[152] The decision, however, met with significant public disapproval, of a kind potentially indicative of democratic error costs; and Congress responded by enacting the *Partial-Birth Abortion Ban Act* of 2003, prohibiting access to D&X procedures in all cases, except where necessary to save the life of a woman.

---

[92] 505 U.S. at 860.
[93] *Id.* at 993 (Scalia J., dissenting).
[94] Maria Cramer, *Here are* Key Passages From the Leaked Supreme Court Draft Opinion, N.Y. TIMES, May 3, 2022, <https://www.nytimes.com/2022/05/03/us/supreme-court-abortion-opinion-draft.html>.

In upholding the Act, in *Carhart II*, the Court clearly gave *some* effect to its prior reasoning in *Carhart I*—most importantly, by noting a range of differences between the 2003 Act and the Nebraska statute, which helped address its prior concerns about constitutional vagueness. Beyond this, however, the Court implicitly chose to overrule almost all its prior reasoning about the necessary scope of a health-based exception on prohibitions relating to late-term abortion. In the face of conflicting medical evidence regarding the comparative safety of D&X and D&E procedures, the Court suggested, it was appropriate to allow the legislature, rather than the Court itself, to determine the relevant "balance of risks."[153] This, as the dissenting Justices pointed out, was also a clear "retreat" from the Court's prior insistence that such restrictions should be subject to "close scrutiny" under the Due Process Clause.[154]

7
Toward Strong–Weak/Weak–Strong Judicial Review and Remedies

A theory of responsive judicial review is premised on two broad ideas about the relationship between judicial review and values of responsiveness: first, that judicial review should seek actively to protect and promote the capacity of a democratic constitutional system to respond to the needs and aspirations of democratic majorities; and second, that in doing so courts should be responsive to their own institutional position and role, including limits on their capacity and legitimacy. One of the most important ways in which courts can do this is also by "weakening" the finality of their decisions.

The distinction between "strong" and "weak" review is often associated with formal choices about constitutional design,[1] but it is also a distinction that applies to a range of choices courts must make in the process of judicial review, including choices about (i) how broadly or narrowly to reason (breadth); (ii) what kind of remedy to rely on, and the timing of those remedies (remedies); and (iii) how strongly to insist on a doctrine of *stare decisis* (the doctrine of precedent).[2] Narrower decisions expressly leave open broad scope for legislators to respond to court decisions—including in ways that express disagreement with aspects of a court's reasoning or logic. Non-coercive or delayed remedies allow legislators an opportunity to respond to courts, including in ways that express disagreement, without facing any form of reverse legislative inertia. Delay in particular can allow time for social and political conditions to shift in ways that increase elite and popular support for, or decrease opposition to, a court decision. And appropriately weakened forms of *stare decisis* allow legislators broad—if somewhat more implicit—scope to engage in "dialogue" with a court, in ways that reduce the danger of reverse burdens of inertia and ongoing democratic debilitation.

---

[1] Mark Tushnet, Weak Courts, Strong Rights: Judicial Review and Social Welfare Rights in Comparative Constitutional Law 22 (2009).

[2] Rosalind Dixon, *The Forms, Functions, and Varieties of Weak(ened) Judicial Review*, 17 Int'l J. Const. L. 904 (2019).

In a responsive approach to judicial review, the risks of reverse inertia and/ or democratic backlash will also provide a powerful argument for courts weakening the finality of constitutional decision-making in some or all of these ways. At the same time, how and when courts should do so will also depend on the nature of the blockage they are seeking to counter—and the specific risk of reverse inertia or backlash they confront.

Where the risk is to the health of the democratic minimum core, a responsive approach suggests that judicial review should be strong–weak in nature—that is, strong, or even "super-strong," and impose coercive limits on legislation or formal processes of constitutional change, and weak—or delayed, or subject to weak precedential force—only in order to avoid an immediate risk of political backlash. In cases involving democratic blind spots or burdens of inertia, in contrast, a responsive approach suggests the value of a weak–strong approach, or a weakened approach to rights combined with stronger judicial remedies. Often, this will involve a preference for delayed but coercive remedies, or engagement-style remedies, accompanied by a form of "penalty default" logic—or greater willingness by courts to uphold legislative action, compared to inaction.[3]

A. Weakened Judicial Review

As originally formulated, the idea of weak-form review was largely used to describe the *formal finality* of judicial review in various systems. In some constitutional systems, for instance, "constitutional" or quasi-constitutional instruments are enacted by way of ordinary legislation. This, as both Mark Tushnet and Stephen Gardbaum pointed out, also limits the finality of judicial review in at least two ways. By enacting constitutional norms via statute, parliaments can ensure that they retain power both to amend and repeal the instrument, or expressly suspend it, by subsequent legislation.[4] They thereby also retain power to override any aspect of a court's interpretation of those norms with which they disagree. This, in most constitutional systems, is understood to be the necessary corollary of the doctrine of parliamentary supremacy.

---

[3] Ian Ayres & Robert Gertner, *Filling Gaps in Incomplete Contracts: An Economic Theory of Default Rules*, 99 Yale L.J. 87 (1989); Eric Maskin, *On the Rationale for Penalty Default Rules*, 24 Fla. St. U. L. Rev. 1 (1997); and Eric Posner, *There are No Penalty Default Rules in Contract Law*, 33 Fla. St. U. L. Rev. 563 (2006). *See also* Ian Ayres, *Ya-Huh: There Are and Should be Penalty Defaults*, 33 Fla. St. U. L. Rev. 589 (2006).

[4] Tushnet, Weak Courts, Strong Rights, *supra* note 1; Stephen Gardbaum, The New Commonwealth Model of Constitutionalism: Theory and Practice (2013).

This is certainly true in countries such as the United Kingdom (UK) and New Zealand, which adopted new constitutional rights charters, and models of judicial review, in the 1990s.[5]

Another way in which constitutions may make judicial review "weak" or penultimate in character is by including an express power of legislative override within the scope of an otherwise entrenched constitutional instrument. In Canada, for instance, section 33 of the *Charter of Rights and Freedoms* 1982 famously created an express power for the Canadian Parliament and provincial legislatures to pass laws "notwithstanding" other key provisions of the *Charter*. This has also been understood by the Supreme Court of Canada (SCC) to give the Canadian Parliament and provincial legislatures power effectively to suspend both the operation of *Charter* rights—and the Court's interpretation of those rights—for a five-year, renewable period.[6] Similar powers of override have been adopted, at various times, in the Constitutions of Poland, Mongolia, Belgium, Luxembourg, and Finland.[7] This is also the model famously proposed in the United States (US) by Judge Bork as a means of altering the strong-form character of judicial review by the US Supreme Court, and recently debated in Israel.[8]

The degree to which Commonwealth countries, and constitutions, have been at the forefront of adopting such a model, however, is one reason why Gardbaum has famously linked the idea of weak-form review to the model of rights protection adopted by various Commonwealth countries between 1982 and 2006. Initially, he did not use the term "weak-form review" to describe the new rights charters found in the United Kingdom, Canada, and New Zealand, but over time, came to see it as "a helpful shorthand for one of their two constitutive features" (the other being pre-enactment political rights review).[9] Tushnet, however, was more skeptical about the idea that weak-form review needed to take this specific form or was linked so clearly to the rise of

---

[5] *See Human Rights Act 1998* (UK); *Human Rights Act 1993* (N.Z.).

[6] On the difference and its potential significance, see Jeffrey Goldsworthy, *Judicial Review, Legislative Override, and Democracy*, 38 WAKE FOREST L. REV. 451 (2003); Rosalind Dixon & Adrienne Stone, *Constitutional Amendment and Political Constitutionalism: A Philosophical and Comparative Reflection*, in PHILOSOPHICAL FOUNDATIONS OF CONSTITUTIONAL LAW (David Dyzenhaus & Malcolm Thorburn eds., 2016).

[7] GARDBAUM, THE NEW COMMONWEALTH MODEL OF CONSTITUTIONALISM, supra note 4.

[8] Rivka Weill, *Reconciling Parliamentary Sovereignty and Judicial Review: On the Theoretical and Historical Origins of the Israeli Legislative Override Power*, 39 HASTINGS CONST. L.Q. 457 (2011). See Tal Schneider & Chen Ma'anit, *Ministers Approve Bill to Override Israel's High Court*, GLOBES (May 6, 2018), <https://en.globes.co.il/en/article-ministers-approve-bill-to-override-israels-high-court-100 1234682>.

[9] Stephen Gardbaum, *What's So Weak About "Weak-Form Review"?: A Reply to Aileen Kavanagh*, 13 INT'L J. CONST. L. 391 (2015).

the "new Commonwealth constitutionalism."[10] Instead, Tushnet was agnostic as to the specific *form* any limitation on judicial finality might take. Indeed, in joint work with me on Asia, he embraced the idea that a range of different functional forms could effectively create an ordinary power of legislative override— including powers of constitutional amendment.[11]

In the United States, Article V of the Constitution makes it extremely difficult to amend the US Constitution: successful amendments require the support of two-thirds of both Congress and the Senate, and three-quarters of state legislatures (or state conventions). In practice, many scholars suggest that this also makes the amendment process more difficult than that of any other current constitutional democracy.[12] Clearly, it limits the capacity for Article V to serve as a mechanism for overriding decisions of the US Supreme Court. It was used for this purpose in the adoption of the Eleventh, Fourteenth, and Sixteenth Amendments,[13] but attempts to rely on Article V to override controversial decisions of the Court during the twentieth century consistently failed.

In many other constitutional democracies, however, the requirements for constitutional amendment are far less demanding. In some countries, the legislature itself has power to amend the constitution, and to do so subject to relatively modest super-majority requirements.[14] In other cases, amendments require the approval of a majority of voters, voting at a national referendum, but in the context of a strong tradition of approving proposed amendments, so that ratification requirements of this kind do not pose a major obstacle to overriding court decisions.[15] And while flexible amendment procedures of this kind allow for constitutional change of a variety of kinds, including changes that update and revise a constitution's architecture, one of their key functions is to allow legislatures to override judicial interpretations of an *existing* constitutional provision with which they reasonably disagree.[16] There are also

---

[10] TUSHNET, WEAK COURTS, STRONG RIGHTS, *supra* note 1.

[11] Mark Tushnet & Rosalind Dixon, *Weak-Form Review and Its Constitutional Relatives: An Asian Perspective*, in COMPARATIVE CONSTITUTIONAL LAW IN ASIA 102 (Tom Ginsburg & Rosalind Dixon eds., 2014).

[12] Donald S. Lutz, *Toward a Theory of Constitutional Amendment*, 88 AM. POL. SCI. REV. 355 (1994).

[13] *See* Geoffrey R. Stone, *Precedent, the American Process, and the Evolution of Constitutional Doctrine*, 11 HARV. J.L. & PUB. POL'Y 67 (1998). Another potential example is the Nineteenth Amendment as a response to *Minor v. Happersett*, 88 U.S. 162 (1875) (finding that women had no right to vote under the Fourteenth Amendment).

[14] Lutz, *supra* note 12; Dixon & Stone, *supra* note 6.

[15] *See, e.g.*, Tom Ginsburg & James Melton, *Does the Constitutional Amendment Rule Matter At All? Amendment Cultures and the Challenges of Measuring Amendment Difficulty*, 13 INT'L J. CONST. L. 686 (2015).

[16] Rosalind Dixon, *Constitutional Amendment Rules: A Comparative Perspective*, in COMPARATIVE CONSTITUTIONAL LAW 96, 98 (Tim Ginsburg & Rosalind Dixon eds., 2011).

numerous countries in which there is a long tradition of legislatures relying on powers of constitutional amendment for exactly this purpose.

India and Colombia are two leading examples. In India, Parliament has relied on the amendment provision of the Constitution (Article 368) with a view to overriding decisions of the Supreme Court of India (SCI) on the right to property, freedom of expression, and non-discrimination, and the scope of judicial review itself.[17] In Colombia, the Congress has relied on amendment to curb decisions of the Constitutional Court on social rights, drug decriminalization, and the terms and conditions of public sector workers.[18] In Ireland, constitutional amendment has likewise been used to modify the effect of a range of Supreme Court decisions, including notably on access to abortion.[19]

Another mechanism for weakening judicial review is the power of legislatures to remove or limit the jurisdiction of courts in certain areas.[20] In the United States, for instance, Article III of the Constitution gives Congress power to make "exceptions" to the Supreme Court's appellate jurisdiction.[21] A range of other countries have also seen legislatures adopt "ouster" clauses in order to protect executive action from judicial review.[22] As Chapter 6 notes, a power of this kind may be used as a tool to attack courts and basic judicial independence. But it may also be used as a more focused tool for weakening the finality of judicial review, or as a means of ensuring that legislatures are able to pass reasonable legislative sequels without the risk of ongoing judicial invalidation

---

[17] Burt Neuborne, *The Supreme Court of India*, 1 INT'L J. CONST. L. 476 (2003); Tushnet & Dixon, *supra* note 11; Dixon & Stone, *supra* note 6.

[18] Rosalind Dixon & David Landau, *Transnational Constitutionalism and a Limited Doctrine of Unconstitutional Constitutional Amendment*, 13 INT'L J. CONST. L. 606 (2015). *See also* MANUEL JOSE CEPEDA ESPINOSA & DAVID LANDAU, COLOMBIAN CONSTITUTIONAL LAW: LEADING CASES (2017).

[19] *See discussion in* Eoin Carolan, *Leaving Behind the Commonwealth Model of Rights Review: Ireland as an Example of Collaborative Constitutionalism*, *in* RIGHTS-BASED CONSTITUTIONAL REVIEW 94 (John Bell & Marie-Luce Paris eds., 2016).

[20] *See discussion in* Walter Murphy, *Who Shall Interpret? The Question for the Ultimate Constitutional Interpreter*, 48 REV. POL. 401 (1986); Cornelia T.L. Pillard, *The Unfulfilled Promise of the Constitution in Executive Hands*, 103 MICH. L. REV. 676 (2005); Gary Lawson & Christopher D. Moore, *The Executive Power of Constitutional Interpretation*, 81 IOWA L. REV. 1267 (1995); Michael Stokes Paulsen, *The Most Dangerous Branch: Executive Power to Say What the Law Is*, 83 GEO. L.J. 217 (1994).

[21] *See, e.g.*, Leonard G. Ratner, *Majoritarian Constraints on Judicial Review: Congressional Control of Supreme Court Jurisdiction*, 27 VILL. L. REV. 929 (1982); Paul M. Bator, *Congressional Power over the Jurisdiction of the Federal Courts*, 27 VILL. L. REV. 1031 (1982). *Cf.* Steven G. Calabresi & Gary Lawson, *The Unitary Executive, Jurisdiction Stripping, and the* Handan *Opinions: A Textualist Response to Justice Scalia*, 107 COLUM. L. REV. 1002, 1008 (2007); Richard H. Fallon, Jr., *Jurisdiction-Stripping Reconsidered*, 96 VA. L. REV. 1043, 1045 (2010); Barry Friedman, *A Different Dialogue: The Supreme Court, Congress and Federal Jurisdiction*, 85 NW. U. L. REV. 1, 34–36 (1990); Gerald Gunther, *Congressional Power to Curtail Federal Court Jurisdiction: An Opinionated Guide to the Ongoing Debate*, 36 STAN. L. REV. 895, 921–22 (1984); James E. Pfander, *Federal Supremacy, State Court Inferiority, and the Constitutionality of Jurisdiction-Stripping Legislation*, 101 NW. U. L. REV. 191, 238 (2007).

[22] In the United Kingdom, see, *e.g.*, *Anisminic Ltd. v. Foreign Compensation Comm'n* [1969] 2 AC 147 (UK); R. (Privacy Int'l) v. Investigatory Powers Tribunal [2019] UKSC 22. In Australia, see, *e.g.*, Plaintiff S157/2002 v. Commonwealth (2003) 211 CLR 476 (Austl.).

of those measures. The logic behind such a dialogue is as follows: a court renders a decision that a democratic majority has reasonable grounds for finding unacceptable; the legislature responds by enacting some form of narrowing legislation or dialogic legislative sequel and, at the same time (or subsequently), passing legislation formally ousting the jurisdiction of courts to hear a challenge to the validity of this broad class of provision.

This logic is not watertight. In cases of decentralized, or diffuse, constitutional review, there are a range of courts that can potentially declare legislative or executive action unconstitutional. Even if the legislature ousts the jurisdiction of the constitutional, or highest, court to hear constitutional cases, other courts may retain jurisdiction to do so. This is especially true in those federal systems that have parallel state and federal intermediate courts. And it is not clear that courts—including the US Supreme Court—would be prepared to give effect to such jurisdiction-stripping legislation if it were to attempt to strip jurisdiction from all courts to hear a constitutional question.[23]

But jurisdiction-stripping is still one important formal legal tool legislatures may rely on when attempting to override the effect of a court decision—and therefore as a tool of both democratic backlash, and reasonable legislative disagreement or dialogue.[24] Thus in the United States, Congress has largely declined to rely on this logic but repeatedly *threatened* to use its powers under Article III to override decisions of the federal courts involving school desegregation remedies, and the civil liberties of communist party members and sympathizers.[25] And in India, Parliament has relied on similar powers as a tool for expressing disagreement with the Supreme Court. It has passed a series of constitutional amendments purporting to redefine the scope of various rights (such as the right to property) under the Constitution, but also to limit the scope for the Court to interpret and enforce such rights—in ways that could allow it to express a different view of the scope and priority of such rights.[26]

---

[23] *Compare* RICHARD H. FALLON, JR. ET AL., HART AND WECHSLER'S THE FEDERAL COURTS AND THE FEDERAL SYSTEM 300–12 (6th ed. 2009); Rosalind Dixon, *Partial Constitutional Amendment*, 13 INT'L J. CONST. L. 391 (2011).

[24] More controversially, some scholars suggest that the *executive* may choose to override court decisions by simply choosing not to implement those decisions. The reflects a long line of "departmentalist" scholarship in the United States, which focuses on the scope for executive rather than legislative officials to override certain court decisions with which they disagree: *compare* Murphy, *supra* note 20; Pillard, *supra* note 20; Lawson & Moore, *supra* note 20; Paulsen, *supra* note 20.

[25] The one case in which Congress did rely on its powers under Art III cl 2 was more prospective: *see* Ex Parte McCardle, 74 U.S. (7 Wall) 506 (1869). Of the other instances of threatened usage, some could also be viewed as unreasonable expressions of democratic backlash, and others as expressions of reasonable, dialogic disagreement.

[26] *See, e.g.*, Neuborne, *supra* note 17; Sajjan Singh v. State of Rajisthan, AIR 1965 SC 845 (India); State of Bihar v. Kameshwar Singh, 1952 1 SCR 889 (India); Karimbil Kunhikoman v. State of Kerala, 1962 AIR 723l; 1962 SCR Supl. (1) 829 (India).

The idea of weakened review has also increasingly been used to describe the ways in which courts themselves may limit the finality of their decisions—through the choices they make about (i) how broadly or narrowly to reason (strong or weak reasoning); (ii) what kind of remedies to rely on, and the timing of those remedies (strong or weak remedies); and (iii) how strongly to insist on a doctrine of *stare decisis* (strong or weak *stare decisis*).[27]

Judicial decisions, as Cass Sunstein famously noted, may be narrow or broad, and shallow or deep in scope.[28] Decisions that are both narrow and shallow are generally understood as truly "minimalist"—that is, they deliberately "say as little as is necessary in order to justify an outcome" in a case—whereas those that are broader or deeper are more maximalist in nature.[29] Narrow or "minimalist" decisions, as Sunstein notes, can have a number of advantages: they can help reduce both "decision" and "error" costs in the process of judicial decision-making.[30] From a democratic perspective, they also leave *express* scope for further legislative action. "They increase the space for further reflection and debate at the local state and national levels, simply because they do not foreclose subsequent decisions."[31]

Courts likewise have a range of choices about the relative strength or weakness of judicial remedies—including both their declaratory versus coercive force, and delayed versus immediate effect. Some judicial orders, such as injunctions, or structural edits, or orders for *mandamus* (the making of a specific decision) or *certiorari* (setting aside of quashing of a decision) are necessarily understood to carry with them the potential for legal coercion, whereas declarations do not. They remain legally binding and authoritative, but without attaching duties on individuals enforceable through coercive sanctions, such as those that follow from a finding of contempt of court.

Declarations themselves can also take stronger versus weaker forms. One of the defining features of the "new Commonwealth" constitutional model, in countries such as the United Kingdom, New Zealand, and several Australian states and territories, is that it adopts a distinctive model of weak declaratory remedies whereby courts are given the power to declare legislation to be incompatible with the constitution, but expressly *denied* the power to declare that it is invalid or lacks effect on that basis.[32]

---

[27] Dixon, *supra* note 2.
[28] *See* Cass R. Sunstein, One Case at a Time: Judicial Minimalism on the Supreme Court (2001).
[29] *Id.*
[30] *Id.* at 3.
[31] *Id.* at 4–5.
[32] See Chapter 5, Section D.3 *supra*.

Remedies can further vary in strength, depending on whether they promise immediate or delayed relief to a plaintiff.[33] In Canada, for example, starting with the *Manitoba Language Rights* case[34] and then more fully with the SCC's decision in *Schachter*,[35] the SCC famously endorsed the idea that it had power to issue suspended declarations of invalidity as part of the power to issue any remedy "appropriate and just in the circumstances."[36] There are at least twenty cases in which the SCC has applied a remedy of this kind.[37] In South Africa, the drafters of the 1996 Constitution gave express recognition to the power of courts to make orders of this kind, providing in section 172(1)(b) of the Constitution that when deciding a constitutional matter, a court may make "any order that is just and equitable," including an order "suspending [a] declaration of invalidity for any period and on any conditions," and the Constitutional Court has held that this extends to the making of a suspended declaration of invalidity. The CCSA issued suspended declarations of invalidity in thirty-eight cases between 1996 and 2016.[38] The same kinds of remedy have been employed by courts in Germany, Italy, Colombia, Korea, and Hong Kong, among others.[39]

Remedial delay of this kind can be implicit as well as explicit. First-order deferral will involve an explicit decision by a court to delay the effect of a remedial order (e.g., by issuing a suspended declaration of invalidity), to give a ruling purely prospective effect, or to endorse a substantive constitutional standard of delayed or "progressive" realization.[40] But second-order deferral will be more implicit, and involve a mix of *Marbury*-style breadth in reasoning and narrowness in result—or "partial confrontation of an issue by a court, combined with partial avoidance or delay at the level of a concrete legal remed[y], or the immediate legal and political consequences of a ruling."[41] In this sense, it is closely related to a range of other modes of judicial "avoidance"—including US-style limits on justiciability (such as doctrines of mootness, ripeness, and standing,

---

[33] *Compare* Kent Roach, *Dialogic Remedies*, 17 INT'L J. CONST. L. 860, 870 (2019); Po Jen Yap, *New Democracies and Novel Remedies*, PUB. L. 30 (2017).
[34] Re Manitoba Language Rts., [1985] 1 S.C.R. 721 (Can.).
[35] Schachter v. Canada, [1992] 2 S.C.R. 679 (Can.).
[36] Canadian Charter of Rights and Freedoms § 24.
[37] Robert Leckey, *The Harms of Remedial Discretion*, 14 INT'L J. CONST. L. 584 (2016).
[38] Erin F. Delaney, *Analyzing Avoidance: Judicial Strategy in Comparative Perspective*, 66 DUKE L.J. 1, 48 (2016).
[39] *See, e.g.*, Yap, *New Democracies and Novel Remedies, supra* note 33; Abortion I, (1975) 39 BVerfGE 1 (Germany); ESPINOSA & LANDAU, *supra* note 18; Decision No. 242 of Nov. 22, 2019 (decision of the Italian Constitutional Court finding a prohibition on assisted suicide unconstitutional).
[40] Rosalind Dixon & Samuel Issacharoff, *Living to Fight Another Day: Judicial Deferral in Defense of Democracy*, 2016 WIS. L. REV. 683, 700–07 (2016).
[41] *Id.* at 699. *See also* discussion in LEE EPSTEIN & JACK KNIGHT, THE CHOICES JUSTICES MAKE 281 (1997).

and the political question doctrine), and substantive doctrines of deference, such as the margin of appreciation doctrine in Europe.[42] These other modes of avoidance, however, are distinct from delay in one important respect: they can often involve permanent avoidance, rather than simply the temporary judicial avoidance of a question. Delay, in contrast, implies that a court must eventually confront a constitutional question, not simply indefinitely postpone or avoid confronting it.[43]

Another variant on weak judicial remedies involves "engagement-style" remedies, which require governments to consult or engage with citizens, prior to any infringement of their rights.[44] Norms of engagement reflect a broad trend in democracies toward an emphasis on consultation as a necessary precondition for effective and legitimate democratic government. The idea of *engagement-style remedies* is also to constitutionalize a requirement of consultation of this kind—both as a sign of respect for those parties and as a means of enlisting and empowering them to help protect and promote relevant constitutional guarantees and assist in defining their content.

Courts must decide, in addition, on the strength of *stare decisis*. Many civil law systems do not recognize any formal doctrine of precedent yet give some weight to prior decisions in a constitutional context—especially a consistent line of decisions or "jurisprudence."[45] Most common law courts also take a somewhat weakened approach to *stare decisis* in a constitutional context. The ultimate source of authority in a constitutional context is the text of a written constitution, not prior case law, and thus prior precedents are often seen to have a lesser claim to authority than in a purely common law context.[46]

Most constitutional systems in the Anglo-American world also recognize at least some limits on *stare decisis* even in a common law context.[47] The US Supreme Court in *Casey*, for instance, noted three broad reasons for departing from a prior ruling under ordinary norms of *stare decisis*: (i) the fact that a prior ruling has "defied practical workability"; (ii) that "related principles of law have so far developed as to [leave] a [prior] rule no more than a remnant of abandoned doctrine"; and (iii) that "facts have so changed or come to be seen

---

[42] Delaney, *Analyzing Avoidance*, *supra* note 38.

[43] Dixon & Issacharoff, *supra* note 40, at 723.

[44] BRIAN RAY, ENGAGING WITH SOCIAL RIGHTS: PROCEDURE, PARTICIPATION AND DEMOCRACY IN SOUTH AFRICA'S SECOND WAVE (2016).

[45] *See, e.g.*, Vincy Fon & Francesco Parisi, *Judicial Precents in Civil Law Systems: A Dynamic Analysis*, 26 INT'L REV. L. & ECON. 519 (2006); JOHN HENRY MERRYMAN & ROGELIO PEREZ-PERDOMO, THE CIVIL LAW TRADITION: AN INTRODUCTION TO THE LEGAL SYSTEMS OF EUROPE AND LATIN AMERICA (2018).

[46] ANTONIN SCALIA, A MATTER OF INTERPRETATION: FEDERAL COURTS AND THE LAW (1998).

[47] Historically, the exception was of course the appellate committee of the House of Lords: *see, e.g.*, Gerald Dworkin, *Stare Decisis in the House of Lords*, 25 MOD. L. REV. 163 (1962).

so differently, as to have robbed the [prior] rul[ing] of significant application or justification."[48] Other courts have also identified the degree to which a case has been affirmed by subsequent courts, and the original strength or weakness of the majority in favor of a particular ruling, as additional factors informing the strength of *stare decisis*.[49]

In practice, many courts further depart from their own prior decisions after some period of time. In the United States, for instance, for most Supreme Court precedents, even under an ordinary norm of *stare decisis*, the greatest chance of citation occurs in the first year of life.[50] Thereafter, the chances of citation decrease progressively, with the probability of a decision being cited falling after five years from 30 percent to 20 percent, after ten years to approximately 13 percent, and after forty-two years to only 5 percent.[51]

Courts, however, may choose *further* to weaken the force of *stare decisis* in certain contexts—for example, in "second look" cases, or cases involving legislative sequels expressing clear legislative disagreement, in ways that affect the *de facto* finality of prior constitutional decisions. As Sunstein notes, "stare decisis adds a temporal dimension to minimalism": "the effect of width and depth is not merely a function of what the court says. It will depend a great deal on the applicable theory of stare decisis."[52] As Chapter 6 notes, the relationship between cases such as *Roe* and *Casey* (though not *Dobbs*), and *Carhart I* and *II*, are prime examples.[53]

In a responsive approach, there will also be clear value to both formal *and* informal modes of weakening the finality of judicial review. All judicial review is weak or nonfinal over the long term. Over time, processes of judicial appointment, and changes in judges' own attitudes and experiences, will almost always lead to some degree of convergence between democratic

---

[48] Planned Parenthood v. Casey, 505 U.S. 833, 854ff (1992) (reliance being a fourth relevant factor that pointed in favor of continued adherence to prior precedent).

[49] *See, e.g.*, Randy J. Kozel, *The Scope of Precedent*, 113 MICH. L. REV. 179 (2014); Earl Maltz, *The Nature of Precedent*, 66 N.C. L. REV. 367 (1988).

[50] *See* Ryan C. Black & James F. Spriggs, *The Depreciation of Supreme Court Precedent* 35 (fig. 1) (Jun. 12, 2009), <http://papers.ssrn.com/sol3/papers.cfm?abstract_id=1421413>. *See also* Frank B. Cross et al., *Citations in the U.S. Supreme Court: An Empirical Study of Their Use and Significance*, U. ILL. L. REV. 489 (2010). *See also* Frank B. Cross et al., *Warren Court Precedents in the Rehnquist Court*, 24 CONST. COMMENT. 3 (2007); William M. Landes & Richard A. Posner, *Legal Precedent: A Theoretical and Empirical Analysis* (NBER Working Paper 1976), <http://www.nber.org/papers/w0146.pdf>.

[51] Black & Spriggs, *supra* note 50.

[52] SUNSTEIN, *supra* note 28, at 19, 21.

[53] *See* Chapter 6, section E *supra*. *Dobbs* goes much further than *Casey* in this context in ignoring as opposed to weakening the finality of decisions such as *Roe*. Compare *Abortion I*, (1975) 39 BVerfGE 1 (Germany), *Abortion II*, (1993) 88 BVerfGE 203 (Germany) as discussed in DONALD P. KOMMERS, THE CONSTITUTIONAL JURISPRUDENCE OF THE FEDERAL REPUBLIC OF GERMANY 339 (2d ed. 1997).

constitutional attitudes and judicial decisions.[54] But the idea behind weakened conceptions of judicial review is that the time frame for this matters, and that in the short to medium term, convergence of this kind will depend on the availability of both formal and informal modes for weakening the finality of court decisions.

One might still ask why judges should weaken judicial review rather than rely on the exercise by *legislators* of formal powers of override. There are two broad responses. First, not all well-functioning constitutional democracies provide meaningful scope for formal legislative override of court decisions, yet they often give courts broad power and discretion to engage in robust forms of judicial review. Second, there are often practical constraints on the use of formal powers of legislative override. For instance, if a power of legislative override is not exercised for an extended period, political understandings may begin to harden against its use. Similarly, where there is a robust "human rights culture" in a country, legislatures can often pay a political price for relying on formal powers of legislative override, even if such an override is democratically justified.[55]

Both factors suggest that formal models of weakened review are generally best understood as a *complement to*, rather than *substitute* for informal judicial approaches weakening the finality of judicial review.[56] This understanding is also borne out by attention to differences in the *de facto* finality of judicial review in countries with a similar degree of formal judicial finality. Both the United Kingdom and Canada, for example, are generally seen as having formally weak systems of judicial review, but one (the United Kingdom) has moved toward *de facto* strong review, whereas the other (Canada) has maintained a weaker, more dialogic model.[57]

The UK *Human Rights Act* 1998, as Chapter 5 notes, confers only weak interpretive and declaratory remedial powers on British courts, under sections 3 and 4. And while British courts have relied on sections 3 and 4 in numerous cases, the UK government has developed an almost perfectly consistent practice of proposing a remedial order when the courts hold that legislation is

---

[54] *Compare* Robert G. McCloskey, The American Supreme Court (1960); Robert A. Dahl, *Decision-Making in a Democracy: The Supreme Court as a National Policy-Maker*, 6 J. Pub. L. 279 (1957).

[55] Goldsworthy, *supra* note 6; Rosalind Dixon, *A Minimalist Charter of Rights for Australia: The UK or Canada as a Model*, 37 Fed. L. Rev. 335 (2009); Aileen Kavanagh, *A Hard Look at the Last Word*, 35 Oxford J. Legal Stud. 825, 836 (2015).

[56] *Compare* David Landau, *Substitute and Complement Theories of Judicial Review*, 92 Ind. L.J. 1283 (2017).

[57] Aileen Kavanagh, *What's So Weak About "Weak-Form Review"? The Case of the UK Human Rights Act 1998*, 13 Int'l J. Const. L. 1008 (2015).

incompatible with the Convention rights, and Parliament has consistently approved the measures.[58] The only occasion on which the government has *not* responded to a finding of incompatibility is in the context of prisoner voting, where the original court decision (*Hirst*) was the decision of a European rather than British court.[59]

Similarly, the Canadian *Charter of Rights and Freedoms* gives Canadian courts a range of strong remedial powers, but almost equally broad powers to Parliament and provincial legislatures under section 33 to override rights protected by the *Charter*. And again, the power in section 33 has rarely been used in practice by provincial legislatures (and never by the federal Parliament).[60] But close attention to the ordinary legislative response to decisions of the SCC reveals a more complex picture of strong and weak review in Canada, compared to the United Kingdom. Most attempts to engage in dialogue with the SCC have succeeded either *de facto* (in the absence of any subsequent court challenge) or because the SCC has upheld them as a reasonable limitation on rights, under section 1 of the *Charter*.[61] The only exception is again in the context of prisoner voting rights, where in *Sauvé II* the SCC declined to uphold attempts to reinstate restrictions on prisoner voting. But this was a case in which the power of override under section 33 of the *Charter* was not available, and was the exception rather than the rule in terms of the SCC's approach

---

[58] Tom Hickman, Public Law After the Human Rights Act (2010); Alison Young, Democratic Dialogue and the Constitution (2020); Aileen Kavanagh, Constitutional Review Under the Human Rights Act (2009); Kavanagh, *supra* note 57; Dixon, *The Forms, Functions and Varieties of Weak(ened) Judicial Review*, supra note 2, at 918. My thanks to Timothy Endicott for helpful discussion on this point.

[59] Hirst v. United Kingdom (No. 2) (2005) ECHR 681. For discussion of the government and subsequent European response to this decision, see, e.g., Ed Bates, *The Continued Failure to Implement* Hirst v. UK, Eur. J. Int'l L. Blog <https://www.ejiltalk.org/the-continued-failure-to-implement-hirst-v-uk/>; Elizabeth Adams, *Prisoner's Voting Rights: Case Closed?*, UK Const. L. Ass'n, <https://ukconstitutionallaw.org/2019/01/30/elizabeth-adams-prisoners-voting-rights-case-closed/>.

[60] Tsvi Kahana, *The Notwithstanding Mechanism and Public Discussion: Lessons from the Ignored Practice of Section*, 44 Can. Pub. Admin. 255 (2008). For more recent uses, see also *Notwithstanding Clause* (Centre for Constitutional Studies, Jul. 2019), <https://www.constitutionalstudies.ca/2019/07/notwithstanding-clause/>.

[61] *See, e.g.*, R v. Vaillancourt, [1987] 2 S.C.R. 636; Ford v. Québec, (A.G.) [1988] 2 S.C.R. 712; Committee for the Commonwealth of Canada v. Canada, [1991] 1 S.C.R. 139; R v. Bain, [1991] 1 S.C.R. 91; R v. Zundel, [1992] 2 S.C.R. 731; R v. Daviault, [1994] 3 S.C.R. 761; Thomson Newspapers v. Canada (A.G.), [1998] 1 S.C.R. 877; Corbiere v. Canada (Minister of Indian and Northern Affairs), [1999] 2 S.C.R. 203; Figueroa v. Canada (A.G.) [2003] 1 S.C.R. 912. *See also* Peter W. Hogg & Allison A. Bushell, *The Charter Dialogue between Courts and Legislatures (Or Perhaps the Charter of Rights Isn't Such a Bad Thing after All)*, 35 Osgoode Hall L.J. 75 (1997); Kent Roach, *Dialogue or Defiance: Legislative Reversals of Supreme Court Decisions in Canada and the United States*, 4 Int'l J. Const. L. 347 (2006). On avoidance of this kind as an important tool of weakness, see, e.g., Delaney, *Analyzing Avoidance*, supra note 38.

to legislative sequels—including what Canadian scholars have called "in your face" legislative replies.[62]

It therefore seems plausible to categorize judicial review under the Canadian *Charter* as *formally* and *de facto* weak in nature.[63] This conclusion, however, depends almost entirely on the willingness of Canadian courts to uphold ordinary legislative sequels or attempts at dialogue, at least in the shadow of section 33 of the *Charter*—not the actual invocation of formal powers of this kind (see Table 7.1).

Table 7.1 Models of the Finality of Judicial Review in Practice

Form/Substance	Strong Stare Decisis	Weak stare decisis
Weak Formal Finality	*De facto* strong	*De jure* and *de facto* weak (e.g., Canada in the shadow of section 33)
Strong Formal Finality	*De jure* and *de facto* strong (e.g., the US in express reasoning in *Casey*, Canada in *Sauvé II*)	*De facto* weak (e.g., the US Supreme Court in practice in *Casey*

B. Why (and How to) Weaken Review

Beyond responding to the constitutional structures in which they operate, courts thus face three broad choices about the scope and *finality* of their decisions. They can choose to reason broadly or narrowly, issue strong or weak remedies, or rely on strong or weak doctrines of *stare decisis*. In a responsive approach, there will also be powerful arguments for judicial weakness of all these kinds—but in a way that is responsive to the specific blockage courts are seeking to counter, and the foreseeable risks of reverse inertia or democratic backlash.

---

[62] Kent Roach, *Constitutional and Common Law Dialogues Between the Supreme Court and Canadian Legislatures*, 80 CAN. B. REV. 481 (2001); KENT ROACH, THE SUPREME COURT ON TRIAL: JUDICIAL ACTIVISM OR DEMOCRATIC DIALOGUE (2001).

[63] *See* Rosalind Dixon, *A New Theory of Charter Dialogue: The Supreme. Court of Canada, Charter Dialogue and Deference*, 47 OSGOODE HALL L.J. 235 (2009); *compare* Roach, *Constitutional and Common Law Dialogues*, *supra* note 62; ROACH, THE SUPREME COURT ON TRIAL, *supra* note 62.

1. The democratic minimum core and the pragmatic argument for weak–strong judicial review

For cases involving attacks on the democratic minimum core, the argument for weakened judicial review will be pragmatic in nature—or linked to a concern to avoid the risk of democratic backlash. There may still be a role for weakening the finality of judicial review in cases of this kind. But the argument for judicial weakness is wholly pragmatic rather than principled in nature: it is not that there is reasonable disagreement about what democracy is, or requires. Rather, it is that narrow rulings, or weakened remedies, may help courts "to live to fight another day" in defense of democracy rather than further opportunities for the expression of reasonable democratic disagreement.[64]

Remedial delay, for example, can allow time for political conditions to shift, and either popular or elite opinion to move in favor of constitutional enforcement.[65] Shifts of this kind do not always occur. Sometimes, opposition to a given constitutional approach may increase, rather than decrease, with time, or delay may signal to opponents that they have an opportunity to prevent the implementation of a decision. This is one way of understanding the effects of the US Supreme Court's adoption of a delayed remedy in *Brown I* and *II*.[66] The notion of "all deliberate speed" may have signaled to opponents of racial desegregation that they had an opportunity to resist its implementation.[67] But often, delay can mean that political conditions do shift, and there is a greater political tolerance for judicial intervention. By "deferring" or delaying the most politically sensitive constitutional decisions to a later date, strong constitutional courts will generally avoid the most damaging forms of institutional backlash.[68]

Delay can also provide courts with an opportunity to lay down certain "doctrinal markers" or statements in dictum that provide *legal* support for later forms of constitutional enforcement.[69] Legal support of this kind can also increase the perceived legitimacy of a court's decision in the eyes of ordinary

---

[64] Dixon & Issacharoff, *supra* note 40.
[65] *Id.*
[66] Brown v. Board of Education, 347 U.S. 483 (1954); Brown v. Board of Education, 349 U.S. 294 (1955).
[67] *See, e.g.,* Jim Chen, *With All Deliberate Speed: Brown II and Desegregation's Children,* 24 LAW & INEQ. 1 (2006); CHARLES OGLETREE, ALL DELIBERATE SPEED xiii, 11 (2004); MICHAEL KLARMAN, FROM JIM CROW TO CIVIL RIGHTS: THE SUPREME COURT AND THE STRUGGLE FOR RACIAL EQUALITY 319 (2004).
[68] Dixon & Issacharoff, *supra* note 40.
[69] *Compare* Rosalind Dixon & Theunis Roux, *Marking Constitutional Transitions: The Law and Politics of Constitutional Implementation in South Africa, in* FROM PARCHMENT TO PRACTICE: IMPLEMENTING NEW CONSTITUTIONS 53 (Tom Ginsburg & Aziz Z. Huq eds., 2020).

judges and lawyers so that by the time courts directly confront the executive or legislative majority on a question, they enjoy greater support for their authority.

Take the *First* and *Second Re-Election* cases in Colombia as an example.[70] In the *First Re-Election* case, the Constitutional Court of Colombia was asked to determine the constitutionality of the attempt by President Uribe to amend the Colombian Constitution to allow for the possibility of presidential re-election—or for Uribe himself to seek a second term in office. The Court also ultimately upheld the validity of the proposed amendment, but in doing so held that there were both procedural and substantive limits on the power of amendment.[71] This allowed Uribe and Congress to pass the relevant amendment, but it laid down clear limits on *any future attempt* at amendment of relevant constitutional limits.[72] And at the time, Uribe had a personal popularity rating over 65 percent.[73] The Court, however, engaged in a form of strong–weak review—that is, it laid down clear procedural and substantive limits on *any future attempt* at amendment of relevant constitutional limits but chose not to apply those limits immediately, or to the specific amendment under challenge.[74]

But in 2010, in the *Second Re-Election Case*, the Court struck down Uribe's attempt to seek a third term.[75] By this time, although Uribe himself remained popular, support for Uribe's government had decreased, in part due to allegations of government corruption and human rights abuses, and there was greater popular support for the decision to require a transition in presidential leadership.[76] The Court's earlier decisions in *Decision C-551 of 2003* and the *First Re-election* case had also laid down important doctrinal markers setting out the Court's power to review the substantive validity of amendments in ways that increased the perceived legitimacy of the Court's decision.[77]

Indeed, the challenge for courts in such cases will often be to ensure that judicial review is *strong enough* to counter the risk of political monopoly. The aim of judicial review, in this context, will be to slow down or deter concerted efforts by legislative or executive actors to erode the democratic minimum core.

---

[70] For a helpful discussion of these and other cases involving the review of amendments in Colombia, see ESPINOSA & LANDAU, *supra* note 18, at 325–82; Vicente Fabian Benitez Rojas, Judicial Power in Constitutional Democracies: Strong and Weak Courts in Colombia and Judicial Review of Constitutional Amendments between 1955 and 2017 (2021) (JSD Thesis, New York University). See also Chapter 4, section C.5 *supra*.

[71] *See* Decision C-1040 of 2005 in ESPINOSA & LANDAU, *supra* note 18, at 343–51.

[72] Dixon & Issacharoff, *supra* note 40.

[73] *Id.* at 32–33.

[74] Dixon & Issacharoff, *supra* note 40 at 691–92.

[75] Jeremy McDermott, *How President Alvaro Uribe Changed Colombia*, BBC NEWS, Aug. 4, 2010, <https://www.bbc.com/news/world-latin-america-10841425>.

[76] *Id.*

[77] Dixon & Issacharoff, *supra* note 40, at 718. See further Chapter 4, Section C.5 *supra*.

To achieve this, courts must be able to impose *immediate* and concrete legal obstacles to would-be authoritarian actors achieving their goals—including by issuing strong remedies, which have the immediate effect of invalidating prior legislative or executive actions, and imposing *coercive* duties on various executive actors to aid in the implementation of a court's order. They may also need to engage in quite broad reasoning, which signals that these obstacles cannot simply be overcome by would-be authoritarian actors putting pressure on a court, or by giving a narrow reading to a court's reasons.

In some cases, as Chapter 3 notes, attempts to erode the democratic minimum core may occur by way of ordinary or sub-constitutional change, but in others, it may occur through formal constitutional amendment. To slow down or deter this kind of "abusive" constitutional change, courts must therefore have power to impose limits on processes of constitutional amendment, and possibly even replacement, as well as ordinary legislation.[78] Given the role formal amendment procedures can play in expressing democratic disagreement, this also implies a quite strong—indeed potentially "super-strong"—form of judicial review.[79] Even still, they may find that there is insufficient political support for independent and effective judicial review.

Consider the decision of the Supreme Court of Kenya setting aside the 2017 presidential election in Kenya and ordering the Electoral and Boundaries Commission (EBC) to conduct fresh elections in conformity with the 2010 democratic Constitution and electoral law. The decision was an attempt by the Court to counter a credible threat of electoral monopoly. As Chapter 3 noted, there were allegations both in the lead-up to and during the presidential election of serious electoral irregularities, and the Court sought to counter this by ordering fresh elections—and greater oversight and intervention by the EBC.[80] The decision, however, was ultimately insufficient to encourage freer and fairer elections.

The Chairman of the EBC publicly admitted that he could not guarantee electoral fairness or prevent electoral misconduct and intimidation.[81] The (then) opposition presidential candidate, Raila Odinga, withdrew from the

---

[78] *Compare* David Landau & Rosalind Dixon, *Constraining Constitutional Change*, 50 WAKE FOREST L. REV. 859 (2015). *See also* David Landau, *Abusive Constitutionalism*, 47 U.C. DAVIS L. REV. 189 (2013).

[79] *Compare* Landau & Dixon, *Constraining Constitutional Change*, *supra* note 78.

[80] *See* Raila Amolo Odinga & another v. Independent Electoral and Boundaries Commission & 2 others [2017] eKLR.

[81] Eyder Peralta, *Kenyan Officials Say They Can't Guarantee Fair Process In Presidential Election*, KPCW (Oct. 18, 2017), <https://www.kpcw.org/2017-10-18/kenyan-officials-say-they-cant-guarantee-fair-process-in-presidential-election>.

election in protest.[82] And while initially promising to abide by the Court's decision, President Uhuru Kenyatta and his allies soon challenged the Court's authority and independence and passed amendments to the electoral law limiting the scope for judicial review of the results of a presidential election.[83] It was thus unsurprising that Kenyatta won re-election by a large margin, even amid accusations of ongoing voter intimidation and electoral manipulation.[84]

To effectively protect democracy in this context, therefore, the Court needed both the power to invalidate the repeat as well as initial presidential elections *and* amendments to the electoral law purporting to prevent them from making such an order. And in the circumstances, it had the power but arguably lacked sufficient political support or efficacy.[85]

2. Blind spots and burdens of inertia: a principled and pragmatic case for weak–strong review

In cases involving legislative blind spots and burdens of inertia, in contrast, there will often be both principled and pragmatic reasons for weakening the finality of judicial review. If judicial remedies are *too* weak, there is a real risk that courts will no longer be able to counter democratic blockages—either generally or in how these blockages affect individuals. The sources of legislative inertia may be too deep, or opposition to a court decision from a mobilized minority too strong. Or, as Chapter 5 notes, there may be little scope for the legislature retrospectively to vary the rights and entitlements of an individual.

Take for instance rights of access to abortion. In Colombia, in *Decision C-355 of 2006*, the Constitutional Court held that under the Constitution, women in Colombia were entitled to access to abortion in a range of circumstances—that is, where a pregnancy threatens a woman's life or her physical or mental health was the result of rape, incest, or another crime, or involved "medically certified malformations of the fetus."[86] And the decision was later codified in new

---

[82] Matina Stevis-Gridneff, *Kenyan Opposition Leader Withdraws From Election Rerun*, W.S.J. (Oct. 10, 2017), <https://www.wsj.com/articles/kenyan-opposition-leader-withdraws-from-election-rerun-1507646147>.

[83] BBC, *Kenya Election Law Amendment Takes Effect*, BBC, Nov. 3, 2017, <https://www.bbc.com/news/world-africa-41859171>.

[84] Jina Moore, *Uhuru Kenyatta Is Declared Winner of Kenya's Repeat Election*, N.Y. Times, Oct. 30, 2017, <https://www.nytimes.com/2017/10/30/world/africa/kenya-election-kenyatta-odinga.html>.

[85] Rael Ombuor, *Kenya Supreme Court Upholds Election Rerun, Sparking Celebrations, Protests*, Wash. Post., Nov. 20, 2017, <https://www.washingtonpost.com/world/kenya-supreme-court-upholds-election-rerun-sparking-protests-celebrations/2017/11/20/f906e310-cdd2-11e7-9d3a-bcbe2af58c3a_story.html>.

[86] Espinosa & Landau, *supra* note 18, at 77–78.

guidelines issued by the Colombian Ministry for Health.[87] There was, however, powerful opposition to the decision, especially among certain Catholic organizations,[88] and public and private actors placed a number of obstacles in the way of effective implementation of the decision. They required specific judicial authorization before performing an abortion.[89] Some health insurers required a judicial order before agreeing to fund abortions. And many healthcare providers refused to perform abortions, citing a conscientious objection to the procedure. Some judges even refused to order access to an abortion on the same grounds. For instance, in *Decision T-388 of 2009*, a case where an insurer had refused to fund an abortion without a judicial order, the judge at first instance refused to hear the case on these grounds.[90] Similarly, in *Decision T-841 of 2011*, a health insurer refused to fund access to an abortion for a twelve-year-old girl, absent a judicial order.[91]

However, the decision of the Court in *Decision C-355 of 2006* was sufficiently strong that these efforts could not entirely defeat women's right of access to abortion in Colombia. When the State Council declared the previous changes to Decree 4444 invalid, in 2013 Colombian women were able to rely on the direct legal right of access to abortion (i.e., strong remedy) recognized by the Constitutional Court in 2006—despite the effect of the 2013 decree, and the broader democratic backlash it formed part of.[92] This access was often limited in practice, which may in part explain why in *Decision C-055 of 2022* the Constitutional Court voted to invalidate almost all legal limits on access to abortion during the first 24 weeks of pregnancy—though again, there may be challenges in implementation, especially if ones thinks the 2022 decision went beyond what current democratic majority opinion in Colombia would support.[93] But the Court's 2006 ruling was still sufficiently strong to guarantee some increased access for Colombian women to legalized abortion.

A similar pattern applied to the recognition of LGBTQI+ rights. In *Decision C-577 of 2011*, the Constitutional Court of Colombia held that Congress was required to create some form of legal recognition for same-sex relationships prior to June 2013, or else same-sex couples would gain the right to go to any

---

[87] Alba Ruibal, *Movement and Counter-movement: A History of Abortion Law Reform and the Backlash in Colombia 2006–2014*, 22 REPROD. HEALTH MATTERS 42, 44 (2014).
[88] *See, e.g., id.* at 46.
[89] *See id.* at 45.
[90] ESPINOSA & LANDAU, *supra* note 18, at 80.
[91] *Id.* at 82; Ruibal, *supra* note 87, at 48.
[92] Ruibal, *supra* note 87, at 48.
[93] Julie Turkewitz, *Colombia Decriminalizes Abortion, Bolstering Trend Across Region*, N.Y. TIMES, Feb. 22, 2022, <https://www.nytimes.com/2022/02/22/world/americas/colombia-abortion.html>.

judge or notary public to formalize their union.[94] Congress extensively debated proposals to amend the law in response to this decision, but the Catholic Church and conservative members of Congress vigorously opposed the change. Thus, even though an increasing number of Colombians supported gay marriage, no legislative change expanding recognition of same-sex relationships was passed by Congress before or after 2013.[95]

To overcome the effect of (arguable) burdens of inertia, therefore, it was again necessary for the Constitutional Court to provide a direct and strong form of relief to same-sex couples. *Decision C-577 of 2011* did this to some degree. The Court's weak–strong approach meant that after 2013, notaries began issuing same-sex couples with a contract marking their "solemn union."[96] And in 2016, the Constitutional Court rendered a decision providing direct access to same-sex marriage, despite the non-response by Congress to the Court's 2011 weak-form or dialogic remedy.[97]

Consider the social rights cases set out in Chapters 3 to 5, as examples of the role that courts can play in promoting greater democratic responsiveness. In South Africa, there was clear evidence of legislative and bureaucratic inertia as a backdrop to cases such as *Grootboom* and *TAC*.[98] In both cases, the CCSA also relied largely on weak remedies, in ways that had limited impact on this form of democratic inertia.

In *Grootboom*, the CCSA declined to use any form of coercive relief in support of its judgment, or to retain supervisory jurisdiction to monitor its implementation.[99] It did not set any time frame within which various levels of government were required to develop a housing plan catering to the need to provide emergency shelter, nor did it grant any other form of injunctive relief against specific government actors. In *TAC*, the Court likewise declined to grant any form of coercive relief, or ongoing monitoring, in support of aspects of the state's duty to protect positive socio-economic rights: namely, its duty to take reasonable measures to expand the testing and counseling services

---

[94] Espinosa & Landau, *supra* note 18, at 91–97. For discussion, see Mauricio Albarracin & Julieta Lemaitre, *The Crusade Against Same-Sex Marriage in Colombia*, 8 Religion & Gender 32 (2018). See also Adriana Piatti-Crocker & Jason Pierceson, *Unpacking the Backlash to Marriage Equality in Latin America* 11 (Paper presented at the Western Political Science Association Annual Meeting, San Francisco, Mar. 29–31, 2018); Mauricio Albarracín Caballero, *Social Movements and the Constitutional Court: Legal Recognition of the Rights of Same-Sex Couples in Colombia*, 8 Int'l J. Hum. Rts. 7 (2011); Macarena Saez, *Transforming Family Law Through Same-Sex Marriage: Lessons from (and to) the Western World*, 25 Duke J. Comp. & Int'l L. 125 (2014).
[95] Albarracin & Lemaitre, *supra* note 94, at 35–37. *See also* discussion in Chapter 4, section C.2 *supra*.
[96] Albarracin & Lemaitre, *supra* note 94, at 35–37 (2018).
[97] Espinosa & Landau, *supra* note 18, at 91–100.
[98] *See* Chapter 4, section C.4 *supra*.
[99] *Id.*

necessary to support the provision of nevirapine.[100] The court overturned that part of the High Court's order which imposed a timetable on governments to report on the measures taken to discharge this duty, and injunctive relief—or a structural edict—to enforce that timetable.

And while it is hard to predict whether a more time-sensitive, coercive remedy, such as a structural edict, would have done more to overcome this inertia, most scholars suggest that it could have. And this would not have been possible if the court were limited to exercising weak remedial powers, or weak powers of judicial review.[101]

At the same time, a responsive approach also points in cases of this kind to the *value* of weakened forms of review, from both a pragmatic and principled perspective. There are certainly important limits to when and how courts should weaken the finality of judicial review. A commitment to the rule of law arguably requires that executive officials should comply with the orders of a court, at least as they concern a specific case. It also suggests that courts should apply a weakened doctrine of *stare decisis* in a way that continues to insist on the binding nature of the narrowest, if not the broadest, reading of its prior decisions. This helps ensure justice to individual litigants *and* promotes broader respect by legislators for legal constraints.

In addition, the idea of reverse burdens of inertia assumes that democratic disagreement is *reasonable*. For a legislative response to a court decision to be entitled to respect, it must therefore be based on a process of reasoned deliberation by legislators, including a willingness to engage with a court's own prior reasoning on a question.[102] Similarly, as Ely himself noted, the idea of reasonableness rules out the idea that courts should uphold legislation that reflects *animus* or hostility toward a particular group.[103]

But even with these caveats, a responsive approach suggests there are both principled and pragmatic reasons for courts to consider the risks of reverse democratic inertia and democratic debilitation as part of the process of constructional choice. Courts in this context will not be seeking to protect or

---

[100] DAVID BICHITZ, POVERTY AND FUNDAMENTAL RIGHTS: THE JUSTIFICATION AND ENFORCEMENT OF SOCIO-ECONOMIC RIGHTS 152–55 (2007); Rosalind Dixon, *Creating Dialogue about Socioeconomic Rights: Strong-Form v. Weak-Form Judicial Review Revisited*, 5 INT'L J. CONST. L. 391 (2007); César Rodríguez-Garavito, *Beyond the Courtroom: The Impact of Judicial Activism on Socioeconomic Rights in Latin America*, 89 TEX. L. REV. 1669, 1692 (2011).

[101] Kent Roach & Geoff Budlender, *Mandatory Relief and Supervisory Jurisdiction: When Is It Appropriate, Just and Equitable*, 122 S. AFR. L.J. 325 (2005).

[102] SUNSTEIN, *supra* note 28, at 70.

[103] JOHN HART ELY, DEMOCRACY AND DISTRUST: A THEORY OF JUDICIAL REVIEW (1980). Compare Rosalind Dixon, *Constitutional "Dialogue" and Deference*, in CONSTITUTIONAL DIALOGUE: RIGHTS, DEMOCRACY, INSTITUTIONS 171 (Geoffrey Sigalet et al. eds., 2019); ROACH, THE SUPREME COURT ON TRIAL, *supra* note 62.

promote the "minimum core" or constitutional democracy—but rather a broader, more contestable notion of what democratic norms require. And if the premise of judicial review is that it seeks to vindicate majoritarian understandings of what the constitution requires, one could expect court decisions to enjoy high levels of public support. Democratic majorities would certainly be unlikely to oppose court decisions and might even be *grateful* to courts for facilitating the expression of popular will. Evidence of popular disagreement, therefore, might be seen as a sign that a court has misread the evolving contours of public opinion in a way that creates a real risk of both democratic backlash *and* reverse democratic inertia.

If court decisions have a weaker, less final quality, however, this risk will be much smaller—because it will be much clearer to the legislature that it is free to modify or narrow the effect of a court decision—or engage in "dialogue" with a court.[104] Weakening the finality of a judicial decision also does not represent any departure from principle. It simply involves a court weighing how best to promote overall democratic responsiveness in the process of constitutional construction by giving appropriate weight to two competing but equally principled concerns about democratic responsiveness.

In Germany, for example, there has been ongoing democratic contestation over decisions of the German Federal Constitutional Court (GFCC) on access to abortion.[105] In 1975, in the *Abortion I* case, the GFCC struck down the attempt by the Bundestag to liberalize access to abortion in the first trimester of pregnancy by endorsing a broad view of the "right to life" of the fetus under the Basic Law, and the "pre-eminence" of that right over a woman's right to self-determination (as opposed to health, for example).[106] The decision met with powerful democratic disagreement, especially after unification, and in 1992, the Bundestag attempted to replicate its 1975 liberalization efforts by decriminalizing abortion in the first trimester of pregnancy, on the condition that women submitted to certain forms of state-sponsored pro-life counseling.[107]

And in the *Abortion II* decision, the GFCC largely vindicated this attempt at dialogue by upholding the decriminalization of first-trimester abortions, on the condition that counseling for unevaluated abortions was explicitly pro-life, rather than neutral, in regard to a woman's abortion decision. To some degree,

---

[104] *See* Chapter 7, *supra*.
[105] Jamal Greene, How Rights Went Wrong: Why Our Obsession with Rights is Tearing America Apart 136 (2021); Julie C. Suk, After Misogyny: Law and Feminism in the Twenty-First Century (2022, forthcoming).
[106] Kommers, *supra* note 53.
[107] *Id.* at 348.

this result was also left open by the Court's earlier ruling, in *Abortion I*.[108] The GFCC in *Abortion I* expressly suggested that it was open to the Bundestag to "expres[s] the constitutionally required degree of disapprobation [for purely discretionary abortion] by means other than penal sanctions," and that what mattered, for this purpose, was that "the totality" of relevant legal measures "in fact guarantee[d]" comparable protection for the fetus as an outright criminal prohibition. This was also exactly the theory on which pro-choice and centrist legislators relied, in 1992, in agreeing to a model based on decriminalization as opposed to legalization, and overtly pro-life as opposed to more open-ended counseling.

This also provides an answer to the question posed in Chapter 6, about how the Supreme Court ought to have approached its decision in *Roe*. A concern about reverse inertia, and the need to preserve scope for legislative dialogue, would have favored the US Court adopting a substantially narrower, more standard-like approach to the question of when the legislature may legitimately limit or burden a constitutional right of access to abortion. In *Casey*, it would likewise have supported the Court narrowing its prior ruling—providing that it insisted on the essential prior holding in *Roe*, of a fundamental right of access to abortion under the Constitution, and the need to defer only to reasonable attempts by the legislature to balance the competing rights of women and the fetus, not legislative reasoning based on animus or disregard toward pregnant women, or preconceived views of women's role. (This is arguably what distinguishes the Court's decision in *Casey* from its later decision in *Dobbs*, to overrule *all* prior recognition of a constitutional right of access to abortion.)

The risk of democratic backlash raises harder questions for a court. Responding to backlash necessarily requires courts to exercise a form of *pragmatic or prudential* rather than purely principled judgment. For some, this raises serious objections: according to this view, courts should be "pure" forums of principle and adopt their own best reading of democratic constitutional requirements, without any regard to risks of this kind.[109] Any departure from this approach, according to those holding this view also threatens to undermine a court's legal legitimacy.[110]

---

[108] GREENE, *supra* note 105.

[109] *See, e.g.*, RONALD DWORKIN, TAKING RIGHTS SERIOUSLY (2013) (limiting pragmatic judgments to those necessary for internal agreement within the Court). For a useful discussion, see Theunis Roux, *Principle and Pragmatism on the Constitutional Court of South Africa*, 7 INT'L J. CONST. L. 106, fn 20–22 (2009).

[110] *See, e.g.*, TREVOR R.S. ALLAN, THE SOVEREIGNTY OF LAW: FREEDOM, CONSTITUTION AND COMMON LAW (2013).

More pragmatic theories of constitutional decision-making embrace the idea that courts should consider limits on their own capacity and legitimacy.[111] Ely's teacher and colleague at Yale, Alexander Bickel, for example, suggested that "no good society c[ould] be unprincipled; and no viable society c[ould] be principle-ridden."[112] The same understanding applies to judicial review. To be legitimate, judicial review must be anchored in commitments to constitutional principle, but it must also accommodate prudential concerns through a form of principled, but strategic approach, or philosophy of "principled pragmatism."[113]

Advocates of "principled pragmatism," however, differ in the degree to which courts should respond to concerns about potential democratic backlash: some pragmatic theories suggest that it will always be permissible for courts to consider and respond to a risk of democratic backlash as part of the process of constructional choice.[114] Other scholars argue that courts should consider this risk only to the extent that it threatens the court's own sociological legitimacy or capacity to implement its orders.[115]

A responsive approach to judicial review favors this second approach. It suggests that judges should be attentive to the risk of democratic backlash as part of responding to limits on their own institutional capacity, but not otherwise. It also suggests that judges should make this judgment responsive to their specific institutional context—that is, considering the existing degree of institutional capital, or legitimacy, enjoyed by the court on which they sit. Some courts, for instance, may have a quite high degree of ingoing sociological legitimacy, which reduces the risk that specific decisions will undermine that

---

[111] On constitutional pragmatism, see RICHARD A. POSNER, LAW, PRAGMATISM, AND DEMOCRACY (2005).

[112] ALEXANDER M. BICKEL, THE LEAST DANGEROUS BRANCH: THE SUPREME COURT AT THE BAR OF POLITICS 64 (1986). See also discussion in Anthony T. Kronman, *Alexander Bickel's Philosophy of Prudence*, 94 YALE L.J. 1567 (1985).

[113] Roni Mann, *Non-ideal Theory of Constitutional Adjudication*, 7 GLOBAL CONST. 14, 38–51 (2018); Malcolm Langford, *Why Judicial Review*, 2 OSLO L. REV. 36, 63 (2015). See also THEUNIS ROUX, THE POLITICS OF PRINCIPLE: THE FIRST SOUTH AFRICAN CONSTITUTIONAL COURT, 1995–2005 (2013).

[114] Fallon, for example, argues that if "upholding a previously unrecognized right would likely trigger a public backlash, more harmful than helpful to the interests that the right would be crafted to protect, the anticipated consequences provide a morally relevant reason for a court to stay its hand": see Richard H. Fallon, Jr., *Legitimacy and the Constitution*, 118 HARV. L. REV. 1787, 1850 (2004). Sunstein likewise suggests that there are strong consequentialist arguments for courts—including courts committed to a principled or "moral reading" of the constitution—avoiding decisions that are likely to be futile or self-defeating: see Cass R. Sunstein, *If People Would be Outraged By Their Rulings, Should Judges Care*, 60 STAN. L. REV. 155, 203–04 (2007).

[115] See, e.g., Aileen Kavanagh, *Defending Deference in Public Law and Constitutional Theory*, 162 LAW Q. REV. 222 (2010).

legitimacy.[116] Others may be far newer or more fragile in ways that point to the need for greater judicial restraint or caution.

Of course, some electoral outcomes may have indirect consequences for a court's institutional role and legitimacy. Considering the electoral consequences of a decision could therefore be viewed as simply a logical part of considering its more immediate, institutional consequences. This view, however, downplays the degree to which judgments of this kind involve an almost entirely consequentialist form of reasoning, with a close connection to electoral politics, and therefore risk undermining both a court's actual and perceived independence from the political branches of government. It also ignores the degree to which judgments of this kind involve a high degree of uncertainty: predicting the outcome of democratic elections is notoriously difficult even for political professionals with access to a wide range of public and private polls, and this is not something that judges are either well-trained or resourced to do.

In a responsive approach, courts should therefore consider concerns about the broader electoral consequences of their decisions if and only if they are confident that these consequences are likely to occur and to threaten their own institutional role. In making these judgments, courts should also consider the degree to which such disagreement is actually reasonable, from a democratic perspective. If a court views disagreement as reasonable, there will be both principled and pragmatic arguments for responding to evidence of disagreement of this kind, whereas if disagreement is perceived to be unreasonable, the only basis for doing so will be pragmatic in nature.

Thus, in a case such as *Roe*, a responsive approach does *not* suggest that the Court should have tried to anticipate or respond to the impact of a constitutional reproductive rights jurisprudence on broader electoral outcomes, or the rise of broader conservative social and political movements—developments that almost no-one, and certainly no judge, could reliably have predicted in 1973. Nor does it suggest that it would have been appropriate for the Court in *Casey*, *Carhart II*, or *Dobbs* wholly to avoid or retreat from the essential finding in *Roe* or *Carhart I*, that the US Constitution requires the protection of women's autonomy and dignity, including through appropriate access to

---

[116] The German Constitutional Court might be viewed as one court that falls squarely into this category: *see, e.g.*, KOMMERS, *supra* note 53; Justin Collings, *An American Perspective on the German Constitutional Court*, *in* THE US SUPREME COURT AND CONTEMPORARY CONSTITUTIONAL LAW: THE OBAMA ERA AND ITS LEGACY (Anna-Bettina Kaiser et al. eds., 2018).

abortion services pre- and post-viability.[117] But it does suggest that in deciding the scope of its decision in *Roe*, the Supreme Court ought to have considered both principled concerns about the scope for reasonable democratic disagreement with its decision *and* prudential concerns about the potential for its decisions to trigger attacks on federal courts' funding, jurisdiction, and composition. The same is true for *Casey* and *Dobbs*, and *Carhart I* and *II*.

C. Toward Strong–Weak/Weak–Strong Judicial Review

A responsive approach thus suggests the value of courts combining reliance on weak and strong modes of review when seeking to counter democratic blind spots and burdens of inertia—that is, a combination of time-sensitive and coercive remedies with less prescriptive modes of review.[118]

"Strong–weak" or "weak–strong" forms of judicial intervention of this kind can also take numerous forms. They can involve broad or strong rights combined with weak remedies (strong rights, weak remedies), a narrow or weak rights approach combined with strong remedies (weak rights, strong remedies), broad or strong judicial reasoning combined with weakened norms *of stare decisis* (strong rights, weak precedent), or a combination of time-sensitive but non-coercive, or delayed but coercive remedies (weak–strong/strong–weak remedies).[119]

As Section B notes, decisions such as *Abortion I* and *II* arguably embodied a weak rights and strong remedies approach, whereas *Roe* and *Casey* were instances of strong rights and weak *stare decisis*.[120] The US Supreme Court's decision in *Lawrence* was arguably a decision involving weak rights but strong remedies, as were early cases in South Africa involving LGBTQI+ rights such as *Satchwell v. President*, *Du Toit v. Minister of Welfare* and *J and B v. Director*

---

[117] Compare *Whole Woman's Health v. Austin Jackson*, Judge, 594 U.S. ___ (2021); Adam Liptak et al., *Supreme Court, Breaking Silence, Won't Block Texas Abortion Law*, N.Y. TIMES, Sept. 1, 2021, <https://www.nytimes.com/2021/09/01/us/supreme-court-texas-abortion.html>.

[118] David Landau, *Aggressive Weak-Form Remedies*, 5 CONST. CT. REV. 224, 245–46 (2013). KATHARINE G. YOUNG, THE FUTURE OF ECONOMIC AND SOCIAL RIGHTS (2019).

[119] César Rodríguez-Garavito also highlights the importance of judicial monitoring as an additional dimension to the strength of judicial remedies: strong remedies involve ongoing monitoring by courts, coupled with the threat of contempt of court for officials who fail to comply with court orders, whereas weak remedies involve a one-off court order: see Rodríguez-Garavito, *supra* note 100, at 1691–92. Compare Dixon, *Creating Dialogue about Socioeconomic Rights*, *supra* note 100; Malcolm Langford, *Judicial Politics and Social Rights'*, in *The Future of Economic and Social Rights* 66–109 (Katherine Young ed., 2019).

[120] *See* Chapters 3 to 6, *supra*.

General.[121] Early Canadian and Colombian decisions on gay marriage, in contrast, involved a mix of strong rights and weak or delayed remedies.[122] Many social rights decisions, in turn, have involved courts relying on a mix of weak and strong rights and remedies.

Take the *IDP* or *Midday Meal* decisions. In *IDP*, the Court created a special chamber of the Court responsible for monitoring implementation and retained jurisdiction in respect of this process.[123] In this sense, it relied on a quintessentially strong form judicial remedy. But it combined this with a form of "weak rights" approach—that is, an open-ended approach to determining how best to protect and realize the rights of internally displaced persons (IDPs)—and a non-prescriptive, participatory remedial process of the kind associated with ideas of weakened or "experimentalist" judicial review.[124] Similarly, in the *Midday Meal Case*, the Supreme Court of India created a special bench responsible for monitoring compliance with the decision, and retained supervisory jurisdiction in respect of its implementation.[125] But, as Chapter 5 noted, it also engaged in a weaker, more experimentalist approach to judicial enforcement. It appointed national and state commissioners to gather information about implementation of the Court's orders, and to make recommendations to the states and the Court about implementation, and relied on these recommendations in crafting follow-up orders.[126]

Weak–strong remedies can themselves also take several different forms. Courts can choose to issue "suspended declarations" of invalidity or declare legislation invalid (the classic hallmark of strong form coercive judicial review)

---

[121] Satchwell v. President of the Republic of South Africa (CCT 45/01) (judicial pensions); Du Toit v. Minister of Welfare and Population Development, 2003 (2) SA 198 (CC) (joint adoption); J and B v. Director General: Department of Home Affairs, 2003 (5) SA 198 (CC) (recognition of the partner of a woman who gives birth to a child by artificial insemination).

[122] *See* Hendricks v. Québec [2002] R.J.Q. 2506; Halpern v. Canada (2003), 65 O.R. (3d) 161; Egale Canada Inc. v. Canada (Attorney General) (2003), 225 D.L.R. (4th) 472, in Chapter 3, *supra*; Decision C-577 of 2011.

[123] *See* discussion in Espinosa & Landau, *supra* note 18; Rodríguez-Garavito, *supra* note 100; Varun Gauri & Daniel M. Brinks, *Human Rights as Demands for Communicative Action*, 20 J. Pol. Phil. 407, 416–17 (2012).

[124] Tushnet, Weak Courts, Strong Rights, *supra* note 1; Michael C. Dorf & Charles F. Sabel, *A Constitution of Democratic Experimentalism*, 98 Colum. L. Rev. 267 (1998); Gaurav Mukherjee, *Democratic Experimentalism in Comparative Social Rights Remedies*, 1 Milan L. Rev. 75, 93 (2020).

[125] Alyssa Brierly, PUCL v. Union of India: Political Mobilization and the Right to Food, in A Qualified Hope: The Indian Supreme Court and Progressive Social Change 8 (Gerald N. Rosenberg et al. eds., 2019); Rosalind Dixon & Rishad Chowdhury, *A Case for Qualified Hope? The Supreme Court of India and the Midday Meal Decision*, in A Qualified Hope: The Indian Supreme Court and Progressive Social Change (Gerald N. Rosenberg et al. eds., 2019); Mukherjee, *supra* note 124; Gaurav Mukherjee & Juha Tuovinen, *Designing Remedies for Recalcitrant Administration*, 36 S. Afr. J. Hum. Rts. 386 (2020).

[126] Nick Robinson, *Closing the Implementation Gap: Grievance Redress and India's Social Welfare Programs*, 53 Colum. J. Transnat'l L. 351 fn 73 (2015); Brierly, *supra* note 125, at 6–13; Dixon & Chowdhury, *supra* note 125.

but delay the effect of such an order for a given period of time.[127] Alternatively, they can choose to issue immediate remedies but without any form of coercive or supervisory relief. Or they may issue "engagement" remedies requiring government officials to engage in dialogue or a consultation prior to, and as a precondition for, any further actions such as eviction orders, redevelopment, or other forms of coercive state action.[128]

Suspended declarations of invalidity combine elements of remedial strength—that is, coerciveness—with elements of remedial weakness, namely delay. That delay may be relatively short, compared to the time a democracy needs to grapple or engage with an issue, or quite long from the perspective of individual litigants. And the length of the relevant delay will inevitably affect the extent to which citizens have time to debate and adjust to a new legal and political *status quo*, and if there is time for intervening political or legal changes to increase support for a constitutional outcome.[129] But remedies of this kind inevitably give legislatures *some* opportunity to take action on issues without the inertia created by a new legal *status quo*, and some time for the polity to debate an issue in ways that can increase both the actual and perceived legitimacy of a constitutional outcome.[130]

Engagement remedies, in turn, implicitly rely on a mix of weak and strong relief. They require that engagement or consultation occurs *before* other actions by the state can occur. But they do not specify any particular time frame in which this must occur, and they are mandatory orders but coercive only in so far as they require that some form of engagement occur, not how and what it should entail. In that sense, they are weak–strong in both the degree of time sensitivity and coerciveness of judicial intervention.

Strong remedies themselves can also vary in their duration and intensity. Courts, for example, may choose to issue one-off coercive orders, or else assume an ongoing role in supervising the implementation of an order. This kind of "structural edict," structural injunction, or supervisory order is also an especially strong judicial remedy.[131] It is ongoing, time-sensitive, and gives courts

---

[127] *See* Chapter 7, section A *supra*.
[128] *See* id, *supra* and discussion in Ray, *supra* note 44. *See also* Kameshni Pillay, *Implementation of Grootboom: Implications for the Enforcement of Socio-economic Rights* 6(2) Af. J. Online 255 (2002); Yap, *New Democracies and Novel Remedies*, *supra* note 33; Landau, *Aggressive Weak-Form Remedies*, *supra* note 118.
[129] For the argument that the delay may not be long enough to allow meaningful democratic debate on an issue, see Robert Leckey, *Assisted Dying, Suspended Declarations, and Dialogue's Time*, 69 U. Toronto L.J. 64 (2019) (in context of assisted dying in Canada).
[130] *Id.*
[131] *See* Landau, *Aggressive Weak-Form Remedies*, *supra* note 118; Yap, *New Democracies and Novel Remedies*, *supra* note 33.

the power to issue a range of coercive orders, including orders for contempt of court.[132] But César Rodriguez-Garavito also highlights the degree to which strong monitoring of this kind may itself be more or less strong or weak, or "monologic" versus "dialogic" in nature. It can either be top-down and court-driven, or bottom-up, participatory, and dialogic in approach—and rely on public hearings, a broad range of civil society actors and government agencies responsible for implementation to help create benchmarks for measuring progress, information on that progress, and suggestions for improving implementation.[133] More top-down models will also tend to involve purer forms of strong review, whereas more bottom-up models combine elements of judicial strength and weakness (see Table 7.2).

Table 7.2 Variants of Strong–Weak/Weak–Strong Review[*]

Weak–strong review	Remedies	Stare decisis
Rights	Strong rights, weak remedies (strong–weak) Narrow rights, immediate and coercive remedies (weak–strong)	Broad rights, weak *stare decisis* (strong–weak)
Remedies	Delayed but coercive or supervisory remedies (weak–strong)	Immediate but declaratory (strong–weak)

[*]*See supra* note 9.

Each model of weak–strong review has advantages and disadvantages; and which is best suited to achieving a balance between overly strong and weak review will depend on the nature of the case, and relevant democratic blockage. Strong rights and weak remedies, for instance, will generally be best suited to cases involving a threat to the democratic minimum core, where courts are seeking explicitly to point out the dangers to democracy of a proposed legislative or constitutional change but in a way that is not so immediate or confrontational as to spark an immediate political backlash. Suspended declarations of invalidity will generally be suited to cases involving legislative blind spots or burdens of inertia—such as those cases discussed above concerning challenges to the criminal prohibition of sodomy, or opposite-sex definitions of marriage. Supervisory remedies will be best suited to responding to cases involving

---

[132] On the significance of this in an Indian social rights context, see, *e.g.*, Robinson, *Closing the Implementation Gap, supra* note 126; Dixon & Chowdhury, *supra* note 125.
[133] Rodríguez-Garavito, *supra* note 100, at 1691–92.

compound burdens of inertia—that is, the failure both by the legislature to supervise and by the executive to implement constitutional requirements.[134] And engagement remedies will be appropriate in cases of actual or threatened rights violations by the executive, and cases of legislative or executive blind spots. They may also have special value in cases where there is a need to build up, as well as respond to, the support structure for litigation in civil society.

There are also differences in the historical willingness of courts in different countries to employ these different forms of weak–strong review, though this may be changing as courts understand and learn from other courts' approaches.[135] In South Africa, for example, the Constitutional Court has tended to issue suspended declarations of invalidity, and engagement remedies, but not supervisory orders or "structural edicts."[136] This may be changing, so that the Court now issues all these different forms of weak–strong remedy, but the extent of this shift remains uncertain.[137] In India and Colombia, in contrast, the Supreme Court and Constitutional Court have been consistently willing to engage in ongoing monitoring of the degree of compliance with their orders.[138] Thus, in both the *Midday Meal* and *IDP* cases, the court assigned a special bench to monitor implementation of its decision. This bench also continues to sit regularly, and hear evidence, more than a decade after the court's initial orders in each case.[139]

But all models of weak–strong review ultimately depend on a common if often unstated logic, namely that courts are willing to show some degree of deference to reasoned and reasonable legislative or executive responses to a weak-form decision. In effect, this will often involve courts applying the same kind of "penalty default" structure that applies in contract law.[140]

In contract law, default rules are terms that parties can contract around by prior agreement.[141] The idea of *penalty* default rules is that they are a special sub-class of default rules that are "designed to give at least one party to the contract an incentive to contract around the default rule and therefore to choose

---

[134] *Compare* Roach & Budlender, *supra* note 101, at 333–34, 339 (noting their usefulness in cases of low state capacity, and/or where regular reporting requirements could help the state achieve a given constitutional goal).

[135] *See, e.g.*, Rodríguez-Garavito, *supra* note 100, at 1692.

[136] Roach & Budlender, *supra* note 101; BRIAN RAY, ENGAGING WITH SOCIAL RIGHTS: PROCEDURE, PARTICIPATION AND DEMOCRACY IN SOUTH AFRICA'S SECOND WAVE (2016).

[137] Roach & Budlender, *supra* note 101.

[138] Rodríguez-Garavito, *supra* note 100, at 1692.

[139] Dixon & Chowdhury, *supra* note 125; Mukherjee, *Democratic Experimentalism*, *supra* note 124; Mukherjee & Tuovinen, *supra* note 125.

[140] *Compare* Landau, *Aggressive Weak-Form Remedies*, *supra* note 118, at 257; David Landau, *The Reality of Social Rights Enforcement*, 53 HARV. INT'L L.J. 189 (2012).

[141] Ayres & Gertner, *supra* note 3.

affirmatively the contract provision they prefer."[142] In a constitutional context, this equates to the idea that courts should stipulate a default rule that will apply should the legislative or executive branch fail to take action, as required by a court's order.[143]

David Landau calls this a form of "aggressive" weak-form review, and Po Jen Yap the idea of "a suspension order 'with bite' "—that is, the idea that a suspended declaration of invalidity is coupled with "a remedial reading-in provision that takes effect automatically, in the event of any legislative default upon expiry of the suspension period."[144] The same "with bite" logic can also apply to engagement remedies, accompanied by a judicially defined default to govern cases in which negotiated outcomes are not possible, or suspended declarations of invalidity, where over-inclusive legislation automatically lapses in effect, upon expiration of the suspension period. It could likewise apply to monitoring by courts under a supervisory order or structural edit or injunction, whereby a court would increase or engage in follow-up monitoring in cases of *prima facie* noncompliance.

In addition, the idea of a constitutional penalty default rule suggests that if legislators or executive actors *do* take action, in good faith and in a reasonable way, the proposed judicial default would *not* apply, and courts would instead defer to the constitutional judgments of the political branches about the best approach to constitutional implementation.[145] Similarly, it suggests that if the executive acts in a reasonable and pro-active way to implement a court's orders, the court should respond by showing increased deference to those efforts— and lifting costly and intrusive forms of judicial monitoring.

A penalty default structure of this kind gives legislators and executive officials a clear incentive to act within the relevant time frame.[146] It means that political actors enjoy freedom to shape constitutional norms and requirements— but only if they take action within a given time frame, and in ways that are responsive to the reasoning of a court. This also gives political actors a reason

---

[142] *Id.* at 91.

[143] As Chapter 1 notes, this has important similarities to the idea of a regulatory pyramid in responsive theories of regulation. *See* Chapter 1 n 25.

[144] Landau, *Aggressive Weak-Form Remedies, supra* note 118; Yap, *New Democracies and Novel Remedies, supra* note 33, at fn 21. *Compare also* Rodríguez-Garavito's idea of "dialogic activism": Rodríguez-Garavito, *supra* note 100.

[145] *Compare* Landau, *Aggressive Weak-Form Remedies, supra* note 118. This also follows the logic of political-legal accountability advocated by Mukherjee: *see* Gaurav Mukherjee, *The Supreme Court of India and the Inter-Institutional Dynamics of Legislated Social Rights*, 53 VRU/WORLD COMP. L. 53 (2020).

[146] Landau, *Aggressive Weak-Form Remedies, supra* note 118. *See also* David Landau, *A Dynamic Theory of Judicial Role*, 55 B.C.L. REV. 1501 (2014).

to overcome inertia, and address an issue which they have previously ignored or overlooked.

To be effective, however, weak–strong review of this kind requires two key things. First, courts must at least raise the possibility of wide-ranging constitutional change, not just the narrowest possible legal reform, as a form of constitutional "default"; and second, as Chapter 4 suggests, courts must show some additional deference or "margin of appreciation" to the active legislative or executive implementation of a constitutional norm, compared to legislative or execution inaction. Some courts, for instance, have issued weak–strong remedies, but without any suggestion that they might be prepared in a future case to go further in requiring legal reform. Predictably, legislatures have responded to this kind of decision in quite narrow, formalistic terms, which have done little to overcome broader democratic inertia in an area. Other courts have gone much further in suggesting that constitutional change may be required in the future, and in doing so, given legislatures much greater incentive to update the law to prevent further challenge.

Take decisions involving the recognition of LGBTQI+ rights. In Hong Kong, in *W v. Registrar*, the Court of Final Appeal (CFA) noted the *Gender Recognition Act 2004* (UK) as a potential model of legislative reform for Hong Kong, and the issues it pointed to as ones calling for legislative attention.[147] But it also explicitly suggested that it was "a matter for the legislature to decide whether such legislation should be enacted."[148] The result was that the government proposed the narrowest possible legislative reform recognizing transsexual marriage, and no other forms of transgender identity recognition (but rather, the creation of an independent working group to examine the issue).[149] And the proposed legislation, the Marriage (Amendment) Bill 2014, was ultimately defeated in the Legislative Council—in part, for this reason.[150]

Failing legislation, the CFA had made clear that it would read in postoperative transgendered persons into the terms of the existing Marriage Ordinance.[151] Hence, for advocates of LGBTQI+ rights, voting for the

---

[147] W v. Registrar of Marriages [2013] HKFCA 39, [141]–[146].

[148] *Id.* at [146].

[149] *See* discussion in Swati Jhaveri & Anne Scully-Hill, *Executive and Legislative Reactions to Judicial Declarations of Constitutional Invalidity in Hong Kong: Engagement, Acceptance or Avoidanc?*, 13 INT'L J. CONST. L. 507 (2015).

[150] Winnie Chan Wing Yan, *Transsexual Marriage in Hong Kong: Reflections on the Journey from the CFA's Decision in W v. The Registrar of Marriages to the Marriage (Amendment) Bill 2014* (Jan. 29, 2015) at 1, 5–6, <https://papers.ssrn.com/sol3/papers.cfm?abstract_id=2556703>; Joy L. Chia & Amy Barrow, *Inching Towards Equality; LGBT Rights and the Limitations of Law in Hong Kong*, 22 WM. & MARY J. WOMEN & L. 303, 322–23 (2016).

[151] *W v. Registrar*, *supra* note 147, at [150]. For this reason, Yap labels it an instance of a suspension order "with bite": *see* Yap, *New Democracies and Novel Remedies*, *supra* note 33.

proposed amendments did nothing to advance transgender rights, and for opponents, it represented an important symbolic defeat and potential slippery slope toward greater *same-sex* relationship recognition. Unsurprising, the bill was therefore defeated by a combination of twenty pro-democratic and twenty conservative legislators voting against it.[152] And while post-operative transgendered persons are free to marry, based on the CFA's decision in *W* itself, as of 2022 there had been no broader legislative attempt to extend transgender identity recognition in Hong Kong.[153]

In South Africa, a similar pattern of legislative non-response was evident following the decisions of the CCSA in the early 2000s finding that legislation that excluded same-sex couples from a range of statutory benefits impermissibly discriminated on the grounds on sexual orientation.[154] The CCSA in these cases did not suggest that *any* legislation drawing distinctions of this kind was necessarily unconstitutional, and read same-sex couples into the operation of the relevant legislation. Unsurprisingly, these decisions also met with no legislative response. None was necessary in order to expand access to the relevant statutory benefits. However, in *Fourie*,[155] the CCSA took a broader approach to the recognition of same-sex relationship rights and adopted a mix of strong and weak rights and remedies.

While the CCSA in *Fourie* avoided holding that same-sex marriage was constitutionally *required*, and remanded the issue to the National Assembly for consideration for twelve months, the Court gave numerous indications that a failure to adopt same-sex relationship recognition could lead to further constitutional challenges.[156] It emphasized both the material and expressive dimensions to same-sex marital equality and suggested that no civil union-based model could discriminate between opposite and same-sex couples at either level.[157] The Court also made clear that if the National Assembly did not act to introduce legislation within twelve months, same-sex marriage would be legalized by a judicial process of reading-in.[158] The message to the National Assembly was therefore clear: if it simply introduced civil unions for same-sex

---

[152] Chan Wing Yan, *supra* note 150, at 6.
[153] *Id.* at 1, 5–6; Chia & Barrow, *supra* note 150, at 322–23; Jhaveri & Scully-Hill, *supra* note 149, at 515–16.
[154] Satchwell v. President of the Republic of South Africa, CCT 45/01; Du Toit v. Minister of Welfare and Population Development, 2003 (2) SA 198 (CC); J and B v. Director General: Department of Home Affairs, 2003 (5) SA 198 (CC). *See* Chapter 4, *supra*.
[155] Minister for Home Affairs v. Fourie, 2005 (3) B.C.L.R. 241 (SCA), 2006 (3) B.C.L.R, 355 (CCSA).
[156] *See* Dixon & Issacharoff, *supra* note 40, at 703–05.
[157] Minister for Home Affairs v. Fourie, 2005 (3) B.C.L.R. 241 (SCA), 2006 (3) B.C.L.R. 355 (CCSA). *See also* Dixon & Issacharoff, *supra* note 40.
[158] Minister for Home Affairs v. Fourie, *supra* note 157. *See* discussion in Yap, *New Democracies and Novel Remedies*, *supra* note 33.

couples and made no change to marriage law, it was likely to face further constitutional challenge to its legislation; and if it did nothing, same-sex marriage would be adopted in any event. This was also an outcome opposed by a range of supporters of the African National Congress (ANC) government.[159]

The most attractive option for the ANC majority in response to the decision, therefore, was to enact legislative measures recognizing same-sex relationship equality, but in a manner that sought to distinguish between opposite-sex and same-sex marriage. This is also exactly what it did via the enactment of same-sex marriage, in all but name, via the *Civil Unions Act* 2006—a law that effectively enacted same-sex marriage.[160]

As Chapter 6 notes, there is also a crucial difference between court decisions that invite a form of constitutional dialogue that is real versus rhetorical in nature.[161] Some court decisions may take a weakened form and invite a form of substantive judicial-legislative dialogue, whereas others may give legislators a purely nominal, "compliance"-focused role in the process of constitutional implementation.[162] The two approaches will also have quite different implications for democracy, and the run the risk that court decisions will lead to dangers of reverse burdens of inertia or democratic debilitation. Decisions that invite real dialogue with legislators provide an important opening for democratic constitutional debate and judgment, and give legislators an incentive to engage in proactive legislative deliberation on constitutional decisions.

Rulings that are formally weak but *de facto* strong, in contrast, provide legislators little meaningful scope to (re)assert democratic constitutional preferences and understandings. They give little incentive for legislators to improve their own capacity or track record on constitutional implementation, considering that doing so does nothing to reduce or remove the likelihood of judicial oversight or sanction. And by requiring a legislative response, without the opportunity for meaningful substantive judgments, they force legislators with limited time and resources to expend those resources complying with judicial decisions, in ways that may simply displace other legislative priorities.

In celebrating weak-form decisions such as *Decision C-355 of 2006* and *Decision C-577 of 2011* in Colombia, or the *Abortion I* case in Germany, it is therefore important to emphasize the particular understanding of those

---

[159] *See* THEUNIS ROUX, THE POLITICS OF PRINCIPLE: THE FIRST SOUTH AFRICAN CONSTITUTIONAL COURT, 1995–2005 (2013).
[160] *See* Dixon & Issacharoff, *supra* note 40.
[161] *See* discussion in Christopher P. Manfredi & James B. Kelly, *Six Degrees of Dialogue: A Response to Hogg and Bushell*, 37 OSGOODE HALL L.J. 513 (1999) in this context.
[162] *See* Rosalind Dixon, *A New (Inter)national Human Rights Experiment for Australia*, 23 PUB. L. REV. 75 (2012).

decisions favored by a responsive approach: decisions such as *Decision C-355 of 2006* and *Decision C-577 of 2011* were decisions that were formally weak–strong and did not lead to a legislative response. But if they had, and that response was reasoned and reasonable, the Colombian Court would have been required to show increased deference to that response as a form of democratic dialogue, even if it meant accepting greater restrictions on access to abortion or a narrower form of marriage-like protection than favored by the Court itself. This was, in effect, what the German Court did in *Abortion II*, and what its decision prefigured in *Abortion I*.

To be effective, weak–strong judicial remedies must also be applied by courts in ways that are suitably dynamic and flexible in nature and sensitive to actual legislative and executive performance. This may also mean either increasing or decreasing the intensity of judicial monitoring over time.

Some courts have taken a static, as compared to dynamic approach to judicial monitoring, or the enforcement of strong judicial remedies.[163] This also includes courts that are otherwise responsive in approach. In the *Midday Meal* and *IDP* cases, for example, courts have maintained regular supervision over the implementation of these orders for more than twenty and seventeen years respectively.[164] And while they have varied the focus of their supervision efforts, based on state performance, they have tended to do so in ways that *increase* monitoring in respect of certain areas or groups, rather than simultaneously increase and decrease it, based on performance. An approach of this kind also dramatically reduces the incentive legislative and executive actors have to implement constitutional requirements proactively. In fact, it can mean that it is rational for legislators and executive officials simply to wait until the court's deadline expires, and the court's order itself takes effect. This can lead to a cycle of further democratic inertia that then compounds problems of state (in)capacity and democratic distrust.

A weak–strong or "experimentalist" approach, in contrast, would encourage a court to take a more flexible and differentiated approach, which explicitly links the intensity of judicial monitoring to evidence of compliance with a court order.[165] In the *Midday Meal Case*, for example, a more variable approach to judicial supervision might have led to more effective monitoring in the parts

---

[163] Landau, *A Dynamic Theory of Judicial Role*, supra note 146.

[164] Dixon & Chowdhury, *supra* note 125.

[165] Dorf & Sabel, *supra* note 124. For its relevance and translation into the context of SER enforcement, see also Katharine Young & Sandra Liebenberg, "*Adjudicating Social and Economic Rights: Can Democratic Experimentalism Help?*" in SOCIAL RIGHTS IN THEORY AND PRACTICE: CRITICAL INQUIRIES (Helena Alviar Garcia et al. eds, 2015); RAY, ENGAGING WITH SOCIAL RIGHTS, *supra* note 136, at 27–28; Mukherjee, *Democratic Experimentalism*, *supra* note 124.

of India where there was greatest need. Or a more flexible and responsive approach to defining the relevant right could have encouraged greater experimentation around the best mode of food preparation and delivery.[166]

Similarly, in Colombia, while the Constitutional Court has been sensitive to the need to engage in ongoing and varied monitoring, including by focusing over time on the groups most vulnerable and adversely affected by the non-implementation of the order—that is, women, children, and teens, and indigenous groups[167]—it could perhaps have done more to focus its monitoring efforts on certain poorly performing areas of the country, or experimented with new technologies for monitoring—including the kinds of cell-phone and other technologies used by health and development economists to promote the effectiveness of public health and development programs.[168]

There is still an important question as to whether weak–strong approaches of this kind will be *sufficient* to counter complex burdens of inertia and thereby avoid dangers of this kind. In cases such as the *Midday Meal* and *IDP* cases, there is clear evidence that the decisions have helped catalyze meaningful improvements in school attendance and childhood nutrition in India, and access to key services for internally displaced people in Colombia.[169] They have also arguably sparked a broader form of rights consciousness, and recognition of the validity of rights claims and the dignity of rights claimants, in the context of the right to food, and right to basic services for IDPs.[170]

But there remain significant gaps in the implementation of the courts' orders. The quality of school meals in India is extremely uneven, and there is mixed evidence on the degree to which it has led to unqualified improvements in childhood nutrition, versus partial substitution of meals from children to adults in a home environment.[171] And many IDPs in Colombia remain in a similar position to where they were in 2004—that is, without meaningful access to housing, healthcare, and education.[172]

Another question is whether there is adequate constitutional litigation to overcome various democratic blockages, especially complex burdens of inertia. For instance, if courts award only weak, non-coercive, or prospective remedies, there will often be limited incentive for individuals to bring constitutional

---

[166] Dixon & Chowdhury, *supra* note 125.
[167] Espinosa & Landau, *supra* note 18, at 187–88.
[168] Valentina Rotondi et al., *Leveraging Mobile Phones to Attain Sustainable Development*, 117 PNAS 13413 (2020).
[169] *See* Chapters 4 and 5 *supra*.
[170] Rodríguez-Garavito, *supra* note 100, at 1687–88.
[171] *See* Dixon & Chowdhury, *supra* note 125.
[172] *See* Chapter 5, *supra*. *See also* Rodríguez-Garavito, *supra* note 100, at 1687.

complaints before a court. This could be one reason that courts such as the CCSA have heard relatively few social rights cases, compared to courts such as the Colombian Constitutional Court. The CCSA defines rights and remedies in a way that provides limited relief to individuals, whereas the Colombian Court provides direct, concrete relief to thousands of individual petitioners each year making social rights claims, through the *tutela* mechanism.[173]

One potential solution to this is also for courts to adopt strong–weak remedies but in a quite specific sense—of granting strong remedies to individuals before the court, and only a weaker remedy for others affected by democratic blockages.[174] Kent Roach, for instance, has recently argued for this kind of "two-track" remedial approach as a means of balancing concerns about judicial under- and over-enforcement of constitutional norms.[175] It was also the approach of the court at first instance (the Cape High Court) in *Grootboom*, where Judge Davis ordered immediate access to shelter for all families with children, and then by consent, immediate access to temporary shelter for all of the named plaintiffs, while engaging in weaker review of the broader housing rights claim raised in the case.[176]

There are, however, also potential dangers to this form of weak–strong remedial approach. It encourages individual litigation in ways that have the potential to impose substantial pressure on a court's caseloads, especially in countries that allow for direct access to a court—such as via *amparo*, *tutela*, or other individualized complaint mechanisms.[177] And in social rights cases in particular, it has the capacity to distort the distribution of resources, toward wealthier individuals who are able to litigate, and away from more marginalized groups indirectly affected by a court order.[178]

One possible response to this is that there is still important work to be done refining the way in which responsive, or weak–strong, forms of review occur. Models of weak–strong judicial enforcement could themselves be made more dynamic or responsive in nature. And the idea of two-track remedies, for example, could potentially be refined to focus on the idea of strong interim

---

[173] I am indebted to Theunis Roux for encouraging me to pursue this point.
[174] Roach, *Dialogic Remedies*, supra note 33. Compare also Gardbaum, *What's So Weak About "Weak-Form Review"?*, supra note 9.
[175] GARDBAUM, THE NEW COMMONWEALTH MODEL OF CONSTITUTIONALISM, supra note 4.
[176] Dixon, *Creating Dialogue about Socioeconomic Rights*, supra note 100.
[177] For discussion of this and related "queue jumping" objections, see, *e.g.*, Roach & Budlender, supra note 101, at 872–73, 880–81.
[178] *Compare* Rosalind Dixon & David Landau, *Constitutional Non-Transformation?: Socioeconomic Rights Beyond the Poor*, in THE FUTURE OF ECONOMIC AND SOCIAL RIGHTS 110 (Katharine G. Young ed., 2019) for discussion of these and related distributional concerns and challenges.

remedies (as in *Grootboom*) combined with a greater emphasis on weak–strong approaches to structural judicial intervention.

Another plausible interpretation, however, is that these are problems of state capacity that are beyond the capacity of courts effectively to address.[179] Judicial review may be able to reduce the effects of democratic dysfunction in such cases but not wholly eliminate or overcome it. And it is important to acknowledge this, even as we seek to highlight the benefits to weak–strong judicial remedies and forms of intervention.

D. Conclusion

Court decisions can be more or less final in nature. They can be subject to formal override by way of constitutional amendment, special legislative override clauses, or other mechanisms that limit the jurisdiction of courts to review or strike down legislation—including legislative "sequels."[180] The finality of courts decisions will also be affected by how courts themselves approach the construction of amendments or legislation of this kind, and the choices courts make about the breadth of their reasoning, the coercive and time-sensitive nature of their remedies, and the strength of *stare decisis*.

Weakening the finality of judicial review, in some or all these ways, will also be highly desirable from the perspective of a commitment to democratic responsiveness. It can allow democratic majorities to play a role in resolving disputes over constitutional rights, the scope and meaning of which are open to reasonable disagreement, and thereby help reduce the risk of reverse burdens of inertia and the potential democratic legitimacy deficit they pose. It can likewise help provide an outlet, or safety valve, for forms of democratic disagreement that might otherwise threaten the court's own legitimacy. Avoiding democratic backlash of this kind is also extremely important to maintaining the stability and effectiveness of judicial review, and sometimes even democratic constitutionalism more broadly.

In a responsive approach, however, how and when judicial review is weakened will also depend on the nature of the case, and the relevant democratic blockages at stake. In cases of legislative blind spots or burdens of inertia, there may be compelling reasons of principle for courts choosing to reason narrowly,

---

[179] *Compare* Landau, *A Dynamic Theory of Judicial Role*, *supra* note 146; Mark Tushnet & Madhav Khosla, Unstable Constitutionalism: Law and Politics in South Asia (2015).
[180] Roach, The Supreme Court on Trial, *supra* note 62; Rosalind Dixon, *The Supreme Court of Canada, Charter Dialogue, and Deference*, 47 Osgoode Hall Law J. 235.

employ weak remedies, or weaken the force of *stare decisis* or equivalent *de facto* norms of adherence to precedent. But in cases of potential electoral or institutional monopoly, the arguments for weakening the finality of review will be far more limited. They will stem solely from the desire to avoid damaging forms of democratic backlash, not any notion that disagreement over the scope of the democratic minimum core is reasonable or principled in nature. Even in cases involving democratic blind spots and burdens of inertia, there may be dangers to courts adopting too weak an approach to review. Doing so may mean that judicial intervention is not sufficient to counter relevant blockages or promote democratic responsiveness.

Responsive judicial review, therefore, will ultimately involve a mix of review that is strong and weak in nature—or as Langford puts it, is neither wholly deferential nor based on independent "enforcer" conception of the judicial role.[181] Weak–strong review of this kind can take numerous forms. Indeed, all judicial review should be understood as "existing somewhere on a spectrum between weak-form and strong-form review."[182] But the core idea beyond responsive judicial review is that courts should adopt a form of "strong–weak" or "weak–strong" review that promotes overall democratic responsiveness—by adjusting the scope of judicial reasoning and remedies to the nature of the relevant case, the democratic blockage courts are seeking to counter, and the risks of reverse inertia and/or democratic backlash.

Weak–strong review in particular will be closely related to the idea of a two-track remedial model, or the idea of "dialogic," "collaborative," and "relational" remedies advanced by a range of other leading comparative constitutional scholars.[183] It also, however, has its own distinctive structure and logic, which at its core depends on a form of penalty default logic. Strong review, in this approach, becomes a form of penalty default which gives powerful incentives for political actors to overcome previous blockages and implement constitutional norms, in ways that ultimately make judicial review weak not strong in effect.[184]

---

[181] Langford, *supra* note 119, at 69–73. *Compare* Landau, *A Dynamic Theory of Judicial Role*, *supra* note 146, at 1504.
[182] *Id.* at 1554.
[183] *Compare* Roach *Dialogic Remedies*, *supra* note 33; KENT ROACH, REMEDIES FOR HUMAN RIGHTS VIOLATIONS: A TWO-TRACK APPROACH TO SUPRA-NATIONAL AND NATIONAL LAW (2021); AILEEN KAVANAGH, THE COLLABORATIVE CONSTITUTION (forthcoming, 2023); Marta Cartabia, *Editorial: COVID-19 and I-CON*, 18 INT'L J. CONST. L. 1 (2020).
[184] *Compare* Charles F. Sabel & William H. Simon, *Destabilization Rights: How Public Law Litigation Succeeds*, 117 HARV. L. REV. 1016 (2004); MICHAELA HAILBRONNER, STRUCTURAL REFORM LITIGATION IN DOMESTIC COURTS (Unpublished manuscript, 2022).

PART 3
RESPONSIVE JUDGING AND COMPARATIVE CONSTITUTIONAL THEORY

8
A Responsive Judicial Voice
Building a Court's Legitimacy

Weak–strong review is one way in which courts can promote the legitimacy and acceptance of their decisions. But it is not the only way. Courts can also contribute to the chances of successful responsive review by helping build the support structure for judicial review,[1] and making careful choices about the (i) authorship; (ii) tone; and (iii) narrative underpinning their decisions.

How and whether these factors influence the response to a court decision will depend on a range of factors, including the audience for court decisions, and how these decisions are explained by intermediaries such as the media. There will also be cases in which strategic choices about these questions are either inappropriate or infeasible. But choices of this kind have an important capacity to shape how parties to a case, or elite or popular audiences, react to a court decision.

The identity of a judge may affect public perceptions of the arguments a judge has been willing to consider as part of their process of reasoning. The specific narrative used to justify a decision may affect the way in which it is received by different audiences. And a public show of respect toward certain parties may encourage reciprocal respect from those parties.

If courts make careful and sensitive choices about judicial authorship, tone, and narrative, therefore, they can enhance both the actual and perceived legitimacy of their decisions; whereas if they make those decisions indiscriminately, or without regard to these concerns, they will often find that their decisions lack public acceptance. Courts, this chapter argues, should therefore deliberately seek to frame their decisions in ways that involve selecting (i) a judicial "author" who speaks directly to the losing party in a case; (ii) a narrative that combines "global" and "local" elements; and (iii) reasoning that shows a posture of respect toward the losing party.

---

[1] David Landau, *Substitute and Complement Theories of Judicial Review*, 92 IND. L.J. 1283 (2017). *See also* Chapter 5, *supra*.

What this means will vary by context, and there may be limits to both the feasibility and desirability of this approach in certain cases. But framing of this kind is an important dimension to many successful instances of responsive judicial review, especially cases involving highly charged issues such as those concerning the recognition of LGBTQI+ rights—where there is clear evidence of legislative inertia but also strongly felt opposition to legal change.

On one level, an approach of this kind is deeply *pragmatic* in nature. It seeks to promote the *effectiveness* of attempts by courts to counter political monopoly, blind spots or burdens of inertia.[2] That is, it aims to contribute to building strong constitutional *courts*, as opposed to strong forms of judicial review.[3] As I noted at the outset, however, there is another more principled level on which an approach of this kind is linked to the idea of judicial responsiveness—that is, the idea that in engaging in judicial review, courts should be responsive to the distinctive nature of adjudication as a practice, and in particular their responsibility to provide a hearing to individuals, and to justify their decisions to individuals and groups disappointed by the result of a decision. In this sense, it is simply another element of a form of principled judicial pragmatism.[4]

A. Why Responsive Judging—or a Responsive Judicial Voice

The right to be heard is a matter of fundamental justice or fairness, but it is also an important determinant of the perceived legitimacy or fairness of a decision, and therefore the willingness of those disappointed by it to abide by relevant outcomes. Social science evidence suggests a powerful relationship between opportunities for voice in processes of decision-making and the *perceived* fairness or legitimacy of decisional outcomes.[5] That is, there are powerful

---

[2] Richard A. Posner, Law, Pragmatism, and Democracy (2005).
[3] Stephen Gardbaum, *Are Strong Constitutional Courts Always a Good Thing for New Democracies?*, 53 Colum. J. Transnat'l L. 285 (2015); Rosalind Dixon, *Strong Courts: Judicial Statecraft in Aid of Constitutional Change*, 59 Colum. J. Transnat'l L. 299 (2021). See also Vicente Fabian Benitez Rojas, Judicial Power In Constitutional Democracies: Strong And Weak Courts In Colombia And Judicial Review Of Constitutional Amendments Between 1955 And 2017 (2021) (JSD Dissertation, New York University).
[4] Roni Mann, *Non-ideal Theory of Constitutional Adjudication*, 7 Global Const. 14 (2018).
[5] *See, e.g.*, E. Allan Lind et al., *Voice, Control, and Procedural Justice: Instrumental and Noninstrumental Concerns in Fairness Judgments*, 59 J. Personality & Soc. Psychol. 952 (1990) (summarizing existing studies finding a "voice effect," relational and instrumental accounts, and providing additional evidence as to the two effects); Derek R. Avery & Miguel A. Quinones, *Disentangling the Effects of Voice: The Incremental Roles of Opportunity, Behavior, and Instrumentality in Predicting Procedural Fairness*, 87 J. Applied Psychol. 81 (2002).

"instrumental" as well as "relational" rationales for a right to be heard; ensuring a right to be heard promotes compliance with court orders, as well as a sense of dignity and respect on the part of citizens.[6] Both accounts also emphasize the notion that voice involves being *listened to*—if not followed in subsequent processes of decision-making.

As Alon Harel, Adam Shinar, and Tsvi Kahana note, at minimum the right to be heard requires three things: (i) the opportunity for an individual to voice a grievance; (ii) a willingness on the part of the tribunal hearing the grievance to engage in "meaningful moral deliberation" or give "good" reasons for the decision; and (iii) for a decision-maker to reconsider its decision, or action, in light of the grievance and that process of reasoning.[7] Each of these stages shows respect for the dignity of those adversely affected by a decision, and as Lon Fuller noted, one of the defining features of the rule of law is the message of respect it sends to citizens.[8]

This is one reason political theorists argue that judicial review has important procedural virtues. It provides individual litigants with the right to challenge decisions adversely affecting them, and to make arguments as to why those decisions are not in fact justified.[9] To do so effectively, however, courts must ultimately offer reasons that could reasonably satisfy "the individual that his or her matter has been considered" in a fair and impartial manner.[10]

This cannot mean that courts must accept the arguments of every individual before them, or group affected by a court decision, or that courts must directly address all of the arguments a party raises in case. Often, as Chapter 7 notes, there may be powerful prudential reasons for them *not* to do so. What it does mean is that courts must assure losing parties, and those more broadly disappointed by a decision, that their arguments and concerns have been heard and treated with respect. They must frame their decisions as a "letter to the loser" in a particular case, and more broadly in civil

---

[6] *Id. See also* Bruce Barry & Debra L. Shapiro, *When Will Grievants Desire Voice? A Test of Situational, Motivational, and Attributional Explanations*, 11 INT'L J. CONFLICT MGMT. 106 (2000).

[7] Alon Harel & Adam Shinar, *The Real Case for Judicial Review*, *in* COMPARATIVE JUDICIAL REVIEW 13, 17–27 (Erin F. Delaney & Rosalind Dixon eds., 2018); Alon Harel & Tsvi Kahana, *The Easy Core Case for Judicial Review*, 2 J. LEGAL ANALYSIS 227 (2010). *See also* Alon Harel & Adam Shinar, *Between Judicial and Legislative Supremacy: A Cautious Defense of Constrained Judicial Review*, 10 INT'L J. CONST. L. 950 (2012).

[8] LON L. FULLER, THE MORALITY OF LAW (rev. ed. 1969). *See* discussion in Jeremy Waldron, *Why Law—Efficacy, Freedom or Fidelity?*, 13 LAW & PHIL. 259, 278–79 (1994); Colleen Murphy, *Lon Fuller and the Moral Value of the Rule of Law*, 24 LAW & PHIL. 239 (2005). I am indebted to Kevin Walton for this suggestion.

[9] Margit Cohn, A THEORY OF THE EXECUTIVE BRANCH: TENSION AND LEGALITY (2021) at 289–320. See also, Margit Cohn, *The Role of Courts in the Public Decision-Making Sphere: A Two-Pronged Argument for Heightened* Review (forthcoming, 2022).

[10] Harel & Shinar, *The Real Case for Judicial Review*, *supra* note 7, at 26 (emphasis in the original).

society.[11] A willingness by judges to reason in a way that acknowledges the perspectives and commitments of constitutional "losers" could also be seen as providing exactly this kind of response or reassurance—that the court has in fact respected the dignity, or standing, of those citizens, and their right to be heard.[12]

There are a number of ways for courts to do this: by selecting a judicial "author" whose identity or life experience speaks directly to the losing party in a case; reasoning that shows a posture or tone of respect toward the losing party, and a narrative justifying their decision that combines appeals to both universal and national values.

None of these techniques will provide a failsafe way to promote the perceived legitimacy of a court decision. Indeed, as I note below, they may sometimes actively undermine not enhance the perceived legitimacy of a court decision. But used carefully, with attention to context and a court's audience, they may help both increase the justifiability and acceptance of certain instances of responsive judicial review.

B. Judicial Framing and Responsive Judicial Review

1. Authorship

The first, and most visible, way in which courts can show respect toward losing parties is by allocating responsibility for writing the court's (or majority) opinion to a judge who shares the same identity and/or lived experience as those most likely to be disappointed by the result. Sharing the same background does not always mean sharing the same experience or perspective.[13] Similarly, sharing the same experience does not always equate to having the same background. And a judge's "identity" will itself be socially constructed. It

---

[11] In the context of a particular case, see, e.g., Nathalie Des Rosiers, *From Telling to Listening: A Therapeutic Analysis of the Role of Courts in Minority-Majority Conflicts*, 37 COURT REVIEW 54 (2000); Sarah Murray, *"A Letter to the Loser"? Public Law and the Empowering Role of the Judgment*, 23(4) GRIFFITH L.R. 545–68 (2014). More broadly, see also Jamal Greene, *Rights as Trumps*, 132 HARV. L. REV. 28 (2018) (calling for a turn by the US Supreme Court to a more flexible, proportionality based approach in preference to a more categorical "rights as trumps" approach, and suggesting that the later tends to alienate one or other side of a constitutional controversy, in ways that undermine their sense of attachment to the overall constitutional project—and to each other, as participants in that project).

[12] ROBERT BURT, THE CONSTITUTION IN CONFLICT (1992).

[13] See, e.g., Rosalind Dixon, *Female Justices, Feminism, and the Politics of Judicial Appointment: A Reexamination*, 21 YALE J.L. & FEMINISM 297 (2009).

will depend which aspects of a judge's personal history or story the media and civil society choose to highlight in public discourse.

But a judge who is *perceived* to share a similar background to disappointed litigants can send a powerful signal to those parties, that even though their claim has been rejected, it has been properly heard and understood.[14]

Judges need not always write the opinion of a court to convey this message. Sometimes the very act of joining or concurring in another judge's opinion may be enough. And there are often benefits to judges *sharing* responsibility for judicial authorship. Doing so creates a fairer and more efficient allocation of a court's workload. It can also increase the degree to which a court's perceived authority is linked to the entire court, rather than a single judge, and thus capable of withstanding changes to a court's membership.[15]

Similarly, there may be cases in which *unanimity* in a court's voice is more important than any proximity to a disappointed party. For instance, where a court fears non-compliance with its orders, it may be especially important for the court to write in a single voice—or issue a *per curiam* opinion—in order to signal that the court is putting its full institutional authority behind a decision.[16] Or if a court fears political interference, as Stephen Gardbaum notes, writing in a single voice may allow a court "to maintain a veil of ignorance between its members and government re-appointers or potential employers."[17]

Conversely, in some cases, there may be strong arguments for encouraging dissenting judgments, including the desire to promote more reasoned, independent forms of judicial decision-making, and the long-term development of the law.[18] Further, dissenting judgments may themselves provide disappointed parties with evidence that their arguments have been heard and considered by

---

[14] In some cases, close parallels between the background of a judge and disappointed party could of course have the opposite effect. They could provoke a sense of increased anger and betrayal on the part of disappointed litigants. This, for example, has arguably been the case for some black litigants and observers of the US Supreme Court in relation to the jurisprudence of Justice Thomas: *see, e.g.,* A. Leon Higginbotham, Jr, *Justice Clarence Thomas in Retrospect*, 45 HASTINGS L.J. 1405 (1993); Mark Tushnet, *Clarence Thomas's Black Nationalism*, 47 How. L.J. 323 (2004); U.W. Clemon & Stephanie Y. Moore, *Justice Clarence Thomas: The Burning of Civil Rights Bridges*, 1 ALABAMA C.R. & C.L. L. REV. 49 (2011); KEN FOSKETT, JUDGING THOMAS (2004).

[15] *See* Rosalind Dixon, *Towering v. Collegial Judges: A Comparative Reflection*, in Rehan Abeyratne and Iddo Porat (eds), TOWERING JUDGES: A COMPARATIVE STUDY OF CONSTITUTIONAL JUDGES (2021).

[16] *See, e.g.,* Ruth Bader Ginsburg, *The Role of Dissenting Opinions*, 95 MINN. L. REV. 1, 3 (2010); Andrew Lynch, *Dissent: The Rewards and Risks of Judicial Disagreement in the High Court of Australia*, 27 MELB. U. L. REV. 724 (2003).

[17] Stephen Gardbaum, *What Makes for More or Less Powerful Constitutional Courts*, 29 DUKE J. COMP. & INT'L L. 1, 15 (2018). Whether this is true, of course, depends in part on how much knowledge of the internal workings of a court becomes public or quasi-public knowledge.

[18] Andrew Lynch, *Introduction—What Makes a Dissent "Great"*, in GREAT AUSTRALIAN DISSENTS 13 (Andrew Lynch ed., 2016), citing CHARLES E. HUGHES, THE SUPREME COURT OF THE UNITED STATES 68 (1928).

the court in ways that contribute to the perceived legitimacy of the majority as well as dissenting opinion. Whether this is the case will depend largely on the tone of the dissent. Some dissents may evidence a notable *lack of respect* for the approach of the majority in ways that only increase the sense disappointed parties have that the majority has not fully heard or understood their arguments.[19] Other dissenting judgments may adopt a tone that shows respect toward losing parties and the majority in ways that may help mediate the gap between the two. But in most cases, judicial authorship is more likely to attract attention from disappointed parties than either concurring or dissenting opinions.

Judicial authorship can be shared across cases, even with appropriate attention to questions of judicial identity. Courts can allocate responsibility for opinion writing, across cases, in ways that are attentive to considerations of both voice and workload. And the power of a *per curiam* opinion may itself depend on the contrast it draws with other opinions in which a court speaks in multiple voices.[20]

Where there is a choice, a court attentive to its own sociological legitimacy should therefore pay close attention to the identity of the judge who authors its opinion, even as it acknowledges the general value of dissent and special value to *per curiam* decisions in certain exceptional cases.

2. Tone: Respect or comity

In private international law, the idea of comity involves "the recognition and implementation of the decisions of courts belonging to other systems."[21] It derives from principles of "courtesy," "mutual respect," and "mutual convenience" among nation states, but is also a means of creating a stable and seamless (or gap-free) global legal order.[22] In this sense, it serves important political

---

[19] *See, e.g.*, Planned Parenthood v. Casey, 505 U.S. 833, 979–81 (1992) (Scalia J., dissenting); Lawrence. V. Texas., 539 U.S. 558 (2003) (Scalia J., dissenting); Bostock v. Clayton County, 590 U.S. —, 32 (2020) (Alito J., dissenting). I am indebted to Erin Delaney for pressing me on this point.

[20] This is less true for the veil of ignorance argument Gardbaum makes above. But on *per curiam* opinions and a court's authority, see, *e.g.*, Cooper v. Aaron, 358 U.S. 1 (1958); Tony A. Freyer, *Cooper v. Aaron (1958): A Hidden Story of Unanimity and Division*, 33 J. Sup. Ct. Hist. 89 (2008); Daniel A. Farber, *The Supreme Court and the Rule of Law: Cooper v. Aaron Revisited*, U. Ill. L. Rev. 387 (1982); Bush v. Gore, 531 U.S. 98 (2000); Laura Krugman Ray, *Road to Bush v. Gore: The History of the Supreme Court's Use of the Per Curiam Opinion*, 79 Neb. L. Rev. 517 (2000); Erwin Chemerinsky, *Bush v. Gore was Not Justiciable*, 76 Notre Dame L. Rev. 1093 (2000); Stephen L. Wasby et al., *The Per Curiam Opinion: Its Nature and Functions*, 76 Judicature 29 (1992); Ira P. Robbins, *Hiding Behind the Cloak of Invisibility: The Supreme Court and Per Curiam Opinions*, 86 Tul. L. Rev. 1197 (2011).

[21] Elisa D'Alterio, *From Judicial Comity to Legal Comity: A Judicial Solution to Global Disorder?*, 9 Int'l J. Const. L. 394, 401 (2011).

[22] *Id.* At 398, 400, 423.

objectives.[23] It is also understood by many international lawyers and scholars as a matter of (at least qualified) legal obligation.[24]

In constitutional theory, scholars such as Aileen Kavanagh likewise argue for comity as a matter of political obligation—or a principle that should guide our understanding of the relationship between courts and legislatures. Comity, Kavanagh notes, is simply "that respect which one great organ of the State owes to another."[25] It arises because of the inter-dependent relationship between courts and other (primarily legislative) actors, which entails requirements of "mutual self-restraint and mutual support."[26]

Reciprocity is also a close corollary of this notion of interdependence.[27] But again, reciprocity is understood as a matter of legal obligation—or as necessary to ensure "the ongoing success" of a system characterized by shared responsibility and interdependence.[28] From a strategic perspective, showings of comity or respect have a distinct, if related purpose. Where Kavanagh's notion of comity *requires* reciprocity, strategic displays of respect simply aim to *encourage* it—through something like the dynamics of "gift exchange."

The basic idea behind gift exchange is quite simple. Those who receive a gift appear to feel a moral obligation to reciprocate in some way, by giving a return gift or benefit of comparable value.[29] This pattern has been found to apply across time and cultures, and in a variety of social and economic settings.[30] It even extends to intangible "gifts" such as demonstrations of respect or trust. Workers who are given more autonomy, and shown more trust, tend to work harder than those who are closely controlled or monitored.[31] Trust begets trustworthiness, and respect begets reciprocal forms of respect and cooperation.[32]

On this logic, courts that demonstrate respect toward a losing party are also more likely to see their own decisions respected, compared with courts that

---

[23] *Id.* At 400, 423.

[24] Compare *Hilton v. Guyot*, 159 U.S. 113 (1895) (suggesting that it is "neither a matter of *absolute* obligation, on the one hand, nor of ere courtesy or goodwill, upon the other") (emphasis added). See discussion in D'Alterio, *supra* note 21, at 400.

[25] AILEEN KAVANAGH, THE COLLABORATIVE CONSTITUTION (forthcoming, 2023), citing *Buckley v. Attorney General* [1950] I.R. 67, 80 (O'Byrne J.).

[26] *Id.*

[27] *Id.* at 21.

[28] *Id.* at 24.

[29] *See, e.g.,* George A. Akerlof, *Labor Contracts as Partial Gift Exchange*, 97 Q.J. ECON. 543 (1982); Sebastian Kube et al., *The Currency of Reciprocity: Gift Exchange in the Workplace*, 102 AM. ECON. REV. 1644 (2012); Armin Falk, *Gift Exchange in the Field*, 75 ECONOMETRICA 1501 (2007).

[30] *See, e.g.,* Akerlof, *supra* note 29; Falk, *supra* note 29; Ernst Fehr et al., *Gift Exchange and Reciprocity in Competitive Experimental Markets*, 42 EUR. ECON. REV. 1 (1998).

[31] *Compare* Akerlof, *supra* note 29; Noel D. Johnson & Alexandra A. Mislin, *Trust Games: A Meta-Analysis*, 32 J. ECON. PSYCHOL. 865 (2011).

[32] JAMES FOWKES, BUILDING THE CONSTITUTION: THE PRACTICE OF CONSTITUTIONAL INTERPRETATION IN POST-APARTHEID SOUTH AFRICA 50 (2016).

show contempt or disregard for a losing party.[33] The relationship between a court and parties to litigation is not identical to that between a gift giver and recipient, or employer and employee.[34] It is more indirect and impersonal and mediated by a range of constitutional structures and duties, but it is still a relationship with potential communicative and expressive dimensions.[35] And some parties may be especially sensitive to the expressive dimensions to constitutional litigation. They may not experience high levels of respect in democratic debate, and therefore place special weight on demonstrations of respect in a judicial setting, which provide them with a right to be heard.[36]

Comity, in this sense, is therefore more about increasing the *perceived* legitimacy of judicial decisions, or compliance with those decisions, than ensuring their actual legitimacy.[37] And it may apply among institutions that are unequal in power, not simply those that enjoy a "heterarchical" relationship.[38]

3. Narrative

Constitutional decisions, as Robert Cover noted, can announce legal rules.[39] But those rules do not exist or operate "apart from the narratives that locate [them] and give [them] meaning."[40] Legal norms also gain both force and meaning from two broad forms of narrative: universalistic or particularistic narratives, or what Cover called "imperialist" and "paedic" norms.[41] The *coexistence* of these norms was especially significant for Cover. Both play a role in sustaining a legal order, but paedic norms in particular "*create* the normative worlds in which law is predominantly a system of meaning rather than an imposition of force."[42]

Indeed, philosophers, such as Thomas Nagel, suggest that the coexistence of narratives of this kind reflects an inherent tension in the nature of political

---

[33] *Compare* Rosalind Dixon, *Constitutional Drafting and Distrust*, 13 INT'L J. CONST. L. 819 (2015).
[34] *Id.*
[35] *Compare* Elizabeth S. Anderson & Richard H. Pildes, *Expressive Theories of Law: A General Restatement*, 148 U. PA. L. REV. 1503 (2000).
[36] Harel & Shinar, *The Real Case for Judicial Review*, *supra* note 7, at 17–27; Harel & Kahana, *Between Judicial and Legislative Supremacy*, *supra* note 7.
[37] *Compare* Roger Masterman & Jo Murkens, *Skirting Supremacy and Subordination: The Constitutional Authority of the United Kingdom Supreme Court*, PUBLIC LAW 800 (2013).
[38] Kavanagh, *supra* note 25.
[39] Robert M. Cover, *Foreword: Nomos and Narrative*, 97 HARV. L. REV. 4 (1983).
[40] *Id.* at 4.
[41] *Id.* at 11–14.
[42] *Id.* See also Robert Cover, *Violence and the Word*, 95 YALE L. J. 1601 (1986).

obligations in a constitutional democracy. Individuals in a political community have both impartial and partial obligations, or impersonal and personal perspectives on questions of justice.[43] Part of the role of political institutions is to mediate this tension between the demands of impersonal and personal notions of justice—or to allow individuals to integrate impersonal and personal perspectives, or understand notions of political obligation through the notion of what is reasonable according to both these perspectives.[44]

Political scientists likewise emphasize the power of different *narratives* to shape public attitudes or responses to certain ideas or issues.[45] Survey evidence suggests that citizens in most democracies have some commitment to global or universal values, including in the form of international law, but also to more specific national or local values and priorities.[46]

Often, courts that appeal to both universalist and particularized constitutional values (i.e., "glocalized values") will therefore have a greater capacity to promote respect for their decisions than courts that adopt either a more singularly global or local approach: doing so allows courts to cite both impersonal and personal values, or national and local values, in ways that can appeal to a broader range of viewpoints *and* citizens.[47]

Of course, there will be variation across countries in the degree to which this in fact helps build support for a court or its decisions. Global norms have traditionally enjoyed quite high degrees of support in most countries, but some countries are witnessing a turn toward an increasingly nationalistic form of politics, or constitutional culture, which openly rejects the idea of shared global norms.[48]

---

[43] THOMAS NAGEL, EQUALITY AND PARTIALITY (1995).
[44] *Id.* at 17–18.
[45] *See, e.g.*, Brett Davidson, *The Role of Narrative Change in Influencing Policy*, ON THINK TANKS (Jul. 10, 2016), <https://onthinktanks.org/articles/the-role-of-narrative-change-in-influencing-policy/. *See also* Robert J. Shiller, *Narrative Economics*, 107 AM. ECON. REV. 967 (2017) (on narrative as an influence on public perceptions about economic growth and outcomes, and therefore also economic behavior); Alexander B. Murphy, *Advancing Geographical Understanding: Why Engaging Grand Regional Narratives Matters*, 3 DIALOGUES IN HUM. GEOGRAPHY 131 (2013) (on narrative as an influence on human geography).
[46] *Compare* Mark A. Polack, *Who Supports International Law and Why? The United States, the European Union and the International Legal Order*, 13 INT'L J. CONST. L. 873 (2015).
[47] On the potential values of appeals to nationalist or nation-specific values, from a liberal democratic standpoint, see, *e.g.*, William Partlett & Dinesha Samararatne, *Redeeming the National in Constitutional Argument*, 54 WORLD CONST. L. (2021).
[48] *See, e.g.*, discussion in David Landau & Rosalind Dixon, *Constraining Constitutional Change*, 50 WAKE FOREST L. REV. 859 (2015) on Zimbabwe and Venezuela. In the United States, see also most recently the rise of "economic nationalist" rhetoric: *see, e.g.*, Monica de Bolle, *The Rise of Economic Nationalism Threatens Global Cooperation*, PETERSON INST. INT'L ECON. (Sept. 4, 2019), <https://www.piie.com/blogs/realtime-economic-issues-watch/rise-economic-nationalism-threatens-global-cooperation>; Adam Harmes, *The Rise of Neoliberal Nationalism*, 19 REV. INT'L POL. ECON. 59 (2012).

Equally, other countries are witnessing increasing internal divisions that threaten the entire notion of shared national or local values. Courts may play some role in constructing a notion of shared values—for example, by persuading either a public or elite audience that there is a connection between highly abstract national commitments (such as the repudiation of Apartheid) and more controversial, concrete values (such as a repudiation of separate systems of customary law, the death penalty, bans on gay sex, or unaddressed homelessness). But there may still be limits to courts' capacity to generate this sense of shared values while, at the same time, relying on those values to build support for their decisions.

In general, however, a multiplicity of overlapping but complementary narratives will help increase public support for the outcome of court decisions and this extends to different narratives that transcend or crosscut the global and local divide. Courts that use different narratives will therefore have greater capacity to build public support for their decisions, than courts that seek to explain or justify those decisions in more singular terms.

This is not to suggest that all judgments can or should have a narrative quality, or that every court can or should reason in a way that grounds its decisions in the stories of individual litigants. Most courts exercising abstract powers of review cannot do so, and some courts engaged in concrete forms of review may have good reasons not to do so, in certain cases. The point is simply that in the process of reasoning, courts should consider the value of relying on reasons that sound in universal and particularistic commitments to justice, or imperial and paedic norms.

C. Responsive Judicial Review and Judging: Building Support for LGBTQI+ Rights

Consider cases involving LGBTQI+ rights in India, South Africa, the United States (US), and elsewhere. In some ways, as Chapter 2 noted, *National Coalition I* was an "easy case": section 9 of the South African Constitution expressly provided that discrimination on the grounds of sexual orientation should be regarded as presumptively unfair and unconstitutional. A legislative ban on anal intercourse between men is also in clear tension with this provision. Yet the decision was made against the backdrop of notable opposition to gay rights among certain parts of the community, especially parts of the Afrikaner and Black Christian community.[49] In other ways, therefore, it was a

---

[49] *See, e.g.*, Louise Vincent & Simon Howell, *"Unnatural", "Un-African" and "Ungodly": Homophobic Discourse in Democratic South Africa*, 17 SEXUALITIES 472 (2014); Thomas Brown, *South Africa's Gay*

much harder case for the Court's sociological legitimacy. In striking down a legislative ban on sodomy as unconstitutional, the Constitutional Court of South Africa (CCSA) could expect to face significant opposition from at least some part of the population, including groups whose faith in the broader democratic project is essential for it to succeed.

The CCSA, however, approached the framing of its decision in a manner sensitive to the principles of responsive judging. In writing for the Court, Justice Ackermann appealed to universal notions of dignity, equality, and privacy, and the "jurisprudence of other open and democratic societies based on human dignity, equality and freedom" as supporting the conclusion that the prohibition of consensual anal intercourse between adult men constituted an unjustifiable limitation on these rights.[50] But he also pointed to the connection between upholding these rights and the "never again" of Apartheid, suggesting that "[j]ust as Apartheid legislation rendered the lives of couples of different racial groups perpetually at risk, the sodomy offence builds insecurity and vulnerability into the daily lives of gay men."[51]

Further, Justice Ackermann himself was one of the few members of the Court from an Afrikaans background.[52] And while liberal, progressive Afrikaners are clearly not core members of the conservative Afrikaans community, they share important cultural and linguistic ties with them. This was also the community (along with Black Christian conservatives) most likely to oppose the Court's decision.

The same pattern can be seen in *Fourie*. The CCSA in *Fourie* linked a willingness to recognize same-sex relationships to universal norms of equality and dignity, noting that a "democratic, universalistic, caring and aspirationally egalitarian society embraces everyone and accepts people for who they are."[53] It also connected this recognition to contextually specific commitments to

---

Revolution: The Development of Gay and Lesbian Rights in South Africa's Constitution and the Lingering Societal Stigma Towards the Country's Homosexuals, 6 ELON L. REV. 455 (2014).

[50] National Coalition for Gay and Lesbian Equality v. Minister of Justice, 1999 (1) SA 6, [26], [28]–[30], [37], [55].

[51] *Id.* at [26]. On this "never again" logic more generally in the Court's jurisprudence, see Rosalind Dixon & Theunis Roux, *Marking Constitutional Transitions: The Law and Politics of Constitutional Implementation in South Africa*, in FROM PARCHMENT TO PRACTICE: IMPLEMENTING NEW CONSTITUTIONS (Tom Ginsburg & Aziz Z. Huq eds., 2020)

[52] On his background, see Historical Papers, *Lourens (Laurie) Ackermann*, Constitutional Court Oral History Project (Dec. 6, 2011), <http://www.historicalpapers.wits.ac.za/inventories/inv_p dfo/AG3368/AG3368-A1-001-jpeg.pdf>; Jonathan Klaaren, *The Constitutional Concept of Justice L Ackermann: Evolution By Revolution*, in MAKING THE ROAD BY WALKING: THE EVOLUTION OF THE SOUTH AFRICAN CONSTITUTION 27 (N. Bohler-Muller et al. eds., 2018).

[53] Minister of Home Affairs v. Fourie, 2006 (1) SA 524, [60].

overcoming the legacy and practices of Apartheid—or "a radical rupture with a past based on intolerance and exclusion," or a "decisive break from, and a ringing rejection of, that part of the past which is disgracefully racist, authoritarian, insular, and repressive."[54] And in doing so, it sought to justify the decision to conservative Black citizens opposed to LGBTQI+ rights.

In addition, the Court showed overt respect for religious South Africans opposed to or disappointed by the decision, and for the importance and sincerity of their beliefs. It noted the importance of religious belief to many individuals' "sense of themselves, their community and their universe," and the important role played by religious groups in South African society.[55] But it also explained to religious opponents of same-sex marriage why respect for their faith and identity did not compel rejection of the petitioners' claims. Rather, the Court held that the "hallmark of an open and democratic society is its capacity to accommodate and manage difference of intensely held world views and lifestyles in a reasonable and fair manner," and that the role of the Court was itself to promote a "mutually respectful co-existence between the secular and the sacred", and not to 'force the one into the sphere of the other.'"[56]

The opinion in *Fourie* was written by Albie Sachs, one the members of the Court with the longest record of service to the African National Congress (ANC). Prior to his appointment to the Court, Sachs was a member of the ANC National Executive and Constitutional Committee, helped draft early versions of ANC's constitution for a democratic South Africa and contributed to negotiations leading to the transition to democracy.[57] He also lost an eye and arm from a letter bomb sent to him, as an ANC leader, by forces loyal to the Apartheid government.[58] He thus could be seen to speak with genuine authority to members of the ANC disappointed by the decision about what the Constitution itself required in terms of equality, dignity and a pluralist society.

In Colombia, in various decisions recognizing same-sex rights, the Colombian Court has relied on a similar mix of universalist (i.e., international and comparative) and particularistic reasoning. For instance, in *Decision C-075 of 2007*, holding that same-sex couples should be included in a common property regime for *de facto* couples, the Court held that the "prohibition on

---

[54] *Id*. at [59]–[60], citing *S v. Makwanyane* [1995] ZACC 3; 1995 (3) SA 391 (CC); 1995 (6) BCLR 665 (CC) [262]. *See* Dixon & Roux, *supra* note 51.
[55] Minister of Home Affairs v. Fourie, 2006 (1) SA 524, [89]–[90] (Sachs J).
[56] *Id*. At [94]–[95] (Sachs J).
[57] Albie Sachs, The Conversation, <https://theconversation.com/profiles/albie-sachs-316094>.
[58] *Id*.

discrimination based on sexual orientation stems from international norms that form part of the constitutional block," or that set of international norms directly enforceable under the Constitution.[59] And in *Decision SU-214 of 2016*, the Court called for submissions from the United Nations High Commissioner on Human Rights and Justice Albie Sachs, and then cited foreign cases, such as *Obergefell*, as supporting the close link between marriage, individual dignity, and equality.[60]

At the same time, the Court in these decisions relied heavily on notions of dignity, autonomy, and equality drawn from the text of the 1991 Colombian Constitution and the Court's own prior case law.[61] For instance, in *Decision C-577 of 2011*, the Court held that the existence of *de facto* relationship recognition was not sufficient to realize the rights to "free development of personality" and "autonomy and self-determination" under the Colombian constitutional order.[62] The Court also noted the series of earlier Court decisions recognizing the rights of same-sex couples (e.g., in the context of rights to property) and the support they provided for finding a deficit of protection in this context.[63] And the Court engaged in a close reading of the text of Article 42 of the Colombian Constitution, holding that the view that Article 42 restricted the definition of families to opposite-sex couples was incompatible with the variety of family forms in Colombia, and the provision in Article 5 of the Constitution for the "family as the basic institution of society." Hence, the Court held that Article 42 should be given a broader, more purposive and less exhaustive interpretation that supported rather than undermined the case for same-sex relationship recognition.[64]

In addition, the Court explicitly affirmed the importance of Congress' role in contributing to the resolution of debates over the recognition of same-sex marriage. And the Court's (unanimous) opinion was authored by Justice Gabriel Eduardo Mendoza Martelo, a former municipal judge and justice of the Council of State, who was arguably one of the most religiously conservative

---

[59] Manuel José Cepeda Espinosa & David E. Landau, Colombian Constitutional Law: Leading Cases 88 (2017) (on the Court's reasoning) and 26–27 (on the constitutional block doctrine in Colombia more generally). *See also* David Landau, *Judicial Role and the Limits of Constitutional Convergence in Latin America*, in Comparative Constitutional Law in Latin America 234–35 (Rosalind Dixon & Tom Ginsburg eds., 2017).

[60] Espinosa & Landau, *supra* note 59, at 98; Adriana Piatti-Crocker & Jason Pierceson, *Unpacking the Backlash to Marriage Equality in Latin America*, Paper presented at WPSA Annual Meeting, San Francisco, Mar. 29–31, 2018, at 11, <http://www.wpsanet.org/papers/docs/crocker_pierceson_wpsa.pdf>.

[61] Espinosa & Landau, *supra* note 59, at 86, 91–97.

[62] *Id.* at 94

[63] *Id.*

[64] *Id.* at 92–93.

members of the Court.⁶⁵ Both the tone, and authorship, of the Court's opinion thus sought to persuade rather than alienate governmental and religious opponents of same-sex marriage.

Likewise in India, in *Johar*, the Supreme Court of India (SCI) reasoned in a way that combined universalistic and contextually specific forms of justification for the recognition of LGBTQI+ rights.⁶⁶ This was evident in all four separate opinions in the case—that is, the judgments of (then) Chief Justice Misra (for himself and Justice Khanwilkar) and Justices Nariman, Chandrachud, and Malhotra. But it was especially notable in the judgments of Chief Justice Misra and Justice Chandrachud. Both judgments relied on universal understandings of autonomy, dignity, privacy, and equality as underpinning the protection of LGBTQI+ rights to sexual freedom, but connected these ideas to specific historical and contemporary commitments in India to a dynamic and "transformative" model of constitutionalism, the elimination of caste and hierarchy, the preamble to and directive principles of state policy found in Part IV of the Indian Constitution, and a distinctly Indian form of "constitutional morality."⁶⁷ Both surveyed international human rights law principles and precedents, and comparative decisions from the European Union (EU), the United Kingdom (UK), the United States, Canada, South Africa, Israel, the Caribbean, Fiji, Nepal, and Hong Kong,⁶⁸ but also emphasized the continuities between the reasoning in *Johar* and earlier decisions of the SCI in *NALSA* and *Puttaswamy*.⁶⁹ Justice Chandrachud in particular cited a range of liberal political theorists, including

---

⁶⁵ *Id.* at 86. The judge who authored Decision C-075 of 2007 (Rodrigo Escobar Gil J.) was also religiously conservative: *see* Landau, *Judicial Role and the Limits of Constitutional Convergence in Latin America*, *supra* note 59, at 234.

⁶⁶ *See* Robert Wintemute, *Lesbian, Gay, Bisexual and Transgender Human Rights in India: From Naz Foundation to Navtej Singh Johar and Beyond*, 12 NUJS L. Rev. 3 (2019). For praise for *Naz* for doing the same thing, see also Madhav Khosla, *Inclusive Constitutional Comparison: Reflections on India's Sodomy Decision*, 59 Am J Comp Law 909 (2011); Sujit Choudhry, How to Do Comparative Constitutional Law in India: Naz Foundation, Same Sex Rights, and Dialogical Interpretation, *in* Comparative Constitutionalism in South Asia (Sunil Khilnani et al., eds., 2013). The SCI in *Koushal*, in contrast, took a notably more nationalist approach, and rejected the relevance of comparative or transnational approaches in this context. And for discussion and criticism of this aspect of the Court's approach, see Arun K. Thiruvengadam, *Forswearing "Foreign Moods, Fads or Fashions", Contextualising the Refusal of Khoushal to Engage with Foreign Law*, 6 NUJS L. Rev. 4 (2013).

⁶⁷ *See, e.g.*, Navtej Singh Johar v. Union of India, AIR 2018 SC 4321, Misra CJ at [88]–[94] (dynamic constitutional tradition); [110] (transformative constitutionalism); [96] (preamble); [114] (Ambedkar); [116] (constitutional morality); Chandrachud J. at [91] (directive principles and health); [141]–[145] (constitutional morality), p 198 (transformative constitutionalism). For the suggestion that the Court could have done more to rely on and develop an anti-caste based form of reasoning and rhetoric in this context, see Gee Imaan Semmalar, *Re-Cast(e)ing Navtej Singh v. Union of India*, 13 NUJS L. Rev. 3 (2020).

⁶⁸ Navtej Singh Johar v. Union of India, AIR 2018 SC 4321, Misra CJ at [191]–[204] and Chandrachud J at [98]–[124].

⁶⁹ National Legal Services Authority (NALSA) vs. Union of India, AIR 2014 SC 1863, Misra CJ at [33], [160]; Chandrachud J at paras [35]–[36]–[52]–[55].

John Stuart Mill, Immanuel Kant, Jeremy Bentham, and John Rawls, the Hart–Devlin debate on the decriminalization of sodomy in the United Kingdom, and more contemporary critical theorists from the United States, such as equality and queer theorists Andrew Koppelman and Eve Sedgwick,[70] *together with* a range of contemporary Indian constitutional thinkers—including one of the key framers of the Constitution, B.R. Ambedkar.[71]

The SCI in *NALSA* adopted a similar approach. In finding that discrimination on the grounds of sex extended to discrimination based on gender identity, the SCI cited the Universal Declaration of Human Rights, international human rights law, and comparative developments in the United Kingdom, the Netherlands, Germany, Australia, Canada, Argentina, and the European Union.[72] But the Court also cited first-person accounts of the transgender experience of young Indians, and Indian scholarship and reports on the distinctive history and experience of the transgender community in India. The Court relied on the Directive Principles of state policy in Part IV of the Constitution as informing its approach to the construction of Articles 19 and 21.[73]

A similar approach can be observed in the United States in decisions of the US Supreme Court recognizing LBGTQI+ rights. *Obergefell* is a leading example. While controversial, the decision was effective in bringing about broad legal change in the recognition of same-sex marriage in the United States.[74] And the Court's opinion had many of the hallmarks of strategic judicial choices about authorship, narrative, and tone. Like *Romer v. Evans* and *Lawrence v. Texas*,[75] the decision of the Court was authored by Justice Kennedy, the leading Republican-appointed justice on the Court in favor of reading the Fourteenth Amendment to protect LGBTQI+ rights.[76]

The Court's opinion combined references to comparative and state-level legislative trends within the United States, and universal and American values. It thus drew upon both general principles of liberty, equality, and dignity, but also the distinctive importance of marriage in the *American* social order, citing de

---

[70] *Id.*, Chandrachud J at [65] (on Rawls), [127] (on Kant), [129]–[131] (on Mill and Bentham), [133]–[134] (on the Hart-Devlin debate), [46] (on Koppelman), [57] (on Sedgwick).

[71] *See, id.* at [106] (citing T Khaitan), [172] (citing D Jain and K Rhoten), [315] (citing M Galanter), [141]–[143] (citing Ambedkar on fraternity and the elimination of inequality).

[72] *Id.*, [35]–[42].

[73] *Id.*, [43]–[46].

[74] For a broader exploration of the decision's significance in this context, see Michaela Hailbronner, *Constructing the Global Constitutional Canon: Between Authority and Criticism*, 69 U. Toronto L.J. 258 (2019).

[75] 517 U.S. 620 (1996); 539 U.S. 588 (2003).

[76] *Supreme Court Justice Anthony Kennedy Will Retire*, N.Y. Times, Jun. 27, 2018, <https://www.nytimes.com/2018/06/27/us/politics/anthony-kennedy-retire-supreme-court.html>.

Tocqueville for the idea that there is "no country in the world where the tie of marriage is so much respected as in America."[77]

It also explicitly affirmed the good faith of those who disagreed with its decision, especially religious believers, noting that much of the opposition to same-sex marriage was based on "decent and honorable religious or philosophical premises," and that neither opponents "nor their beliefs" were disparaged by the decision.[78] But like the Court in *Fourie*, the Court explained why this was insufficient to favor rejection of the petitioners' claim, noting that "when that sincere, personal opposition becomes enacted law and public policy, the necessary consequence is to put the imprimatur of the state itself on an exclusion that soon demeans or stigmatizes those whose own liberty is then denied."[79]

The same is true of *Bostock*, the decision of the Court holding that the prohibition on discrimination on the grounds of sex under Title VII of the *Civil Rights Act* 1964 extends to discrimination against gays and lesbians *and* transgender Americans. The decision had several hallmarks of responsive judging. It expressly acknowledged the legitimacy of the concern, on the part of opponents of the decision, that protections of this kind could undermine religious freedom, noting that free exercise of religion lies "at the heart of [a] pluralistic society."[80] It further suggested that these concerns might give rise to claims for certain exceptions to be recognized, in future cases.[81] The opinion of the Court was written by Justice Gorsuch, the first member of the Supreme Court appointed by President Trump and a committed *legal* conservative (i.e., textualist).[82] The authorship of the opinion thus sent a powerful message to religious conservatives disappointed by the decision that the Court understood their concerns, both religious and constitutional, and had taken those concerns seriously in arriving at its decision.[83]

This may not have been enough to persuade religious conservatives of the correctness of the decision. Many Republicans regard Justice Kennedy as a "Republican in name only" (RINO), or member of the coastal elite rather than a true representative of Republican voters, especially evangelical

---

[77] Obergefell v. Hodges, 576 U.S. 644, 647–48, 652–54, 656–57, 660 (2015).
[78] *Id.* at 663.
[79] *Id.*
[80] Bostock, *supra* note 19.
[81] *Id.* at 32.
[82] Nina Totenberg, *Supreme Court Delivers Major Victory to LGBTQ Employees*, NPR (Jun. 15, 2020), <https://www.npr.org/2020/06/15/863498848/supreme-court-delivers-major-victory-to-lgbtq-employees>; Alexander Chen, *Gay Rights and Trans Rights Are Indivisible: SCOTUS Just Showed Why*, WilmerHale Legal Serv. Ctr. (Jun. 19, 2020), <https://legalservicescenter.org/alexander-chen-gay-rights-and-trans-rights-are-indivisible-scotus-just-showed-why/>.
[83] *Compare* Ezra Ishmael Young, *Bostock is a Textualist Triumph*, Jurist (Jun. 25, 2020), <https://www.jurist.org/commentary/2020/06/ezra-young-bostock-textualist-triumph/>.

Christians.[84] Justice Gorsuch's opinion for the majority in *Bostock* was also accompanied by a highly critical dissent by another Trump appointee, Justice Kavanaugh, and the reaction to the decision among conservatives was not positive.[85] But the Court's responsive approach may still have increased the willingness of key actors to comply with the decisions. Compliance with *Obergefell* has been widespread even in many Republican-controlled states, and President Trump acknowledged the need to respect the Court's authority in *Bostock*—despite opposing the relevant position before the Court, and adopting parallel attempts to wind back transgender rights in healthcare.[86]

D. Responsive Judging and the Democratic Minimum Core

Responsive judging tools and techniques can likewise help bolster the perceived legitimacy of attempts by courts to protect the democratic minimum core. Consider the recent constitutional experience of Fiji. Since gaining independence, Fiji has witnessed three separate military coups overthrowing a democratic government, the first in 1987, bringing Lieutenant-General Sitiveni Rabuka to power.[87] The second occurred in 2000, led by General George Speight, and the third in 2006, led by Commodore Frank Bainimarama. Fiji courts were also called on to review the legality of both coup attempts. In one case, *Prasad v. Fiji*, the court succeeded in restoring democratic constitutional rule, whereas in the other, *Qarase v. Bainimarama*, its decision provoked a complete and immediate suspension of the democratic constitution.[88]

While there are many differences between the two cases, one key difference is in the degree to which the court in each case engaged in a form of responsive

---

[84] *See, e.g.*, Ed Kilgore, *This Day in RINO Betrayal!*, WASH. MONTHLY. (Mar. 19, 2012), <https://washingtonmonthly.com/2012/03/19/this-day-in-rino-betrayal/>.

[85] Bostock, *supra* note 19, at 1822 (Kavanaugh J., dissenting). *See, e.g.*, Josh Blackman, *Conservative Justices Do Not Need to Apologize for Making Socially-Conservative Rulings*, REASON (Apr. 23, 2021), <https://reason.com/volokh/2021/04/23/conservative-justices-do-not-need-to-apologize-for-making-socially-conservative-rulings/>.

[86] *See* Natasha Lennard, *Supreme Court Upholds Trans People's Workplace Protections: But Trans Lives Remain Under Constant Threat*, THE INTERCEPT (Jun. 16, 2020), <https://theintercept.com/2020/06/15/transgender-rights-supreme-court/>.

[87] Stephanie Lawson, *Indigenous Nationalism, "Ethnic Democracy," and the Prospects for a Liberal Constitutional Order in Fiji*, 18 NATIONALISM & ETHNIC POL. 293, 298 (2012). *See* discussion in Jon Fraenkel, *The Origins of Military Autonomy in Fiji: A Tale of Three Coups*, 67 AUSTL. J. INT'L AFF. 327, 333 (2013); Nicholas Aroney & Jennifer Corrin, *Endemic Revolution: HLA Hart, Custom and the Constitution of the Fiji Islands*, 45 J. LEGAL PLURALISM & UNOFFICIAL L. 314, 324–25 (2013).

[88] Prasad v. Republic of Fiji [2000] FJHC 121; Qarase v. Bainimarama [2008] FJHC 241. The following discussion and analyses of these cases draw on Rosalind Dixon & Vicki Jackson, *Hybrid Constitutional Courts: Foreign Judges on National Constitutional Courts*, 57 COLUM. J. TRANSNAT'L L. 283 (2018).

judging—that is, delivered an opinion that showed a responsive approach to questions of authorship, tone and narrative.

In *Prasad v. Fiji*, in 2000, the High Court of Fiji found that the actions of the military in responding to the crisis created by the Speight coup—including the taking of various high-level government officials as hostages—were valid under the doctrine of "necessity."[89] But the Court also held that the 1997 Constitution remained in effect and had not been successfully abrogated.[90] The Court of Appeal confirmed that finding, holding that the contention that the Constitution had been abrogated was not supported by either the doctrine of necessity, or the idea of an "effective" constitutional revolution.[91] The Court further held that the Parliament had been prorogued rather than dissolved, that the President had effectively resigned, and thus that the Vice President was entitled to perform the functions of the President until a new President could be appointed.[92] Remarkably, the military and the interim government complied with the Court's ruling.

It is rare for a coup-installed government to respect a court decision purporting to invalidate the entire legal basis of the government itself.[93] Yet this is exactly what happened following the *Prasad* case. After Vice President Rata Josefa Iloilo was appointed as President by the Council of Chiefs, he called fresh democratic elections for August 2001.[94] Political parties allied with both ethnic-Fijian and Indo-Fijian interests further chose to participate in the election, and members of Speight's party ultimately agreed to form a coalition government with the ethnic-Fijian SDL party.[95]

---

[89] [2000] 2 FLR 115.
[90] *Id*. For discussion, see George Williams, *Republic of Fiji v. Prasad*, 2 MELB. J. INT'L L. 144 (2001); Noel Cox, *Republic of Fiji v. Prasad: A Military Government on Trial*, ALRJ 5 (2001). ; Anne Twomey, *The Fijian Coup Cases: The Constitution, Reserve Powers and the Doctrine of Necessity*, 83 AUSTL. L.J. 319 (2009); Brij V. Lal, "*The Process of Political Readjustment*": Aftermath of the 2006 Fiji Coup, in THE 2006 MILITARY TAKEOVER IN FIJI: A COUP TO END ALL COUPS? (JON FRAENKEL et al., eds. 2009); Venkat Iyer, *Restoration Constitutionalism in the South Pacific*, 15 PACIFIC RIM L. & POL'Y J. 39 (2006).
[91] Prasad v. Republic of Fiji [2001] FJCA 2. The Court also added certain findings in relation to the role of Bainimarama which were distinct from the findings of Justice Gates in this context. For discussion, see further Williams, *supra* note 90; Cox *supra* note 90; Twomey, *supra* note 90; Brij V. Lal, *supra* note 90; George Williams, *The Case That Stopped a Coup? The Rule of Law and Constitutionalism in Fiji*, 1 OXFORD U. COMMONWEALTH L.J. 73 (2001).
[92] *See also* discussion in Williams, *supra* note 90; Cox, *supra* note 90; Twomey, *supra* note 90; Iyer, *supra* note 90.
[93] Fraenkel, *supra* note 87, at 334.
[94] On the degree to which this is unusual in comparative terms, see, *e.g.*, Aroney & Corrin, *supra* note 87, at 324–25; Fraenkel *supra* note 87, at 334; Iyer, *supra* note 90, at 61–66; Williams, *supra* note 90, at 561.
[95] Fraenkel, *supra* note 87, at 334–35. The SDL won thirty-two seats, the Indo-Fijian-aligned Labor Party twenty-seven seats and Speight's Conservative Alliance–Matanitu Vanua Party (CAMV) six seats.

The bench that delivered the judgment was a truly multinational bench comprised of judges from New Zealand, Australia, Tonga, and Papua New Guinea (i.e., the Hon. Sir Maurice Casey, Sir Ian Barker, Sir Mari Kapi, Gordon Ward, and Kenneth Handley), and the Court issued a single *per curiam* opinion in the case. The Court adopted a tone of respect toward the government, which effectively assumed that steps had been taken to preserve rather than undermine democratic government. And the Court relied on a mix of global and local narratives—that is, on both international human rights law and the 1996 Fijian Constitution, and the degree of public approval it enjoyed during the period of consultation prior to its adoption.[96] Justice Handley in particular indicated that this reflected a conscious attempt by the Court to enhance the perceived legitimacy of its decision.[97]

This result, and approach, was in stark contrast to the decision handed by the Court several years later, in *Qarase v. Bainimarama*, following another coup—this time by Commodore Bainimarama.[98] In December 2006, under the leadership of Bainimarama, the military staged a coup to overthrow the elected government, citing the doctrine of necessity, and the need to protect Indo-Fijian interests. Bainimarama appointed himself as President, then Prime Minister, and Mahendra Chaudhry as a senior minister.[99] Once again, these actions were challenged before the Fijian courts. Initially, the High Court rejected these challenges, holding that the actions of President Iloilo in appointing Bainimarama as Prime Minister were a valid exercise of his prerogative power.[100] But on appeal, in *Qarase v. Bainimarama*,[101] the Court of Appeal held that Bainimarama's actions were illegal, there was no basis for his appointment as Prime Minister, and that the 1997 Constitution remained in full force and effect.[102] The Court therefore ordered that the President should appoint an

---

[96] Prasad, *supra* note 91.

[97] Interview with Handley Nov. 17, 2017. For broader analysis of the role of Fijian law and norms in this context, see also Aroney & Corrin, *supra* note 87; Theodor Schilling, *The Court of Justice's Revolution: Its Effects and the Conditions for its Consummation: What Europe Can Learn from Fiji*, 27 Eur. L. Rev. 445, 451 (2002).

[98] For discussion, see, *e.g.*, Justice Rachel Pepper, *Back to the Future: Qarase v. Bainimarama* (International and Comparative Perspectives on Constitutional Law Conference, Nov. 27, 2009), <https://lec.nsw.gov.au/documents/speeches-and-papers/PepperJ271109QARASEvBAINIMARAMA.pdf>.

[99] Qarase, *supra* note 88; *Bainimarama Appoints Himself President of Fiji*, Scoop (Dec. 5, 2006), <https://www.scoop.co.nz/stories/HL0612/S00089/bainimarama-appoints-himself-president-of-fiji.htm>.

[100] *See* Qarase, *supra* note 88.

[101] Qarase v. Bainimarama [2009] FJCA 9.

[102] *Id*. For discussion, see, *e.g.*, Pepper, *supra* note 98.

interim Prime Minister to advise on the calling of fresh elections. The government, however, chose not to comply with this order, and instead purported to abrogate the 1997 Constitution.[103]

Qarase was also a decision that *lacked* almost all of the hallmarks of a responsive approach to questions of authorship, tone, and narrative. The Court that decided the case was comprised exclusively of Sydney-based appellate lawyers and judges, Francis Douglas QC, Ian Lloyd QC, and Randall Powell SC, when Australia was widely perceived as exerting a problematic degree of influence over the government of Fiji.[104] In its reasoning, the Court was openly critical of Bainimarama's actions, suggesting that the actions of Bainimarama himself amounted to "a military coup or an unlawful usurpation of power."[105] And the Court placed strong emphasis on universal over local norms, citing the House of Lords, Privy Council, and comparative sources in the course of its opinion.[106]

Some of these dimensions to the decision may have been difficult to change (for instance, the composition of the bench, once appointed). There were also legitimate questions about the actions and good faith of Bainimarama himself, and whether the reference to global authority had the potential to increase the persuasiveness of the opinion for certain audiences, especially external ones, and those in Fiji with a cosmopolitan outlook or ties. But the Court did have the option of adopting a more conciliatory tone, and drawing on local as well as international jurisprudence, as a means of avoiding the perception that it was engaged in a process of colonial imposition rather than participating in a universal project of democratic constitutional protection. And in each case, the contrast with the decision in *Prasad* could not have been more stark. The Court's failure in *Qarase* even to attempt to engage in a more responsive approach, therefore, could be seen as predetermining that judicial attempts to protect the democratic minimum core would not succeed, when earlier experience in Fiji suggested that they might have been able to do so.

---

[103] Pepper, *supra* note 98, at 19–20.
[104] *See* discussion in Dixon & Jackson, *supra* note 88. *See also* Interview with Francis Douglas QC, Former Judge, Fiji Court of Appeal 27/6/17.
[105] *Id.* at [132], [162].
[106] *See* Qarase, *supra* note 88, at [80], [82], [97]–[98], [114], [117], [120], [121], [131], [163].

E. Responsive Judging: Limits and Cautions

What, if any, limits are there to judicial framing techniques of this kind? Can all courts engage in techniques of this kind? And are there any dangers to responsive judging as an approach?

1. Limits on responsive judging

Not all courts will be able to frame their decisions in this way. There may be important variation across countries in the degree to which the size and composition of the bench, and norms of judicial authorship (i.e., those relating to concurrence and dissent), allow full use of these tools and techniques.

Some courts have historically been quite diverse and included judges from a range of different backgrounds—including judges from different professional backgrounds, judges of different races, genders, religions, and judges identifying as gay, HIV positive, and with lived experience of disability.[107] Other courts have a much more limited history of diversity and a system of judicial appointment that does far less to produce diversity of this kind. And without some minimum degree of visible or professional diversity on the bench, it will be almost impossible for a court to ensure that its opinion is authored by a judge whose life experience speaks directly to the parties, or broader public.

Similarly, some courts may have a quite high degree of internal diversity, but a history of political or ideological polarization that limits the scope for the chief justice (or senior judge in the majority) to choose from among the entire bench when deciding who should write for the court.

Some courts may have a convention of randomly assigning responsibility for opinion-writing to certain judges.[108] And others, especially those in the continental or civil law tradition, may have a convention of unsigned or unanimous opinions, or convention *against* judges issuing dissents and concurrence in their individual name.[109] As Section B noted, concurring and dissenting

---

[107] *See, e.g.*, the past and current judges on the Constitutional Court of South Africa: at *Current Judges*, Constitutional Court of South Africa, <https://www.concourt.org.za/index.php/judges/current-judges>; and *Past Judges*, Constitutional Court of South Africa, <https://www.concourt.org.za/index.php/judges/former-judges>.

[108] This is true in Colombia, for example, and in some US Circuit Courts of Appeal.

[109] *See, e.g.*, Ruth Bader Ginsburg, *Remarks on Writing Separately*, 65 WASH. L. REV. 133 (1990); Rosa Raffaelli, *Dissenting Opinions in the Supreme Courts of the Member States*, POL'Y DEPT. C. CITIZENS' RTS. & CONST. AFF., PE 462.470 (Nov. 2012), <https://www.europarl.europa.eu/document/activities/cont/201304/20130423ATT64963/20130423ATT64963EN.pdf>; Katalin Kelemen, *Dissenting Opinions in Constitutional Courts*, 14 GERMAN L.J. 1345 (2013).

opinions can also play an important role in expanding the scope for a court to frame the authorship of different opinions in ways that speak directly to the losing party, or those in civil society disappointed by a court decision—including in cases where the court lacks discretion over the allocation of the lead author of an opinion.

There may be differences in the degree to which judges are known to the public. Some judges are widely known among lawyers and politicians and even among the broader public.[110] This may be because these judges occupy a specific institutional role (as president or chief justice of a court), or because of the substance and significance of their decisions. Or it may be a product of the media attention given to those decisions, or the televising of court proceedings. But public knowledge of a judge's identity and background will clearly be important to the capacity of that judge to speak to disadvantaged parties or groups.

Courts worldwide will also vary in the degree to which they issue lengthy opinions, accompanied by extensive reasons, or shorter judgments with only quite abstract justifications. In India, for example, opinions of the Supreme Court sometimes exceed 1,000 pages, whereas in France, the decisions of the *Conseil Constitutionnel* are often less than a single page.[111] This implies quite different opportunities for courts to use a mix of global and local narratives, or different persuasive techniques.

There may likewise be differences across countries in the degree to which there is public and media attention directed toward courts and court decisions, and thus obvious channels of influence for different approaches to judicial reasoning.[112] In the United States, for instance, Nathaniel Persily and his co-authors suggest there is often little public awareness of court decisions, and even less of the reasons behind those decisions.[113] There are clearly multiple publics for a court's decision, and certain elites, and the media, can play an

---

[110] *See* Rosalind Dixon, *Towering Versus Collegial Judges: A Comparative Reflection*, in TOWERING JUDGES: A COMPARATIVE STUDY OF CONSTITUTIONAL JUDGES (Iddo Porat & Rehan Abeyratne eds., 2020); Chad M. Oldfather, *The Inconspicuous DHS: The Supreme Court, Celebrity Culture and Justice David H. Souter*, 90 MISS. L.J. 183 (2020).

[111] Compare, *e.g.*, *Kesavananda Bharati v. Kerala*, 4 SCC 225/1973; Decision No. 2020-806 DC DU 7 AOUT 2020.

[112] In the US, see PUBLIC OPINION AND CONSTITUTIONAL CONTROVERSY (Nathaniel Persily et al. eds., 2008). *Cf.* in other countries: Jay N. Krehbiel, *The Politics of Judicial Procedures: The Role of Public Oral Hearings in the German Constitutional Court*, 60 AM. J. POL. SCI. 990 (2016); James L. Gibson et al., *On the Legitimacy of National High Courts*, 92 AM. POL. SCI. REV. 343 (1998); FLORIAN SAUVAGEAU ET AL., LAST WORD: MEDIA COVERAGE OF THE SUPREME COURT OF CANADA (2011); Joshua Rozenberg, *The Media and the UK Supreme Court*, 1 CAMBRIDGE J. INT'L & COMP. L. 44 (2012).

[113] *See* PUBLIC OPINION AND CONSTITUTIONAL CONTROVERSY, *supra* note 112.

important role as intermediaries between the court and the broader public.[114] But there may still be limits on the capacity of courts to persuade the public of certain positions.

In some cases, there will also be logical and political limits to the idea of comity in a court's tone. It is only in cases of doubt that a court should assume, at least publicly, that the conduct of parties is motivated by good faith. And in some cases, there may be little room for doubt of this kind. Parties before a court may have engaged in sufficiently *bad faith* conduct that it would be patently inappropriate for a court to credit their actions as carried out in *good* faith.[115] Doing so would simply add to the perceived legitimacy of that conduct, when in fact it is conduct that a court needs directly to confront and challenge if it is to protect and promote constitutional democratic norms.[116]

2. Democratic legitimacy versus legitimation

It is also important to note the potential for techniques of this kind to be deployed in ways that ultimately undermine, rather than promote, democratic legitimacy. Unlike the ideas in Chapters 3 to 7, which have a clear pro-democratic orientation, techniques of this kind may ultimately be deployed in aid of judicial approaches that either help overcome *or* compound existing democratic blockages or pathologies. And in the latter case, they may assume a distinctly troubling cast—as effectively co-opting members of disadvantaged groups, or the specific narratives that speak to those groups in aid of the *legitimation* of that disadvantage, rather than the promotion of legal or political legitimacy.

A potential example is Justice Frankfurter's opinion in *Gobitis*.[117] The petitioners in *Gobitis* were Jehovah's witness children who were expelled from their local US elementary school after refusing to salute the US flag at a pledge of allegiance ceremony. They (and their father) claimed it was against their religion to pledge allegiance to any authority other than God, and therefore that it was in violation of the Free Exercise Clause to require them to salute the flag

---

[114] *See* Kent Roach, *Dialogic Review and its Critics*, 23 Sup. Ct. L. Rev. (2D) 49, 54, 69 (2004); Roy B. Flemming et al., *Attention to Issues in a System of Separated Powers: The Macrodynamics of American Policy Agendas*, 61 J. Pol. 76, 84 (1999).

[115] On bad faith generally in a constitutional context, see David E. Pozen, *Constitutional Bad Faith*, 129 Harv. L. Rev. 885 (2015).

[116] In South Africa, for example, Roux and I argue that this is exactly what occurred in the *Nklanda* case, and what necessitated the shift in approach by the CCSA from an earlier posture of comity and deference to one of more direct confrontation with the threat of political monopoly: *see* Dixon & Roux, *Marking Constitutional Transitions*, supra note 51.

[117] Minersville Sch. Dist. v. Gobitis, 310 U.S. 586 (1939).

in this way.[118] In an 8:1 decision authored by Frankfurter, however, the Court dismissed their First Amendment claim. The petitioners' interest in religious freedom, the Court held, was outweighed by the government's interest in promoting respect for and allegiance to the kind of "ordered society ... summarized" by the flag as a national symbol.[119]

Frankfurter's opinion in *Gobitis* also displayed almost all the key hallmarks of a responsive approach to framing a judicial opinion. As a Jewish immigrant and naturalized American citizen, Frankfurter was the closest among the members of the Court to sharing the petitioners' experiences as religious "outsiders."[120] In the course of his opinion, Frankfurter emphasized the importance of religious freedom in a way that was respectful of the petitioners' claims and employed a mix of globalist and particularistic narratives recognizing the importance of religious freedom in the US constitutional tradition. The right of free exercise, Frankfurter suggested, was "a precious right" only "brought into question ... when the conscience of individuals collides with the felt necessities of society." He likewise suggested that "the affirmative pursuit of one's convictions about the ultimate mystery of the universe and man's relation to it [was] ... beyond the reach of the law." And he tied this to universal notions of the importance of religious freedom (as interests that were "subtle and dear") and the more specific struggles over religious freedom that led to the adoption of the Bill of Rights in the United States.[121]

Yet the decision was ultimately met with broad *disapproval*. Both at the time and subsequently, constitutional scholars have criticized the decision as adopting too strong a norm of deference toward state legislative authority, and as generally unpersuasive in its reasoning.[122] The decision was also criticized as insufficiently protective of religious freedom. Even President Franklin Delano Roosevelt and his wife, Eleanor, expressed their disappointment with the decision, and sought to counter its influence.[123] Only three years later, in *West Virginia v. Barnette* the Court reversed itself and held that *Gobitis* was "wrongly decided."[124] Frankfurter, however, continued to maintain his prior position,

---

[118] *Id.* at 591–92.
[119] *Id.* at 599–600.
[120] *See* Thomas Halper, *Felix Frankfurter and the Law*, 7 Brit. J. Am. Legal Stud. 115, 118–20 (2018); Nomi M. Stolzenberg, *Un-covering the Tradition of Jewish Dissimilation: Frankfurter, Bickel, and Cover on Judicial Review*, 3 S. Cal. Interdisc L.J. 89 (1993).
[121] See Gobitis, *supra* note 117, at 594.
[122] *See, e.g.*, Stephen W. Gard, *The Flag Salute Cases and the First Amendment*, 31 Clev. St. L. Rev. 419 (1982); Melvin I. Urofsky, *The Failure of Felix Frankfurter*, 26 U. Rich. L. Rev. 175, 178 (1991).
[123] Robert L. Tsai, *Reconsidering Gobitis: An Exercise in Presidential Leadership*, 86 Wash. U. L. Rev. 383–91, 402–04 (2008).
[124] 319 U.S. 624 (1943).

and explicitly suggested that as a member of "the most vilified and persecuted minority in history" he was not insensitive to the importance of religious liberty, but duty-bound to give effect to constitutional requirements.[125]

The substance of the decision in *Gobitis* is also hard to square with a responsive approach to judicial review. A mandatory flag salute requirement does not account for the full diversity of children's religious and philosophical backgrounds; and to that extent, any law that authorizes it suffers from clear blind spots of perspective.[126] It likewise ignores the possibility of allowing children to show allegiance other than by saluting the flag, in ways that evidence potential blind spots of accommodation. Rather than promoting democracy, deference to legislative constitutional judgments in such circumstances will therefore tend to compound democratic blockages. And a responsive approach to judicial review suggests that courts should orient processes of constitutional construction to *countering* such blockages.

The techniques of "responsive judging" should therefore be viewed with caution. In embracing these tools, judges should not lose sight of the substantive democratic values or goals they are designed to serve, or the need to tether them to an appropriately responsive or pro-democratic approach to judicial review. And observers of the court should be careful to maintain a distinction between the techniques of responsive judging and substance of responsive judicial review.

Responsive judging techniques can and often are used by courts in aid of countering democratic blockages, but they need not be. And to that extent, opinions that use such techniques should always be assessed with an appropriately critical and context-sensitive eye.[127]

3. A responsive judicial voice beyond the bench

This is true for responsive approaches both on and off the bench. Some judges have sought to communicate with the public beyond the courtroom—by giving speeches, issuing media releases, granting media interviews, and authoring

---

[125] West Virginia. v. Barnette, 319 U.S. 624, 646–47 (1943) (Frankfurter J., dissenting). *See* discussion in Stolzenberg, *supra* note 120, at 826–27.

[126] In *Gobitis* itself, there was no such legislation, but legislation of this kind was passed in a number of states following the decision. *See* discussion Gard, *supra* note 122.

[127] Rosalind Dixon & David Landau, *1989-2019: From Democratic to Abusive Constitutional Borrowing*, 17 INT'L J. CONST. L. 489 (2019); ROSALIND DIXON & DAVID LANDAU, ABUSIVE CONSTITUTIONAL BORROWING: LEGAL GLOBALIZATION AND THE SUBVERSION OF LIBERAL DEMOCRACY (2021).

opinion pieces explaining their decisions.[128] There is also a strong argument for courts framing communications of this kind in a way that is mindful of considerations of authorship, narrative, and tone. Framing of this kind increases the chances that relevant judicial communications are in fact effective in helping build support for the court as an institution or achieve the purpose they are designed to serve.

Whether courts should in fact engage in practices of this kind is less clear. Judicial outreach of this kind is patently inconsistent with a traditional view of judicial independence,[129] but largely consistent with evolving conceptions of the separation of powers in the Global South.[130] The harder question is whether they are in fact likely to increase a court's sociological legitimacy. There are clearly benefits to courts publicizing their opinions, especially when it comes to putting pressure on executive actors to comply.[131] Moreover, actions of this kind can help build increasing awareness of, and support for, a court's role in a new democracy.[132] This was certainly true, for example, in Hungary and Indonesia in the early years of the operation of those countries' constitutional courts.[133] But communication of this kind can also embroil courts and judges in broader media and political controversies, which they may be poorly equipped to respond to. And for some judges, it may encourage an expanded conception of their own role in ways that are ultimately quite dangerous to courts' perceived independence and institutional standing.

A responsive approach therefore suggests that any communications of this kind should be framed in light of concerns about judicial authorship, narrative, and tone, but that judges should be cautious about engaging in communications of this kind. Whether the benefits of doing so outweigh the risks will depend entirely on the specific sociopolitical context and should be carefully considered by a judge before deciding to engage in such practices.

---

[128] Jeffrey K. Staton, Judicial Power and Strategic Communication in Mexico (2010); Lee Epstein & Jack Knight, The Choices Justices Make 284–85 (1997); Rosalind Dixon, *Constitutional Design Two Ways: Constitutional Drafters as Judges*, 57 Va. J. Int'l L. 57 (2017).

[129] *See, e.g.*, Randall T. Shepard, *Telephone Justice, Pandering, and Judges Who Speak Out of School*, 29 Fordham Urb. L.J. 811 (2002); William H. Rehnquist, *Act Well Your Part: Therein All Honor Lies*, 7 Pepp. L. Rev. 227 (1980); Lord Dyson, Justice: Continuity and Change 31–32 (2018).

[130] On new separation of powers ideas and theories, developed with special attention to the Global South, see, *e.g.*, The Evolution of the Separation of Powers: Between the Global North and the Global South (David Bilchitz & David Landau eds., 2018).

[131] Staton, *supra* note 128.

[132] *See, e.g.*, Jimly Asshiddiqie, analyzed in Stefanus Hendrianto, *The Rise and Fall of Historic Chief Justices: Constitutional Politics and Judicial Leadership in Indonesia*, 25 Wash. Int'l L.J. 489 (2016); Dixon, *Constitutional Design Two Ways*, *supra* note 128.

[133] Dixon, *Constitutional Design Two Ways*, *supra* note 128.

9
Conclusion

Toward a New Comparative Political Process Theory?

A responsive theory of judicial review offers general guidance for courts as they seek to construe a democratic constitution, namely that in exercising constructional choice under a democratic constitution, they should:

(1) Seek to counter risks of antidemocratic monopoly power and democratic blind spots and burdens of inertia, and calibrate the scope and intensity of constitutional doctrines accordingly;
(2) Be mindful of inevitable limits on their own competence and legitimacy, which can lead to risks of reverse democratic inertia and democratic backlash, as well as broader risks of democratic debilitation; and given this, adopt a weakened—or weak–strong, or strong–weak—approach to the finality of their decisions; and
(3) Seek to actively promote the actual and perceived legitimacy of representation-reinforcing review of this kind by making careful and sensitive choices about: the authorship of, tone, and narrative used in judicial opinions.

In each case, the underlying logic of judicial review is a commitment to protecting and promoting the capacity of a democratic system to respond to minority rights claims *and* considered majority understandings under a range of real-world, non-ideal conditions. This translates into an embrace of both active and restrained judicial review in different contexts, and a carefully calibrated, contextual approach to the intensity of judicial review under both a US-style form of tiered scrutiny and test of structured proportionality.

Further, implicit in this approach is a "generic" notion of constitutional legitimacy. That is, it assumes that the legitimacy of judicial review derives from a combination of its responsiveness to minority rights claims and democratic majority understandings *and* consistency with formal modalities of constitutional argument within a particular system (such as the text, history, and structure of a constitution, as well as its prior case law).

A responsive theory of judicial review likewise combines elements of both strength and weakness—or breadth, coerciveness, and immediacy, together with narrowness, non-coerciveness, and delay—in judicial decision-making. It does so out of a concern to promote the revisability of judicial opinions, both as a matter of principle and pragmatism, or in order to avoid the risk of democratic debilitation, reverse burdens of inertia, and damaging forms of democratic backlash.

It further emphasizes both the principled and pragmatic value of courts making choices about authorship and tone that signal respect to losing parties, and reasoning in ways that draw on both global and local narratives. By taking this approach, courts can hope to persuade a broader range of actors of its preferred constitutional position but also show respect for those disappointed by a court decision, and their standing as citizens, and their right to a hearing in contexts where the law bears most harshly on them.

But how truly global in scope are these ideas? Does a responsive theory of judicial review in fact succeed in contributing to a form of new, truly "comparative political process theory"? The tension between judicial review and commitments to democratic self-government is certainly one felt in many constitutional democracies worldwide. The idea of the "counter-majoritarian difficulty" with judicial review is most famously associated with debates in the United States (US), and the work of Alexander Bickel.[1] But it is an increasing part of constitutional discourse and debate elsewhere. In Europe, for instance, countries that experienced fascist or totalitarian governments during the twentieth century remain firmly committed to the role of constitutional courts in protecting and promoting democratic values, including thicker democratic ideas of rights and deliberation. But they are seeing new forms of pluralism and polarization which strain the idea of shared constitutional principles and values, and put new emphasis on the need to engage with democratic values in ways that recognize the existence of reasonable disagreement about the concrete scope and content of those values.[2]

The same is true in many parts of Eastern Europe and the post-Soviet world, which continue to grapple with the legacy of communism but also new forms

---

[1] ALEXANDER M. BICKEL, THE LEAST DANGEROUS BRANCH: THE SUPREME COURT AT THE BAR OF POLITICS 181, 216 (1986). *See also* Barry Friedman, *The History of the Countermajoritarian Difficulty, Part Four: Law's Politics*, 148 U. PA. L. REV. 971 (2000).

[2] I am indebted to Marta Cartabia for this way of understanding the European debate.

of democratic pluralism and disagreement.[3] And it is arguably true in many parts of the Global South, where it is widely agreed that post-independence constitutions are designed to achieve constitutional independence, social and economic "transformation," and a truly democratic form of government, but where again there is significant disagreement or contestation over what the ideal of transformative constitutionalism means in practice.[4]

Inevitably, however, there will be variation in the degree to which these ideas have relevance in different contexts. Any constitutional theory has potential global reach but also geographic limits. Constitutional law is ultimately a mix of what might be considered "generic" constitutional norms and norms that respond to specific legal, social, and economic conditions and demands in a particular nation state, at a given point in time.[5] Constitutional theories, therefore, must also combine generic and more context-specific elements. Throughout this book, I emphasize the need for careful attention to the relevant legal and political context in implementing or applying generic constitutional principles, such as democratic responsiveness or representation-reinforcement, and I suggest that a court's capacity to engage in successful forms of responsive review will depend on a range of context-specific factors, including:

(1) A court's degree of formal and actual independence;
(2) The degree of political support for judicial review generally and in a specific context;
(3) The broader support structure for constitutional litigation in civil society; and
(4) The range of remedial tools available to a court.[6]

Without judicial independence, what appears to be an instance of responsive judicial review may in fact be a form of *abusive* judicial review in action.[7]

---

[3] William Partlett & Dinesha Samararatne, *Redeeming "the National" in Constitutional Argument*, IACL-AIDC BLOG (Feb. 1, 2022), <https://blog-iacl-aidc.org/new-blog-3/2022/2/1/redeeming-the-national-in-constitutional-argument>.

[4] *See, e.g.*, GAURAV MUKHERJEE, JUDICIAL PATHOLOGIES & LEGITIMACY OF TRANSFORMATIVE CONSTITUTIONALISM (work in progress, 2022); Karl E Klare, *Legal Culture and Transformative Constitutionalism*, 14 S. AFR. J. HUM. RIGHTS 146 (1998); Armin von Bogdandy et al. (eds.), TRANSFORMATIVE CONSTITUTIONALISM IN LATIN AMERICA: THE EMERGENCE OF A NEW IUS COMMUNE (2017); GAUTAM BHATIA, THE TRANSFORMATIVE CONSTITUTION: A RADICAL BIOGRAPHY IN NINE ACTS (2019); Michaela Hailbronner, *Transformative Constitutionalism: Not Only in the Global South*, 65 AM. J. COMP. LAW. 527 (2017); Heinz Klug, *Transformative Constitutionalism as a Model for Africa?*, in PHILIPP DANN ET AL. (eds.), THE GLOBAL SOUTH AND COMPARATIVE CONSTITUTIONAL LAW (2020).

[5] David S. Law, *Generic Constitutional Law*, 89 MINN. L. REV. 652 (2004).

[6] *See* Chapter 5, *supra*.

[7] *See* David Landau & Rosalind Dixon, *Abusive Judicial Review: Courts Against Democracy*, 53 U.C. DAVIS L. REV. 1313 (2020). *See also* Chapter 5, *supra*.

Abusive judicial review, as David Landau and I have noted, arises where judicial review actively furthers, rather than constrains, the erosion of the minimum core of democracy. And it can arise where courts are loyal to an authoritarian or would-be authoritarian regime, or else coerced or co-opted into upholding or advancing its objectives. The precondition for both of these outcomes is a lack of true judicial independence.

A lack of independence, or true political support for independent review, may also mean that courts have scope to engage in some, but not all forms of responsive review. For instance, in some settings the dominance of a single political party may mean that any attempt by a court to counter political monopoly would be futile or self-defeating, unless and until political conditions shift.[8] Courts, in dominant party democracies, might thus have the capacity to engage only in the strong–weak or dialogic, rather than stronger anti-monopolistic, forms of judicial review implicit in a responsive approach to the judicial role.[9]

Similarly, as Chapter 5 notes, not all *judges* will be equally well placed to engage in successful forms of responsive review. To engage in responsive judicial review, judges must be skilled in orthodox forms of legal reasoning but equally able to develop legal doctrines capable of countering democratic blockages. They must have the capacity to write in ways that persuade a broad range of audiences, and which draw on a tone and narrative that shows respect to diverse audiences, but especially those disappointed by a court's decision. This will mean understanding the perspective of those disappointed by a court's ruling, and the kind of tone and arguments most likely to be seen as responsive to their concerns. This also demands a considerable amount from judges in terms of their capacity for empathy—and even humility about the degree to which their own experiences and perspectives are shared by others.

To engage in responsive forms of review, judges must likewise have the capacity to anticipate and respond to limits on their own sociological legitimacy, or the perceived legitimacy of certain decisions. This will require a degree of political skill and sensitivity, including an ability to gauge the extent of democratic majority support for and likely political opposition or democratic backlash to a particular decision.

Whether judges have these skills will depend on a range of factors, including a judge's personal attributes, prior professional experience, and length of time on a court.[10]

---

[8] *See, e.g.*, Yvonne Tew, Constitutional Statecraft in Asian Courts (2020).
[9] *Id.*
[10] Rosalind Dixon, *Constitutional Design Two Ways: Constitutional Drafters as Judges*, 57 Va J. Int'l L. 1 (2017).

Successful forms of responsive review may also be self-perpetuating; the more experience a court, or judge, has in engaging in review of this kind, the more skilled they will be at navigating the tension between the dangers of overly strong and weak review, or between compounding versus creating new forms of legislative blockage. And the more accustomed the public and political elites are to the exercise of independent judicial review, the more they may support forms of review that aim to be representation-reinforcing in nature.[11]

This does not mean that only long-established courts can engage in successful forms of responsive review. New courts can and have succeeded in doing so. The Constitutional Court of South Africa is a leading example. The Court was an entirely new court established in 1994 to interpret and enforce the new democratic constitutional order created as part of the transition from apartheid.[12] And while members of this court had served previously on courts of appeal, those justices were in the minority. Most of the justices were practicing lawyers and academics with limited judicial experience, and yet together they created one of the most effective and respected constitutional courts worldwide, and a court that increasingly assumed an active role in both countering democratic blind spots, burdens of inertia, and risks of electoral and institutional monopoly.[13] But it does suggest that the likelihood of successful forms of review may vary, according to the country and its history of independent judicial review.

The political *valence* to responsive judicial review may vary across democracies. One of the recurrent arguments I make is that judicial review should seek to conform to legal and political notions of legitimacy, but also that courts occupy a unique role that effectively traverses the distinction between law and politics. Courts are able to help counter blockages or dysfunction in the democratic process partly because judges understand and are sensitive to political dynamics and processes. Furthermore, the status of courts as independent institutions, and judges' distinctive legal training, tools, and modalities of reasoning allow them to effectively identify and counter democratic blockages.

---

[11] Some of the most important factors influencing the chances of successful representation-reinforcement by courts will thus be those relating to judicial appointment and retirement. *Cf. Cape Town Principles on the Role of Independent Commissions in the Selection and Appointment of Judges*, British Institute of International and Comparative Law (Feb. 2016), <https://www.biicl.org/documents/868_cape_town_principles_-_feb_2016.pdf?showdocument=1>.

[12] *Role of the Constitutional Court*, CONST. CT. S. AFR., <https://www.concourt.org.za/index.php/about-us/role>.

[13] *See, e.g.*, Rosalind Dixon & Theunis Roux, *Marking Constitutional Transitions: The Law and Politics of Constitutional Implementation in South Africa*, in FROM PARCHMENT TO PRACTICE: CHALLENGES OF IMPLEMENTING NEW CONSTITUTIONS (Tom Ginsburg & Aziz Huq eds., 2020); JAMES FOWKES, BUILDING THE CONSTITUTION: THE PRACTICE OF CONSTITUTIONAL INTERPRETATION IN POST-APARTHEID SOUTH AFRICA (2016).

In proposing a responsive approach to judicial review, I argue for courts to embrace this "dualist" understanding of their role and avoid an approach that is seen to veer too far toward either a wholly political or legal(ist) approach to the judicial role. Each of us, however, will conceptualize constitutional theory from a different tradition and vantage point, and therefore have somewhat different reactions to what it suggests about the judicial role.

In some countries, where there is an established tradition of robust and creative judicial review, the idea of responsive judicial review may be understood as a call for increased judicial restraint or for greater judicial sensitivity to limits on judicial competence and legitimacy. If the prevailing understanding of a court's role in a particular country is to protect minority rights (no matter what disagreement there may be as to the scope or priority of those rights), a responsive approach to judicial review may be seen as a variant of theories that call for increased constitutional "dialogue" between courts and the legislative branch, or weaker—that is, either more restrained or non-final—approaches to judicial review. Like these other theories, a responsive approach to judicial review emphasizes that in certain circumstances there are both pragmatic and principled reasons for courts responding to evidence of disagreement with their past or proposed approach to judicial review. This kind of responsiveness to political disagreement is also quite foreign to, or at least radical in, many constitutional systems with long-standing traditions of independent and strong-form judicial review.

Consider constitutional systems such as India, Brazil, and Colombia. At various times, courts in these countries have clearly issued quite broad and strong judicial orders that have had limited practical effect. A responsive approach to judicial review, in these countries, could thus rightly be seen as a call for a more restrained—and weak–strong—approach to judicial intervention that takes more seriously the limits on courts' own competence and legitimacy in certain cases.

Conversely, if the dominant legal tradition in a country is one of judicial restraint, the idea of responsive judicial review may be understood as a call for a quite radical expansion in judicial power or notions of judicial creativity. This would arguably be the case, for example in Japan, which has a long-standing tradition of judicial restraint in constitutional (if not sub-constitutional) cases,[14] and even in countries such as Australia, which has a longer and more

---

[14] *See, e.g.*, David S. Law, *The Anatomy of a Conservative Court: Judicial Review in Japan*, 87 TEX. L. REV. 1545 (2012). Another leading court in this category historically was the Supreme Court of Chile, but in recent years it has engaged in a more activist approach, of both a conservative and progressive variety. *See, e.g.*, Javier Couso & Lisa Hilbink, *From Quietism to Incipient Activism: The Institutional and Ideological Roots of Rights Adjudication in Chile, in* COURTS IN LATIN AMERICA 99

active tradition of *Marbury v. Madison*-style judicial review, but a legal culture that continues to prize a commitment to "legalism" and traditional notions of the separation of judicial and non-judicial power.[15]

Even in the United States, where there is a long-standing tradition of strong judicial review, the Supreme Court has adopted a relatively restrained view of its own remedial power, or the scope of constitutional implications capable of responding to systemic government inaction. It has certainly not adopted the kind of engagement remedy, or suspended declaration of invalidity, embraced by courts in Canada, South Africa, Colombia, Korea, and Taiwan, or the "unconstitutional state of affairs" doctrine adopted by the Constitutional Court of Colombia.

In the United States, a call for a more responsive approach to judicial review could thus, again rightly, be seen as a call for a quite significant expansion in the court's willingness to embrace novel constitutional remedies and doctrines—including doctrines capable of responding to systemic burdens of inertia, such as those that exist in relation to climate change and gun violence. Imagine the idea of a future (Democrat-majority appointed) court declaring an "unconstitutional state of affairs" in relation to the current level of gun violence in the United States, and imposing a twelve-month deadline for Congress to take action—or face the court itself imposing a default model of uniform background checks and a ban on assault weapons sales. Given the pervasive and persistent burdens of inertia in Congress taking action in this area, an approach of this kind would be entirely consistent with a responsive approach to judicial review. Yet it would clearly be quite radical within current US constitutional understandings. The same would be true for a decision by the court to require Congress to update the coverage formula under section 5 of the *Voting Rights Act*, or to adopt a more radical response to the threat posed by climate change.[16]

(Gretchen Helmke & Julio Ríos-Figueroa eds., 2011); Javier Couso, *Models of Democracy and Models of Constitutionalism: The Case of Chile's Constitutional Court*, 89 TEX. L. REV. 1517 (2010); Sergio Verdugo, How Can Constitutional Review Experiments Fail? Lessons from the 1925 Chilean Constitution (unpublished manuscript) (on file with author).

[15] *Compare* Theunis Roux, *Reinterpreting "The Mason Court Revolution": An Historical Institutionalist Account of Judge-Driven Constitutional Transformation in Australia*, 43 FED. L. REV. 1 (2015); Rosalind Dixon, *The High Court and Dual Citizenship: Zines and Constitutional Method 30 Years On*, in CURRENT ISSUES IN AUSTRALIAN CONSTITUTIONAL LAW: TRIBUTES TO PROFESSOR LESLIE ZINES (John Griffiths & James Stellios eds., 2020).

[16] On s 5 of the *Voting Rights Act*, see *Shelby County v. Holder*, 570 U.S. 529, 534–47, 549, 553 (2013) (Roberts CJ). On climate change decisions of this kind, compare *Leghari v. Federation of Pakistan* HCJD/C-121, and recent decisions of the German Federal Constitutional Court: BVerfG, 1 BvR 2656/18, 1 BvR 78/20, 1 BvR 96/20, 1 BvR 288,20 (Mar. 14, 2021), <https://www.bundesverfassungsgericht.de/SharedDocs/Entscheidungen/DE/2021/03/rs20210324_1bvr265618.html>.

Similarly, the valence to responsive judicial review may differ, depending on the degree to which judges already embrace the notion of judicial statecraft, either publicly or in the context of confidential deliberations within a court. In some contexts, an existing appreciation of pragmatic considerations by judges may mean that the ideas set out in Chapters 4, 7, and 8 are seen as quite orthodox, or having limited additional value beyond the ideas that judges already intuitively apply, as part of a concern to promote a form of principled yet pragmatic approach to the judicial role.[17] I would still suggest there is value for these judges in engaging with a more formalized and explicit account of this kind of approach. But the benefits to doing so will be modest; it may offer useful clarification and sharpening of an existing approach but not any radically new insight or source of guidance.

In other contexts, however, the notion of judicial statecraft may be much more foreign. Judges may approach their role with much greater focus on principle, over pragmatism, and give little consideration to how they might frame their opinions—in ways that both increase support for the implementation of court orders, and the actual legitimacy of those orders as capable of responding to the distinctive position, identity, and experience of those disappointed by court decisions.

There may also be some difference in the degree to which a responsive approach to judicial review fits with existing common law versus civilian constitutional traditions. The idea of responsive judicial review draws explicitly on theories of responsive law and regulation that have been developed in Germany, as well as in the United States and Australia. This book also draws at various points on examples of responsive judicial review in civilian systems, including in Colombia, Germany, and Korea. This lends some support to the relevance of responsive judicial review as an approach that can inform and guide civilian as well as common law judges as they approach the interpretation and enforcement of democratic constitutional norms.

But there may still be some differences in the degree to which judges in different systems have the tools and perspective necessary to counter various forms of democratic blockage.[18] Blind spots, for example, are generally most effectively identified and countered by courts exercising concrete forms of judicial review, involving the parties adversely affected by a law, and not all civil law systems will permit or have a long-standing tradition of concrete review of

---

[17] Compare Roni Mann, *Non-ideal Theory of Constitutional Adjudication*, 7 GLOBAL CONST. 14, 38–51 (2018); THEUNIS ROUX, THE POLITICS OF PRINCIPLE: THE FIRST SOUTH AFRICAN CONSTITUTIONAL COURT, 1995–2005 (2013).

[18] *See* Chapter 5, *supra*.

this kind. Similarly, one useful tool for countering burdens of inertia will be the capacity of courts to help draw broader media and public attention to an issue, and not all courts will be equally well-situated to do so—especially if, as in the civilian tradition, they are staffed by government lawyers whose work does not generally attract broad public attention.

Constitutional theory, therefore, may provide a bridge across different (families of) constitutional systems but also an incomplete bridge, which cannot overcome the need for attention to the specific limits on such a theory in varying constitutional systems. My hope is that, over time, others will join me in considering what it would mean for courts to protect and promote commitments to democratic responsiveness within a much broader range of constitutional systems and contexts. If they do, we can also hope both to extend this bridge and perfect its foundations.

Index

For the benefit of digital users, indexed terms that span two pages (e.g., 52–53) may, on occasion, appear on only one of those pages.

Tables are indicated by *t* following the page number

abortion 81
  LGBTQI+ rights and 48, 49–50
  non-intact (D&E) dilation and extraction procedures 105, 202
  partial-birth procedures 202
  pro-life counselling 224
  restricted access to 53, 188–93
  right of access to 25–26, 27–32, 40–41, 48, 49–50, 57, 102–8, 158, 182, 195n.65, 198–99, 201–3, 208, 220–21, 224–25, 227–28, 236–37
  right-to-life movement 198
  rights 25–26, 46–47, 102–8
  Roe v Wade, significance of 27, 102, 182, 183n.4, 188, 198, 202
  same-sex marriage and 27–32
  sexual privacy and 27–32
  see also maternal health; pregnancy
accountability
  democratic 197
  electoral 62
  institutional 61
  judicial responsiveness, and 12, 196–97, 246
  political-legal logic 233n.145
  of political power 75
activism
  civil rights 54
  dialogic 233n.144
  judicial 96–97
  LGBTQI+ 111
  political 195
  social movement 172
advertising, political 33
advocacy, political 173–75
affirmative action 40n.91, 136, 137, 138–39
African National Congress (ANC) 71, 90–91, 109, 118, 235–36, 256

Ambedkar, B. R. 258–59
amicus curiae 144, 145, 174
amparo procedure 152, 239
animus 17–18, 45, 127, 223, 225
anticompetitive practices 78–79
antiretrovirals 118, 172
antitrust law 78–79
apartheid 4–5, 29–30, 71, 109, 254, 255–56, 275
appellate courts 18, 131, 151–52, 154
Arab-Israelis, rights of 48–49, 51n.144, 117
Argentina 152, 259
Arrow, Kenneth 150–51
assault, sexual 31–32, 191–92
assault weapon sales 277
Australia 9–10, 16–17, 176, 263, 264, 276–77
  Constitution 115, 116
  equality rights 26, 33
  High Court (HCA) 57, 115, 116–17
  human rights 177
  Law Reform Commission 116
  new Commonwealth constitutional model 210
  political system 115–16
  responsive judicial review 7, 278
  same-sex marriage 32
  sex discrimination 259
Austria 151–52
authoritarianism
  competitive 65–66
  stealth 59n.4
authorship, judicial 21, 245, 249–50, 257–58, 259, 260, 261–62, 264, 265–66, 269–70, 271, 272
autocracy, electoral 68–69, 138–39
autonomy, decisional 44–45

backdoor strong remedies 179
backsliding, democratic 56–57, 71–72, 138–39, 146
Badgley Committee 106
Bainimarama, Frank 261, 262n.91, 263–64
Bangalore Principles of Judicial Conduct 126n.137
Bangladesh 59, 68
banks, central 75, 148
Barak, Aharon 38
'baseline' of rights protection 46–47
Bayesian decision-making 184
Beetz, Justice 193
behavioral economics 184
Belgium 206
Benin 70
Bentham, Jeremy 258–59
Bharatiya Janata Party (BJP) 68, 112–13
biases 72, 125–26, 147
    cognitive 184
bicameralism 88
Bickel, Alexander 151, 226, 272
Biden, Joe 89–90
bills of rights 176–77
    Australia 43
    Hong Kong 30–31, 69–70
    New Zealand 176–77
    United States 177, 268
bisexuality 28
    see also LGBTQI+ rights
bite, 'with bite' logic 128, 233, 234n.151
Blackmun, Justice 188–89, 202
'blind spots', democratic 106, 117–18, 153
blockages, democratic 18, 106, 107, 178, 231–32, 241, 278–79
bodily integrity 26n.4, 39, 121
'boiled down' account 80–81
Bolivia 67–68, 155n.39, 170n.116
Bolsonaro, Jair 67–68
Bork, Judge 206
borrowing, abusive constitutional 73–74, 156
Botswana 32n.37
'bottom-up' models 230–31
Braithwaite, John 7
Brandeis, Louis 145
Brazil 29–30, 34–35, 42–43, 67–68, 128–29, 152, 276
    Constitution 29–30
    structural social rights 49

breaches of constitutional rights 17–18, 178–79
broadcast media 127–28
budgets 119, 164–65, 170, 183
Building Bridges Commission 36–37, 167
Bulgaria 65–66
burdens, democratic 107–8, 149–50, 188–89
    of inertia 2, 6, 60
bureaucratic inertia 56–57, 121–22, 222
Burundi 70, 170n.116
Bushell, Alison 186–87
business community/practices 69–70, 78–79

cadre deployment 76–77
Calabresi, Guido 83
Cambodia 68–69
Cambodian People's Party (CPP) 68–69
Canada
    abortion law reform 28, 106–7, 193
    assisted dying 230n.129
    constitutional courts 16
    discrimination and equality rights 129–30, 136, 206–7, 211, 259
    LGBTQI+ rights 29, 49–50, 108–9, 158–59, 258–59
    proportionality doctrine 128–29
    Supreme Court (SCC) 101, 158–59, 186–87, 206
    weak and strong judicial review 9–10, 214, 215–16, 216t, 277
capabilities approach (CA) 39
Caribbean countries 258–59
carve-outs, constitutional 136–37
caste 4–5, 136, 258–59
Catholic Church 109–10, 220–22
cautions 265–70
Cepeda, Manuel 55–56, 57–58
certiorari (setting aside/quashing decisions) 176, 210
Chan, Cora 130n.167
Chandrachud, Justice 258–59
charters 28–29, 129–30, 136, 158–59, 177, 205–7, 215–16
Chaudhry, Mahendra 263–64
Chávez, Hugo 67, 90
    'Chavez playbook' 74n.80
Cheung, Alvin 73–74

childbirth 202
    see also abortion; artificial insemination; pregnancy
children
    monitoring 238
    nutrition 120, 122, 163–64, 238
    religious background 267–68, 269
    same-sex parenting 42
    shelter, access to 239
    see also family
Chile 276–77n.14
    Recurso de protección 152n.28
China
    Constitution 128–29
    South China Morning Post 111
Choudhry, Sujit 75
Christianity
    Black community 254–55
    churches 188–89
    evangelical 260–61
    see also Catholic Church
civilian systems 18, 101n.21, 278
civil law tradition 38, 178, 212, 265–66, 278–79
civil partnerships 160
civil service 66, 126–27
civil unions 29–30, 159, 235–36
clientelism 148
climate change 35, 120, 121–22, 277
Climate Change Commission 35
coalition-driven inertia, forms of 84–85, 108–9, 118, 138
coercion, judicial 169–70
coerciveness 230, 272
cognitive bias 184
collegium 125
Colombia
    abortion legislation 107, 220–21, 236–37
    actio popularis 151–52
    childhood nutrition 238
    climate justice 119–20
    Constitution 36, 119, 122–23, 218, 257
    constitutional courts 16, 28, 29–30, 34–35, 42–43, 106, 120–22, 126, 174–75, 195n.65, 208, 211, 218, 220–21, 232, 238–39, 277
    constitutional system 276, 278
    Indigenous Authorities of Colombia (AICO) 174–75

internally displaced persons (IDPs) 164–65, 238
LGBTQI+ rights 49–50, 109–10
monitoring technologies 238
National Association of Displaced Afro-Colombians (AFRODES) 174–75
National Indigenous Organization of Colombia (ONIC) 174–75
same-sex relationships 159–60, 221–22, 228–29, 256–57
structural social rights 49
tutela petitions 152, 171
unconstitutional amendment doctrine 165, 166–67, 170
colonialism 31–32, 264
color see race
comity 250–52, 267
commercial speech 127–28
Commonwealth 16–17
    constitutional model 176, 178n.147, 206–7, 210
communism 209, 272–73
Communist Party 112–13
comparative political process theory (CPPT) 2, 14–15, 16, 55–56, 57, 271–79
comparativists, constitutional 143
compensation 136
competitiveness 72–73, 115–16
complaints 171, 238–39
confidentiality 147–48, 278
conscience vote 85
conscientious objection 220–21
consensus approach 49–50, 61–62, 112–13, 150–51
consequentialist approach 226n.114, 227
Conservative Party (UK) 110
conservativism 255
constitutional morality 98, 258–59
constructional choice 4–5, 20, 27, 43, 48, 55, 57, 58, 95, 102, 108, 223–24, 226, 271
    abortion 27–32, 40–41, 48
    constitutional theory and 37–43
    equality rights 33, 41–42, 48–49
    implied speech 33, 48–49
    judicial review and 27–37
    same-sex marriage 27–32
    sexual privacy 27–32, 41–42
    structural social rights 33–35, 42–43, 49
    unconstitutional amendment doctrine 36–37, 49

consumers 78, 86
continental law tradition 171, 265–66
contraception 50, 190–91
Copenhagen principles 63
Corporation Women's House (*Casa de la Mujer*) 174–75
Corrin, Jennifer 262n.94, 263n.97
corruption 76, 87, 218
  anticorruption commissions 148
counseling services 173, 190, 222–23, 224–25
courtesy, principles of 250–51
COVID-19 pandemic 122
creativity, judicial 96–97, 119–20, 276–77
criminalization
  abortion 224–25
  consensual sexual intercourse 30–32
  drugs 126–27, 208
  sodomy 258–59
criminal justice 46–47
criminal prohibitions
  abortion 28, 107, 158, 192, 224–25
  gay sex 32n.37, 41, 110, 112–13, 231–32
  libel/defamation 74
criminals 41
criminology 192
custodial sentences 52–53
customary law 254
Czech Republic 65–66

Dalits 136
Davis, Judge 239
decisional privacy 39, 40
declaratory remedies 176, 179, 180, 210, 214–15
decriminalization
  abortion 107–8, 224–25
  consensual sexual intercourse 30–31
  drugs 126, 208
  sodomy 112, 258–59
defamation 73–74
defection, political 73
deference, judicial 140–41
deferential review 1–2, 56–57, 128, 130n.167, 139, 141–42
degradation *see* democratic degradation
Delaney, Erin F. 19n.70, 215n.61
Delano, Franklin 268–69
Democracy and Distrust 1, 20, 27, 59–60, 80, 143
democracy-forcing constitution 200n.90

democracy-protection 17–18
democracy-sensitive theories 141–42
democratic accountability 197
democratic backlash 9–10, 20, 181–82, 185, 194–99, 201, 205, 209, 216–17, 221, 223–24, 225, 226–27, 240–41, 271, 272, 274
democratic backsliding 56–57, 71–72, 138–39, 146
democratic blind spots 106, 117–18, 153
democratic blockage 18, 106, 107, 178, 231–32, 241, 278–79
democratic burdens 107–8, 149–50, 188–89
  of inertia 2, 6, 60
democratic commitments 55, 62, 88–89, 112, 149
democratic constitutionalism 60, 125–26, 128–29, 146, 197, 240
democratic constitutions 4, 74, 76–77, 194
democratic debilitation 9, 56–57, 200–1, 204, 223–24, 236, 271, 272
democratic degradation 57–58, 71–72, 89
democratic deliberation 44, 47, 60, 88, 142, 151
democratic dialogue 181–82, 192, 194
democratic disagreement 5, 10–11, 88–89, 191, 217, 219, 223, 224, 227–28, 240
democratic dysfunction 1–2, 95–96, 135–36, 143, 175
  antidemocratic monopoly power 65–80
  concepts and notions of 20, 58
  courts and 2–8
  detection of 145–51
  effects of 240
  forms of 2, 95
  judicial strength and weakness 56–57
  relevance of 131
  sources of 3, 6, 10–11, 20, 64, 88–89, 139–40, 143, 154, 200
democratic elections *see* elections
democratic erosion 4, 15, 69–70, 76, 146
democratic experimentalism *see* experimentalism
democratic government 47, 74–75, 82, 212, 261, 263
democratic hedging 56–57
democratic inertia 10–11, 100, 117, 121–22, 181, 182, 188, 192, 201, 222, 223–24, 234, 237, 271

democratic institutions 55–56, 80–81, 90n.141
democratic legislation 2, 84, 156, 201
democratic legitimacy 47, 240
    legitimation vs. 267–69
democratic majority 2–3, 8–9, 10–11, 64, 83, 112, 149–50, 151, 155, 188–89, 190, 200, 208–9, 221, 274, 277
    understandings 8, 59, 61, 88, 96–97, 101, 104n.31, 182, 190–91, 271–72
democratic malfunctions 1, 47–48, 59–60
democratic minimum core 10–11, 14, 63–64, 65, 67–71, 73, 78, 79, 89–90, 95, 102, 124–26, 132, 133, 139, 147–48, 169–70, 205, 218–19, 264
    concept of 60, 61–62, 146
    corruption, effects of 148
    responsive judging 261–64
    stealth attacks 59
    threats to 6, 61, 115–16, 124, 139–40, 146–47, 166, 170, 199, 231–32, 240–41
    weak–strong judicial review, argument for 217–20
democratic norms 10, 73–74, 223–24, 267
democratic opinion 145, 149–50, 151, 153, 181
democratic pathology 153
democratic perspective 37–38, 63, 181, 191, 191n.53, 193–94, 210, 227
democratic pluralism 5–6, 157, 272–73
democratic politics 42, 44, 57, 82, 88–89, 201
democratic preservation 18–20
democratic representation 4–5, 27, 51, 144–45, 201
democratic responsiveness 8–9, 10–11, 15, 18, 20, 54, 61, 64, 95–96, 99, 100, 112, 132, 133, 172, 181, 182, 185, 194, 197, 199–200, 222, 224, 240–41, 273, 279
    promotion of 2–8
democratic self-government *see* self-government
democratic systems 3–4, 52, 61–62, 65, 72, 75, 84–86, 87, 88, 89–90, 99, 141–42, 271
democratic understandings 64, 85–86, 88, 103–4, 135, 149–50, 179–80
democratic values 1, 14–15, 45–46, 47, 49–50, 193–94, 269, 272
departmentalism 196–97, 209n.24

destabilization 18–19
    rights 56–57
de Tocqueville, Alexis 259–60
devolution of power 68–69
die, right to 114–15
dignity, individual 6, 38, 42–43, 116, 120, 135–36, 139, 140*t*, 256–57
disability 53–54, 128, 136, 265
disadvantage, political 53–54, 138–39
discrete and insular minorities 47–49, 51, 52, 53, 54, 89, 128, 135
discrimination
    calibration of judgments about 134–40, 140*t*
    elimination of 39–40, 48
    employment 29
    historical patterns of 53, 136
    human dignity and 53–54
    LGBTQI+ rights and 28, 29–30, 109, 110–12, 114–15, 160, 161, 254–55, 256–57, 259, 260
    non-discrimination principle 30–31, 33, 39–40, 44–45, 116, 208
    political actors, against 132
    positive 40, 136–37, 139–40
    unfair 129–30, 136
disease 120–21
    control 75
    see also COVID-19 pandemic; epidemics
disenfranchisement 46, 52–53, 83, 186
diversity goals 136
docket 154–55
doctor-patient relationship 103
doctrinal markers 217–18
documents, government/official 161
Dorf, Michael C. 7–8, 141–42
driving licenses 161
drought 163–64
drugs
    dealers and users 68–69
    decriminalization of 126, 208
    trafficking 68–69
dualist approach 276
due process 27–28, 46–47, 49, 103, 104, 105, 119, 203
Duterte, Rodrigo 68–69
Dworkin, Ronald 13, 44–45, 80, 225n.109
dysfunctional democracies 81

286 INDEX

Economic Freedom Fighter (EFF) Party 71, 90–91
economics 39
economists
  behavioral 184
  development 238
Ecuador 67–68, 170n.116
educational development 120, 163–64
effectiveness of judicial review 240
egalitarianism 44, 255–56
elections
  ballot boxes 72–73, 135–36
  democratic 227, 262
  electoral autocracy 68–69, 138–39
  multiparty 61, 65, 72–73, 79–80
Electoral and Boundaries Commission (EBC) 219–20
electoral irregularities 70, 219
electricity 118n.103
Ely, John Hart 1–2, 4–5, 13, 14–16, 20, 27, 47–58, 59–60, 65, 88, 89, 111, 128, 130, 132, 135, 143, 147, 151, 223, 226
Elyian approach/neo-Elyian scholarship 2, 47–58
emergency powers 66
empathy, judicial capacity for 274
employment discrimination 29
entrenchment problem 89, 147
environmental justice 119
epidemics 118, 162
epistemic approach 44
epistolary jurisdiction 171
Epp, Charles 171–72
Epstein, Lee 168
equality
  commitments to 112, 137–38
  constitutional doctrines 138–39
  economic 42–43, 191
  formalist view of 113–14, 134–35
  freedom of expression and 115–17
  guarantees of 136
  legal 38–39, 50
  liberty and 46–47
  of opportunity 40, 53–54, 134–35
  political 46, 138–39, 186
  principles of 47, 259–60
  rights 26, 30–31, 33, 39–40, 48–49, 53
  same-sex 235–36
  sexual privacy and 41–42
  substantive 5, 53, 136–37, 138–39

equal protection, right to 25–26, 28, 48, 53, 128
Erdogan, Recep Tayyip 66
erosion of democracy *see* democratic erosion
error, judicial 184
ethnic origin 136
ethnic violence 70
European Court of Human Rights (ECtHR) 62, 160
European Union (EU) 54–55, 62, 258–59
evaluative judgment 27, 40, 52, 88–89, 95–96, 130, 133, 146, 151
eviction
  forced 162
  formal housing, from 117–18
  orders for 162, 164, 229–30
  protection from 30–31
evidence-based approach 7–8, 75–76
experimentalism 56–57, 76, 229, 237–38
  democratic experimentalist approach 7–8, 141–42
extraction procedures 105, 202
  see also abortion

fairness 7
  electoral 76, 219–20
  perceived 246–47
  political process 132n.170
  responsive judging 246–47
Fallon, Richard H. 97–98, 226n.114
family
  basic institution of social, as the 257
  forced removal 162–63
  Hong Kong 111
  LGBTQI+ rights 110, 158–60
  life 42
  planning 199
  security 162–63
  see also children; marriage
famine 163–64
fascism 272
federalism 65, 88, 138
Federalist Papers 168
fetal life 27, 41, 188, 189, 190–91, 192, 202
  see also abortion
Fidesz party 65–66
Fiji 16–17, 59, 139n.192, 258–59, 261–64
Finland 206
first-order deferral 211–12

food
  preparation and delivery 237–38
  right of access to 33–34
  'right to food' campaign 163–64, 175, 238
  shortages 163–64
  see also nutrition
formalism 113–14, 136–37, 187, 234
France 151–52, 266
  Conseil Constitutionnel 266
Frankfurter, Justice 267–69
fraternity 259n.71
freedom, individual 5, 38–39, 43
'free rider' problems 86–87
functionalism 179
funding
  civil society groups 74
  counselling services 173
  federal allocation 199, 227–28
  political parties 33, 74
  school 33–34

Gallup opinion polls 188–89
Gandhi, Indira 165–66
Gargarella, Roberto 44
gay community
  citizens 65–66
  Gay Pride parades 109–10, 112
  marriage 221–22, 228–29
  media personalities 109–10
  men 255
  rights 108–10, 159–60, 195n.65, 254–55
  sex 32n.37, 41, 254
  see also LGBTQI+ rights
gender
  discrimination 50, 53
  equal protection clauses 128, 138
  government documents 161
  identity 30–31, 114–15, 160, 259
  minorities 53–54
  pay gap 52
  quotas 139n.191
  recognition 160, 234
  structural inequality 191
  see also LGBTQI+ rights; sexuality; transgender
Germany 7, 211, 259, 278
  abortion rights 192, 224, 236–37
  German Federal Constitutional Court (GFCC) 41
  Nazi rule 4–5

gift exchange 251
globalism 268
globalization 14–15
glocalized values 253
good faith 6, 12, 80, 88, 233, 260, 264, 267
goodwill 251n.24
Graber, Mark 85
grass-roots organizations 174–75
Greene, Jamal 248n.11
Greenhouse, Linda 188–89
Grove, Tara Leigh 199n.83
Guinea 70
gun violence 122, 277

habeas corpus, writ of 152n.28
Habermas, Jürgen 44
Hailbronner, Michaela 56–57, 96n.1, 259n.74
Hamilton, Alexander 168
harassment 72–73, 161
hardball, constitutional 89–90
Harel, Alon 247
Harlan, Justice 103
Hart-Devlin debate (sodomy) 258–59
hate speech 46–47
healthcare 26, 33–34, 41–42, 48, 90, 117, 120–21, 199, 220–21, 238, 260–61
hearing, right to a 12, 272
hedging, democratic 56–57
heterosexual models 42, 50
HIC 34
Hinduism 68
Hirschl, Ran 16–17
HIV/AIDS 109, 118, 162, 265
Hogg, Peter W. 186–87
'hollow hope' of change 13
homelessness 117–18, 162, 163, 254
homosexuality 110
Hong Kong 16–17, 258–59
  Basic Law 128–29
  constitutional system 69–70
  Court of Final Appeal (CFA) 30–31
  LGBTQI+ rights 49–50, 234–35
  media 69–70
  rainbow community 111
  remedies 211
horizontal constitutional checks 4, 59, 76
House of Lords (UK) 30–31, 110, 179, 212n.47, 264

housing
  emergency 117–18, 222–23
  national plans 172–73
  rights of access to 26, 42–43, 117–18, 119, 120–21, 238, 239
  shortages 161–62
human rights 63, 75
  abuses 218
  culture 214
  institutions 76
  international law 259, 263
  legislation 26n.4, 29, 30–31, 176–77, 214–15, 259
  norms 35n.62
  principles 258–59
  UK legislation 30–31, 176–77, 214–15, 258–59
Hungary 65–66, 270
Hyde Amendment 199

ideology, political 197
illegal actions 263–64
illegitimate court 197
immigration 41–42
impartiality 197, 247, 252–53
impeachment 55n.161, 67–68
imperialist norms 252
impersonal notions of justice 251–53
incompatibility, declaration of 176–77, 179, 180, 214–15
inconsistency, declaration of 176–77
India 123–26, 136, 164
  childhood nutrition 34–35, 119–20, 122, 163–64, 237–38
  Constitution 30–31, 36, 77, 124–25, 258–59
  constitutional court 16, 232
  constitutional system 276
  democratic minimum core 68
  democratic power, abuse of 77
  High Court of Delhi 112–13, 161n.64
  LGBTQI+ rights 49–50, 111–14, 161, 254–55
  Penal Code 30–31
  Rajasthan, drought and food shortages 163–64
  Reserve Bank of India (RBI) 148n.11
  structural social rights 49, 231n.132
  Supreme Court of India (SCI) 30–31, 112–13, 154n.33, 160, 171, 175, 200n.86, 208, 209, 229, 232, 258–59, 266
  transgender community 259
  unconstitutional amendment doctrine 36, 122–23, 165–66
Indo-Fijian interests 262, 263–64
Indonesia 270
inequality 44, 84, 122, 136–37, 191n.51, 259n.71
inhuman treatment 39–40, 44–45
injunctions 176, 210
  structural 230–31, 233
injunctive relief 222–23
injustice 64
institutionalism 5–6
insular minorities see discrete and insular minorities
insurance, health 192
insurers, health 220–21
integrity
  bodily, right to 26n.4, 39, 121
  democracy/electoral 62, 72–73, 76, 78–79, 85–86, 89
  legislative process 55–56, 57
  office 75
  personal, right to 30–31
  political process 132n.170
interdependence, notion of 251
internally displaced persons (IDPs) 34–35, 119–21, 164–65, 174–75, 229, 232, 237, 238
  see also refugees
interpreters, constitutional 16–17
interpretivism 51
intimacy, personal 41, 162–63
intimidation 69–70, 72, 219–20
Ireland 208
irrationality 193
Israel 16–17, 26, 32, 33, 48–49, 66, 116–17, 128–29, 206, 258–59
Issacharoff, Sam 56–57, 73, 74n.80, 81n.112, 81–62nn.114–15
Italy 211

Jackson, Vicki 16–17, 170n.115, 261n.88, 264n.104
Japan 125, 276–77

Johnson, Boris 54–55
journalists 66, 89–91
jurisdiction-stripping measures 196–97, 209
justiciability 211–12
justifiability 11, 98, 142, 248

Kahana, Tsvi 247
Kant, Immanuel 5, 39, 258–59
Kavanagh, Aileen 201, 251
Kelly, James B. 187
Kelsen, Hans 18, 151–53
Kenya 31–32, 36–37, 70, 123–24, 167, 219
Kenyatta, Uhuru 36–37, 70, 124, 167, 219–20
Khaitan, Tarunabh 148n.11
Klarman, Michael J. 195
Kleinlein, Thomas 133n.172
Knesset, *Basic Law* 26, 33, 117
Knight, Jack 168
Koppelman, Andrew 258–59
Korea, Republic of 16–17, 49–50, 106, 211, 277, 278
  see also South Korea
Kothari, Jayna 161
Kumm, Mattias 141–42

Labour Party (UK) 110
Landau, David 55–58, 60, 62, 71–72, 87, 156, 169, 233, 273–74
landlord's right to 'peaceful enjoyment' 179n.149
Langford, Malcolm, 8
lawfare, definition 73
'least common denominator' approach 63
legal aid 171
legalism 276–77
legitimation 267–69
LGBTQI+ rights 50, 102, 108–15, 161, 228–29, 234–35, 255–56, 259
  abortion and 48, 49–50, 198
  activism 111
  Canada 29, 49–50, 108–9, 158–59, 258–59
  Colombia 49–50, 109–10
  discrimination and 28, 29–30, 109, 110–12, 114–15, 160, 161, 254–55, 256–57, 259, 260
  equality and sexual privacy 41–42
  family rights 110, 158–60
  Hong Kong 49–50, 234–35
  identity and 112–15
  India 49–50, 111–14, 161, 254–55
  legal recognition of 28, 29–31, 108–10, 221–22, 234, 246, 258–59
  Mexico 29–30
  opposition to 255–56
  political support for 111, 254–61
  South Africa 49–50, 228–29, 254–55, 258–59
  United Kingdom 110
  United States 48, 259
  violence 159–60
  see also gay community; gender; lesbians
libel 74, 127–28
liberal democracy 68–69
liberalism 46–47, 62n.12, 66, 98
liberty, right to 103
  religious 267
litigants
  individual 171, 223, 230, 247, 249, 254
  responding to 11–12
Lloyd, Ian 264
'lumpers' 13
  see also 'splitters'
Lustig, Doreen 1
Luxembourg 206

macroeconomic management 75–76
Maduro, Nicolás 67
majoritarian decision-making 5, 112
  'counter-majoritarian difficulty' 272
  democratic politics 88–89
  groups 55–56, 57
Malaysia 68–69
Malema, Julius 90–91
malfunctions *see* democratic malfunctions
Mali 70
malnutrition 120, 121, 163–64
  see also food; nutrition
managerial judicial review 56–57
mandamus (making of a specific decision) 176, 210
mandatory orders 230
Manfredi, Christopher 187
Manitoba language rights 211
marijuana, criminalization of 126–27
market failure *see* political market failures

marriage
  equality 42, 235–36
  law 235–36
  Marriage Ordinance 30–31, 234–35
  opposite-sex definition of 29–30, 158–59, 231–32, 236
  same-sex 25–26, 29–30, 31–32, 41–42, 48, 49, 57, 109–10, 158–60, 183n.3, 222, 235–36, 256, 257–58, 259, 260
matching 158
maternal health 188–89, 190
  see also abortion
Mbeki, Thabo 118
media
  broadcast 127–28
  Colombia 166, 174–75
  court decisions 245, 266–67, 270
  gay personalities 109–10
  government 74
  Hong Kong outlets 69–70
  independence 54–55, 66n.31, 67, 68–69
  interviews 269–70
  regulation 65–66
  scrutiny 154, 155
Medicaid program 199
medical treatment 103
Mendoza Martelo, Gabriel Eduardo 257–58
mental health 107, 190–91, 220–21
Mexico
  amparo procedure 152
  LGBTQI+ rights 29–30
  Supreme Court 28, 29–30
migrants 66n.30
military *coup d'état* 59n.3, 139n.192, 261, 262, 263–64
Mill, John Stuart 258–59
minimal impairment 129
minimalism, judicial 213
minimum level of subsistence 119
minorities *see* discrete and insular minorities
misconduct 68–69, 156, 165–66, 219–20
Mongolia 206
monologic approach 230–31
monopoly 143–44
  antidemocratic power 2, 5, 10, 19, 20, 58, 60, 65–80, 99, 126, 132, 143–44, 155, 157, 169, 185, 271

electoral 12, 72–74, 78, 89, 123–25, 219, 240–41, 275
institutional 2–4, 5, 10, 12, 17–18, 20, 60, 67–68, 74–77, 78, 99, 102, 123–25, 146–47, 155, 240–41, 275
intent vs effect 78–80
political 3, 74, 81, 89, 95, 99, 104–5n.32, 116–17, 126, 184, 218–19, 246, 267n.116, 274
threats of 171
mootness doctrine 190, 211–12
morality, constitutional 98, 258–59
multiparty elections 61, 65, 72–73, 79–80
Muslim community, attacks against 66n.30
Myanmar 59

Nagel, Thomas 252–53
narrative 12, 21, 245, 252–54, 259, 261–62, 264, 269–70, 271, 274
'narrow tailoring' of laws 133
nationalism
  economic 253n.48
  nation-specific values 253n.47
'natural born' citizens 25
natural disasters 117–18
Nazism 4–5
Nepal 258–59
Netherlands 259
nevirapine 34, 118, 162, 173, 222–23
New Zealand 9–10, 176–77, 205–7, 210, 263
NGOs (non-governmental organizations) 54, 74
Nicaragua 67, 170n.116
Niger 70
Nigeria 70
nonbinary identity 160
non-coerciveness 204, 228, 238–39, 272
non-compliance 233
non-deliberativeness of the legislature 55–56
non-discrimination principle 30–31, 33, 39–40, 44–45, 116, 208
Nonet, Philippe 6
non-responsiveness, democratic 64, 88, 120–21, 222, 235
Nussbaum, Martha 39, 100n.17, 191–92
nutrition 119, 122, 163–64, 238
  see also food; malnutrition

Odinga, Raila 70, 124, 167, 219–20
ombudsman, national 75, 174–75
one-off court orders 228n.119
  coercive orders 230–31
opposite-sex relationships
  age of consent 30–31, 110
  civil partnerships 160
  de facto relationships 158–59, 257
  equal recognition of 53, 160
  eviction, protection from 30–31, 162–63, 164, 229–30
  families, defining 257
  marriage, defining 29–30, 158–59, 231–32, 236
  statutory benefits 29
ordinances
  anti-discrimination 28
  Bill of Rights 30–31, 69–70
  crimes 30–31
  marriage 30–31, 234–35
Ordóñez, Alejandro 109–10
originalism 37–38
Ortega, Daniel 67
orthodox forms of legal reasoning 50, 144, 274, 278
over-enforcement, judicial 181, 182, 185, 239
oversight, judicial/legislative 11, 54–55, 86, 87, 96, 121–22, 219, 236

packing, court 197
paedic norms 252, 254
Pakistan 35, 119–20, 121–22
Papua New Guinea 263
Pareto efficiency 150–51
parliamentary supremacy, doctrine of 205–6
participatory approach 6, 7–8
particularistic approach 252, 254, 256–57, 268
partisan lock up 73
Partlett, William 253n.47
party discipline 85–86
pathology, democratic 153
patriarchal concepts 190–91
patronage, political 148
pavement dwellers 164
penalties 73, 176
pensions, judicial 29–30, 229n.121

peremptory judicial review 56–57
Persily, Nathaniel 266–67
Petersen, Niels 55–56
petitions 107n.43, 119, 152, 154–55, 171
Philippines 31–32, 68–69
philosophers 252–53
philosophy 39, 226
Pildes, Richard 73
plebiscites 4, 32n.41
pluralism
  democratic 5–6, 157, 272–73
  ethnic and religious 101
  forms of 272
  institutional 5–6, 51, 61, 65–66, 68, 71, 90–91, 125–26, 139–40, 143–44, 146, 165, 166–67
  political 59, 74–75, 147n.9
Poland 65–66, 206
polarization 47, 88–89, 150–51, 265, 272
police 41
political democracy 62n.12, 131
political disadvantage 53–54, 138–39
political dysfunction 81
political market failures 55–56
polling 149
polycentricity 184
populism 89–91
poverty 90, 163
Powell, Randall 264
Pozen, David E. 267n.115
pre-clearance procedures 138
pregnancy 27, 31–32, 103n.23, 106, 107–8, 188, 189, 190, 191–92, 202, 221, 224
  see also abortion
prejudice 47–48, 52, 161
preservation, democratic 18–20
pricing, competitive 78
prima facie noncompliance 233
prisoner voting rights 215–16
privacy
  decisional 39, 40
  right to 39, 102–3, 114–15, 198
  sexual 27–32, 41–42
  spatial 39, 41
private international law 250–51
Privy Council (UK) 264
pro bono legal representation 171, 173–74
pro-democracy movements 69–70, 111
professionalism 126–27

proportionality doctrine 5–6, 20, 95–96, 127–41, 134t, 248n.11, 271

Québec 101, 158–59
queer
 rights 28
 theory 258–59
quotas, electoral 138–39

rabbinical court jurisdiction 32n.41
Rabuka, Sitiveni 261
race 39–40, 50, 128, 136, 137
racial minorities/politics 39–40, 49, 137n.181
racism 255–56
rape 107–8, 189, 220–21
rationality 82–83, 193
Rawls, John 44–45, 62n.12, 80, 98, 185n.14, 258–59
'reading-down' provision 176, 180
'reading-in' provision 233, 235–36
Reagan, Ronald 198
realism 14, 117n.99
reasonableness 49, 191–92, 223
reason-giving, public norms of 44
reciprocity 251
referendums 115, 207–8
refugees 66n.30
 see also internally displaced persons (IDPs)
regulatory pyramid 233n.143
religion 26n.4, 136, 260, 265, 267–68
remedial power/tools 3, 14, 20, 144, 155, 177, 214–16, 223, 273, 277
 jurisdiction and 176–80
representation-reinforcement 1, 2, 3–5, 9, 11–12, 27, 48, 51, 54–58, 95, 130, 143, 144–45, 153–54, 157, 171, 182, 273
reproductive healthcare 48
Republican in name only (RINO) 260–61
republicanism 104n.31, 198, 259, 260–61
respect, demonstrations of 251–52
responsiveness, democratic 2–9, 10–11, 15, 18, 20, 54, 61, 64, 95–96, 99, 100, 112, 132, 133, 172, 181, 182, 185, 194, 197, 199, 200, 222, 224, 240–41, 273, 279
restitution 40, 136
retaliation, democratic 181–82, 194–95
retirement, judicial 275n.11

reversibility, concept of 6, 100, 143–44, 147, 157
revisability of judicial opinions 272
rhetorical dialogue 11, 236
right to food (RTF) campaign 163–64, 175, 238
rights
 consciousness 155, 164–65, 238
 human see human rights
 LGBTQI+ see LGBTQI+ rights
 violations, seriousness of 119, 120–21
ripeness doctrine 178n.147, 186–87, 232n.134, 239, 239n.177
Roach, Kent 211–12
Rodríguez-Garavito, César 35n.55, 164n.87, 228n.119, 230–31, 233n.144
rolling best-practice standards 7–8, 141–42
Romania 65–66
Roosevelt, Eleanor 268–69
Roosevelt, Franklin D. 268–69
Rosenberg, Gerald N. 13, 199
rot, democratic 71–72
Roux, Theunis 61n.11, 73n.77, 81n.111, 141–42, 147n.9, 225n.109, 239n.173, 255n.51, 267n.116
Ruto, William 124
Rwanda 70, 139nn.190–91

Sabel, Charles F. 7–8, 56–57, 141–42
Sachs, Albie 256–57
safeguarding integrity of the legislative process 55–56, 57
safe harbor-based approach 136–38
same-sex relationships 109–10, 112, 158–60, 178–79, 221–22, 234–36, 255–56, 257
 see also LGBTQI+ rights; marriage
sanctions 7, 41, 210, 224–25
Santos, Juan Manuel 109–10, 166–67
Scalia, Antonin 202
Schauer, Fred 154–55
Scheduled Castes 136
Schleicher, David 76–77
Schumpeter, Joseph A. 43, 44–45, 61
SDL party 262
secularism 66, 68
self-determination, right to 224, 257
self-entrenchment problem 89, 147
self-government 42, 45–46, 49, 63, 69–70, 91, 272

self-identity 30–31
self-interest 97–98
Selznick, Philip 6
semi-procedural judicial review 6, 142
Sen, Amartya 39
Sen, Hun 68–69
Senegal 70, 170n.116
sex
  age of consent 30–31, 110
  intercourse 30–31, 110, 113–14, 161
  intimacy 41
sexual assault 31–32, 191–92
sexuality 53, 109, 128
  see also gender; homosexuality;
    transsexuality
shelter
  basic emergency 42–43, 161–62, 172–73, 222–23
  home and 162–63
  right of access to 33–34, 42–43, 119, 239
Shinar, Adam 247
Siegel, Reva 187
Singapore 31–32
slavery 4–5
Smith, Miriam 108–9
socialism 14n.53
social justice 162n.67
socioeconomic rights 46–47, 185
sociological legitimacy 21, 97–98, 101n.20, 185, 194, 196, 226–27, 250, 254–55, 270, 274
sociopolitical context 13–14, 270
sodomy 30–31, 109, 112–13, 231–32, 254–55, 258–59
South Africa 155n.39, 267n.116, 277
  African National Congress (ANC) 71, 90–91, 256
  antiretrovirals 172
  Constitution 50, 71, 77, 109, 128–29, 136, 211, 254–55
  Constitutional Court (CCSA) 16, 29–30, 34, 129–30, 159, 222, 232, 235, 254–55, 265n.107, 275
  democratic minimum core 70–71, 147n.9
  Diepsloot area 118n.103
  LGBTQI+ rights 49–50, 228–29, 254–55, 258–59
  national housing shortages 161–62

religious groups 256
structural social rights 49, 117–18
South Korea 28, 107–8, 128–29
Soviet era 272–73
spatial privacy 39, 41
speech
  freedom of 102
  implied 26, 33, 48–49
  low value 127–28
  protected 127–28
  speeches 148, 269–70
speed bumps, institutions as 143–44, 156
Speight, George 139n.192, 261, 262
'splitters' 13
  see also 'lumpers'
spouses 179
  spousal notification requirements 103–4, 190–91
Sri Lanka 68
stacking, court 197
standing doctrine 211–12, 247–48
stare decisis 103, 240–41
  'contrived' version of 202
  doctrine of 198, 204, 210, 216
  weak vs. strong 9–10, 212–13, 216, 216t, 223, 228–29, 231t
state aid 163
statecraft, judicial 18–19, 278
stereotypes 39–40, 41, 53–54, 137
stigma 52–53, 137, 260
Stone, Adrienne 127n.143
Stone, Justice 48
stricto sensu 129, 133
strong-form judicial review 14, 49–50, 56–57, 206, 241, 276
strong-weak judicial review 17–18, 205, 218, 228–40, 241, 271, 274
  variants 231t
structural edicts 222–23, 230–31, 232
subconstitutional context 49–50
Sudarshan, Ramaswamy 123
suffrage, adult 80
suicide, assisted 211n.39
Suk, Julie 191n.51
Sunstein, Cass R. 6, 210, 213, 226n.114
super-strong judicial review 10, 205, 219
supervisory jurisdiction/orders 9–10, 222–23, 229, 230–31, 232, 233
surrogacy 32

taboo-breaking actions 195n.63
Taggart, Michael 154n.31
Taiwan 128–29, 277
Tamil Nadu 163–64
Tanzania 70
taxation 41–42, 178
technocratic forms of judgment 170
technologies 86–87, 121, 238
televising court proceedings 266
territory law 32n.41, 177
testing services 34, 162, 173, 222–23
Tew, Yvonne 19n.69
textualist approach 260
Thailand 59
Thatcher, Margaret 110
Thiruvengadam, Arun K. 258n.66
Thompson, Dennis 44
Thornton, Alison 186–87
tolerance interval 8–9, 168–70
tone 12, 21, 245, 248, 249–52, 257–58, 259, 261–62, 263, 264, 267, 269–70, 271, 272, 274
Tonga 263
top-down approach 230–31
topical majorities/minorities 82
totalitarian governments 272
transgender
  community 28, 111–12, 259, 260
  identity 111, 160, 179, 234–35
  marriage 41–42, 234–35
  rights 30–31, 111–12, 113–14, 161, 234–35, 260–61
  same-sex relationships 178–79, 234–35
  see also LGBTQI+ rights; transsexuality
transnational institutions 4
transsexuality 31–32, 234
  see also transgender
treason 68–69
Tribe, Laurence H. 52
Trinidad and Tobago 32n.37
Trump, Donald J. 54–55, 89–90, 260–61
trumps, 'rights as trumps' approach 248n.11
trustworthiness 89, 251
truth, pursuit of 131
Turkey 66
Tushnet, Mark 9–10, 46–47, 79n.103, 200, 205–7

tutela system 34–35, 119, 152, 171, 238–39
two-track remedies 178n.147, 239–40, 241

Uganda 70
Umbrella movement 111
unanimity 249
unconstitutional constitutional amendment (UCA) doctrine 26, 36, 49, 57, 122–25, 158, 165, 170
unconstitutional state of affairs doctrine 34–35, 119–20, 121–22, 277
United Kingdom (UK)
  British constitutional courts 16
  constitutional democracy 54–55, 180, 205–6
  gender recognition 234
  human rights legislation 30–31, 176–77, 214–15, 258–59
  judicial review, system of 9–10, 19, 214, 215–16
  LGBTQI+ rights 110, 258–59
  new Commonwealth constitutional model 176, 210
  rights of access 49–50, 206–7
  same-sex marriage and relationships 160, 178–79
  sex discrimination 259
  sodomy, decriminalization of 258–59
  transgender issues 160, 178–79
  Westminster politics 160
United States (US)
  abortion, access to 31–32, 107, 158, 182, 188, 189, 225
  affirmative action 139
  African-American voters 53
  Bill of Rights 268
  categorial approach 127n.143
  citizen participation 44
  Congress 209
  Constitution 1, 25–26, 27–28, 33–34, 48, 49, 52, 105, 207, 208–9, 227–28
  constitutional construction 25, 277
  constitutional courts 16
  constitutional traditions 267–68
  counter-majoritarian difficulty 272
  court decisions, public awareness of 266–67
  critical theorists 258–59

cultural values 259–60
democracy 1, 51, 54–55
democratic dysfunction 145
discrimination 53
economic nationalist rhetoric 253n.48
Federal Reserve 148n.11
gun violence 277
human rights law 258–59
judicial confirmation process 198
justiciability, limits on 211–12
originalism 37
LBGTQI+ rights 48, 259
legal realism 37–38, 97n.7
legislative intent 139–40
legislative trends 259–60
political elections 76–77, 90n.141
presidency 25, 50, 54–55, 89–90
Qualifications Clause 25
rational basis review 130–31
responsive judicial review 7, 95–96, 254–55, 277, 278
same-sex marriage 259
scrutiny, levels of 5–6, 127, 130, 132, 136, 139, 271
structural social rights 33–34
Supreme Court 16, 25–26, 27–28, 33–34, 39, 102, 136, 137, 154–55, 155n.35, 177, 188, 193, 201, 206, 207, 209, 212–13, 217, 248n.11, 249n.14, 259
Voting Rights Act (VRA) 138
Warren Court 1, 13, 15–16, 143
weak and strong judicial review 49–50, 206, 216t, 277
universalistic approach 252, 255–56, 258–59
unlawful power 264
urban overcrowding 164
Uribe Vélez, Álvaro 109–10, 165, 166–67, 218

vagueness, constitutional 203
valence, political 135, 195, 275, 278
V-dem index of democracy 61n.10
veil of ignorance 249, 250n.20
Venezuela 67, 74n.80, 90, 151–52, 170n.116, 253n.48

veto, judicial 47, 125
violation of rights 120–21
violence
    gun 122, 277
    political 70
    protection from 33–34
    threats of 160n.57
vulnerability
    Apartheid legislation 255
    historical 135
    political 52

Waldron, Jeremy 45–46, 80–82, 83, 185–86
Ward, Gordon 263
warfare, legalization of 73n.77
Warren Court 1, 13, 15–16, 143
water, access to 26, 117–18, 118n.103
weak-form judicial review 14, 56–57, 155n.35, 205–7, 222, 233, 236–37, 241
weak-strong judicial review 204–41
    pragmatic argument for 217–20
    rights and remedies 228–29, 235
    see also *stare decisis*
weapons, assault 277
Weberian notions of legitimacy 97–98
Weiler, Joseph 1
Williams, George 262nn.90–92
Wilson, Justice 193
women's rights 104, 202, 221
    see also abortion
World War II 128–29
written constitution 4–5, 25, 37, 100, 102, 212

Yap, Po Jen v–vi, vii, 17n.63, 233, 234n.151
Young, Ezra I. 260n.83
Young, Katharine G. 43n.106, 56–57, 133n.172, 164n.84, 175n.139, 237n.165, 239n.178

Zimbabwe 253n.48
Zondo Commission 71n.65
Zuma, Jacob 71